Global Financial Markets

Global Financial Markets is a series of practical guides to the latest financial market tools, techniques and strategies. Written for practitioners across a range of disciplines it provides comprehensive but practical coverage of key topics in finance covering strategy, markets, financial products, tools and techniques and their implementation. This series will appeal to a broad readership, from new entrants to experienced practitioners across the financial services industry, including areas such as institutional investment; financial derivatives; investment strategy; private banking; risk management; corporate finance and M&A, financial accounting and governance, and many more.

More information about this series at
http://www.palgrave.com/gp/series/15011

Ross McGill

US Withholding Tax

Practical Implications of QI and FATCA

Second Edition 2019

Ross McGill
TConsult Ltd
Yateley, Hampshire, UK

Global Financial Markets
ISBN 978-3-030-23087-6   ISBN 978-3-030-23085-2 (eBook)
https://doi.org/10.1007/978-3-030-23085-2

© The Editor(s) (if applicable) and The Author(s), under exclusive licence to Springer Nature Switzerland AG 2013, 2019
This work is subject to copyright. All rights are solely and exclusively licensed by the Publisher, whether the whole or part of the material is concerned, specifically the rights of translation, reprinting, reuse of illustrations, recitation, broadcasting, reproduction on microfilms or in any other physical way, and transmission or information storage and retrieval, electronic adaptation, computer software, or by similar or dissimilar methodology now known or hereafter developed.
The use of general descriptive names, registered names, trademarks, service marks, etc. in this publication does not imply, even in the absence of a specific statement, that such names are exempt from the relevant protective laws and regulations and therefore free for general use.
The publisher, the authors and the editors are safe to assume that the advice and information in this book are believed to be true and accurate at the date of publication. Neither the publisher nor the authors or the editors give a warranty, express or implied, with respect to the material contained herein or for any errors or omissions that may have been made. The publisher remains neutral with regard to jurisdictional claims in published maps and institutional affiliations.

This Palgrave Macmillan imprint is published by the registered company Springer Nature Switzerland AG.
The registered company address is: Gewerbestrasse 11, 6330 Cham, Switzerland

Foreword

The first edition of this book was hailed across the industry because of its clarity and consistency in explaining a very complex subject. This second edition has continued that tradition and includes now additional diagrammatic descriptions as well as new topics such as Code 871(m) in Part I and intergovernmental agreements (IGAs) in Part II that were either in their infancy or non-existent when the first edition was published.

McGill has, as always, taken a complex subject with many dimensions and given a very practical description not just of what the regulations are as background knowledge for the reader, but what they mean in the day-to-day operations of financial services firms. In his consulting and training work, he has come across almost every permutation of financial institution by size, geography and status in IRC Chapters 3 and 4. As a result he is perfectly placed to know and understand the kind of issues that face financial institutions and the types of approach to regulatory and operational compliance that work and can be considered best practice.

In particular, his work in Asia-Pacific is outstanding, not least because he understands the linguistic and cultural issues that can affect compliance. Exposure to the US securities market does not come without obligations and taxation of income and anti-tax evasion are the two largest issues. It's not enough to look at the regulations themselves; they are almost impenetrable to any normal person. Firms need to understand what their counterparties are doing in this space and why. They also need to understand what they need to do to comply on the one hand but manage risk and cost on the other. Many firms are worried about becoming qualified intermediaries because they don't fully understand what it means, but the alternative of staying as a non-qualified intermediary is fast becoming an untenable status. Most US withholding agents and QIs are wary of non-qualified intermediaries (NQIs), not just because the US administration believes them to be facilitating tax evasion, but because the operational cost and risk of having such clients are becoming too high. This book answers many of those concerns and questions so, while the material is useful for firms that are already QIs, it's almost required reading for any NQI considering QI status.

So, this book, while explaining the basics, and some of the more advanced aspects of QI and FATCA, is invaluable because it gives practical context. As McGill often says, 'it helps you understand what you'll be doing differently tomorrow than you were doing yesterday—and why'.

Professionals in delivering custody and prime services across Asia-Pacific and the rest of the world will find this book an eye-opener and a 'must have' on the desk, not just the bookshelf.

Chairman & Managing Director　　　　　　　　　　　　　　Robert Dombrowski
Viewtrade Holding Corp.

Preface

This is the second edition of this book. Since the publication of the first edition, a great deal has changed.

It is important for the reader to be aware at the outset that this book does not attempt to describe the regulations (QI and FATCA) in detail. The original regulations total over 1600 pages between them, with many hundreds more pages of subsequent guidance and interpretation in the intervening 17 years since their inception.

My objective here is purely practical. It's an attempt to take the experiences I have had in the last 18 years, dealing with financial institutions and their customers, and highlight the big practical issues that these regulations represent in an everyday financial services and investment environment.

If this book leaves any legacy at all, I hope it is that regulators will realise that a far greater proportion of their time needs to be spent increasing awareness, explaining to and collaborating with the industry if they want to have really workable regulation that meets its objective.

Today's world is becoming filled with more and more extraterritorial regulation. QI went under the radar mainly because, for the most part, the intent of the US was to have matters dealt with via commercial contracts with non-US financial institutions rather than a complex way of making foreign institutions subject directly to US regulation. FATCA then took that exact route leading us to a complicated web of intergovernmental agreements that led to domestic legislation and guidance. In this new world, regulators increasingly need to understand that language and culture will have played an important part in the operational approach of financial firms. While the IRS has improved its communications substantially over the last few years, it has, nevertheless, suffered from continued budget cuts and resource challenges (and that's not including government shut downs). All of this has an effect and many firms still struggle to understand and implement the basics and are bemused if they get penalty notices going back three, four or five years and are unable to get responses in a 'commercial' time frame. So, while this is a story about experiences from the financial side, it must not be forgotten that there are two sides to QI and FATCA.

Our industry is not fundamentally against regulation; it's against inefficient, uncoordinated regulation that creates more cost and risk than the expected benefit. I also hope that financial institutions and their customers will see and understand what the big practical issues are and hopefully in enough time be able to consider and come to some workable solutions that engender compliance.

Yateley, UK   Ross McGill

Acknowledgements

I would like to acknowledge the invaluable help, support and assistance, whether they realised it or not, of:
  Mrs. Kirsty Pitkin, TConsult
  Mr. Stuart Lipo, TConsult
  Mr. Neil Moorhouse
  Mr. Bob Dombrowski, Viewtrade
  Mr. Kenneth Chan, Viewtrade
  Mr. Tony Petrilli, Viewtrade
  Mr. Andy Liao, Viewtrade
  Mr. Michael Lempert, GlobeTax
  Mr. Haydon Perryman, TAINA
  Mr. Ali Kazimi, Hansuke Consulting

Disclaimer

The views and opinions expressed in this book are solely those of the author. Although the author has made reasonable efforts to ensure the accuracy of the text, the author does not accept any legal responsibility whatsoever for consequences that may arise from errors or omissions or any opinion given or statement made. Nothing in this book is intended to constitute the provision of tax, legal or investment advice. Readers are strongly advised to take professional independent advice on these matters. Unless context to specific regulation is given, any text inferring or appearing to infer a view or opinion of the US Internal Revenue Service (IRS), US Treasury or US government directly or indirectly is purely an editorial device to make the content more easily readable and is an opinion or inference of the author and which has not been endorsed by or verified by the IRS.

Contents

Part I	The QI Regulations	1
1	Principles of IRC Code Chapter 3	3
2	Contracts: The QI Agreement—With Commentary	23
3	Documentation	39
4	Withholding and Depositing Tax	63
5	Information Reporting and Tax Returns	79
6	Control and Oversight	101
7	Penalties	119
8	Issues for Non-qualified Intermediaries	127
9	871(m) and QDD	145
Part II	FATCA	155
10	An Introduction to FATCA	157
11	Principles of FATCA	165

12	Due Diligence	183
13	Simplifying FATCA	199
14	FATCA Withholding	217
15	Reporting	223

Part III	Related Global Tax Initiatives	231
16	International Context	233
17	Conclusions	259
18	Further Reading	273

Index		407

About the Author

Ross McGill is the founder and Chairman of TConsult, a regulatory and operational compliance firm based in the UK with active clients in 15 countries.

McGill is a prolific author with this being his ninth published work, including such subjects as technology management in financial services, global custody and clearing, data protection, withholding tax reclaims and relief at source, Sarbanes Oxley and, of course, US withholding tax in the form of qualified intermediary (QI) and Foreign Account Tax Compliance Act (FATCA).

McGill is a well-known industry figure and frequent speaker. He has contributed to many international initiatives and industry groups including the ISO20022 Standards groups for corporate actions, proxy voting and funds evaluation, the European Commission FISCO committee and Tax Barriers Business Advisory Group (T-BAG), International Securities Services Association (ISSA) and the International Capital Markets Services Association (ICMSA).

List of Figures

Fig. 1.1	IRC Chapter 3 processes. Source: Author's own	7
Fig. 1.2	Common account structures and payment flows. Source: Author's own	8
Fig. 1.3	Cascade nature of US reporting. Source: Author's own	15
Fig. 1.4	Reporting in a disclosed cascade. Source: Author's own	17
Fig. 3.1	Chain of documentation	41
Fig. 3.2	QI with client and proprietary assets	44
Fig. 3.3	QI with multiple business lines	45
Fig. 3.4	W-8IMY validation on the face—hot spot method. Source: Author's own	53
Fig. 3.5	W-8IMY validation on the face—simple flow method. Source: Author's own	54
Fig. 3.6	W-8IMY validation on the face—detailed method. Source: Author's own	54
Fig. 4.1	Withholding model for a withholding QI. Source: Author's own	67
Fig. 4.2	Withholding model for a non-withholding QI. Source: Author's own	68
Fig. 4.3	Withholding model for a non-withholding QI with rate pool statements. Source: Author's own	69
Fig. 4.4	Deposit formula. Source: Author's own	73
Fig. 5.1	1042 and 1042-S reporting explained	88
Fig. 5.2	Tax return completion for a withholding QI. Source: Author's own	93
Fig. 5.3	General structure of 1042-S ASCII file. Source: Author's own	94
Fig. 5.4	Constructing the data for 1042-S reporting. Source: Author's own	95
Fig. 5.5	Multiple withholding agents. Source: Author's own	96
Fig. 5.6	Form 1099-X report data layout. Source: Author's own	97
Fig. 6.1	The need for a responsible officer	102

Fig. 6.2	Certification deadlines. Source: Author's own	106
Fig. 6.3	Formula for determining sample size in Periodic Reviews	107
Fig. 6.4	Periodic Review assessment phases. Source: Author's own	108
Fig. 6.5	Process flows for Periodic Review and assessment of controls. Source: Author's own	109
Fig. 7.1	Penalties for failure to file 1042-S (gross receipts > $5 m). Source: Author's own	121
Fig. 8.1	Account structures. Source: Author's own	130
Fig. 8.2	Effects of disclosure on payments and reporting for NQIs. Source: Author's own	135
Fig. 8.3	Nested NQI chains of custody. Source: Author's own	143
Fig. 9.1	Who determines if a transaction is 871(m)? Source: Author's own	148
Fig. 9.2	871(m) Determination workflow. Source: Author's own	150
Fig. 9.3	How to calculate the net Δ exposure? Source: Author's own	152
Fig. 9.4	How to calculate the 871(m)amount? Source: Author's own	153
Fig. 9.5	How to calculate QDD tax liability? Source: Author's own	154
Fig. 10.1	Structural elements of FATCA. Source: Author's own	159
Fig. 10.2	Legal structures for FATCA. Source: Author's own	160
Fig. 11.1	Effect of QI status on FATCA	172
Fig. 12.1	W-8 validation for W-8 in FATCA and QI indicia strategies. Source: Author's own	187
Fig. 12.2	Is your client an American? Source: Author's own	189
Fig. 12.3	Types of account holders under FATCA. Source: Author's own	190
Fig. 15.1	Selection of accounts for FATCA reporting. Source: Author's own	224
Fig. 15.2	Cyber risk. Source: Author's own	227
Fig. 17.1	Operational structure map (OSM). Source: Author's own	268
Fig. 17.2	Digital compliance map (DCM). Source: Author's own	269

List of Tables

Table 6.1	Application of multiple rules for determining sample size	108
Table 16.1	Comparison of TRACE IP, FATCA, QI and code of conduct	235
Table 17.1	FATCA GIIN issuance by jurisdiction	261

Introduction

What This Book Is About?

This book is intended to be an explanation of the US withholding tax system as it applies, in a very practical sense, to non-US financial institutions and their customers.

It is also important to state what this book is *not*. Apart from the natural caveats found elsewhere, that this book is not intended to provide (and should not be construed as providing) tax, legal or investment advice. Neither is it intended to be an exhaustive tax technical exposition of the entire US internal revenue code.

It's meant to be a reasonably understandable explanation of the regulations in practical context to the typical operational and compliance changes that non-US financial institutions and their customers face when receiving US-sourced income.

I've received many compliments over the years, about the readability and usefulness of the first edition of this book. I intend to continue that tradition in this, the second edition. In order to do that, I need to provide a little explanation of how this book is structured.

Learning the Language and Dialects

Before you read this book, you need to learn a new language. US tax regulations are not written in English. They are not even written in American English; they are written in tax technical American. Within the language of tax technical American, there are two dialects—IRC Chapter 3 and IRC

Chapter 4. You need to understand and use both if you are to work effectively in this space. IRC is used in this context to refer to the US Internal Revenue Code (IRC) and should mean that the reader can differentiate a reference to a chapter of the IRC as opposed to a chapter of this book.

Most of this book is predicated on a financial institution located outside the US receiving US-sourced income that is FDAP in nature, being fixed, determinable, annual or periodic, on behalf of its customers. As soon as that occurs, the financial institution becomes subject to various 'Chapters' of the US Internal Revenue Code (IRC). Two of these IRC chapters have different dialects of tax technical American to describe structures and entities that receive or distribute US income.

In IRC Chapter 3, financial institutions are either QIs or NQIs. Their customers are entities and individuals, intermediaries or flow throughs. Individuals and entities are either treaty entitled, not treaty entitled, tax exempt or US. Intermediaries, again, are either QIs or NQIs. Flow-through accounts are either partnerships or trusts.

In IRC Chapter 4, foreign financial institutions (FFIs) have three types of client—individuals, entities or other FFIs. Each category can have multiple sub-categories. FFIs are the most complex and can have one of many categorisations depending on whether they are in a jurisdiction with an intergovern-

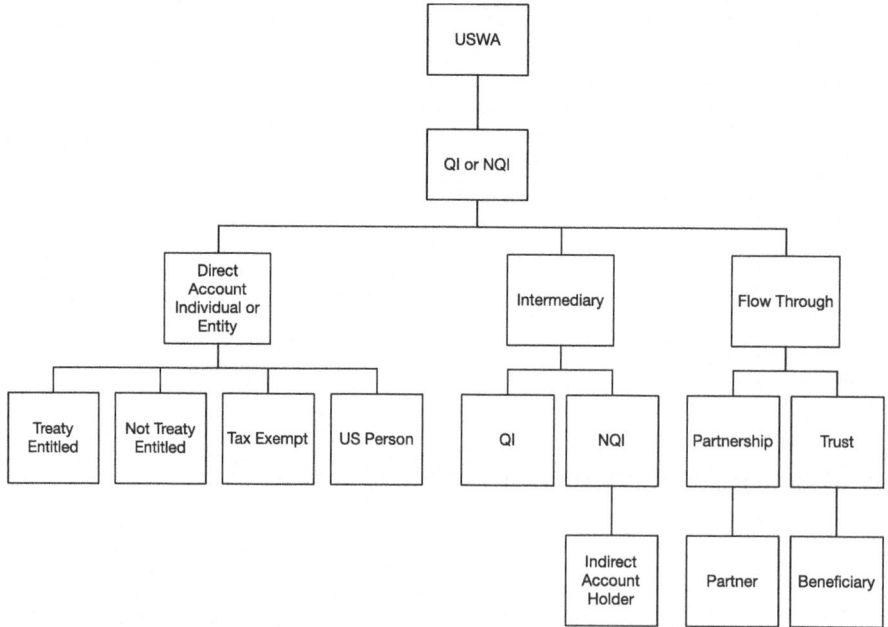

Fig. 1 IRC Chapter 3 dialect. Source: Author's own

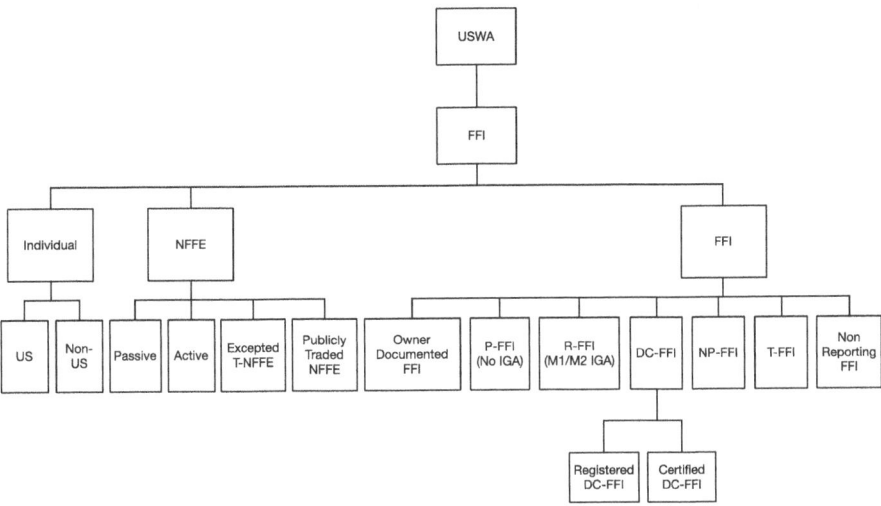

Fig. 2 IRC Chapter 4 dialect. Source: Author's own

mental agreement (IGA), or whether they are required to report and the type of IGA. Certain other FFIs can be 'deemed' compliant in either registered or certified form and they could be located in a US territory. Figure 0.2 is not an exhaustive list (see form W-8IMY).

The message here is that discussion of IRC Chapter 3 should use Chapter 3 dialect terms and IRC Chapter 4 should use Chapter 4 dialect terms.

Where income is received there are two simple rules: (1) apply IRC Chapter 4 first, then IRC Chapter 3; (2) if tax is withheld in IRC Chapter 4, do not withhold in IRC Chapter 3—the principle of non-duplicative taxation.

Code Sections Covered

For non-US financial institutions and for investors with bank accounts outside the US (including both non-US investors and US investors), there are several elements of the US Internal Revenue Code (IRC) that this book addresses. In particular, the IRS brought together several, previously disparate parts of the revenue code into the QI Agreement that is now in its third iteration under Revenue Procedure 2017-15.

Code Chapter 3 Sections 1141, 1442, 1443, 1461, 1463 and 1464 deal with the taxation of US-sourced FDAP income paid to non-US recipients outside the US, including the provision of tax treaty relief and the exemption of withholding on portfolio interest.

Code Chapter 4 Sections 1471, 1472, 1473 and 1474, often referred to as FATCA, deal with the identification and reporting of US account holders outside the US.

Code Chapter 6 Sections 6041, 6042, 6045, 6049 and 6050N deal with the identification, and reporting, of US non-exempt recipients on forms 1099.

Code Chapter 31 Section 3406 deals with the taxation (backup withholding) and reporting of US or presumed US recipients without a valid claim of exemption from backup withholding.

Code Chapter 1 Section 871(m) deals with withholding and reporting on dividend equivalents.

I'm making no attempt to go through every line in these regulations. I'm much more concerned in this book with getting the general message across. It will become clear as you read this book why that is. There is little point in going into that level of detail when most firms have not yet grasped the basics or even the larger picture.

Fundamentals

We'll cross the bridge of trying to integrate all these issues into one whole in due course. The IRS has tried on several occasions to issue 'converging regulation' as well as transition arrangements for particularly complex parts of the regulations, but, more often than not, this just creates more confusion as well as a lot of duplicated effort in meeting both transitional and final regulations. Financial firms, whatever you've been told, are rarely set up to handle change well.

For those unfamiliar with Chapters 3 or 4 and who are reading this book as a fundamental reference work, I provide the following top-level summary of both IRC Chapters that form the backbone of QI and FATCA regulation. I'll bring in the other Code sections to the discussion as they become relevant.

IRC Chapter 3

Chapter 3 of the US Internal Revenue Code has the overall effect of making a non-US financial institution into an unpaid collector of US taxes on behalf of the US government. It's about the proper taxation of investment income.

In the practical sense, Chapter 3 is all about four steps in a repeating process—documentation, withholding, depositing and reporting US-sourced FDAP income payments made to non-US beneficial owners through non-US financial intermediaries. 'FDAP' means income that is Fixed, Determinable, Annual or Periodic. For most financial institutions, 95% of FDAP received comprises dividends and interest.

The procedural and compliance obligations of financial intermediaries in this model are set out based on whether they are 'qualified' or 'non-qualified'.

So, the first, most important issue to understand, is that a financial institution is subject to these US tax regulations as soon as it receives US-sourced FDAP income. The default status of such firms is 'non-qualified intermediary' or 'NQI'. If the firm decides to enter into a separate agreement with the IRS, then it becomes a 'qualified intermediary' or 'QI'. The base regulations apply to both types of intermediary but the QI Agreement effectively makes compliance and procedural changes to how those regulations are implemented that benefit a QI and make their life easier. The QI Agreement also adds another, fifth step, into the repeating process, that of control & oversight, that is, the IRS wants to make sure that, if you become a QI, that you meet the terms of the contract. In 2009, former President Obama made a speech in which he referred to NQIs as being deemed by the US to be facilitating tax evasion. That should tell you all you need to know about what the regulations are likely to be like when applied to NQIs—they get no favours.

It's also important to know that the tax withheld from non-US beneficial owners (payees or recipients) in this model is *only* on US-sourced FDAP income and is based on the nature and validity of appropriate documentation available to the financial institution (payor) on the pay date of the income.

A word about trading. These regulations don't really apply to trading. They apply to the receipt, taxation and reporting of *income* resulting from trading. So, while trading is a key preparatory act, the activities described in these regulations are not about trading; they are about what to do with investment income derived from trading, if and when it turns up.

Chapter 4: FATCA

Chapter 4 of the Internal Revenue Code on the other hand is an anti-tax evasion regulation, the forerunner of the OECD's Automatic Exchange of Information (AEoI) and associated Common Reporting Standard (CRS).

FATCA is all about soliciting and maintaining information and documentation about *all* account holders in order to correctly understand whether the account is a US reportable account and subsequently report the *global* income paid to accounts that are deemed to be 'US' for the purpose of FATCA.

In the same way that Chapter 3 regulations apply based on receipt of income and can be procedurally adjusted based on whether or not the financial institution has entered into a QI Agreement or not, Chapter 4 has a similar, albeit slightly more complex structure.

In FATCA, the world outside the US is split into those jurisdictions that have signed 'intergovernmental agreements' or 'IGAs' with the US and those that have not. In those that have not signed an IGA, a basic Foreign Financial Institution Agreement (FFIA) is required to be signed in order to avoid the default status of 'non-participating foreign financial institution' or 'NP-FFI'.

In a jurisdiction with an IGA, there is usually no FFI Agreement to sign because the terms of the FFI's compliance have been negotiated between the governments. IGAs are universally required to be translated into domestic statute so that the terms apply directly to that jurisdiction's financial institutions.

The object of the IGAs (as well as the FFIA) is to determine how, when and to what extent, a financial institution must document its account holders and perform due diligence beyond Know-Your-Customer (KYC) or Anti-Money Laundering (AML) rules in order to determine whether that account is (1) reportable as US, (2) recalcitrant or (3) an NP-FFI. The result of that activity is annual reporting to the IRS directly or indirectly and the imposition of penalties on any account holder that does not comply with the requests of their financial institution under FATCA.

FATCA also has rules that apply to the reportable subjects—US persons. FATCA requires them to comply with requests and also to separately report their non-US global assets to the IRS.

So, when looked at in the whole, FATCA has elements that apply to non-US financial institutions and also elements that apply to US persons with accounts at those institutions.

In 2019 we have already seen some extraterritorial 'sting' operations performed by the IRS with subsequent extraditions and initial indictments brought for flouting FATCA regulations. So, be of no doubt, they're serious.

What is critical to understand, and will be described in detail in the following chapters of this book, is that both systems are 'cascade' in nature. This means that there are obligations at *all* levels and that non-compliance at any level is automatically visible to the IRS through compliance at the higher level, usually through information reporting.

What should also be clear, even from these two brief descriptions, is that Chapter 3 and Chapter 4, even though they have some similarities of structure, are very different in purpose.

Practical Versus Tax Technical

There are two other things to know about the content of this book and the way in which I've chosen to write it.

First, while it may not always seem so, it is written from a practical perspective, not a tax technical perspective—although the two may be difficult to distinguish at times and I will try to 'bring it back to reality' as often as possible. Whatever the tax language may be, there is usually a practical consequence. In fact, there is usually more than one consequence and many of these individually, in turn, interact with each other to create new and often unforeseen effects.

For a financial institution, that may be a change in client on-boarding procedures, policies or entirely new processes such as tax information reporting. For an investor it might be a new form they have to know about or the consequence of not filling in a form that they need to be aware of.

Second, while many, but by no means all, of those on the receiving end of these regulations have a good command of English, as I said earlier, these regulations aren't actually written in English. They are written in 'American tax technical' language. This language can be difficult to master and failing to understand it can have serious consequences.

I was also tasked, when thinking about how to structure this book, as to why I would want to include IRC Chapter 3 at all. IRC Chapter 3 came into force on 1 January 2001, over 18 years before this edition of the book was written. From outside the industry, one would naturally assume that, after nearly two decades of supposedly knowing what the 'rules' are, both financial institutions and investors would not only understand what they are supposed to do, but would have taken steps to comply. You'd also naturally expect that compliance to these regulations would have been progressively standardised and automated to the point where a book on the subject would be, well, pointless.

In practice, nothing could be further from the truth. It is true that Global Custodians and larger financial institutions have embraced the implications of IRC Chapter 3. However, if you draw a line from Washington DC eastwards, the level of knowledge, understanding and compliance to IRC Chapter 3, even after 18 years, falls rapidly with distance. By the time you get to Asia, levels of engagement and understanding are very low, English (let alone 'American tax technical') is not the back-office language of choice and thus levels of awareness, understanding and compliance are lower still.

Why is this important? First, it evidences a continuing need to explain IRC Chapters 3 and 4 in practical terms that everyone can understand. The consequences of non-compliance to IRC Chapter 3 (and 4) are very severe. To date, the IRS has had, at best, a fragmented approach to enforcing its own regulations. However, relying on 'they'll never find us', 'not getting caught' or using ignorance as a defence is not a realistic risk management strategy in today's highly regulated financial environment.

QI Versus FATCA

I've mentioned language a couple of times so far and language is one of my passions, particularly in the context of being clear and concise. This probably originates from my early science-based education, but I still find it a prevalent need in my consulting, educational and training work today. There are several aliases under which these two chapters are more commonly known by or referred to. IRC Chapter 3 is commonly known as the 'QI regulations' or sometimes '1441' or '1441 NRA', a reference to the section of the Code that applies. Equally, IRC Chapter 4 is also commonly known as 'FATCA'. The seeds of confusion and non-compliance are sown by these terms.

The 'QI regulations' is a reference to a principle of IRC Chapter 3 in which a foreign (i.e. non-US) financial institution may choose, if it fulfils certain criteria, to engage in a contractual agreement with the IRS and thus become a 'qualified intermediary' or 'QI'. However, the regulations themselves relate to the tax and reporting treatment of specific types of income sourced from the US and paid to *anyone* resident outside the US. The net result of the term 'QI regulations' is that (1) many financial institutions believe that because they haven't signed a QI Agreement with the IRS, they are not affected by the regulations, and (2) many investors believe that because they are not US residents, they aren't covered by US tax regulations. Both are incorrect. The regulations are triggered by the receipt of US-sourced FDAP income. So, a financial institution receiving a payment of US-sourced income *is* subject to the regulations *in full*, irrespective of whether it has signed a QI Agreement or not. All that changes are the procedures that follow on from being either a QI or a NQI. Equally, for example, a South African investor receiving US dividends to his online brokerage account operated by a European financial firm *is* subject to these US tax rules because the payment was sourced from the US. Many rant against this 'extra-territoriality', but, since the system is cascade and starts with a US withholding agent bank, the IRS has all the control it needs to enforce the regulations, irrespective of where the beneficial owner is or where his or her account is located outside the US.

'FATCA' does not, tax technically, exist at all. It did once, in draft form only, in 2009, as a Congressional Bill (HR3933). However, that Bill never got passed. Its content, adjusted and amended, ended up in a different piece of US law known as Title V of the Hiring Incentives to Restore [American] Employment Act or 'HIRE' Act, passed in March 2010. Unfortunately, FATCA sounds very like 'Fat Cat' and is a reference to the distaste expressed by many in the US electorate for those rich Americans evading US taxes by holding their investments off-shore and then failing to declare not just their US-sourced income but also their global income from these accounts. So, even though the original name has no reference point in current US law, it has stuck to the point where even the IRS uses the term.

So, while, as a purist, I may not, and do not, like such loose terminology, I'm forced to use it in this book since it has entered the industry's lexicon.

On the subject of lexicons, it's also important to note that there is one other area of potential misunderstanding that can occur between IRC Chapters 3 and 4 and it's best that I highlight this in the introduction, although I will go into more detail later. A 'financial institution' to most ordinary people would include banks and brokerage firms and to a large extent that is also the implied meaning of the term in IRC Chapter 3. A payment of US-sourced income would typically be made from a US corporation that issues a financial instrument, like a bond or share ('Issuer'), through a US withholding agent bank (USWA) to a foreign, that is, non-US financial institution, again typically a bank or broker who would have the status of either QI or NQI under the regulations and adopt the required procedures accordingly. IRC Chapter 4, on the other hand, very specifically creates a new and wider definition of 'financial institution' whose purpose I will discuss in Part II of this book. This wider definition brings many funds, hedge funds, collective investment vehicles, insurance companies, credit card companies and the like into the definition of 'financial institution' and therefore places them under the IRC Chapter 4 regulatory rules. So, for readers of this book it's important to realise that when we talk about 'financial institutions', this means different things in IRC Chapter 3 to IRC Chapter 4.

Global Context

While the vast majority of this book is focussed on IRC Chapters 3 and 4, I want to make an important point about the principles that IRC Chapters 3 and 4 establish for the global tax landscape. IRC Chapter 3 is a withholding tax system designed to provide 'at source' relief for foreign investors based on proper documentation of beneficial owners prior to, or on pay date. IRC Chapter 4 is a tax evasion detection system providing the IRS with enhanced reporting of foreign accounts of its citizens and punitive penalties for financial institutions and account holders who fail to disclose themselves and/or their accounts.

The principles of IRC Chapters 3 and 4 are not unique. They are shared by many, if not all, tax jurisdictions around the world. Application and collection of the correct tax on income and deterring, identifying and punishing tax evasion are the two basic principles.

It should come as no surprise therefore that the US is not alone in seeking to enhance the operative elements of these principles. In particular the Organisation for Economic Co-operation and Development (OECD) and the European Union (EU) both have parallel projects under way.

The OECD Tax Relief and Compliance Enhancement Implementation Protocol (TRACE IP) and the European Union's Withholding Tax Code of Conduct (WTCC) seek to create an enhanced, standardised and automatable way in which investors can have the correct tax applied 'at source'. Both models draw heavily on ideas in IRC Chapter 3.

Equally the EU and OECD markets have settled on a version of FATCA—AEoI supported by CRS as the primary anti-tax evasion framework. Again, both AEoI and CRS draw heavily on IRC Chapter 4, but take the opportunity to simplify where possible.

My point here is that I don't believe that a financial institution, or an investor, can afford to look at QI and FATCA in isolation from the more global context of taxation of cross-border income and anti-tax evasions frameworks. These may not be connected systems (yet), but there is commonality of purpose and similarity of solutions which, if ignored, place financial institutions at high risk, but if accepted, offer the prospect of efficient compliance.

So, with this brief introduction in mind, we will move on to a more layered discussion of QI.

Part I

The QI Regulations

1

Principles of IRC Code Chapter 3

In this chapter, I will look at the overarching principles of Code Chapter 3. Later chapters will deal with the granular aspects of meeting these regulatory obligations.

Part of the need to understand the principles first is that many of these principles have more than one way of being implemented in practice. While the system is very much 'rules' based, it cannot and does not take into account every possible permutation of entity type, account structure and so on. Regulators are also, by their very nature, always in catch-up mode to what happens 'out on the street'. So, while the principle may say one thing, it's often the case that the way in which the investment chain is structured either precludes that principle or provides several different ways for it to occur.

IRC Chapter 3 is essentially a way to codify a generalised relief at source taxation system so that US-sourced income (e.g. dividends or bond interest) paid to recipients outside the US can be distributed net of tax withheld at the correct rate.

There are several tax rates that apply to these kinds of income, including—0%, 10%, 15%, 20%, 25%, 30% and 39.4%. The 'correct' rate will depend on the nature of the paying instrument, the legal form and residence of the ultimate beneficial owner, the existence or otherwise of a double tax treaty, and to some extent the nature, location and status of any intervening financial intermediaries and the type of accounts they hold with upstream and downstream counterparties in the payment chain.

In order to achieve this relief at source, IRC Chapter 3 lays down rules by which non-US financial institutions, those usually closest to the beneficial owner recipient, can properly identify and communicate those tax entitlements to those who need to withhold the tax. As with any system of regulation, the IRC Chapter also includes both oversight mechanisms and enforcement penalties to ensure that foreign financial firms are complying with the rules and not allowing those with no entitlements to gain them.

Key Principles

Relief at Source

Most tax jurisdictions fall into one or more of four categories:

1. relief at source;
2. quick refund;
3. standard (post pay date) refund;
4. a combination of (1), (2) and (3).

In a relief at source only jurisdiction, failure to provide adequate evidence of treaty entitlement or exemption prior to pay date leaves the beneficial owner with no 'post pay date' procedure to apply. There may be a quick refund process available on occasion, for example, France, where an appointed agent remits tax to its tax authority once a month—so claims for relief at source that failed the pay date deadlines can still be filed as long as the claim is received before the agent remits the tax to the tax authority.

Equally, in a standard refund-only jurisdiction, there is no pre-pay date procedure by which a beneficial owner can access the correct rate of tax on the pay date. Clearly combination jurisdictions offer the best solution with multiple processes—relief at source available to those who can provide the evidence prior to pay date, a quick refund process or, finally, a standard refund process for those who can't.

There are many reasons why a beneficial owner may have a treaty entitlement but be unable to access tax relief processes. This establishes the important difference between *having* an entitlement and *realising* that entitlement.

Having an entitlement is based on certain known factors—owning securities on record date, tax residency, legal form and existence of a double tax treaty. While there may be some associated interpretive issues, generally, having an entitlement is a fixed thing. If you meet the criteria, you have an entitlement.

Realising an entitlement, on the other hand, requires that there be a process or mechanism acceptable to a tax authority and implemented usually by either the tax authority or a financial institution authorised by it. Some tax authorities make these processes very simple, while some make them very complex in terms of what documentation is required to substantiate an entitlement.

Of course, unless legally challenged, for example, under EU anti-discrimination laws, the final arbiter of whether any given beneficial owner is entitled to relief is the tax authority of the source country—the country where the income originated. However, given the very large numbers of beneficial owners involved, most tax authorities have moved from assessing these documents themselves to using the financial services infrastructure to perform this task for them. This allows them to reduce their workload and costs by pushing the assessment to the financial institutions, using regulation to generate the rules under which this happens. This raises important issues for the financial services industry, particularly where interpretation of the treaties is not clear, since, in most cases, tax authorities will hold the financial intermediary financially and strictly liable if it applies the wrong withholding tax on pay date.

Rules-Based Regulation

The US is technically a combination jurisdiction that permits both relief at source and standard (post pay date) refunds. That said, the Internal Revenue Service (IRS) requirements make it almost impossible for beneficial owners to successfully file standard refunds.

There is a kind of quick refund system in the US but it can only be operated by qualified intermediaries (QIs) via a refund, set-off or reimbursement process built into the QI Agreement.

The concepts that underpin relief at source are:

1. 'Qualified Intermediary' (QI) status by means of a contractual relationship with non-US financial intermediaries to undertake withholding obligations in return for less onerous reporting;
2. Approval of a jurisdiction's Know-Your-Customer (KYC) rules as a pre-requisite to enabling financial institutions to apply for Qualified Intermediary status;
3. Documentation of account holders using US self-certifications or use of documentary evidence (KYC/Anti-Money Laundering [AML]), or both, to establish legal form, residency, eligibility for tax rate and any applicable penalties;

4. Deposits of withheld tax to US Treasury;
5. Full disclosure of all beneficial owners by non-qualified intermediaries (NQIs);
6. Tax Information Reporting on an annual cascade basis including:

   (a) Limited disclosure and pooled reporting for QIs
   (b) Full disclosure and beneficial owner level reporting for NQIs

7. Oversight through triennial Periodic Review and certification of effective internal controls by an appointed Responsible Officer;
8. Enforcement through the application of penalties for compliance failures including late returns, inaccurate returns and under- or over-withholding.

The impact of each of these principles will be discussed in detail in the following chapters. However, in summary:

1. Non-US financial institutions become unpaid tax collectors and report filers on behalf of the IRS;
2. QIs sign up to a six-year, non-negotiable, unilaterally changeable (by IRS) contract under which they agree to:

   (a) Know the IRC Chapter 3 status of their account holders using documentary evidence (KYC/AML), documentation (forms W-8 or W-9), 'reason to know', 'actual knowledge' rules or, in the absence of these, 'presumption rules';
   (b) Appoint a Responsible Officer who must implement a written compliance programme, have sufficient authority to make changes in the business to meet the QI Agreement obligations;
   (c) Submit to two certifications within each six-year contract cycle unless they fall within the rules for waivers;
   (d) Make deposits of tax to US Treasury if they elect to be withholding QIs or instruct a US withholding agent (USWA) bank to make such deposits if they do not so elect;
   (e) Be liable for any under- and/or over-withholding plus penalties and interest.

The overall process is described in Fig. 1.1.

NQIs, who hold their status either by reason of being ineligible for QI status or by choosing not to, can still access tax relief at source on payments made to them, but only subject to full disclosure of their customers to another financial institution which is either a QI or a US withholding agent. NQIs are

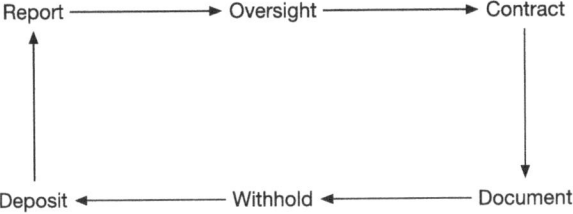

Fig. 1.1 IRC Chapter 3 processes. Source: Author's own

also subject to the reporting and enforcement elements of the regulations, but they don't get the special treatment afforded to QIs. Hence their reporting to the IRS is at the beneficial owner level, not pooled. In other words, for NQIs receiving US-sourced income, all beneficial owners must be disclosed either to another intermediary (in order to get tax relief) or to the IRS (to meet reporting obligations).

As mentioned briefly in the introduction, the trigger for being subject to these principles is simply the receipt of US-sourced Fixed, Determinable, Annual or Periodic (FDAP) income.

There are some common misconceptions about how and when an institution becomes subject to these regulations.

Some hold that not being in the US means that the US tax regulations have no force at all. This is incorrect.

Others hold that they become subject to the regulations because they trade US securities. This also is incorrect; IRC Chapter 3 is about receiving income, not trading. You could trade all you want and receive gross proceeds from the purchase and sale of those securities, as long as you don't receive a dividend, interest or the regulations and rules don't apply (i.e. for the purpose of IRC Chapter 3 gross proceeds are not FDAP income).

The regulations and associated rules also have to take account of the way in which the income flows out and down to the ultimate recipient.

These income payments are typically made by a US withholding agent bank to the account of its customer, who will typically be a non-US financial institution. The ultimate beneficial owner of this US-sourced income may be several levels down in this chain with several financial entities in between. Below the level of the US withholding agent, the way in which the regulations are applied depends very much on the status of the institution receiving the US-sourced income, the tools available to it to meet its obligations, the nature and structure of accounts leading down to the ultimate beneficial owner and the commercial decisions it takes when there are options available within the regulatory framework.

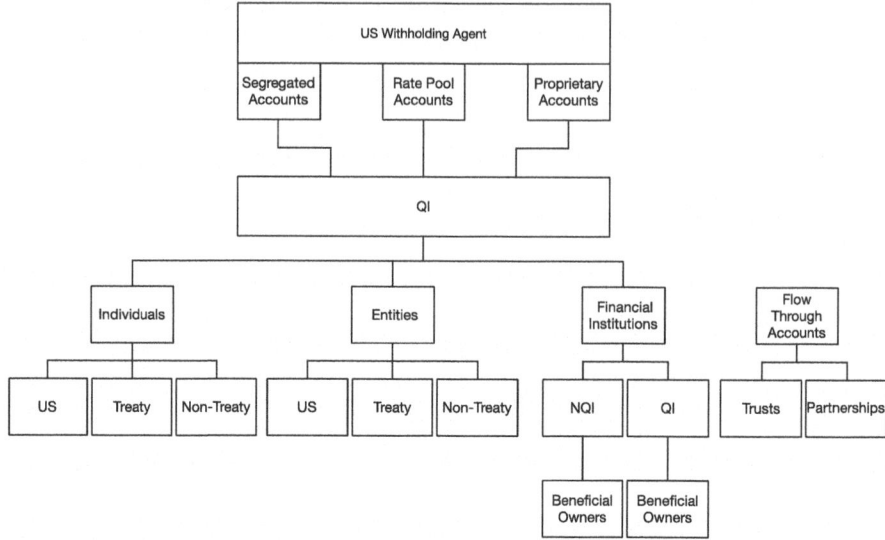

Fig. 1.2 Common account structures and payment flows. Source: Author's own

Figure 1.2 shows a common structure in IRC Chapter 3. A US withholding Agent (USWA) makes payments to accounts operated by its client, a QI. In this model, the QI is not adopting primary withholding and so all client assets are held in 'rate pool accounts'. These are omnibus accounts co-mingling client assets that attract the same tax rate. For US income those would typically be a 0%, 15% and 30% rate pool account. As its client is a QI, the USWA has no interest in whose assets are in which account. The USWA merely pays out for any given corporate action based on the tax rate applicable to that account.

As can be seen, the QI in this model has several types of account holders—individuals, entities, financial institutions and flow-through entities—most with appropriate sub-classifications.

It's important to note, from this diagram, the two outliers—segregated accounts and proprietary accounts. For purposes that will become clear later on, if a QI has proprietary assets, these would need to be held in an account separated from client assets. This also means that a QI would need to document itself separately for each type of account. For the proprietary assets, it's not acting as a QI—it's acting as a beneficial owner so it would present a form W-8BEN-E—while for accounts containing client assets, it would present a form W-8IMY.

The segregated accounts are becoming less popular. These would typically each be a mirror image of the account that a QI holds for a financial institution client (usually an NQI). These are not entirely necessary, as the rate pool accounts are perfectly OK to be used to co-mingle all assets of the same tax rate. However, it's common for QIs to open a segregated account for a QI at a USWA so that they can separate assets of their direct clients from their indirect clients.

The message here for anyone in this field is that mapping out your exposure to the US market and the structure of the cascading chain of custody are vital to getting operational compliance correct.

Most of the practical issues associated with IRC Chapter 3 require an understanding of this chain to be able to make good commercial decisions as well as comply efficiently.

It's very easy to drop down to the granular level too quickly when thinking about practical implications of these regulations. When all this is boiled down, we can state the high-level principle of these regulations as follows, from the perspective of a financial institution:

> Withhold 30% from all payments of US-sourced FDAP income unless you have, in hand, on the pay date, reliable evidence of the recipient's entitlement to a lower rate, exception or exemption from tax on that income. Pay this tax to the US treasury in a timely manner according to the rules and report the income and tax withheld annually to the IRS and to the recipient.

The above rule applies to all financial intermediaries irrespective of whether they are QIs or NQIs. All that changes, with the type of status, is the method by which this overall rule is implemented in practice.

While that may be a reasonably simple concept, there are some important issues that are created by these principles that need to be considered first at this higher level.

The Foreign Intermediary Concept

Most people think the regulations are just for QIs. Actually, the regulations apply to *all* foreign intermediaries, provided they receive US-sourced FDAP income. It is a common misconception that if an institution has not signed a QI Agreement with the IRS, then it is not subject to the regulations. This is not true.

The default status of all non-US financial intermediaries is that of Non-Qualified Intermediary (NQI). NQIs are subject to the regulations as soon as, and for as long as, they receive US-sourced FDAP income. As NQIs they are subject to the full disclosure and reporting of all their customers both to the IRS and to their upstream counterparties.

NQIs and QIs can apply relief at source on payments of US-sourced FDAP income.

So, now we have two top-level categories: QI and NQI. While NQIs have no sub-structure in the regulations, there are two major categories of QIs—withholding QI (WQI) and non-withholding QI (NWQI).

Since the primary objective of the regulations is to control withholding tax, as the description implies, a withholding QI is directly responsible for assessing and making the withholding, or in the vernacular of the regulations, 'assumes primary withholding responsibility'. As such, any US-sourced payment it receives from a US withholding agent bank would be received gross, that is, with no withholding applied. The withholding QI (WQI) is then responsible for calculating the withholding and making deposits of tax directly to the US Treasury.

A non-withholding QI, again as the name implies, does not directly withhold on payments. There are two important points to note. First, as far as the US is concerned, every intermediary in a financial chain is technically a withholding agent even if it does not *actually* withhold. Second, since the non-withholding QI (NWQI) is not actually withholding tax, by definition, someone else is, and in this model, the expectation is that a US withholding agent bank would be doing the actual withholding.

Of course, under normal commercial circumstances, a US withholding agent (USWA) will not know how much to withhold on any given payment since it does not know who the underlying beneficiaries of its customer (the NWQI) are, nor does it know the amounts, eligibility or tax residencies of each of those underlying beneficiaries. This means that a system to allow for information to flow from an NWQI to a USWA must exist in order that the USWA can do its job. We will discuss how this happens in more detail later.

It's important to realise that even though an NWQI is not withholding, since it's technically a withholding agent, it still holds responsibility and liability for correctly organising the withholding. In essence, what's happening is that an NWQI is actually outsourcing its withholding responsibilities to a third party.

As an aside, there are also some other types of entities that can engage in contractual arrangements with the IRS; these are foreign partnerships and private arrangement intermediaries (PAIs). The former are popular with banks that are QIs where they have partnerships as customers.

Of course, as I have pointed out, there are far more NQIs than QIs. It's a critical principle to understand that simply being an NQI does not mean that the intermediary is not subject to the regulations. It just means that it has different rules to follow. The regulations are triggered by the receipt of US-sourced income, not by any firm's status. The NQI population is composed of those who choose not to be QIs (i.e. they are capable under the geographical/approved KYC rules but elect not to engage with the IRS), those who cannot be QIs (because they are in non-approved jurisdictions) and those who are NQIs because they are not aware that they are subject to the regulations. Irrespective of the reasons, the key issue is that the NQI has no contract with the IRS. This also means that the IRS has no *direct* means to control the NQI's compliance to its regulations. President Obama in 2009 went so far as to overtly describe NQIs as 'presumed by the US [government] to be facilitating tax evasion'. As such, where a QI is given some procedural leniency due to its contract, for example, pooled-level reporting, an NQI gets no such perks. Because it is viewed as a natural conduit to engage in treaty shopping, the regulations require full disclosure by NQIs both to upstream withholding agents and to the IRS.

KYC Rules

There are two issues related to 'being a QI'. First is whether any given institution is even capable of being a QI from a geographical perspective. Second, even if the geographical hurdle is overcome, there are different types of QI and associated agreement. Both these issues have a major impact on subsequent practicalities.

The basis of being a qualified intermediary is that the institution concerned must be resident and operating in a tax jurisdiction whose Know-Your-Customer (KYC) rules have been approved by the IRS. There is a list of current approved jurisdictions on the IRS website (http://www.irs.gov/businesses/international/article/0,id=96618,00.html). There is a fundamental principle involved in this rule. The concept of the regulation is to outsource the process of assessing eligibility for relief, part of which also satisfies the IRS objective to deter treaty shopping by its residents. In order to have confidence that any foreign financial institution had adequate systems and controls in place, IRS looked to international rules that might help it. KYC rules are internationally recognised, as are Anti-Money Laundering (AML) rules. For the IRS' purpose, KYC rules were seen as a good tool to use since KYC in all markets is overseen by domestic regulatory bodies.

In the early days of the regulations, it was possible to be a QI in a non-approved jurisdiction using what was termed the 'Home Rule'. Under this rule, for example, a German QI could operate as a QI in, say Kyrgyzstan, provided that it applied the German KYC rules (which are approved) to their

Kyrgyzstan customers. This rule has since been withdrawn. There is another loophole in the system in that, presuming one has a US customer that is trying to treaty shop or evade US tax, the early system would allow a financial institution that was part of a group to take the customer in under one of its NQI subsidiaries and hold the assets in an omnibus account. This would enable the QI parent to meet its obligations without 'knowing' its customer directly. If the NQI subsidiary did not know or meet its disclosure obligations, the US person had successfully by-passed the objective of the system. This loophole has also been closed, not by regulatory means but by commercial pressure and risk aversion in the custody chain as I will explain later.

For those considering QI status, it's important to know that an application to become a QI must be accompanied by a list of the KYC-approved rules for the jurisdiction concerned. However, if the KYC rules for a given jurisdiction do not appear on the IRS list, this does not prevent an applicant from submitting a QI application, provided it also makes an application for the KYC rules to be accepted. If they are, then all other financial institutions in that market also become eligible to be QIs. There are some jurisdictions that have changed their KYC rules since 2001 and these are also listed at the IRS website. As far as the IRS is concerned, the approved KYC rules are based on 18 questions posed by the IRS for each jurisdiction. These will be shown later.

Documentation

From a principle perspective the US system allows QIs and NQIs to use either KYC or its own self-certification forms. This is, of course, on the basis that it has pre-approved the KYC rules of each jurisdiction and it knows that if the QI fails in its KYC documentation in support of the US rules, it will also, by definition, have breached those rules under its own domestic regulatory framework and be subject to penalties. To that extent, there's a certain amount of trust used that the QI would not be likely to breach its own KYC rules, since these are among its core business activities. However, the US also allows for the use of the form series W-8 and also the form W-9, the latter being used to document US persons. As will be detailed later, the W-8 series actually has five forms in it (BEN, BEN-E, EXP, ECI and IMY). However, the big difference between the self-certification concept and the KYC concept is that the W-8 concept places the liability for an incorrect assessment (and subsequent withholding/reporting) at the door of the beneficial owner and not the financial institution. Each W-8 is signed by the beneficial owner 'under penalties of perjury' in US law and an intermediary using such a form is absolved of liability if it is later found that the form was fraudulently presented. Of course, liability is not absolved if the intermediary fails to meet its obligations to verify that the form is valid on the face and meets the relevant requirements for processing.

The documentation issue is also cascade in principle. Not only do beneficial owners have to document themselves to their financial institution, the institutions themselves must also document themselves to upstream institutions. The principle is that everyone must know everyone else that they are dealing with upstream and downstream so that everyone can identify both their role and their obligations.

The net result is that institutions need to spend some time working out whether they will use the KYC documentation they collect, solicit forms W-8 and W-9 from their clients, or both. This has major implications for cost, risk and liability.

Withholding

As I have referenced earlier, there are two types of QI, withholding and non-withholding. The act of withholding is a calculation of the appropriate tax rate based on the evidence in hand on the pay date of a security. That evidence can be KYC/AML (documentary evidence), documentation (W-8 and W-9) and the application of reasons to know, actual knowledge and presumption rules. The actual withholding, thus calculated, can be deducted from a gross payment, with the net being credited to a client's account and the tax being remitted to the US Treasury either directly, by a withholding QI, or indirectly by a non-withholding QI. The use of the rate pool account structures shown in Fig. 1.2 facilitates this on an operational level. The use of rate pool accounts also facilitates an easier reconciliation of payments that is required later on in the cycle at reporting.

For most financial firms, the principles of Chapter 3 apply because they receive simple dividends on long securities positions. However, the IRS has also determined that IRC Chapter 3 withholding (and reporting) should also apply to securities-lending transactions and derivatives dealing. A financial firm that has exposure to these activities and the US market is open to much higher levels of compliance and risk because the rules are inordinately complex. For securities lenders, in addition to the concepts of withholding and non-withholding QI, we also have the concept of a qualified securities lender (QSL). For firms engaged in derivatives dealing, the IRS also adds the concept of a qualified derivatives dealer (QDD).

In securities lending, the IRS determines that, providing there is a US touch point in the transaction, substitute dividends are subject to US withholding tax. Equally, on the derivatives side, if the financial firm creates or trades in products that are equity-linked instruments, notional principal contracts and such like, there is a US withholding tax exposure on dividend equivalents. The rules are very complex and a description of the treatment of these activities is included, at high level, later in this book. Suffice to say, at this stage, that, other than the relatively simple custodial activities relating to simple investments, more exotic activities bring QSL and QDD rules into play at both the withholding and reporting stages in the cycle.

Deposits

It's a critical principle to understand the difference between the IRS and the Treasury in the US model and that there is a difference. Many people that I meet only ever reference the IRS, but in the US withholding tax model, the IRS and the Treasury perform very different roles and therefore have very different agendas.

The US Treasury is responsible for receiving tax dollars, while the IRS is responsible for drafting and communicating regulatory rules and receiving reports. Therefore it's an entirely consistent argument that a QI (or NQI) could be penalised for failing to meet its reporting obligations (to IRS) even though the maximum withholding (30%) had been applied to payments made during the year and deposited (to US Treasury). Equally, it's entirely consistent that a withholding QI could be penalised for failing to deposit tax dollars to the US Treasury in a timely manner, despite its information reporting being on time. Understanding this is important to creating a compliant structure.

Reporting

Reporting is a very important aspect of the US withholding tax system. It's what follows operational compliance and is essentially the first and preparatory stage of oversight of the system. The principle of the system is cascade. Each institution in the chain between a US withholding agent and the final institution servicing an ultimate beneficial owner must file a tax return and submit supporting information returns of some kind to the IRS and to its customers, with only limited exceptions. In the case of IRC Chapter 3, the institutions file a tax return on form 1042 and supporting information returns on form 1042-S. US resident reporting on form 1099 comes under a different chapter of the Code.

Reporting by financial institutions is mandated to be electronic, irrespective of the number of returns involved. This is achieved through the use of an IRS system called—FIRE (Filing Information Returns Electronically).

In addition, the rules for reporting vary depending on the status of the institution involved, that is, QI or NQI. The reports themselves essentially inform the IRS of the gross income by type, the tax withheld on that income and the nature of the recipients. As you can see from Fig. 1.3, the 'recipient' in a chain of investment may well be another financial institution and only at the base of that chain will the recipient be the 'ultimate beneficial owner'. QIs, by reason of their contract with the IRS, gain a benefit in that they are allowed, to an extent, to pool the income of groups of their non-US customers by the rate of tax that was applied to the income during the year. However, it's important to recognise that this is not always the case and there are defined circumstances where QIs are not permitted to pool their reports. This will be discussed in later chapters.

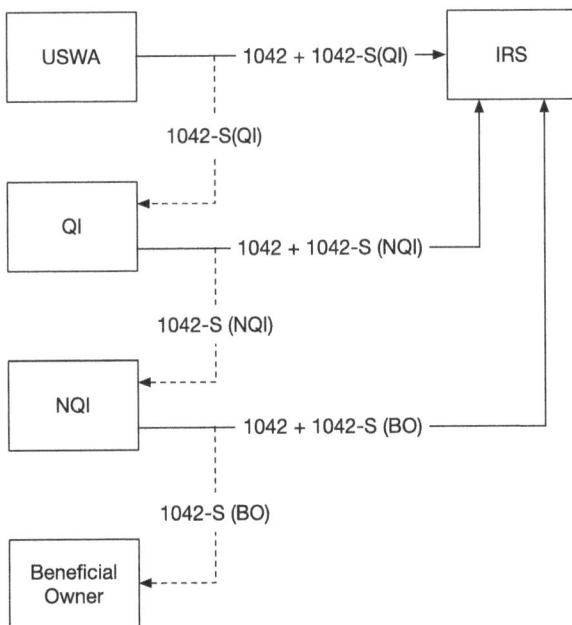

Fig. 1.3 Cascade nature of US reporting. Source: Author's own

The net effect of this pooling concept is that, to a large extent, QIs are permitted under the regulations to protect the identity of their non-US direct customers whilst providing them with relief at source on their US-sourced income. NQIs on the other hand have no such protection and *all* US-sourced income paid to every one of their customers individually and by income type must be reported to the IRS. As we will explore later, who has this obligation depends on a number of circumstances.

The most important aspect for financial institutions to understand is that, in theory, there is no hiding place. As far as a US withholding agent is concerned, the 'recipient', in Fig. 1.3, is a QI. The US withholding agent will know this (1) because it must document its customer under KYC rules and (2) because additionally under IRC Chapter 3, it will have requested and received one of the self-certification forms in the W-8 series (in this case a W-8IMY). The documentation that each intermediary in the chain receives about its customers triggers and determines the way in which the withholding agent treats the account of the QI and also what the end-of-year report contains and looks like.

So, in summary, documentation flows up, while information returns flow out (to IRS) and down.

The US withholding agent, for example, will report to the customer, naming them and identifying them as a QI (based on the W-8IMY) and provide all the relevant information about the US-sourced income and tax withheld on their account(s). Here's the important bit: a copy of that report will be sent to the IRS. Since each entity in the chain must do the same thing, each entity is essentially identified to the IRS as a recipient together with its status. That status determines what the IRS will be expecting to see in the way of reporting from the next entity downstream.

To achieve this electronically in an efficient manner, the regulatory system contains a number of areas where identification numbers are used. At the top of that chain are QIEINs (Qualified Intermediary Employer Identification Numbers), which are assigned to QIs. NQIs, presuming they are meeting their obligations, don't get QIEINs; they just get EINs. These numbers appear on all reports from all levels so that when each level has filed its information reports, the IRS can, in theory, reconcile each level with the lower one. The importance of this will become obvious when we come to discuss oversight and enforcement.

Here are two final comments at this stage that should help the reader understand the context of compliance. First, these EIN numbers are not 'assigned' automatically; they are applied for. And, almost without exception, you can be sure of one thing: if you have to apply for it, there'll be a form for it. Handling these regulations is just as much about form filling and knowing which ones to fill in and when, as it is about day-to-day operational issues. Second, the EIN is just one example of the identity concept. There are several others—Transmitter Control Codes (TCCs); Tax Identification Numbers (TINs), which are issued by the IRS; and Social Security Numbers (SSNs), which are issued by the Social Security Numbering Agency (SSNA), being just three. Administration of compliance is just as big an issue as compliance itself.

Second, in Fig. 1.3, the model shows what happens when an NQI does not disclose its customers to its upstream counterparty. This is extremely common but does not reflect what the IRS expects to happen. The regulations are written in a way that assumes that the default setting is that an NQI should disclose all its clients to its upstream counterparty. If this does occur (and we will explore the details later), then all the NQIs' clients become indirect clients of the QI and the reporting obligation flows to the upstream institution. Needless to say, apart from disclosing your clients to a competitor that makes the NQI and beneficial owner unhappy, the upstream institution has lots of additional work to do. The 'disclosed model' is shown in Fig. 1.4 below for completeness, but no one really wanted it.

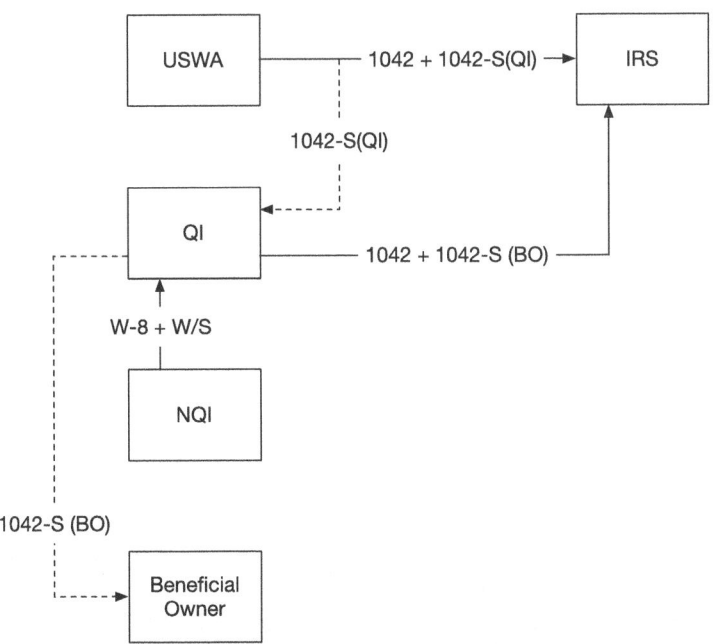

Fig. 1.4 Reporting in a disclosed cascade. Source: Author's own

Oversight

As with any regulatory framework, the regulator needs to have some oversight of the framework in order to know whether it's working or not. IRC Chapter 3 is no exception. The IRS uses two mechanisms to create an oversight system. First, it will not enter into a QI contract with any institution unless that institution is resident in a tax jurisdiction whose Know-Your-Customer rules have previously been approved. When you think about it, this is quite a clever idea. KYC rules are set by each jurisdiction as part of its own oversight of its own institutions. Those domestic rules also have domestic penalties, often financial, if not criminal. So, in accepting the KYC rules of another jurisdiction, the IRS is essentially acknowledging that if an institution breaches the US regulations, it will also be highly likely to be breaching its own domestic regulations. The assumption is that most institutions will be fully compliant with their own domestic regulations and take great pains to stay compliant. This first oversight system of the US leverages that expectation.

The second area of oversight is direct, but only applies to those institutions that have signed a QI Agreement. In the QI Agreement, a QI accepts oversight in the form of the appointment of a Responsible Officer (RO), whose role, amongst other things, is (1) to oversee compliance through a written compliance programme documenting the firm's policies and procedures for compliance to the QI Agreement and (2) to make a triennial certification of effective internal controls to the IRS, which is in turn predicated on the obligation of the RO to have an independent Periodic Review of the firm's compliance.

Since NQIs will almost always receive their US-sourced income either via accounts at a QI or via a US withholding agent, NQIs will also be caught indirectly in these reviews. So, while many NQIs think that they are below the IRS radar, this is very far from the truth. Not only are NQIs reported to the IRS each year unless they fully disclose, the accounts they maintain at other institutions are subject to indirect scrutiny as part of the Periodic Review system.

Enforcement

The major problem the IRS faces is how to 'motivate' compliance among the world's financial institutions. After all, there's only one IRS and many thousands of financial institutions in over 200 countries with diverse languages and cultures. All of these factors add to the already complex basic rules of the system to create risk that somewhere, someone won't do what they are supposed to do whether deliberately, by accident or through lack of awareness.

The US government, including both the IRS and the US Treasury, defines and applies penalties for compliance failures at various levels. Again, these will be discussed in more detail in other chapters. However, the important things to understand are (1) that penalties may be financial and/or reputational and (2) that just because you have no contract with the IRS, it does not mean that you are not subject to either the regulations or their penalties. As I've already pointed out, this system is cascade in nature. I often speak with people at financial institutions that are NQIs who comment that they aren't subject to Code Chapter 3 because they have no contract with the IRS. This is worrying because it demonstrates a fundamental failure in understanding the regulations. Because NQIs operate through accounts at other institutions to access the US equity and debt markets, any penalties that the IRS or the Treasury seek to enforce can be applied indirectly via an upstream account if the subject refuses to pay directly.

I mention financial and reputational enforcement. Financial is obvious, but equally, where a QI is failing to meet its obligations through material failures or events of default or where an NQI is deemed to be breaching the regulations, it's entirely within the remit of the IRS to terminate the contract of a QI or request the closure of the account of an NQI at an upstream institution. Both scenarios have practical consequences, which would make it almost impossible for an institution thus affected to avoid being 'visible' in the market, together with the reputational damage that would ensue.

Penalties

There are a wide range of penalties that can be applied for non-compliance. These include for example:

1. Financial

    (a) Failure to file information returns on time to the IRS
    (b) Failure to file accurate information returns to the IRS
    (c) Failure to use the correct reporting method
    (d) Failure to send reports to recipients
    (e) Periodic Review failure related penalties, for example, under-withholding
    (f) Failure to deposit taxes on time

2. Reputational

    (a) Termination of the QI Agreement
    (b) Closure of accounts (for NQIs via QI or USWA)

One of the biggest problems that has besieged the industry and the IRS for some years, and why most of the industry considers IRC Chapter 3 a failure, is that there has been very little transparency from the IRS on the subject of penalties. Indeed, anecdotally, the IRS is pretty sanguine about, for example, imposing penalties on non-reporting NQIs and has no formal mechanism to publish the results of Periodic Reviews on QIs nor any penalties associated with them. This leaves the industry in a very difficult situation. On the one hand, operations staff in most financial institutions are under enormous daily pressure to do their core business. Quite naturally, with most firms divesting many thousands of jobs over the last few years, the industry is faced with a smaller number of people doing an increasingly complex daily job. With that as a backdrop, it's natural that, if no one is going to penalise you for it, there's a good chance that, even though it may be a regulatory obligation, there's no operational driver to comply. Contrast this with the legal, compliance and risk functions in the same institutions whose objective is not the day-to-day operations such as income processing, but more to protect the company's reputation and minimise risk. In these functions there is no doubt that, just because no one has been subjected to a penalty, it is not a good reason to ignore the risk.

How the IRS Communicates

All of the preceding information thus makes communication and clarity absolutely imperative to proper compliance. The IRS has a number of communication methods, some formal, some informal.

1. Agreements
2. Announcements
3. Attachments
4. Bills
5. Code
6. Forms
7. Guidance
8. Instructions
9. Notices
10. Publications
11. Regulation
12. Revenue procedures

When the IRS issues these forms of communication, it uses a numbering system formed of the type of communication (as noted above) followed by the year (e.g. 2011) and a sequential number of the communiqué. For the most part, the differences between these types of communication are self-explanatory. However, readers should be aware that it's very easy to get confused. There's no reason why there wouldn't be a duplication of numbering (year + sequence number) where the only difference is the type of communication. So, for example, Revenue Procedure 2017-15 is the current QI Agreement, while Notice 2017-15 on the other hand provides guidance on the interpretation of a US legal case on an applicable exclusion amount under the Code and use of the generation-skipping transfer exemption under section 2631. One (the former) is absolutely of interest; the other is not germane to this subject matter at all.

The IRS also has a useful website (www.irs.gov), although visitors should note that this website is primarily oriented to a domestic US audience and so finding material pertinent to the foreign aspects of the US tax system can sometimes take a little time.

On a more informal basis, the IRS sometimes attends meetings with industry interest groups, for example, banking associations and so on.

So, to summarise, IRC Chapter 3 is a true withholding tax system designed to act primarily as a relief at source framework. In this framework, all non-US financial institutions receiving US-sourced FDAP income are, by default, non-qualified, that is, NQIs. NQIs must, under the regulations, document all their customers and disclose these customers to a QI or USWA. Failure to do so can result in IRC Chapter 3 withholding at 30%, if there is no IRC Chapter 4 penalty that would otherwise need to be pre-applied.

Intermediaries that choose to (and are eligible to) can apply to sign a QI Agreement with the IRS that provides certain additional benefits that mitigate the cost and risk of compliance to the regulations.

The main benefits are the ability to keep direct non-US customers' identities confidential from competitors and report the income to those accounts on a pooled basis to the IRS.

In all cases, any customer of an NQI or QI that is an American must be separately reported. Failure to meet the obligations of the regulations and, if you are a QI, the terms of your QI Agreement, carries significant financial and reputational risk.

I'll end this chapter with an observational response to a common question. Many who hear of these regulations are outraged by the seemingly disproportionate scale of the regulations to their purpose and the fact that they appear to be very extraterritorial in nature. Consider the US securities market to be a sand pit. It's the biggest sand pit of its type in the world and it's pretty difficult, if not impossible in the global trading environment, not to want or need to play in this particular sand pit. So while we may not like it, and many don't, we don't make the rules of the sand pit, but we have to abide by them if we want to continue to play in it.

All that said, we should now move on to look at the actual QI contract and the impact it has on financial firms.

2

Contracts: The QI Agreement—With Commentary

The Internal Revenue Service (IRS) default position is that it wants and prefers any non-US financial institution that receives US-sourced Fixed, determinable, Annual or Periodic (FDAP) income to be a QI. The geographically oriented constraint is that such institutions must be located in jurisdictions whose Know-Your-Customer (KYC) rules are approved by the IRS. However, there is a procedure by means of which applicants in non-approved jurisdictions can apply for approval of their KYC rules at the same time as applying for QI status.

The current QI Agreement is Revenue Procedure 2017-15. This is the third main QI Agreement. It was preceded by Revenue Procedure 2014-39 and the original QI Agreement—Revenue Procedure 2000-12.

Just prior to 2001, the IRS was promoting the concept of QI status to many institutions around the world. At that time, the financial world was a very different place to that which we find ourselves in today. That said, financial institutions had and still have major concerns over the cost, risk and implications of this new status of 'qualified intermediary'.

As of today there are estimated to be around 5000 QIs. All the major tier 1 custodian banks, brokers and ICSDs are QIs. There is less certainty elsewhere in terms of both market segment and geographically.

As has been alluded to elsewhere, all intermediaries that receive US-sourced FDAP income are subject to the IRC Chapter 3 regulations. The QI Agreement does not replace the regulations. It adds certain obligations on both sides using the regulations as the starting point.

If you want to be a QI, presuming you are an eligible institution, you are resident in a jurisdiction with approved KYC rules and you receive US-sourced income, you can provide relief at source to your non-US customers without disclosing their identity. Your reporting obligations are simplified, but you will be subject to closer scrutiny through triennial Periodic Review and subsequent certification to the IRS that you have effective internal controls. All this and more is contained in the QI Agreement.

From a practical perspective, we come into contact with many QIs and we have conducted many compliance reviews. To date not one QI has demonstrated to us that it is meeting all the obligations of its QI Agreement and most have both material failures and events of default occurring on a multi-year basis. With that in mind let us look in more detail at the QI Agreement.

Key Principles

Eligibility

There are several aspects to eligibility for QI status. These are:

1. Legal form;
2. Capacity in which acting; and
3. Location.

The QI status is not open to just anyone. Clearly the concept of an 'intermediary' implies that the institution seeking QI status must act in the capacity of an asset servicer or similar with regard to the accounts of its customers. Banks, brokers, prime brokers and custodians all fit neatly into this category. However, the IRS accepts other types of QI, which is useful. These include withholding foreign partnerships (WFPs) and withholding foreign trusts (WFTs). Contracts can also be executed with other types of entities as Private Arrangement Intermediaries (PAIs) in which the QI takes on the responsibility for performing the obligations of a QI for one or more of its customers that are not QIs.

Location is also important. Underpinning the regulations is the concept that a non-US entity seeking QI status is regulated in its own home country and is subject, in particular, to Know-Your-Customer (KYC) rules. The inference is that since a firm is regulated and faces penalties in its home jurisdiction if it does not comply, this establishes a level of control and oversight.

Amendments

It's one of those rather incongruous facts that the QI Agreement can be changed by the IRS unilaterally (cf the foreign financial institution [FFI] terms) but can't be changed unilaterally by the QI.

Withholding or Non-withholding

There are two main types of QI: withholding intermediary (WQI) or non-withholding intermediary (NWQI). The principal difference, as the names suggest, is that a withholding QI takes on the primary responsibility of withholding tax. This means that any US-sourced FDAP income it receives, usually from a US withholding agent (USWA), will be paid gross, that is, no withholding will be applied. A non-withholding QI has the same obligations in contract with the exception that the withholding, and therefore depositing, is performed upstream, again, usually by a US withholding agent. The practical implication of this, given that the QI status allows an institution to protect the identity of its customers, is that an NWQI must find a way to inform its upstream withholding agent how much to withhold from any given payment of US-sourced income.

As noted elsewhere, if the QI is also a Qualified Derivatives Dealer (QDD), there are circumstances in which it cannot act as a non-withholding QI; it must act as a withholding QI.

Renewal

Renewal of a QI Agreement is not automatic. In fact, if the renewal instrument is not submitted to the IRS on their website in sufficient time, a QI can spend up to two years as a non-qualified intermediary before being able to re-submit for QI status. It's therefore imperative for those firms that want to be QIs to understand not just the operational requirements of being a QI, but also the administrative elements that flow from the contract itself.

Account Designation

QIs don't have to act as QIs for every single account that they have. They don't even have to act as a QI for every single account they have that receives US-sourced FDAP income. There are important implications of 'account designation' for QIs. However, at this stage, it's good enough to understand that each QI can make a decision with respect to any account as to whether it needs to or will act in the capacity of QI with respect to that account. This is termed 'account designation'. This has implications not only for what activities take place at the QI account level but also for what kind of accounts the firm might have upstream in the chain of custody and how the upstream counterparty is made aware of the difference through documentation.

Obligations

The other obligations of the QI Agreement cover the main aspects of the IRC Chapter 3 regulations. They set out what the QI must do in terms of:

1. documenting its customers;
2. reviewing and validating documentation;
3. applying presumption rules in the absence of such documentation;
4. depositing taxes to US Treasury;
5. information reporting; and
6. Periodic Reviews and certifications.

As all these activities are the main subject of the other chapters in Part I of this book, I won't go into them in detail here. It will suffice to say that it's in the QI Agreement that a financial institution obtains its ability to have different rules apply to its activities than apply to non-qualified intermediaries (NQIs). Most important among these are

1. the ability to protect the identity of its non-US direct beneficial owners;
2. the ability to provide relief at source on US-sourced FDAP income; and
3. the ability to pool its information returns to the IRS, thus significantly reducing its operational burden.

The QI Agreement by Section

The QI contract can be found in Revenue Procedure 2017-15 (Rev. Proc. 2017-15). The contract has 12 sections and 2 appendices:

1. Purpose, scope and parties
2. Definitions
3. Withholding responsibility and QDD tax liability
4. Arrangements for PAIs, partnerships and trusts
5. Documentation
6. QI certificate and disclosure rules
7. Tax Return obligations (form 1042)
8. Information reporting (form 1042-S)
9. Adjustments and refunds
10. Compliance procedures

11. Expiration, termination, merger and default
12. Miscellaneous
13. Appendix I Information and certification requirements
14. Appendix II Sampling safe harbour for periodic reviewers

Section 1: Purpose and Scope

This section establishes that the QI recognises that it is a withholding agent under IRC Chapter 3 and a payor (of US-sourced FDAP income) under IRC Chapter 61 and Section 3406. This part of the agreement also establishes the concept of designated accounts.

Another important and almost always ignored part of this section of the QI Agreement is that the QI is agreeing that it will comply with the obligations 'as from the effective date'. I don't know of *any* QI, in 18 years, that has met this requirement. The complexity of the agreement is such that a financial institution would have had to spend at least six months, probably more, prior to making its application, in preparing and physically changing its operating and compliance structures in order to be able to be compliant 'on the effective date'—assuming that its application was successful. No, what actually happens is that a prospective QI gathers enough information, if it is lucky, to make some kind of informed decision about being a QI—*then* it applies. Once it obtains its Qualified Intermediary EIN (QIEIN), it begins the process of changing its operating and compliance structures.

Technically, this means that, at the end of its first certification period, it will, by definition, have some degree of non-compliance from the first year in that period. All that said, the term in this section is pretty clear.

This section also has commentary about scope. This is where the scope of QI is expansive and includes Chapter 4 (Foreign Account Tax Compliance Act [FATCA]) compliance, inclusion of the rules for QIs that act as sponsoring entities and permitted permutations of withholding status relating to QDD and Qualified Securities Lender (QSL).

Section 2: Definitions

Self-explanatory, but essentially defines key terms. Of particular interest is the differentiation of the term 'documentary evidence', which refers to KYC material and 'documentation', which refers to the combination of documentary evidence and IRS form W-8 or W-9 (or substitutes of them).

This section of the QI Agreement, and the recitals that precede it, also starts to mention Chapter 4, QSL and QDD rules. While this book is segregating QI and FATCA from an explanatory perspective, the QI Agreement requires that, as a pre-condition of being a QI, the financial institution must comply with all its Chapter 4 obligations. This is important because a QI will have a different and additional obligation in FATCA because it is receiving US-sourced FDAP income so, if necessary it will also have the ability to withhold a FATCA penalty, while an FFI without receipt of US-sourced FDAP income has nothing on which to withhold.

As far as QDD is concerned, there are conditions under which the QI's freedom to act in a non-withholding capacity is restricted. The Home Office Rule that appeared in prior QI Agreements also re-appears in a different form in the current agreement, applying solely to QIs that are also QDDs.

The important takeaway here is not to ignore this section because, while rules are explained in later sections, they are summarised within the section—often in a way that makes far more sense than the tax technical areas deeper in the agreement.

Section 3: Withholding Responsibility and QDD Tax Liability

This section of the agreement deals with the responsibilities referenced by a QI's decision to either accept primary withholding responsibility or not accept in both IRC Chapters 3 and 4 as well as tax deposit requirements. This section of the contract also deals with backup withholding, which is due on undocumented US accounts. The original backup withholding rate was reduced to 24% from 28% in 2018.

This section effectively describes the options open to a QI that it will then be able to use with its upstream counterparties—adoption of primary withholding (or not) in IRC Chapter 3; adoption of primary withholding (or not) in IRC Chapter 4; adoption of withholding as a QDD (or not); adoption of backup withholding and 1099 reporting (or not).

It's important to note here that all these are tick boxes that have major consequences for processing. They are also tick boxes that can be applied, in many cases, differently with each upstream counterparty. So, for example, a QI with a custody business line, a prime brokerage business line and proprietary assets could (may have to) act as a withholding WQI for the prime brokerage side while acting as a non-withholding QI for its custody operations and of course as a beneficial owner for its proprietary assets.

Section 4: PAIs

Section 4 of the QI contract allows a QI to essentially outsource many of its obligations to a third-party intermediary as long as certain conditions are met. The third-party intermediary is called a Private Arrangement Intermediary (PAI). Importantly, QIs may choose to outsource some elements of their obligations, but they cannot outsource their liability. PAIs are rare not least because most QIs struggle to meet their own obligations, let alone meet the obligations of others and are often unprepared to take the risks.

Section 5: Documentation

This is probably the most important part of the QI contract and certainly the foundation of good operational compliance. This section generally describes the requirements for treaty/KYC documentation as well as the W-8 series of forms and W-9s. It also describes the extent to which documentation cannot be relied upon if there is 'actual knowledge' or 'reason to know' that statements made on documents are either unreliable or incorrect. This section of the agreement also describes how QIs must apply 'presumption rules' and coordinate their efforts in IRC Chapter 3 with IRC Chapter 4.

Section 6: Certification and Disclosure

This section of the QI Agreement deals with how a QI can certify its status to a USWA or other QI using a form W-8IMY. As noted, the certification, on form W-8IMY including all the various permutations of ways in which the QI is allowed to act, is specific at the account level to specific counterparties.

Section 7: Tax Return Obligations

This section deals with the US tax return—form 1042, not to be confused with the form 1042-S which is an information return.

In simpler terms consider the 1042 tax return as a kind of summary and the 1042-S information returns as a kind of breakdown of that summary.

The section deals with deadline for filing and methods by which the deadline can be extended. The reality is that everyone in the custody chain files for and gets extensions on both 1042-S and 1042. The extension for the tax return goes to 14 September. The operational complexity, as we will see, for the tax return is that it must reconcile not just to the original 1042-Ss filed earlier in the year, but also to any amended 1042-Ss that were issued after the original filing.

Finally this section also references form 945 returns. A 945 return is required if the QI adopted primary backup withholding responsibility AND actually backup withheld during the year.

Section 8: Information Reporting Obligations

This section is about form 1042-S and sets out the rules for QIs. It's this section that removes the obligation for a QI to provide recipient copies to direct clients (which remains a requirement for NQIs) and allows pooling of those direct clients for the purpose of reporting.

This is also where the requirement is located for separate reporting for clients of a QI that are other financial institutions or flow-through entities, that is, pooling for the purpose of reporting is only for direct accounts (i.e. individuals and entities) that are not financial institutions or flow-through entities (partnerships and trusts).

While this section provides much relief for QIs, it also highlights the speed with which 1042-S processing volumes can escalate for an NQI. If that NQI is disclosing its clients to a QI, that QI in turn is on the receiving end of those escalating volumes. Given that the penalties for late and inaccurate filing apply per form, this highlights how a disclosing NQI represents risk for a QI.

I've also mentioned elsewhere that this book is constructed, for simplicity of explanation, with QI and FATCA issues separated. The QI Agreement does not do this. The convergence of the regulations, despite their very different purposes, has meant that IRC Chapter 4 and IRC Chapter 3 are effectively 'mashed' together in each section of the QI Agreement. This approach has also been taken with QDD and QSL rules, leaving a QI Agreement that is extremely difficult to interpret clearly and operationalise.

Section 9: Adjustments for Over- and Under-Withholding

It is a continuing challenge to explain to QIs that a default position of 'if in doubt, tax at 30% and you'll be fine' is not OK. This is very different from the correct statement that 30%, which is the default statutory US withholding rate, is applied only when a QI does not have reliable documentation or documentary evidence to substantiate a different rate or a client is not eligible or does not claim a different rate. Nor does a QI, as many do, get to choose whether to apply a treaty rate when a client claims it. The base principle of appointing a QI as a withholding agent is that the QI does the job properly. If a client claims a treaty rate and that claim is reliable, the QI is required by the QI Agreement, to provide that rate. We see many QIs applying a 30% rate even when their clients are in treaty jurisdictions *and* make a treaty claim, on the basis that they can make some kind of commercial decision not to apply a claimed rate. No, they can't. This is an example of over-withholding and while perhaps not viewed as seriously from a cash perspective as under-withholding, it is nonetheless both a material failure and an event of default under the QI Agreement.

Under-withholding is more common than over-withholding. The failure rate of W-8 validation procedures, even 18 years into the mission, is still lamentably high, easily over 70% on average in Asia and over 30% on average in Europe, Middle East and Africa (EMEA).

So, this section of the agreement provides some clarity on what procedures are available to QIs to correct over- and under-withholding. To be clear, the IRS has very little incentive, given the scale of the QI regulations and agreement, to accept standard post pay date, post-reporting refunds directly from beneficial owners. QIs cannot just leave their clients out in the cold and this section makes it clear that the IRS expects its appointed withholding agents to step up to the plate and make sure that withholding is done correctly first time and where that doesn't happen, they have to be the solution, not part of the problem.

Section 10: Compliance Procedures

It's often difficult to say which section of the QI Agreement is the most important, because all of them are important. However, this section is the one in which the IRS defines how its contract is monitored and compliance effectively assured. It does this, not by holding out direct oversight, but embedding indirect oversight through the appointment of a Responsible Officer (RO).

Interestingly, as we speak of the convergence of FATCA and QI regulations, FATCA does not have the concept of an RO and so many firms think they don't need one. The reality is that because the QI Agreement does require an RO and the QI Agreement embeds FATCA compliance into its fabric, essentially for firms that are QIs, there is a requirement for an RO that covers both IRC Chapters 3 and 4.

This section of the agreement provides details on the requirement for an RO and the scope of their remit. It cites the requirement for effective controls through adequate systems, change monitoring and training. It cites the requirement for a written compliance programme. Most importantly it provides the framework for triennial independent Periodic Reviews and subsequent certifications to the IRS. This will be explained in more detail in the relevant chapter.

Section 11: Expiration, Termination, Merger and Default

Fairly self-explanatory, this section deals with the conditions under which the agreement is terminated and what happens then. Given that several processes go beyond the US tax year, for example, tax return, information reporting and certifications, the section deals effectively with those obligations that survive the termination of the agreement.

The QI Agreement has several defined terms. Two important ones are 'material failures' and 'events of default'. The definition of material failures contains limitations that restrict activities that were accidental from being included in the definition. However, importantly the limitation has two parts to it. What might be deemed accidental in one part may not be easy to assume as accidental in the other (failure of an RO to adequate policies and procedures). So, the limitations on material failures take what appears clear and concise and makes the issue more interpretive, which can be a good thing for QIs but makes it a more principles-based approach even though it looks rules based.

The standard term of a QI Agreement is six years. To be more precise, the agreement terminates automatically on 31 December of the fifth full year after the year in which the agreement was executed. While the agreement can be terminated by either party, the IRS does note that it won't terminate the agreement unless there has been a 'significant' change in circumstances or an event of default has occurred.

The flaw in the event of default mechanism is that the QI Agreement requires that the only party that can issue an Event of Default Notice is the IRS. The problem is that the same agreement does not explicitly require the RO of a QI to formally disclose any failure other than as part of a triennial certification process. So, while it would seem natural that an RO having knowledge of an event of default would inform the IRS, there is no such requirement built into the agreement.

Section 12: Miscellaneous

There is nothing major in this section, although this is where the IRS gets the right to change the terms, but you don't.

Becoming a QI

Most institutions I speak with make the mistake of not fully understanding what it means to be a QI. In particular, while anyone can read the contracts and other documentation, most do not make any analysis of the practical implications. These include the following.

Resource

The IRS fully expects that a QI has connected the issues associated with meeting its obligations with the resources it will need to implement and maintain those obligations. However, it's common for QIs to maintain a very low resource level, often just one or two people, with any overall knowledge. When these people go on holiday, are sick or worse, leave the business, their knowledge often goes with them. It's therefore more likely that a QI with limited resources will see its relative performance and compliance go up and down with time to the extent that it does not incorporate QI obligations into its corporate memory.

QIs should also build up a library or 'centre of excellence'. Building the QI obligations into corporate memory is vital to avoid the pitfalls of lack of resource and/or lack of training. I recently consulted with one QI who could not even find a copy of their signed QI Agreement. There are a number of different elements to a QI library or resource centre. My own resource centre contains the following sections in which I store both historical and current material:

- Agreements, for example, QI Agreement, Renewal Instrument, Withholding Statement;
- Announcements;
- Attachments, that is, approved KYC attachments for each jurisdiction
- Bills;
- Code, that is, the actual internal revenue codes that are referenced by the QI Agreement;
- Forms, for example, historical forms W-8, 1042, 1042-S, 1099 and various other forms;
- Guidance both from the IRS and other 'trusted' sources;
- Instructions, that is, the instructional material usually related to forms, who should request them, who should complete them, when and how;

- Notices;
- Official explanations, for example, IRS technical documents explaining impacts and also helpful explanations from other 'experts', for example, me;
- Publications, for example, Publication 515, both current and historical;
- Research and background papers, for example, explanatory and other helpful background information provided from time to time by various experts in the field;
- Revenue procedures, for example, Rev Proc 2017-15;
- Validation procedures, for example, control procedures for W-8 forms.

This library concept is structured by the type of communication. An equally valid structure would be one based on the process:

- Contract
- Documentation
- Withholding
- Deposits
- Reporting
- Compliance

The important issue here is to have a library and that it contains both current material and a record of historical material. In some cases, if the IRS changes a form, for example, the form used by a QI must be the right one for the year in question.

Siloes

The financial services industry, like many others, is riddled with inefficiencies that have grown over time. It takes a disruptive force to change those legacy ideas. One such is grouping of activities into departments (siloes) in such a way that communication, sharing of common best practices or even awareness of the bigger picture is either minimal or non-existent. These are the seeds of failure in QI matters because the nature of the agreement requires close coordination across nearly every function in a financial institution. Notwithstanding corporate politics, which can be just as toxic as siloes, the only way that a QI can be effective is through good communication and a corporate culture that facilitates, not prevents, cross-pollination.

Training

Almost every aspect of a financial institution's activities is impacted by QI status, mainly because the US markets often represent a significant part of their business. However, many compliance failures exist because QIs believe that operational compliance is mainly a back-office issue focused on income processing. Many also believe that since the contract is relatively static and the regulations haven't changed much, there's no need for training once the QI status has been achieved. I run training courses on a regular basis and find that (1) staff have extremely low levels of knowledge and understanding and (2) QIs do not apply sufficient resources to meet their obligations. QIs need to have a multi-disciplinary approach to QI status including tax, operations, sales, legal, compliance, risk and IT. All these departments need an overall understanding of the regulations in order that they can prepare appropriately for the impact on their part of the business and importantly, discuss how decisions in one part of the business might impact the needs of other parts.

I should also mention here the issue of QIs with NQI customers. Typically the IRS does not approve of QIs having large percentages of their customer populations represented by NQIs—a fact known at the time of the Periodic Review and annually via the QI's reporting. NQIs are a source of risk in the chain. In the main, most QIs seem to take the view that an NQI's position is entirely up to it and does not affect the QI itself. This is not quite true. Particularly as you travel east from Washington DC and into Asia Pacific, it's not that NQIs are particularly ignoring the regulations (although some are), it's that they don't even know about them. Culture and language all play a part, but so too does the relationship with their upstream counterparty through whom they receive US-sourced payments. Whether or not an NQI is compliant can directly affect the standing of a QI even if only in reputational terms. In my opinion, QIs should take a much more active role in educating their NQI customers about their expected obligations and, in many cases, encouraging them to become QIs at the very least or to be able to indicate at review that they can organise a training programme for their NQIs.

IT and Account Structures

If the QI Agreement is the beginning, the preparation must include some account of the way in which a QI is set up. This will vary depending on what type of QI is involved and what counterparties are able to support. In general

NWQIs operate one of two models. They can operate withholding rate pool accounts so that once a customer is documented, its assets can be moved into the relevant tax rate pool account of the QI at its USWA. In theory, an NWQI could also operate an omnibus account at a USWA and achieve the same result by receiving a record date notification from a USWA to be responded to with a Withholding Rate Pool Statement (WRPS).

While both achieve the same objective, it will clearly take some consideration internally and discussion with US counterparties before a workable solution can be put in place. Other similar issues can easily overwhelm a new QI unless addressed beforehand. How will a QI know whether the income received is US sourced? An obvious question, but not with the most obvious of answers, as around 5% of payments are of a nature where counterparties disagree on whether the income is actually US sourced or not.

What happens if an NWQI receives a payment with incorrect withholding? Again, not an obvious answer, but, despite being an NWQI, if there is under-withholding at the higher level, then it falls to the NWQI to withhold the balance so that the ultimate beneficial owner receives the payment with the correct amount of tax withheld for the documentation on hand.

Since acting as a QI only commences once the intermediary has been allocated its QIEIN by the IRS, in theory these technical aspects (and many others like them) don't need to be addressed until after the QI Agreement is signed. However, I'd always recommend a full internal review of how the firm intends to operate, let alone comply, prior to signing the agreement.

Application

There is a form to complete (SS-4), but the application itself is made on the IRS' QI web portal. The application process is fairly simple and requires the SS-4, 'Attachment A', a business description, and 'Attachment B', the KYC rules that apply to the prospective QI. In addition, the prospective QI will need to enter certain data that provides a sort of profile of the QI in terms of the number of accounts it has with US exposure, the value of those accounts and the types of account. In addition, the prospective QI is required to give the name of its auditor. The prospective QI must indicate if it is going to adopt primary withholding responsibility and whether any of its affiliated businesses is to be included in the agreement.

So, the basic QI Agreement for most financial firms is fairly straightforward and deals with the main processes of documentation, withholding, depositing, reporting, control and oversight.

The complexity in the agreement stems from the fact that it has to take account of convergence of rules with IRC Chapter 4, rule variations that would apply in different circumstances—PAIs, whether the applicant is part of an expanded affiliate group (EAG), whether the applicant is also a QSL or QDD and whether the applicant is planning to adopt any of the primary withholding and reporting obligations.

All these should really be explained and understood prior to making the application so that a prospective QI can make an informed decision about its options (whether optional or mandatory) and how those might affect its operations.

In my experience the only firms that come anywhere close to this level of prior knowledge and gap analysis are tier 1 financial institutions, because they have the resources to be able to analyse and plan. Tier 2 and lower institutions suffer from a much lower level of resource availability and also a lack of understanding at the senior management level.

3

Documentation

Documentation is at the core of these regulations. Get this bit right and most of the rest should follow with much less pain. The converse is also true. In my experience, those firms that either do not understand the documentary requirements of the regulations or choose to try to get around them with commercial expediencies generally fail not only evidential requirements but also withholding and reporting obligations.

This chapter, it follows, is not only one of the most important but also one of the longest.

In this chapter I will explain that:

1. The requirement to document clients is cascade and applies to all firms in the chain of custody irrespective of their status as a qualified intermediary (QI) or non-qualified intermediary (NQI);
2. There is a difference between 'documentary evidence' and 'documentation';
3. Use of documentation, particularly the W-8 series forms and W-9, generally removes liability from a financial institution, while use of documentary evidence does not.
4. Documenting clients serves more than one purpose;
5. Documentation submitted is with respect to specific accounts;
6. Having robust validation procedures that are regularly updated and trained into front line staff is fundamental;
7. Substitute forms, electronic signatures and e-W-8 systems with or without an MoU with the Internal Revenue Service (IRS) are now all possible;
8. The output from the validation process is connected to and drives withholding processes and ultimately information and tax returns.

The Cascade System

The objective of the US QI regulations is to deter treaty shopping and tax evasion. Ironically, if the QI regulations had been more widely adopted between 2001 and 2008, we may never have seen Foreign Account Tax Compliance Act (FATCA) appear at all.

The net result is that the regulations are written in such a way as to require financial institutions to document themselves and *all* their customers in order to determine this.

It's very important to know that in the three primary operational obligations—documentation, withholding *and* reporting—IRC Chapters 3s and 4 are part of a 'cascade' system.

Each entity in the chain between a US withholding agent and the ultimate beneficial owner must provide evidence of their status to the entity upstream from themselves. In this way, all financial institutions outside the US will need to provide a self-certification of status to the upstream institution where they have accounts including but not limited to those that may receive US-sourced income.

At each level, depending on status, each institution will also have to document its account holders. From a practical perspective, it's very common for NQIs, less so for QIs, to misunderstand the rules and assume that it's only their customers that need to be documented, not themselves.

The reader will note from Fig. 3.1 that there are two types of materials described. In the US context, there is a difference between 'documentation' and 'documentary evidence'.

Documentary evidence is material such as Know-Your-Customer (KYC) and Anti-Money Laundering (AML), but NOT the W-8 series or W-9.

When we use the term 'documentation', the IRS means everything in the definition of documentary evidence PLUS the W-8 series. From a practical perspective, all QIs will automatically have a domestic legal obligation to meet KYC and AML laws, so for all practical purposes, most QIs treat 'documentation' as meaning the W-8 forms.

The main reason this is an important difference is that it differentiates liability for the financial institution and determines certain other requirements that I will discuss later. The W-8 series and W-9 are also sometimes referred to as withholding certificates or self-certifications.

In addition, in Fig. 3.1, you will see mention of a withholding statement. There are several places where the language of the US tax rules can be confusing. A withholding certificate (W-8 or W-9) is not the same as a withholding statement. We will discuss withholding statements later on in the withholding process. It is mentioned here because the withholding statement effectively

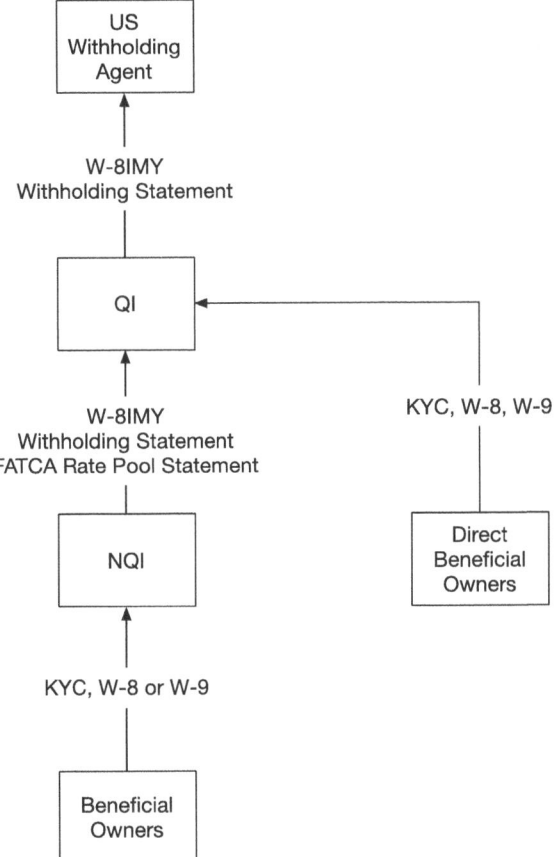

Fig. 3.1 Chain of documentation

goes with the documentation and, together, they establish not just who the counterparty is from a US tax perspective but also allocations of withholding with respect to accounts covered by the documentation.

Documentation in particular has effects on all stages in the compliance process. The nature and way in which documentation is obtained, how it's completed and what validations took place, all have effects on withholding, reporting and even the Periodic Review and the certification stage.

KYC Versus Self-certification

The US regulations take two approaches to documentation. As I've noted in prior chapters, the US makes reference to Know-Your-Customer (KYC) rules when deciding if any given jurisdiction is acceptable as a location for qualified intermediaries to take on the task of documenting non-US customers. So, if you are a QI, by definition, you are resident in a jurisdiction with approved KYC rules. The US government knows that, apart from its own documentation rules outlined below, you will be meeting your own domestic KYC rules in documentary processes and that you are a regulated entity. A list of the approved jurisdictions together with their country attachments can be found on www.irs.gov.

The 'country attachments', as they are called, are a summary of the KYC documents and rules to which financial institutions in that jurisdiction are subject. Note that these can be updated from time to time and the responsibility for updating the IRS with any changes is an obligation of QIs. In fact, failure to do so is an Event of Default of the QI Agreement.

The purpose of the documentation process is to determine five things:

- The identity of the account holder;
- Whether the account holder is a beneficial owner or an intermediary;
- The country where it resides for tax purposes;
- Whether it is a US or non-US person;
- Whether the account holder is entitled to any favourable rate of tax on US-sourced income.

In addition to KYC documentary evidence, institutions are permitted to rely on documentation, specifically the US W-8 series of forms. These are:

- W-8IMY used to document intermediaries
- W-8BEN used to document beneficial owners that are individuals
- W-8BEN-E used to document entities i.e. corporations or 'bodies corporate'
- W-8ECI used to document beneficial owners with 'effectively connected income' from the US
- W-8EXP used to document beneficial owners who are exempt entities

For a full description, readers should refer to the forms and the instructions for each form. Since these forms are 'self' certifications and most financial institutions are not authorised to give tax advice, the institution should not even normally give direction to its customers as to which form they should complete. However, in practice I come across many situations where the instruction from an institution in its marketing or relationship management material references just one form, usually the W-8BEN. While this is indeed the most commonly used form, it's the *beneficial owner's responsibility* to choose which of the forms is most appropriate to his or her circumstances.

The reason for this is related to liability.

'Self-Certifications' are different from 'Certifications of Residency'. Certifications of Residency, for example, the US form 6166, are issued by a tax authority or government agency at the request of a resident. Self-certifications are completed by the residents without recourse to their own tax authority.

Under the US regulations, an institution is allowed to rely on statements made by its customers on a self-certification without any liability, provided the institution properly validates the certification.

That validation process is critical. It consists of three elements:

1. Validation on the face—are statements made on the firm consistent with other statements made on the form? Is it signed and dated and are all mandatory fields completed?
2. Validation to KYC/AML—are the statements on the form consistent with KYC and AML records?
3. Reason to Know and Actual Knowledge—is there any other information that would lead the firm to know that statements made on the form are unreliable?

Only if these three processes lead to a proper validation can the form be relied on and liability thus transferred from the financial form to the person signing the form.

This of course begs the question as to whether the self-certification was consistent with the KYC documentation obtained by the institution, under which the institution *would* have a liability to its domestic regulator. The regulations are clear that financial institutions have an obligation to check that a self- certification form received has no inconsistencies with other information available to it. Many firms adopt a risk mitigation policy and require *all* customers to provide self-certifications. The problem they face is that, for the US, there are five such forms, not one.

This often causes confusion. On the one hand, the institution (QI or NQI) is not normally in a position to give tax advice or guide its customer into which form to complete, even though it may have a good idea based on its other KYC documents. On the other hand, once a form is received, the institution must 'validate' the form, which includes comparing the information on the form to external information, for example, KYC documentation.

This, in turn, may mean that the institution may have to indicate to the client that it can't accept or validate the form because, based on the comparison, it appears to be the wrong form. The two are different issues and trying to reduce the incidence of the latter by essentially pre-judging which form to send will only cause problems.

The US market is still the largest trading market in the world and as such it's difficult for most institutions to avoid some exposure to it. Hence, in documentation terms it's often easier for institutions to add these additional US documents to their account-opening policies and procedures than to try to filter out only those with a US trading exposure. The net result is that many firms will not allow any account to be opened, even if the account holder has no intention of trading in the US markets, without providing one of the US self- certification forms.

I've mentioned the W-8 series above and its focus on non-US account holders. Any US person or US entity would be providing a form W-9 to their institution to evidence their status. Which form is provided determines all subsequent actions by the intermediary?

Account Designation

When financial institutions hold accounts at upstream counterparties or when beneficial owners hold accounts at a financial institution, the documentation provided is usually account specific. It provides status and instruction with respect to those accounts. This is called 'account designation'. Two examples that will help explain are shown in Figs. 3.2 and 3.3 respectively.

A financial institution maintains two accounts at an upstream counterparty from which it receives US-sourced Fixed, Determinable, Annual or Periodic (FDAP) income. The first is an account that co-mingles client assets, and the

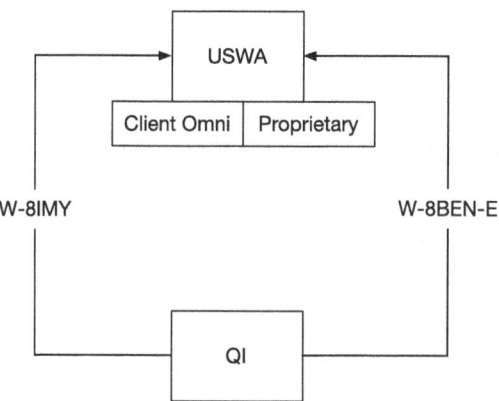

Fig. 3.2 QI with client and proprietary assets

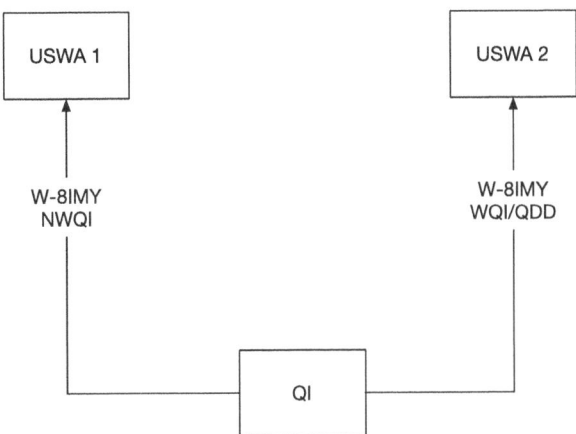

Fig. 3.3 QI with multiple business lines

second is an account for the firm's proprietary assets. So, when we speak of documentation in this context, we would expect two forms W-8—one with respect to the client account in which the financial institution is acting as an intermediary and one with respect to the other account where the financial institution is a corporate beneficial owner.

In the second example, a financial institution, a single legal entity, has two lines of business, a custody operation and a prime brokerage operation, each with separate upstream counterparties. In the custody operation, the firm acts as a non-withholding QI. In the prime brokerage operation, because the firm engages in derivatives dealing, it must act as both a withholding QI and a Qualified Derivatives Dealer (QDD). This firm will need to present two different sets of the form W-8IMY to each upstream counterparty differing based on their different QI statuses.

The message is simple. Do not assume that because you have 'a' client, you will only receive one form of documentation from them. If they have multiple accounts, they may be acting in different capacities for each of those accounts. This is normal.

Documentation Obligations

Documentation and documentary evidence obligations of financial institutions flow from two sources: (1) the regulations themselves, which apply to any financial institution receiving US-sourced FDAP income, and (2) contractual obligations between the IRS and those financial institutions that sign QI Agreements (QIs).

QIs assume certain responsibilities under their QI Agreement with respect to documentation.

- Solicitation. They must, first of all, determine the status of each designated account holder, that is, for each account for which they are acting in the capacity of QI, they must solicit using 'best efforts' all documentation required under their QI Agreement. This will include both KYC and W-8 series or W-9 forms.
- Review. They must review, validate and make sure they track the validity of the documentation that they receive.
- LOB. If their customer is an entity claiming treaty benefits, they must ensure the account holder has properly completed the 'Limitation of Benefits' (LOB) clauses relating to the applicable treaty with the US.

This may sound simple, but in fact it is an extremely complex issue and other operational practices can impact compliance.

It's also important here to note that documentation obligations are codified both in the regulations and in the QI Agreement. So, an NQI cannot generally avoid the documentation obligations since it is subject to them via the regulations, while QIs are subject to them both via the regulations and also their QI Agreement.

Solicitation

There are a number of different issues related to solicitation.

The first is for an institution to remember that it is likely to be at the receiving end of an upstream solicitation request from any institution where it maintains accounts that receive US-sourced income. Equally, it must solicit documentation from its downstream customers, including those that are intermediaries themselves. There are fewer operational issues associated with the upstream solicitation chain since most of those involved are 'in the business' of managing the assets of others. In this world, the knowledge levels and understanding of the tax forms are fairly good.

However, unlike the documentation that a financial institution prepares under IRC Chapter 3, for upstream distribution, the account-level documentation downstream is often being requested of people who (1) have little or no cultural connection to the US; (2) may have English as their second language, at best; and (3) tax technical American English is not understood at all.

Further, most of the received documentation will be paper based and handwritten. There are relatively few systems available to automate these documents.

Most of the KYC-level documentation that is obtained during account opening or review is of course generally, culturally and linguistically aligned. How it's communicated and what language it's in will reflect the domestic regulation that underpins it. However, the US tax forms don't have either of these benefits. I estimate that around 70% of W-8BEN forms received and reviewed are not reliable or valid for purpose. As a result there is a substantial under-withholding and over-withholding taking place even today.

Much of this very high error rate is due to the way in which the forms are solicited. The recipients are not tax experts, nor are they familiar with the way in which US tax language is phrased. In addition, most of the US tax forms (W-8 and W-9) are received hand-written. This means that, in addition to any cultural or linguistic issues, most QIs have to receive and validate handwritten tax forms. The combination of these three issues creates many opportunities for the solicitation process to go wrong.

There are two ways around this kind of problem.

First, the regulations do provide for the use of a 'substitute' form. Second, to the extent allowed, some market participants have developed systems to both assist beneficial owners in understanding the forms and provide electronic methods by which to complete them.

Substitute W-8s

The concept of a substitute form is very simple and I will use the W-8BEN to explain, since this is the most common form involved. The principle is that a financial institution (QI or NQI) can develop its own forms provided it meets certain terms. Language is the most common reason for considering a substitute form with culture coming a close second.

If an institution's clients are mainly individuals who do not have English as a first language, the probability rises that the received forms will be unreliable. So, an institution can design its own form. Typically this might be a 'lookalike' of the form with a foreign language translation for each part of the form placed 'in situ'. The other common method is to translate the whole form and provide the recipient with the English version and the translation, essentially two documents.

Clearly this will be most helpful to customers. The main rule is that, while the institution can *add* information to the form, that is, ask additional questions if it wishes, all the information requested on the *original* form *must* be on the substitute form.

The second rule is that the certification must include the terms of the 'penalty of perjury' clause on the original form.

The third rule is that if a translation is offered, the recipient must be made aware that the English version is the one that is considered to have legal force. In other words, the translation is being provided only as a courtesy.

This to some extent addresses issues of understanding whether cultural or linguistic. The next problems are of readability and consistency. Since most beneficial owners hand-write their responses, the degree to which their writing is legible can cause problems. Also, when writing, beneficial owners have a tendency to paraphrase or abbreviate, particularly when the space available on the form is not large. For the receiving institution, this can cause higher rejection rates. Part of the obligation on receiving institutions is to compare the form with their other records. If a beneficial owner has paraphrased or abbreviated their name, this may not match the institution's account of record. If the writing is not legible, again, technically, this may render the form unusable.

Digitisation

Much effort has gone into the standardisation and digitisation of these forms in recent years. As at the date of writing, the IRS will allow both 'electronic W-8s' and 'electronic signatures' on W-8s. The IRS goes further and allows firms to develop their own systems for solicitation and validation of W-8s forms via software systems. These electronic systems are technically generating substitute W-8 forms. Some commercial firms have leveraged some or all of these options to different degrees. Some large financial institutions, typically at the top of the chain of custody and with indirect clients, have also built their own systems.

In essence, the IRS has taken a three-layer approach to digitisation.

First, the rules have changed to allow an electronic W-8. This would typically be a scanned image or .pdf of a manually produced W-8 that had the original 'wet' signature on it. The resultant 'electronic W-8' can be emailed from a beneficial owner to a financial institution. Generally, these are acceptable as long as the receiving institution has some way to verify that the electronic form originated from its customer. This would typically mean that the email address of the sender should be the email address of record on the customer's account file.

Most financial institutions and third-party vendors still require the paper original to be delivered within 90 days.

The second and more recent change is the acceptance of an electronic signature. The IRS provides rules for the standards of acceptance and there are a few electronic and digital signature vendors that have quickly adopted the approach. Docusign and Signeasy are two examples that can easily be embedded into existing systems or processes. The benefits of an electronic signature are obvious again, provided that the signature can be associated reliably with the customer and that there is traceability and non-repudiation, that is, the data cannot be changed after the e-signature is created.

Finally, the IRS has, for some time, had an eW-8 programme using a Memorandum of Understanding (MoU). The principle is that a commercial vendor or a large financial institution can build its own software system to solicit and validate the W-8 series of forms. The MoU application requires the builder to answer a series of questions that give the IRS comfort that the system will meet the regulations. It's important to note that the regulations themselves allow for an e-W8 system. The MoU is a way to ensure that such a system has credibility in the market, but it is not technically a requirement. This is useful because the MoU programme, at the time of writing, is in moratorium.

The usual access to such systems today is of course via websites. This may be via links to vendor websites or increasingly via APIs between proprietary banking systems and vendors (which are opaque to the end user). Financial institutions with an MoU can, of course, embed their system directly into their custody or brokerage offering.

In order to develop an eW-8 system, a firm would obviously need a compelling business case that the effort would offset either risk or manual processing costs (or both). So, generally eW-8 systems are in the realm of tier 1 financial institutions or commercial vendors where the cost can be offset to large volumes of the forms.

The IRS methodology requires developers to consider certain key objectives in terms of how the business rules of such systems meet the regulatory requirement and, in particular, identify US indicia. The use of electronic signatures is increasing in the US and even within the IRS but it is not yet ubiquitous by any means. In addition, the US knows that electronic signature standards vary across the world and are constantly evolving. So, when it comes to the MoU for an eW-8 system, the technical requirements for electronic signatures are fairly vague, talking more about what the output needs to demonstrate rather than how the output is to be created.

Review and Validation

For those not using an electronic system for solicitation and validation, as I have strongly intimated earlier, getting the documentation right stands at the heart of compliance to IRC Chapter 3 (and of course IRC Chapter 4 too). One of the primary principles of documentation is that, once the form is received, there is an expectation that the recipient will review and validate it for its various purposes.

Unfortunately, in my travels, I come across many more occasions where review and validation does not take place at all and received forms are merely 'filed'. So, I want to spend some time addressing the procedural issues of review and validation.

At the top level there are four things that must be done with any W-8 form received:

1. Completeness—are all mandatory parts of the form completed?
2. Internal consistency—is there any information on the form that is inconsistent with information on any other part of the form?
3. External consistency—is there any information on the form that is inconsistent with external data and/or documentation held by the institution?
4. Indicia of US status—is there any information on the form that might indicate that the beneficial owner may be a US person or has connection through control or ownership, in the case of entities, with US persons?
5. Fitness for purpose(s)—given tests 1–4 have been passed, what purpose can the form be used for? This will depend on which form is being reviewed and what policies the requestor is applying in their compliance programme.

The reason for this fifth item, fitness for purpose(s), is very important. There are firms that choose to use the W-8 forms for both IRC Chapter 3 and IRC Chapter 4 and also for the assessment of exemption on portfolio interest (where all you have to prove to be eligible is that the recipient is not US). However, some firms bifurcate these assessments preferring, for example, to receive IRC Chapter 4 status through a separate self-declaration form.

The usual reason for this is that the firm is aligning its IRC Chapter 4 assessments with its Common Reporting Standard (CRS) assessment because both IRC Chapter 4 and CRS share the same purpose (anti-tax evasion).

While entirely doable, this bifurcation can create operational problems and risk. The CRS documentation process uses self-declarations, as opposed to self- certifications. Self-declarations do not usually carry the penalty of perjury clauses and so liability remains with the financial institution in such circumstances.

So, while the document solicitation and validation processes are critical to getting the other processes of withholding and reporting running smoothly, it is equally important that, before deploying processes, firms make sure they have a robust policy context for them and understand the risks they are accepting, that is, be clear about what purposes you are, and are not, using the forms for, as well as a clear statement about the liabilities and risks associated with your chosen methodology (and how you mitigate them). Such is the world of a QI.

Clearly, just receiving such a W-8 document and filing it (as many do) is insufficient to the requirements of the regulations. A review under any of the above test types may also mean that the recipient has to do further work before being able to use the document in any operational sense. This could mean rejecting the document entirely and requesting a replacement or it could merely mean a clarification with the beneficial owner. The important things to remember are that if there is any remediation work to be done (1) it should be documented so that there is a clear evidence trail of what was done, by whom and when, and (2) until such remediation is complete, the beneficial owner may need to be treated as undocumented and taxed at 30% and the financial institution may need to apply the 'presumption rules'.

Another common error at financial institutions is to misconstrue the purpose of the form and particularly the operational impact of such misconstruction. I'll take two typical examples—the W-8IMY and the W-8BEN.

W-8IMY

The W-8IMY is a self-certification form typically presented by an intermediary, that is, an entity that is not a beneficial owner, but that acts on behalf of one or more underlying beneficial owners. Typical examples might be a broker or certain kinds of trust.

So, on receipt of a W-8IMY, a financial institution immediately knows that its account holder is not a beneficial owner but an intermediary. This fact has an effect on the receiving institution's withholding procedures and information reporting each year. QIs are permitted to 'pool' all their US-sourced income for the purpose of withholding, but they can only pool direct clients for the purpose of reporting. On receipt of a W-8IMY, a receiving institution must immediately know that it will need to separately report the US-sourced income paid to its intermediary client and not pool it. The way in which the report is constructed also depends on the way the W-8IMY is filled in. I will deal with this aspect in more detail in a later chapter.

Further, the answers to many questions on this form are critical both to the receiving institution and to the intermediary.

Most important for IRC Chapter 3 status assessment is whether the intermediary is 'qualified' or not, that is, a QI or NQI. If the intermediary is an NQI, are they prepared to disclose their underlying customers?

If the intermediary is qualified, are they adopting primary withholding responsibility, that is, are they a withholding QI?

What is their stance towards backup withholding and 1099 reporting for US non-exempts? We'll see at various points in this book the overlap between IRC Chapter 4 and IRC Chapter 3, but this is rarely more evident when a financial institution has US (or presumed US) clients.

The W-8IMY also has a trigger section for IRC Chapter 4 status and each status has a separate section in the remainder of the form, meaning that the W-8IMY is not only important but also one of the most complex to understand and complete.

I came across a financial institution recently that presented a client's W-8IMY. After a quick review I said that I could tell two things from the form—first, that the receiving party had no clue what they were doing and second that the presenter also had no clue what they were doing. The presenter had specified that they were a withholding QI on their W-8IMY and the receiver was taxing their US assets at 15%. I knew that both parties were clueless because, if the presenter had known the implications of their status as a withholding QI, they would have been asking their counterparty why their assets were being taxed at all (withholding QIs are paid gross). The receiver had clearly not properly understood what the form was telling them to do, otherwise they would not have been taxing the income.

Ultimately, the lesson here is that there are major operational and compliance implications that flow from how these withholding certificates are completed and interpreted.

So, the W-8IMY not only identifies the account holder but also triggers different operational and compliance processes, depending on how it has been completed.

W-8BEN

The W-8BEN is generally the most common of all the W-8 forms and is often presumed to be just a self-certification of (non-US) residency. Similar to the W-8IMY, what is completed on the form and how it is completed triggers several different processes that the receiving institution must be aware of if it is to avoid problems.

The form establishes the account holder to be a non-US individual both in IRC Chapter 3 and IRC Chapter 4. The IMY and BEN-E forms both have separate classification sections for IRC Chapter 4 whereas the BEN does not.

Validation on the Face

For those not using an automated system—which is most firms—we recommend one of three methods to validate W-8 forms: the 'hot spot' method, the simple flow chart or the detailed flow chart method.

One of the key things about validation of these forms is, depending on volumes, how to do it efficiently. For example, in all three methods we suggest, the validation process is not linear as one might expect. We do not start at the top left and move through the form to the bottom right. That's because 70% of forms that fail validation fail for well-known reasons. These should be checked first. I can reliably manually validate a W-8 form in less than 30 seconds as a result (Figs. 3.4, 3.5, and 3.6).

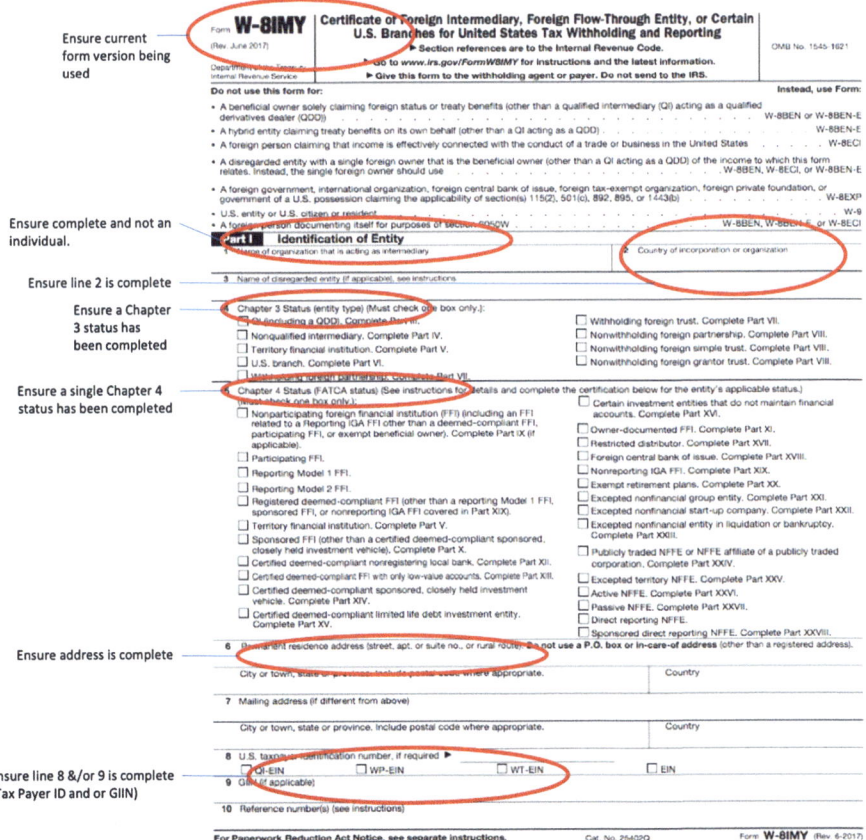

Fig. 3.4 W-8IMY validation on the face—hot spot method. Source: Author's own

Fig. 3.5 W-8IMY validation on the face—simple flow method. Source: Author's own

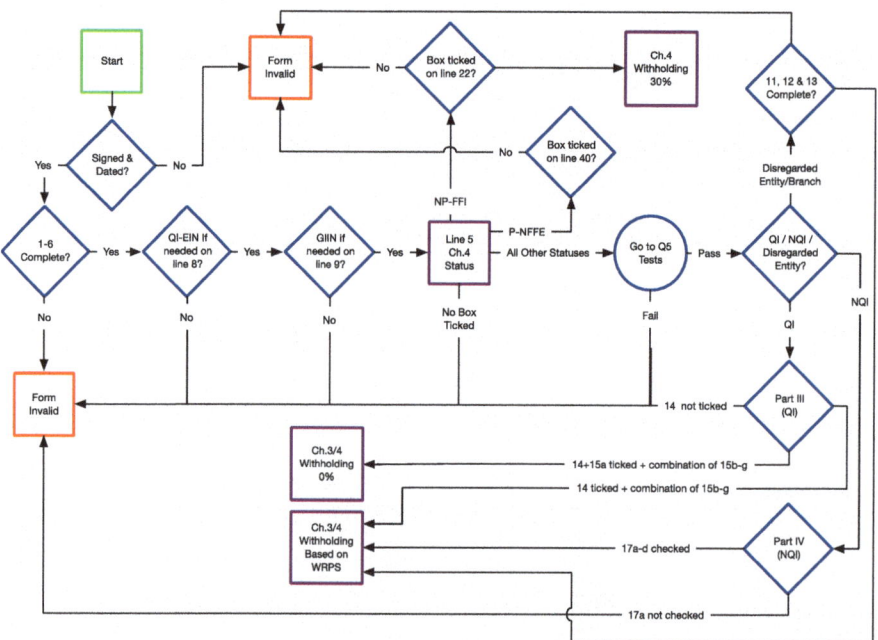

Fig. 3.6 W-8IMY validation on the face—detailed method. Source: Author's own

Practical Consequences

The first point of note is that the rate of withholding that can be applied to US-sourced income received by a financial institution on behalf of a beneficial owner depends on how the form is completed. The most obvious application of this principle is in Part II of the form which clearly states that this part of the form is a 'claim of treaty benefits'. There are several sub-parts to this section, but for our purpose at present, if the form is correctly completed, the institution should be able to ensure that the beneficial owner receives US-sourced FDAP income at the relevant preferential treaty rate applicable between their residence jurisdiction and the US.

However, while FDAP covers a number of income types, for most non-US financial institutions, US-sourced income is usually dividends and portfolio interest. However, only Part I of the W-8BEN would need to be completed for the beneficial owner to receive US-sourced portfolio interest on a gross (no withholding) basis. This is because, currently, the income classification is what drives the 0% (as an exemption) on portfolio interest distributions, while it's the residency of the beneficial owner that drives a preferential rate on dividends where a double tax treaty applies.

Therefore, a receiving institution must know, once it has reviewed and validated the form, how to process different income distributions that would attract different rates—all from one form. Since the Hiring Incentives to Restore Employment (HIRE) Act came into force, under the guise of FATCA in 2013, the portfolio interest exemption to which this applies has been clarified. The exemption used to apply simply because the recipient was not a US person. As part of its crackdown on tax evasion, the US repealed this unlimited exemption with effect from 1 January 2013 and now the exemption only applies if the recipient is not a US person *and* the instrument (bond) that generated the income (portfolio interest) was both immobilised and in registered form.

Registered form merely means that the exemption cannot be granted to portfolio interest payable on an instrument that is in bearer form, or can be converted to, or is fungible with, bearer form instruments.

Immobilised means that the instrument must only be capable of being traded through an electronic book-keeping system (i.e. not a physical form).

Both these examples hopefully highlight that soliciting a W-8 form is the relatively easy bit. Reviewing and validating the form is critical to having a document on which the institution can act and yet is the process most commonly under-addressed. Properly interpreting valid W-8 forms into correct operational withholding and reporting practices is the third element.

So far, I have only looked at the top-level issues associated with these forms.

Man Walks into a Bar

There's another scenario that is worth remembering. The regulations, both in IRC Chapter 3 and IRC Chapter 4, have the concepts of 'reason to know' and 'actual knowledge'. This is particularly important for relationship managers who may well come into contact with customers outside the formal business environment.

The example is that a man walks into a bar and sees his relationship manager there. They have a drink and a chat. The man is documented in the intermediary's systems as non-US. During the conversation, the relationship manager mentions how tough a time he has getting through the queues at JFK when he visits the US. The man sighs and says, he doesn't have the problem because he has a second passport (US). The RM has just been given 'reason to know' that his customer may be a US person and that the bank's records may be unreliable. The technical definition of reason to know is:

> Reason to Know: Information that requires only an ordinary level of intelligence to infer from it that a certain fact exists, or that there are reasonable and sufficient grounds for its existence. Reason to know implies that a reasonable person may accordingly proceed, relying on the fact's likely existence. (Source: BusinessDictionary.com)

The RM doesn't even need to see the passport to go over the 'reason to know' line. The same situation might occur for example, if the conversation covered how many times the man had travelled to the US in the last three years, or that his mother was an American. Both of these also take the relationship manager over the reason to know line and action would have to follow. Clearly this raises an important training issue for many firms (or more likely a directive not to engage in apparently meaningless chat).

Now, let's suppose that the same conversation took place but that this time, the man, instead of just mentioning that he had a US passport, actually takes one out of his pocket and waves it in front of the relationship manager 'I don't get that problem because I have one of these'. Now, the relationship manager has crossed the second line and has 'actual knowledge' that his client is an American. Again, action must be taken, even though it resulted from a chance meeting or one in which business was not a priority. The definition of actual knowledge is:

> Actual Knowledge: Direct and clear cognizance of a circumstance or fact, resulting from information that would lead a reasonable, prudent person to investigate further. (Source: BusinessDictionary.com)

US Indicia

One of the most practical issues associated with these forms and also KYC documents is triggered by the presence of what is called 'US indicia' or 'indicia of US status' in an account. As the term implies, this is the presence of any information that might indicate US status for tax purposes. In IRC Chapter 3, these indicators are based on the KYC and W-8 requirements. In IRC Chapter 4, as we'll see, the indicia become more finely defined. Ultimately, the whole of IRC Chapter 4 (FATCA) is about finding and reporting these US accounts in the fight against tax evasion. In the QI Agreement, it's about correctly processing income and reporting of payments to US persons under IRC Chapters 31 and 61. So, these US indicia are important because they trigger a series of events that can have very unfortunate consequences if it goes wrong.

Accidental Americans

The main data in client onboarding that triggers this extra due diligence includes:

1. either parent born in the US,
2. unrevoked green card,
3. born in the US,
4. US hold mail address,
5. US telephone number,
6. US passport,
7. substantial presence (more than 180 days in the US over three years).

The presence of many of these indicia may have a completely benign reason, but their presence does trigger the requirement on the financial institution to do more work to establish actual status. The directive to do this extra work is so strong that, with US indicia, a W-8 form, for example, will be unreliable until resolved by getting further responses from the account holder, dependent on the nature of the account holder.

The main negative reaction to FATCA has been from Americans who have been denied banking facilities by financial firms that just don't want the hassle of the additional procedures that the US status triggers. However, a very close second are those individuals who don't think of themselves as US citizens at all—Accidental Americans.

The US operates a taxation system based on citizenship. The US also operates a system in which citizenship is automatically granted to those born in the US or whose parents were born in the US. The combination of these two can bring someone into US citizenship without them even realising it. In addition, parents in the US often register their childrens' births and almost contemporaneously apply for a US Social Security Number (SSN) for the child. If the child is removed from the US and has an SSN, it is both automatically a US citizen (by virtue of place of birth) and fully documented as a US citizen. If the child is removed from the US after birth but without having an SSN, the child is still a US citizen. Many years later, if this person now wants to open an investment account, he or she will have major problems and the financial institution will have an uphill relationship battle with its client. Technically, in the first example, the person will have to file three years of US tax returns, then renounce their US citizenship and have a certificate to prove it. In the second example, the person will have to apply for an SSN as an adult and then file three years of US tax returns before renouncing their US citizenship. All this because someone, who probably has had no point of contact with the US since birth, wants to open a bank account.

The unrevoked green card and substantial presence issues are similar in that, people, as they go about their daily lives, rarely contemplate their historical actions could have inadvertently made them subject to a US tax liability. Green card issues are hitting those who usually have spent time in the US working whilst acquiring an education. The substantial presence issue hits those who travel frequently to the US and can, without realising it, cross the magical 183-day line and become subject to US tax liability as a result.

The problem in all these cases is that, under the strict rules of FATCA and QI, a financial firm must 'cure' these indicia when they find them. Unfortunately, statements by the account holder that they have never had any real meaningful exposure to the US just won't be accepted.

The cure has two parts. First, the account holder must provide evidence of their non-US status—that would typically be a W-8 form, a non-US passport and KYC/AML documentation showing non-US status. The second, and more difficult, part of the cure is that they must demonstrate loss of US citizenship (Certificate of Loss of Nationality—CLN). In other words, it's not enough to certify that you are a national of another country; you must also prove that you have revoked your US citizenship. For most people, as I note above, this process is complex and burdensome.

The difficulty they have is that the option of just 'going away' isn't really available. The extraterritorial nature of FATCA and the reach of the IRC Chapter 3 regulations mean that this situation will occur wherever they go.

Worse, assuming they can get the first half of the cure procedure implemented easily enough, but the second half (CLN) is too hard, the financial institution will have no option but to apply what are called the 'presumption rules'. These will force the institution, usually to mitigate risk, to presume their client to be a US non-exempt individual. Because they are unlikely to have a US SSN or be prepared to present a W-9, their account will be flagged as recalcitrant in IRC Chapter 4 (and may be penalised at 30% if they are in a non-intergovernmental agreement [IGA] jurisdiction). In the QI Agreement they will receive a form 1099 and be taxed at 24% (if they weren't penalised in IRC Chapter 4). A copy of the 1099 will go to the IRS.

So, what started as just trying to open an account or trade the US market ends up with the account holder being reported to the IRS in two separate ways, income being taxed at a punitive rate and no real way for the account holder to fix the problem. In other words, a mess.

It's not uncommon for an intermediary to have an upstream account in which it maintains proprietary assets, as well as omnibus client accounts. What can easily confuse a QI is receiving both a W-8BEN-E and a W-8IMY. This would be the case in the example cited.

Spotting Avoidance Tactics

One other comment I would make here is that those receiving forms W-8 should take care to do sufficient due diligence. This is particularly important when it comes to the W-8BEN-E.

Given that much of these regulations are either about correct taxation of income or the detection of potential tax evasion, the latter does not usually occur by people opening individual accounts. It occurs by opening accounts of entities in complex structures designed to hide the underlying owners.

However, there is also another effect of the W-8: that, on receipt by a QI, its assets will be pooled for both withholding and reporting, and there is no reporting to the entity itself. Whether through lack of knowledge or through intent, there are many firms that present a W-8BEN-E when they should be presenting a W-8IMY. This is more common in the brokerage world than it is in the custody world, but it highlights that, while the mantra is that a self-certification can be relied on by a QI without liability, that only applies if the QI applies sufficient due diligence to the form. The validation 'on the face' and to internal materials is the starting point. Reason to Know and Actual Knowledge are also predominantly treated as passive activities. In our work, all it usually takes to spot a W-8BEN-E that should be rejected, or at least questioned, is a visit to the presenter's web site. If that site talks about investments and client assets, it's a pretty good indicator that the presenter is actually an intermediary and not a beneficial owner. They could, of course, as described earlier in this chapter, have both client assets and proprietary assets and you, as the receiver, may only be seeing their proprietary assets, but that should be challenged, because the alternative is that this is a firm that knows it can evade US tax regulations by representing itself as an entity beneficial owner when it is in fact acting as an intermediary.

W-9

This, however, is not the whole story. The forms we have discussed have, so far, only been those needed to evidence non-US status. Many financial institutions have customers who are US persons. On the same principle as the W-8 series, if a QI or NQI receives a W-9, it must treat its customer as a US person. This also has implications for processing payments and withholding.

The most important element of the W-9 from a QI's or NQI's perspective is the presence or absence of a US tax ID (in the case of an entity) or social security number (in the case of an individual). We must remember that documentation is important, not just for its own sake, but because it's the first stage in a five-stage process. Several aspects of the W-9 have to be correct in order to avoid backup withholding on the beneficial owner and form 945 reporting by the institution.

If

1. there is no US tax ID or SSN on these forms, or
2. the given identifiers do not match the IRS database, or
3. the beneficial owner has failed to check the box for exemption from backup withholding, or
4. the form is not properly signed and dated.

The receiving institution will need to apply the backup withholding rules discussed in a later chapter. They may also fall foul of 1099 reporting issues and B and C-Notices where the Tax Identification Number (TIN) eventually provided, does not match the IRS' records.

I often get confused about the subject of US tax identifiers, particularly that intermediaries use the terms SSN and TIN as if they are interchangeable. While the effect may be interchangeability inasmuch as the presence of either one on a W-9 is enough to validate the form, these two numbers are otherwise very different. TINs are issued by the IRS, while SSNs are issued by the Social Security Numbering Agency (SSNA).

Connection to Compliance

As stated at the beginning of the chapter, documentation is fundamental because it is the first of several obligations connected in series and parallel for QIs. The overarching process in the QI Agreement is that of control and oversight.

In the control phase, the Responsible Officer for the firm must have a written compliance programme (CP) documenting policies and procedures by means of which a QI intends to meet its contractual obligations. This CP is formally tested every three years indirectly via a Periodic Review and directly by the RO under his or her obligations elsewhere in the QI Agreement.

One of the most common failures found in Periodic Reviews is under- and/or over-withholding caused by failures of document validation. If the documentation is unreliable, it is likely that the wrong rate of tax gets applied and may also be mis-categorised. That means that the reporting of the withholding will also be inaccurate. When this kind of thing is caused by inadequate procedures in the CP, it's deemed a material failure.

In the first edition of this book, I cited the average failure rate of W-8 validation to be between 30% and 75% with strong bias to higher failure rates in Asia where culture, language and understanding (or lack thereof) of US tax-centric forms have a major effect. Today that failure rate has not improved much and many of the forms I am asked to look at are almost immediately easily identifiable and unreliable.

For QIs it's important to realise that the documentation drives withholding and that withholding must be correct. The IRS is appointing non-US financial forms as withholding agents with special benefits that flow from the commercial contract they engaged in. The requirement is not to apply a 30% rate as a risk prevention strategy, but to apply the correct rate of tax for the conditions on pay date.

Conclusions

So, what have we learned in this chapter?

1. Correctly documenting accounts that are US, Presumed US or receive US-sourced FDAP income is fundamentally important for financial institutions;
2. The US system of documentation is cascade;

3. Every financial institution in the chain must document themselves to their upstream counterparty with respect to any accounts they operate there;
4. Documentation serves multiple purposes but predominantly identifies the correct rate of withholding on US-sourced FDAP income (in Chapter 3) and identifies reportable accounts (in Chapter 4 FATCA);
5. Documentation obligations flow from both the regulations and, additionally for QIs, from their contract with the US government and that these obligations require some significant effort from the recipients to validate the forms;
6. Use of the W-8 forms removes liability from the receiver, provided they apply correct due diligence validation procedures including 'on the face', comparison to KYC/AML, application of reason to know, actual knowledge and presumption rules;
7. Use of the W-9 forms for US non-exempt recipients has similar validation procedures to ensure correct withholding and reporting. Unreliable W-9 forms can trigger backup withholding, form 945 reporting as well as 1099-X reporting IRS B and C-Notices.
8. The best way to avoid the use of complex (and client annoying) presumption rules is to have robust document validation policies and procedures in place so that they (the presumption rules) are never required.
9. Depending on volume and scope of documentation requirements, consider using an automated system either from a third-party vendor or by developing one of your own under an MoU with the IRS.
10. The CP must have robust policies and procedures to control how documentation is solicited, validated and applied in order to avoid consequential material failures in the Periodic Review and risk of loss of QI status.

4

Withholding and Depositing Tax

While documentation is important, the main object of that activity is preparatory to processing income payments to recipients. There is therefore a requirement for some entity in the chain to (1) withhold tax and (2) deposit it with the appropriate authority. In this chapter we will look at some of the practical issues that flow from these two activities and some of the common pitfalls.

Key Principles

Income

There are two issues to deal with:

- Is the income US sourced?
- Is the income of a type that is subject to withholding?

US-sourced income may seem a rather self-explanatory term; however, many institutions, including unfortunately US withholding agents, mistake US-sourced income for income paid in US dollars. The two are different. The latter, for example, would include American Depositary Receipts (ADRs), which are not US-sourced income even though they are paid in US dollars. ADRs are derivative instruments that represent non-US underlying securities. The tax applied to these instruments is therefore determined by reference to the underlying non-US stock, that is, a French ADR is taxed based on the

French stock even though it pays in US dollars. There are some US withholding agents that mistakenly withhold *both* the underlying tax *and* the US tax, mainly because their computer systems are unable to differentiate.

In the complex world of equity instruments, it's also not a foregone conclusion that income coming from the US (ADRs aside) is US-sourced income. Some distributions by Luxembourg entities are deemed US sourced. Some distributions of Delaware entities are also not US sourced. As usual, it depends. Operationally, the further down the payment chain you are, the more likely it is that the determination of whether a payment is US sourced or not will have been done somewhere up the chain and most institutions rely on this upstream determination. However, that means that someone has to make that determination and that will depend on the status of the institution. At the top of the chain, of course, is the US withholding agent (USWA).

However, a withholding QI (WQI) would receive its income gross from a USWA and thus it becomes the top-level determinant, that is, the primary withholding agent. Unfortunately, there can still be disagreements further down the chain since everyone must report, and account, for these deductions. Many firms have tax departments that disagree with the determination and, to ensure that everyone's reporting is consistent, these must be resolved. That said, the number and frequency of these occurrences is, proportionately, relatively small.

The first issue to understand is what to withhold tax on. IRC Chapter 3 withholding is performed on 'FDAP' sourced from the US. FDAP is Fixed, Determinable, Annual or Periodic income. For most QIs this means dividends on equities and interest on bonds. However, there are over 20 different income codes that are defined by the Internal Revenue Service (IRS).

Tax Rates

Most qualified intermediaries (QIs) and non-qualified intermediaries (NQIs) assume that there are only three applicable tax rates—0% for portfolio interest and exempt entities; 15%, which is the general treaty rate that the US has with most of its treaty partners; and 30%, which is the default statutory rate. The withholding rates below are in relation to general dividends issued by US corporations. Other types of income can attract different treaty rates. So, step 1 for any QI is to map their client base by jurisdiction to the types of income received in order to identify the applicable rates. The various rates can be found at https://www.irs.gov/pub/irs-utl/Tax_Treaty_Table_1.pdf.

0%	paid to US non-exempts with a valid W-9, non-US recipients presenting a valid W-8ECI or W-8EXP and those receiving portfolio interest;
10%	paid to treaty claimants in certain jurisdictions, for example, Bulgaria, China;
15%	paid to treaty claimants in most common jurisdictions
20%	paid to treaty claimants in certain jurisdictions, for example, Turkey, Tunisia;
24%	backup withholding rate on US or presumed non-US non-exempt recipients without a valid form W-9;
25%	paid to treaty claimants in certain jurisdictions, for example, India, the Philippines, Israel;
30%	penalty rate in IRC Chapter 4 Statutory rate in IRC Chapter 3;
39.4%	rate applicable to certain distributions from US partnerships.

This can cause problems if a QI or NQI has established its business and operational model on the assumption of only three rates, especially when, out of the blue, a payment is required to be made that falls into one of the other rates. Therefore, it's important for QIs and NQIs to plan for all rates, rather than just some.

Status

It's also important to understand that the IRS defines any non-US financial firm that receives US-sourced FDAP income on behalf of clients as a withholding agent. This also applies to partnerships and trusts, which are not intermediaries per se, but 'flow through entities'. This means that, as far as the IRS is concerned, in a chain of custody, if any one player fails to withhold correctly and this is identified by another intermediary or flow through, they are all withholding agents and thus required to correct the upstream error and account for it in their reporting.

Withholding Mechanisms

There are several mechanisms for withholding. The IRS allows QIs, foreign partnerships and foreign trusts (foreign, in this context, means not the US) to choose whether to adopt primary withholding responsibility or not—in the popular vernacular, whether to be withholding or non-withholding.

The difference is who actually is making the deposit of tax to the US Treasury.

Given that QIs are permitted to pool the assets of their clients for the purpose of withholding, this leads the way open to the use of omnibus accounts that are categorised by the rate and type of withholding applied to any assets held in those accounts.

As I noted in an earlier chapter, the way in which this is communicated between counterparties is via the form W-8IMY at an account-specific or designated account level. The two operational factors are (1) whether the firm is adopting primary withholding in IRC Chapter 3 and/or 4 and also whether it is adopting backup withholding responsibility, and (2) whether or not the firm is using omnibus accounts.

From the tax technical perspective, the first of these is communicated via the W-8IMY and, on that form, the firm is establishing that, in choosing one or more of these options, it will provide a withholding statement as a method to certify that the assets they are handling, are entitled to the rate given. This is done operationally via omnibus accounts. For QIs, these withholding statements do not disclose the underlying beneficial owners, they certify that the account is a 'rate pool' at a given tax rate and categorisation. For NQIs, the withholding statement must identify each recipient individually.

Withholding QIs

As I noted, a withholding QI (WQI) has adopted primary withholding responsibility usually in IRC Chapters 3 and 4 and thus receives US-sourced income gross as shown in Fig. 4.1.

In the withholding QI model, all the WQI needs is an omnibus account and a tax accrual account at a USWA. In essence, the WQI is responsible for the payment of tax to the US Treasury. The USWA will pay the WQI's omnibus account gross. The WQI then only needs to move the appropriate cash into the tax accrual account so that it can then (1) pay the clients net and (2) pay the tax out to the Treasury. This latter is usually done via a US bank using the Electronic Federal Tax Payment System (EFTPS). There does not need to be a tax accrual account for every USWA relationship, so effectively if a WQI has multiple USWAs, it can still operate just one tax accrual account at one institution to move the cash to the US Treasury.

Obviously, sitting behind this principle is that the WQI has correctly documented its clients and can allocate any payment to those holding those assets on record date.

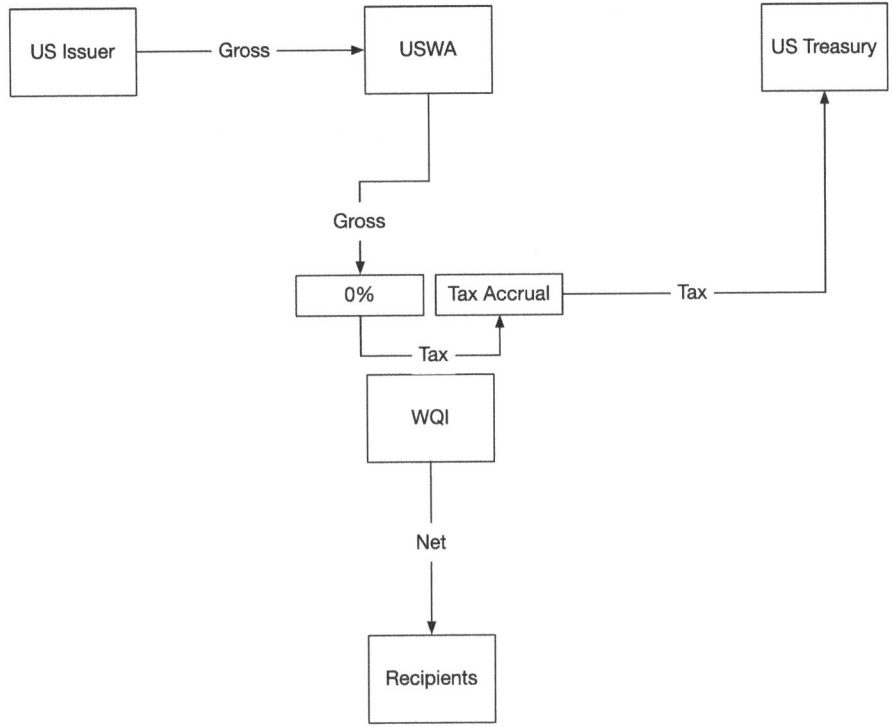

Fig. 4.1 Withholding model for a withholding QI. Source: Author's own

As we will see later, at this stage, it is important for the WQI to correctly categorise the tax it is withholding as well as the rate. It must also record the tax liability (as opposed to the tax paid) as this is required in the reporting part of the cycle.

Non-withholding QIs

A non-withholding QI (NWQI) is effectively outsourcing the activity of withholding to an upstream counterparty.

In addition, despite being an NWQI, if a payment is received and an NWQI sees that there has been under-withholding, the regulations would require that the NWQI then withhold and remit tax to the IRS so that, overall, the correct amount is deposited. In the real world, it's more likely that the NWQI would work with its USWA to correct the error.

Applying Withholding

Typically, an NWQI will either operate segregated rate pool accounts (see Fig. 4.2) or provide a withholding rate pool statement to its withholding agent (see Fig. 4.3). As an aside, because it impacts the reporting phase of the regulations, all QIs and NQIs need to remember that they are *all* defined as withholding agents by the IRS, irrespective of whether they actually withhold tax or not and irrespective of their status as a QI or an NQI.

In the segregated rate pool account model, the NWQI will set up several custody accounts at its USWA, each named for the tax rate that should be applied to the assets in that account. The NWQI then performs its documentation and Know-Your-Customer (KYC) obligations to assign a tax rate for each income type that its customer may receive. As a result of that work, the assets of those clients are allocated to one of the rate pool accounts. So on pay date, the upstream withholding agent already knows how to tax the payment—it just applies the tax based on which account the assets are in. So, for example, if an NWQI has 1,000,000 shares in Microsoft, held in custody by one USWA, it may place some of those shares into a 15% custody account and the remainder in its 30% custody account—the amounts of shares in each account being determined by its underlying documentation of the

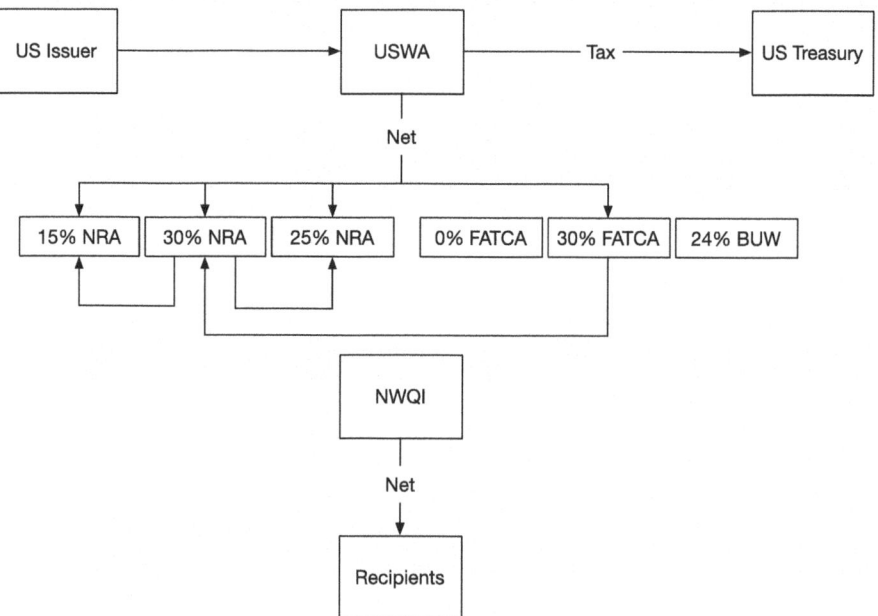

Fig. 4.2 Withholding model for a non-withholding QI. Source: Author's own

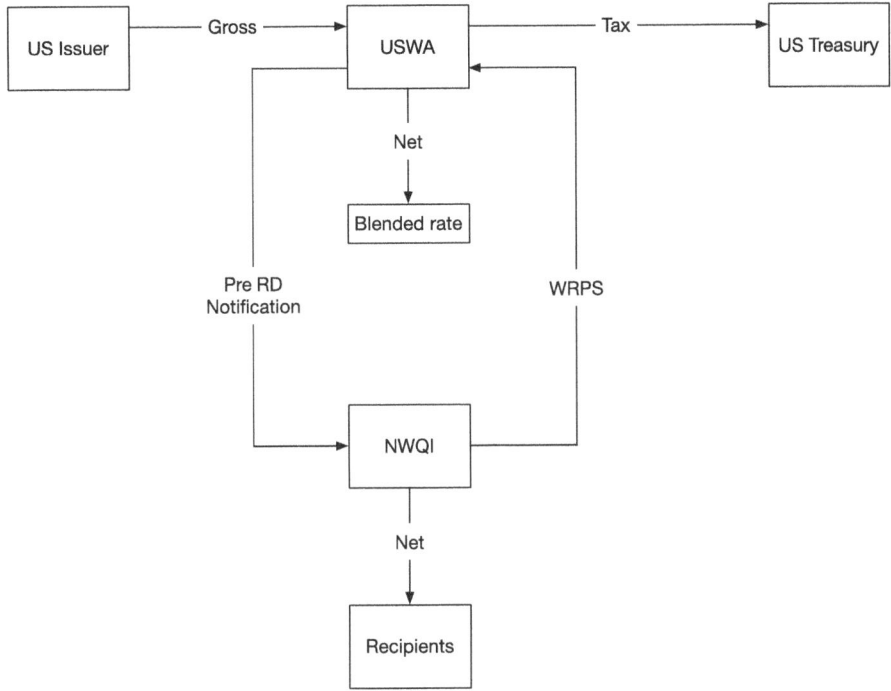

Fig. 4.3 Withholding model for a non-withholding QI with rate pool statements. Source: Author's own

account holder on whose behalf it is acting as custodian of the shares. The practical problem with this type of model is that the NWQI must make sure that the assets are correctly allocated to the right accounts. In a practical scenario, if the NWQI is relying predominantly on W-8 documentation, in order to avoid liability, there may be a period in which there is no W-8 on hand on pay date (assets should be in the 30% account). Then a W-8 turns up (assets moved into the 15% account). If there is a significant change, the W-8 may no longer be valid, OR, if there is no Tax Identification Number (TIN) on the W-8 form, it will become invalid in any event on 31 December three years after the year of signing. In either case, the NWQI must keep track of all this since, for any of the above, the assets would need to be moved into the 30% account, pending new and valid documentation being on hand. Now multiply this effect for many clients.

The alternative to segregated rate pool accounts is the withholding rate pool statement shown in Fig. 4.3. In this model, the NWQI needs only to maintain an omnibus account at its USWA. However, now, in order to withhold correctly, the USWA needs to receive an instruction from its customer as to how much to withhold on any given payment. In order to give the instruction, the USWA needs to inform its customer that a payment is impending. This is usually done prior to record date. The NWQI then assesses all its customers, their tax status and the portion of the impending payment allocable to their holding. The NWQI can now send a simple instruction to its USWA that summarises the tax to be withheld in each of the tax rate categories—this is a withholding rate pool statement (WRPS). Please don't confuse this with a Full Withholding Statement—these are two completely different things.

The result is that the payment made to the omnibus account is effectively at a blended rate. This does mean that in the reporting phase the QI will need to 'tease out' the individual transactions in order to reconcile and report correctly. The WRPS system is also event driven, that is, a WRPS is required for each and every income event, meaning that pre-record date and WRPS messaging needs to be robust. However, if the cost of operating multiple omnibus rate pool accounts is high, this can be an effective system.

Backup Withholding

Backup withholding applies to several scenarios. It applies to any account of a US non-exempt recipient that fails to provide a valid W-9. That includes an unsigned or undated form, a form on which the TIN or Social Security Number (SSN) cannot be validly associated with the IRS database or a form on which the beneficial owner has not ticked the box to certify that they are exempt from backup withholding. It also applies to any account that must be presumed US under presumption rules. In the latter case, almost every 'presumed' US person will not in fact be a US person ergo they are almost certain not to have a US SSN or TIN and by definition, backup withholding will apply. It's important to note also that if backup withholding is actually applied, the financial firm involved becomes liable for the burden of additional form 945 reporting as we shall see later.

Many QIs, and most NQIs, fail to understand backup withholding and how to apply it. There are two main facets to backup withholding: first, the election to perform the activity and second the activity itself. Speaking first of the election issue, some entity in the payment chain must take up the backup withholding responsibility. A QI can adopt this status but equally, it can request that its upstream counterparty (withholding agent) perform this role. As with other aspects of IRC Chapter 3, if an upstream entity is taking up the primary backup withholding responsibility, there will need to be some level of disclosure, this time of US account holders, so that the upstream entity is capable of performing its obligations.

For an NWQI adopting primary backup withholding, the consequence is that it will need to have additional structures in place to allow for another rate of tax to be applied to payments. For example, an NWQI would typically either provide a withholding rate pool statement to its withholding agent between record date and pay date OR maintain rate pool accounts at its withholding agent where it segregates assets based on the applicable tax rates. In both cases, in addition to the non-US tax rates the NWQI would need to establish a 24% account to handle those assets subject to backup withholding in Chapter 31.

Depositing

From the perspective of this book, depositing tax withheld applies mainly to withholding QIs. All NWQIs have the tax withheld on their behalf by an upstream entity, either a withholding QI or a US withholding agent. There are three issues to address here:

- Who the tax is sent to
- When to deposit the withholding tax
- How to deposit the withholding tax

The common assumption in IRC Chapter 3 is that everyone is dealing with the IRS. As noted elsewhere, in fact QIs deal with two segments of the US government: the IRS and the Treasury. From this perspective, tax is deposited with the US Treasury, and tax returns and information returns are submitted to the IRS.

For NWQIs, tax is deposited by an upstream withholding agent and therefore the 'when' is rather immaterial except to say that there is a business obligation that the NWQI should know that its agent, in effect, understands its responsibilities and is meeting them.

For withholding QIs, there is a formula that determines how frequently tax should be deposited. The frequency of payments rises from 'annually' where the annualised withholding amount is small, through to 'every three business days' where it's very large.

In most cases, tax is deposited using the US' Electronic Federal Tax Payment System (EFTPS). While mainly useful for WQIs, the Treasury encourages all QIs to enrol in EFTPS, since they may need to make balancing payments as noted earlier if there is under-withholding elsewhere in the chain.

Penalties

Penalties are assessed by the Treasury for tardiness of depositing tax. These are reviewed regularly and published.

The penalties for late filing are dependent on the lateness of the deposit and the amount of the deposit. If the deposit is 1–5 days late, the penalty is 2%. If the deposit is 6–15 days late, the penalty is 5%. If the deposit is more than 16 days late, the penalty is 10%. In and of itself, this would not normally really be an issue if the payment times were simple, but they aren't.

The time to make a deposit is based on the total amount of tax expected to be deposited.

First, if the amount of tax in a calendar year is expected to be $200 or less, the intermediary can just make the deposit at the same time as they file their tax return (1042).

Second, if at the end of any month, the total amount of tax to be deposited is more than $200 but less than $2000, then the deposit must be made within 15 days.

Third, if the amount of tax is greater than $2000 in any quarter month period, then the tax must be deposited within three business days of the end of the quarter month period.

This formula based 'three-rule' approach means that withholding intermediaries will need to have a very good tracking system to calculate when to make deposits at EFTPS (see Fig. 4.4). Most intermediaries I speak to mitigate this risk simply by paying their tax, at whatever level, assuming rule three that is, three business days.

Intermediaries must also remember that the timings on payments are based on the business days in the US and on the District of Columbia in particular. If you're an intermediary in Asia, for example, it'll be important to understand the impact of the time difference since you'll effectively have almost a day less to effect payment.

Impact on Reporting

It is one final element in this chapter, which will be repeated in the chapter on reporting; for USWAs and WQIs, form 1042 must be completed in full. That form has a table which provides for tax amounts paid to be reported in date order. This must be correct, and based on the tax liability. NWQIs do not have to break these figures out. As a result, most NWQIs merely put the total amount in December and the same amount in the annual total. Life gets

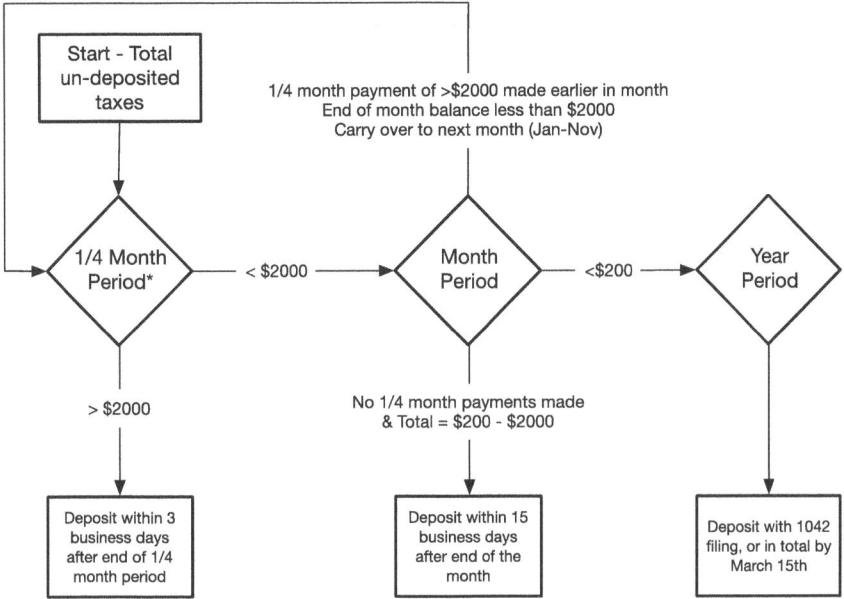

A quarter month period ends on the 7th, 15th, 22nd and last day of the month
A business day is any other than Saturday, Sunday or legal holiday in the District of Columbia

Fig. 4.4 Deposit formula. Source: Author's own

really complicated when a QI has dual status, for example, a business line where it acts as an NWQI and another business line where they act as a WQI.

Refunds and Adjustments

Getting it right would be nice, but in a real world this does not happen. If there is under-withholding, clearly you must make the deposit as soon as possible since the amount will essentially be 'late' and subject to penalties. If there is over-withholding, there are three scenarios available to correct this. The over-withholding may have been a simple mistake, but more likely it's due to new information or new documentation. For example, if you do not have valid documentation, such as a W-8BEN on hand for six months of the year (perhaps a tardy customer), then you receive a valid form; under normal circumstances, there has been no over-withholding because you withheld 30% correctly when the customer was undocumented and then, say, 15% after they became documented. However, if the beneficial owner also provided you with an affidavit of unchanged status, you now have sufficient information and documentation to correct the original withholding and essentially 'make the client whole'. Which one of the three possible methods to adjust withholdings applies depends on when you discover and/or intend to make the adjustment. There's a lot of conflict in this area between what an intermediary is able to do using the available procedures and what it actually may choose to do in a commercial environment.

The primary process would apply if you discover an over-withholding before 15 March of the year after the over-withholding took place. In this case, all an intermediary needs to do is reduce the amount of the next tax deposit to offset the amount refunded to a customer. Of course, this works easily if you, as an intermediary, are a withholding QI, since you're in full control. However, if you're non-withholding, then you'll need to liaise with your upstream QI or USWA, since they are the ones depositing the tax on your behalf. Whether this, or the following procedures, is actually available to you is then not dependent on the regulations, but on whether your counterparty will be supportive. The regulations are so complex and interact with reporting so closely that it's actually quite rare to find a USWA or QI that will support these refund mechanisms.

If there is insufficient undeposited tax to do this or if you've already deposited all the tax at EFTPS, then there are two more methods that can be used—Reimbursement and Set-Off.

In essence, you can use the reimbursement procedure up to 15 March of the year following the over-withholding (or the next available business day if the 15th is on a US weekend or holiday). All you need to do is reimburse your customer out of your own funds (document this with a receipt). You can then reimburse yourself by reducing your future tax deposits (you only have until 31 December of the year after the over-withholding to compete this). That sounds simple enough, but there is an operational twist.

The rule is that, if you intend to use this method, it has to be reflected in your information reporting (1042-S) and US tax return (1042). So, while you have until 31 December to reimburse yourself, you must (1) have already refunded the client and be able to prove it (by 15 March) and (2) show this on your 1042-S information reports, which MUST be filed by the regulatory deadline (15 March) and not under a filing extension. Most intermediaries automatically file for extensions of time to file on form 1042-S, which provides an additional 30 days to file. In this case, the act of filing for the extension would remove the ability of the intermediary to use the reimbursement procedure anyway. The period January to 15 March is very busy for most QIs, so, fiddling with reimbursements while trying to figure out your base reporting obligations, then getting them all to reconcile, in a very practical way, makes the reimbursement procedure very difficult to apply and get right.

The other method available is the 'set-off' procedure. In this model, you are effectively setting off the amount you want to refund the client against an amount of tax that it is due to pay on income it receives in the future. This method is only available up to the date you file 1042-S forms. That would be, in a typical operational environment, 15 March at the earliest and 14 April at the latest.

Finally, if the over-withholding is discovered after 15 March of the year after the over-withholding, none of these methods applies. The only way that the client can recover the over-withheld tax is through a long form claim. In this model, the intermediary does nothing: no changes or amendments to reporting, no payments to the beneficial owner. The beneficial owner will have to file a claim themselves.

This raises another quirk of the system that causes problems for beneficial owners. A standard refund claim, filed by a beneficial owner, has to be supported by evidence of the over-withholding. That would typically be a form 1042-S. However, QIs, by reason of their QI Agreement, are not obliged to produce and distribute 1042-S forms to their direct customers. So, in this case, a direct customer of a QI would find it very difficult to file a claim. That said, the regulations provide that if a direct client of a QI asks for an individual 1042-S, the QI cannot refuse. Having produced such a form, the QI is then obligated to amend its own reporting to reduce its pool by the amount that was separately reported. This will be a nightmare for the QI even if just one client asks for this. It's quite common for QIs to discourage clients from this process and 'its regulation' is often used as the excuse where the real reason is commercial expediency.

Equally, most NQIs are actually in breach of the regulations by never having filed information reports or tax returns to the IRS. So, if the beneficial owner is a customer of a non-disclosing NQI, they too will be unable to file a claim. The latter is described in its own chapter of this book.

Finally, in order to pay a standard refund claim, the IRS wants to know who the primary withholding agent was, that is, who paid the tax and also confirmation that the tax claimed was actually deposited. This information is almost impossible to get unless you are a direct customer of a USWA or a WQI. In effect, the way the rules are written, any claims of under- or over-withholding, must be resolved by QIs within the parameters of the QI regulations. Any other type of claim is very unlikely to succeed.

That said, the standard refund process, when it can be used, is different than for most other markets, in that the 'claim' is actually a tax return. Essentially, while the claimant is not a US person and therefore not subject to

US domestic tax issues, they'll need to file a US tax return (on forms 1040-NR or 1120-F depending on their legal form) in order to claim a refund.

This kind of refund brings its own challenges. From a relationship management perspective, clients can often feel angry that their institution is essentially leaving them out in the cold. However, there is a practical reason why this is usually so. Most investors have accounts with more than one financial institution. If a claim to the US were just that, and similar to say, the EU model, then the investor could file individual claims to the IRS. However, the US claim is actually a tax return and so should contain information about all the investor's US-sourced income from *all* sources. In this respect it's highly unlikely that any one financial institution will have access to all the information needed to make the claim. In addition, the US has been changing the rules associated with standard refunds, which will also make it much more difficult. This includes, for example, a requirement for an original passport to accompany a claim, or a certified copy (certified by an authorised agent outside the US).

The Italian government, amongst others, has tried this tactic before. In the Italian case, the government required, for a short time, that a foreign person claiming a treaty benefit would need an Italian tax identification number. The problem was that, in order to get an Italian tax ID, a foreigner would need to have an Italian residential address. It was observed by many that this could constitute 'abuse of treaty'; however, the procedural change was quickly withdrawn. I suspect that the same situation, or reason, sits behind the US move too. Changing the rules is often a good way to change behaviour without changing policy. The net result of the US changes will be to reduce drastically the number of refund claims filed by non-US persons.

Conclusions

So, what have we learned in this chapter?

1. Withholding is fully dependent on the outcome of the documentation process.
2. All financial intermediaries are technically withholding agents and must correct errors when they see them by withholding appropriately.
3. There are three operating models generally available to QIs:
    (a) 0% Omnibus account model for WQIs
    (b) Rate pool accounts, or
    (c) a blended rate WRPS model for NWQIs

4. Tax deposition is outsourced by an NWQI, but while the activity can be outsourced, the liability cannot.
5. Tax deposition for WQIs is determined by a formula.
6. Under- and over-withholding are material failures of the QI Agreement if too frequent.
7. Refunds are expected to be done using one of the three mechanisms open to QIs. Which one is used is dependent on when the over-withholding was discovered.
8. Refund claims by beneficial owners are complex and unlikely to succeed.

5

Information Reporting and Tax Returns

We began with documentation, the foundation of compliance. We then moved on to withholding and deposition of taxes to the US Treasury. In this chapter we will discuss the practical implications of reporting.

Reporting is a key component of the US system of control and oversight of both qualified intermediaries (QIs) and non-qualified intermediaries (NQIs). It is unlike any other tax relief at source system. However, as the Organisation for Economic Co-operation and Development (OECD) and the EU are converging on a similar model, readers would be wise to assume that, at some point, a reporting mechanism will be added to most jurisdictions' rules.

The principle of the US relief at source system is that the US government is contracting commercially with a non-US financial institution to act as a collector of taxes on its behalf (withholding agent). It's thus not unreasonable to expect that, in that contract (and the regulations), the US has included some ways to monitor and oversee what's going on. Reporting is effectively the US way of monitoring the ongoing adherence to its withholding rules. This is done annually. Oversight, the subject of a different chapter of this book, is performed triennially and through the mechanism of the appointment of a Responsible Officer and the conduct of an independent Periodic Review.

For the US, reporting occurs in several different chapters of the Code. The extent to which any of these reporting requirements apply, and how they apply, depends on the status of the financial institution and the nature of its client base.

Generally, reporting will include:

- Withholding on US-sourced Fixed, Determinable, Annual or Periodic (FDAP) income paid to non-US recipients under IRC Chapter 3 reported on forms 1042-S and 1042
- Withholding on US-sourced FDAP under IRC Chapter 4 on forms 1042-S and 1042 relating to income paid to:
  - unreported intergovernmental agreement (IGA) recalcitrant accounts;
  - NP-FFIs;
  - US non-exempt persons in a FATCA 0% rate pool;
- backup withholding under IRC Chapter 31 reported on form 945;
- income paid to US non-exempt recipients under IRC Chapter 61 on forms 1099-X;
- payments that are not withholdable payments but are reportable amounts.

One of the difficulties in writing this book is that several aspects of the US regulations crossover each other and do not always make sense in isolation. So, for example, if a financial institution has to apply a Foreign Account Tax Compliance Act (FATCA) penalty of 30% to a client in IRC Chapter 4, this will get reported on forms 1042-S and 1042 (even though those forms, for the most part, are reserved for reporting of non-US recipients). Equally, reporting of dividend equivalents under section 871(m) of Chapter 1 is also on forms 1042-S.

So, as with many aspects of these regulations, to properly assess the scope of impact, it's important to map your own exposure not least because, often, many types of reporting (as well as documentation and withholding) may not be relevant to your circumstances.

Even so, reporting rules change on an irregular basis, so the analysis of reporting presented here is necessarily general in nature.

Key Principles

IRS Versus Treasury

It's a commonly held belief that the relationship with the US government is with the Internal Revenue Service (IRS). This is not completely accurate and leads to some common misunderstandings, which in turn can lead to non-compliance.

The IRS is a department or 'arm' of the US Treasury. However, from a practical perspective, when it comes to IRC Chapter 3, the US Treasury deals with tax—the physical cash—while the IRS deals with reporting.

Hence, the Treasury deals with EFTPS, the Electronic Federal Tax Payment System, by means of which QIs and US withholding agents (USWAs) physically transfer tax to the US government.

It is common that an NQI will believe that because it has suffered the maximum withholding (30%) on all its US-sourced income, that it has no reporting obligation. This is not correct.

The regulations are clear; even though maximum withholding has taken place, the IRS still requires reporting to be submitted by means of which the IRS, in theory, can reconcile actual tax dollars received by the Treasury with the amounts reported to the IRS. Think of it another way; no matter how much tax you pay, the US government needs a report so it can reconcile all the different levels in the cascade. It's been estimated by this author that the amount of financial penalties that could be imposed on NQIs globally for this failure to report could be as much as $87 billion a year. Yes, you read that right—in the region of US $87 billion. This is derived from the fact that most financial firms are NQIs not QIs and most are either not reporting at all, ever or if they are, they are reporting inaccurately.

Cascade

As with documentation, information reporting under IRC Chapter 3 is, as I've mentioned above, a cascade system. Everyone in the financial chain must file a report to the IRS of some kind. The system is a top-down cascade. So, at the top, a USWA will provide reports to the IRS and send copies to its customers. As we go further down the chain, the same principle applies. Each entity must file a report to the IRS, with a copy to its customers. The nature of each entity at each level determines just what that reporting should look like and we'll discuss that presently. The important thing to understand is that the cascade system provides the IRS with the ability, in theory, to reconcile reports from one level to those received from the lower level.

Deadlines

One of the most frustrating parts of the regulations relates to the deadlines associated with reporting. Given that the system is a cascade in which there can be many levels, *all* levels have the same deadline—15 March each year.

This causes much angst for a couple of reasons. First, before a QI or NQI in the chain can file its reports, it must make sure that it reconciles to the total of those payments received from its upstream counterparties. It's almost impossible to do this if everyone has the same deadline. The second reason is that there are some forms of US-sourced income that can be reclassified after the end of the US tax year. Such re-classifications are outside the control of the financial intermediaries in the system. Mutual funds and real estate investment trusts (REITs) are two good examples where distributions can be reclassified typically from dividends to return of capital. The former is subject to withholding; the latter is not. This leads to the need to adjust information reports in a very short time span.

The IRS has provided two mechanisms to handle these issues. While there is a single deadline (15 March), it's possible to request an extension of time to file. This is done on forms 8809 (for forms 1042-S) and 7004 (for form 1042). There is no form for a request to have an extension of time to file copies of reports to customers. This is done with a simple letter, but it's an application that requires approval. While the extension of time to file for form 1042 is six months, the extension for Forms 1042-S is only 30 days. In theory this would provide those downstream in the chain sufficient time to receive final reports from their upstream counterparties, reconcile and file their own reports. What actually happens is that everyone in the chain requests an extension. So the problem persists but moves to 14 April (or nearest business day after that). While on this subject, I would observe that it's entirely possible to request a second extension of time to file. The reality is that the world has to be ending (or something close to it) before a second extension would be granted.

Amended Reporting

The second solution is the concept of 'amended reporting', such that, once reports have been filed, institutions can amend previously submitted reports.

The difference between the extension periods for 1042 and 1042-S is explained by amended reporting. Here's what happens. Let's assume that an intermediary has filed for an extension for both forms 1042 and 1042-S. They now have until 14 April to submit their 1042-S forms and 14 September to submit their tax return (1042). The important thing is that the tax return should be as correct as possible. In the industry vernacular, by that time, it should be netted out of all errors and so on. Now let's assume that the intermediary analyses its data to prepare its 1042-S reports for submission on 14 April.

Whatever its own data says about payments it made to its customers, the intermediary must make sure that its 1042-S reports are going to reconcile to the sum of the 1042-S reports it receives from any upstream intermediaries (remember, reporting is cascade). So, even if it can get all its data together *and* it looks accurate, it will have to wait until it receives all its upstream 1042-S reports to be sure that its numbers reconcile. If they don't reconcile, even by a small amount, they risk being penalised for inaccurate reporting. The performance of US withholding agents on this issue is very patchy. Most downstream institutions ask for quarterly reconciliations of data so that, by the time the deadline nears, the outstanding data to reconcile is relatively small. However, many USWAs' systems are not set up to give this kind of support.

Now let's move the calendar on and say that they have received their upstream 1042-S forms and that they do reconcile. Now, they can file their information reports 1042-S, BUT they do not yet need to file their tax return 1042. Many intermediaries mistakenly believe that, even though they have additional time, the fact that their reports reconcile is enough and that they can just file all together. This would be unwise. Here's why: let's presume that they reconciled their reports and filed their 1042-S package to the IRS. Now they start getting 'amended reports' from their upstream institutions due to re-classifications of income (or perhaps even just correction of errors). This sort of thing can go on for some time, often late May or early June. The intermediary must realise that what reconciled on day 'one' will now not reconcile, because the upstream institution has changed its reports. This forces the intermediary to change its 1042-S reports in order to avoid an inaccurate filing penalty. If the intermediary has already filed its tax return as well, it will have to start amending that too, which is much worse. So, the general practical rule is to hold back on filing your tax return for as long as possible, so you only have to do it once.

The other scenario I come across is one where either the deadlines or the lack of upstream reports causes an intermediary to feel that it should delay submitting its 1042-S reports, even after the extension deadline. This is a bad thing. First, this happens to many intermediaries. The further up the financial chain you go, the less concerned the financial institutions appear to be about the woes that the customers of their customers might suffer as a result of their using the maximum time to distribute 1042-S reports. Even without this, many intermediaries will know that their data is not perfect. The simple rule in practical terms is 'it's better to file something than file late'. If you think about it, the feature of the system that provides a difference in extended deadlines gives a certain amount of time (14 April to 14 September) to get things right. It's not just re-classifications that can trigger an amended information report. Clearly, no one wants to be doing this complex onerous process on multiple occasions. However, if an intermediary knows its data is not perfect, it should, from a simple financial risk perspective, submit its 1042-S reports to the IRS before or on its maximum deadline (including any extensions). This immediately means that the intermediary avoids any significant IRS penalty for failure to file reports 1042-S. The intermediary now has time to (1) wait for any re-classifications and (2) correct any errors. Once it has done that, it can file its amended reports together with its tax return (1042) in September. Hopefully, this example shows why it's important to understand the difference between an information report and a tax return. The practical consequences of misunderstanding can be significant.

It's also worth noting here that 'amending' is a specific term. If, as a result of changes and re-classifications, a new 1042-S is created that did not exist before, that would attract a late-filing penalty because it's not amending a 1042-S; it's filing a new one.

Reportable Amounts Versus Reportable Payments

One of the common errors in reporting is that the filer does not include all the income that should be reported. Typically, foreign intermediaries concentrate on US-sourced income paid to their clients on which tax was withheld—these are reportable payments. It's understandable that they would focus on this. However, information reporting requires intermediaries to also report certain amounts on which there may not have been a payment of income, or even a withholding. These are reportable *amounts*. Intermediaries preparing their report packages should be mindful that they report the correct amounts.

The Forms

QIs and NQIs have reporting obligations that differ, even though they sit within the same cascade system.

The IRS requires reporting of all US-sourced income paid to recipients outside the US. This falls into two categories—(1) income paid to non-US recipients and (2) income paid to US recipients. The forms used for each are radically different, although the information on the forms is similar.

US-sourced income paid to non-US recipients is reported using forms on the form 1042-S. The intermediary submitting such reports is also subject to a US tax return (which will summarise all the income and tax withheld from all sources) on form 1042.

5 Information Reporting and Tax Returns

While the tax return 1042 is relatively simple, the 1042-S form is less so, because the number and way in which the 1042-S forms must be completed depends on a number of factors, including:

1. Whether the filer is a QI or an NQI
2. If the filer is an NQI, the extent to which there has been 'disclosure' to a QI or USWA

This is discussed in more detail below.
Income paid to US recipients is reported on forms in the 1099 series.

Disclosure

As a general principle, all US persons receiving US-sourced income in the chain must be reported, that is, disclosed, at the individual level. This is done using forms 1099, which are grouped by type of income received, that is, 1099-DIV for dividend income paid to a US person, 1099-INT for interest and so on.

The main issue to remember is that while forms downloaded from the internet can be used for 1042 and 1042-S reporting (presuming them to be the correct forms for the reporting year in question), this is not the case with 1099 forms. While they can be downloaded, they should not be used for filing.

When it comes to non-residents, reporting takes on a slightly more complex flavour. A QI is able, due to its contract with the US government, to protect the identity of its non-US *direct* customers. This takes the form of so-called pooled reporting in which the QI aggregates all its direct customers' US-sourced income by the tax rate and income type that were applied during the year. The important word here is 'direct'. QIs do not have the luxury of pooling the reporting their indirect clients and many QIs trip over this distinction. If a QI has five customers, two direct beneficial owners and three indirect customers, it would be able to pool the income from the first two into one 1042-S report, thus protecting the identity of those two customers. The other three would have to be reported separately on individual forms 1042-S. This concept connects with the cascade nature of the system. There is also one important extra issue for QIs. If a QI has an indirect customer, the question is whether that indirect customer is also a QI or, far more likely, an NQI. The QI will determine this by reference to the documentation process and would typically expect to receive a form W-8IMY from such account holders. The way in which the W-8IMY is completed by the account holder and the subsequent actions taken will determine what reporting obligations the QI has and, in many cases, what obligations the NQI has. Ultimately, the IRS only permits QIs to protect the identity of their customers and that, only to a limited degree. Where there is no contract, the general principle is that the IRS expects the individual beneficial owners to be reported directly to the IRS. This concept supports the principle that the regulations are intended to deter US persons from hiding their assets in a chain of intermediaries.

So, now we know that information reporting under IRC Chapter 3:

1. is a fundamental and important activity within the regulations which is unrelated to the activity of withholding and depositing taxes;
2. is cascade in nature, with each entity in the chain generating a report of some kind, both downstream to its customers and to the IRS;
3. has a single deadline for all entities in the chain to file reports;
4. provides for different reports for US persons (1099-X) from those of non-US persons (1042 and 1042-S);
5. generally expects reporting in electronic format;
6. allows some entities to protect the identity of their customers in these reports, but requires complete disclosure of others.

Overlap to FATCA

It's also worth noting something that confuses people greatly. The forms 1042-S and 1042 are generally associated with reporting of US-sourced FDAP income paid to non-US recipients. In general, this is true. However, there are some exceptions. The most common exception is with respect to FATCA or IRC Chapter 4. There are some places in the regulations where IRC Chapter 3 and IRC Chapter 4 converge and this is one of them.

The basis of the logic starts with the fact that, for any payment, a withholding agent is required to assess the payment for IRC Chapter 4 (FATCA) penalties and only if there are no FATCA penalties to apply, then to assess the payment for IRC Chapter 3 taxation of US-sourced income. Remember that IRC Chapter 4 is about anti-tax evasion in which the penalty is applied through the tax system, but it is a penalty for not doing something that should have been done—that is, it's not really a tax.

So, the first convergence in reporting is that, for payments made to non-US recipients, the 1042-S forms must have a coding to confirm whether a FATCA penalty was applied and if not, why not.

The second convergence is with respect to payments made to US non-exempt recipients. If a withholding agent has clients that are US, and if they are properly documented and validated, the tax rate to apply is 0% (because they should be declaring and paying tax on these foreign assets domestically in the US). However, this is not IRC Chapter 3 reporting. The assets of these US clients would be pooled (by a QI) into what is called a 'FATCA rate pool of US non-exempt recipients'. Hence, in withholding terms, a QI could have two FATCA omnibus accounts—a 0% for the assets of US clients and a 30% for FATCA penalties on recalcitrants (in non-IGA markets), unreported recalcitrants (in IGA markets) and non-participating FFIs (anywhere). The reporting of payments made in these categories is, obtusely, on forms 1042-S.

1042 and 1042-S Reporting Mechanisms

As soon as we use the terms 1042 and 1042-S, we know that we are talking about reporting to the IRS with respect to US-sourced FDAP income paid to non-US recipients.

As noted, form 1042 is actually a tax return, whereas forms 1042-S are information reports. I tend to explain it, from a practical perspective, as a summary and breakdown. The 1042 is the summary and the 1042-Ss are the breakdown.

The level to which the breakdown goes will depend on the nature of the financial institution, the types of customers it has and their status with the IRS.

Using Fig. 5.1, I will explain how this reporting takes place. The diagram may look complex, but this is only so that I can explain how some of the decision processes work. There are three factors at work:

1. The nature of the financial chain between the beneficial owner and the USWA
2. The nature of the accounts held up- and downstream by each intermediary
3. The way in which certifications have been completed by each party

The reader may note that, from a reporting perspective, it looks quite simple, and in principle, it is. Each level must file reports and tax returns to the IRS each year.

The way in which the IRS 'connects' all these reports is through the intermediaries' Employer Identification Number (EIN), which is obtained from the IRS. For QIs, this will be a Qualified Intermediary EIN (QIEIN) and for

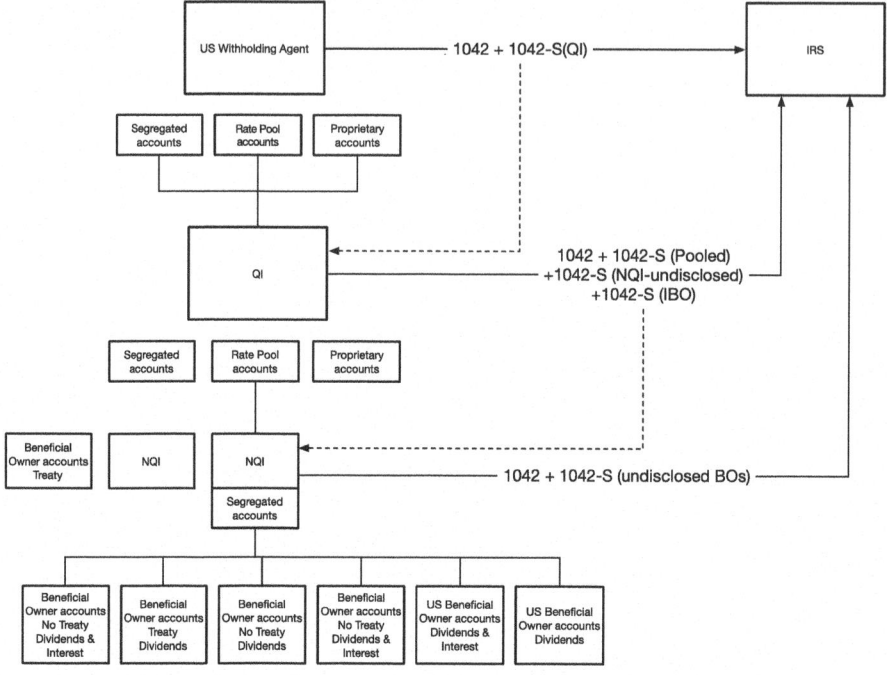

Fig. 5.1 1042 and 1042-S reporting explained

NQIs, it will just be an EIN. So, the first pre-requisite to reporting is that any intermediary receiving US-sourced FDAP income should apply for an EIN of the relevant type.

However, the number of reports and the level of reporting is different depending on the above factors.

The diagram exemplifies that in real life, the financial system is a 'broad cascade'. In other words, each level will have multiple counterparties at the next level down. So, a USWA does not have just one customer but many. The QI in Fig. 5.1 has three customers—a direct beneficial owner and two NQIs. The NQI on the far right of the diagram has a number of direct beneficial owners, each of which has a segregated account at the NQI. Some are US persons and some are not. Of the customers who are not US persons, some are resident in jurisdictions with a treaty with the US and some are not. So far so good. We see that the cascade is something more like a pyramid in that it's relatively simple at the top, but gets more complex as we drop down the financial chain. I have shown only three levels here and that is very common, but deeper levels are certainly possible.

Now we have to consider how the assets, purchased by the beneficial owner at the bottom of the chain, are held at each level in the chain ending with the USWA. Typically, beneficial owners of financial intermediaries have securities accounts at those institutions. These would be called, for this purpose, client 'segregated' accounts. The NQI, however, is not safekeeping these assets directly. They are ultimately held in the accounts of a USWA (and the QI in between). To do that, the NQI typically opens an omnibus account at a qualified intermediary. They could do this directly with a USWA too. The omnibus account is chosen because it's a cheaper way of safekeeping the assets. It also means that the NQI does not disclose the positions, or identity, of its individual customers to what is effectively a competitor. While this is sensible commercial practice, it does have reporting consequences, as we will see. Many financial institutions also have their own money which is invested in securities. Typically, these assets would not be held in the same omnibus account as client assets, so, in the model shown, the NQI has both an omnibus account and a 'proprietary' account with its upstream counterparty, the QI.

Equally, the QI faces the same issues; however, it also now has to consider some of the practical aspects of the US regulations and its own status in order to structure its accounts at a USWA. If the QI is a withholding QI (WQI), it would only need an omnibus account at the USWA, because the USWA will not be physically withholding any tax and the QI needs only to have a mechanism to receive the gross payments. If the QI is a non-withholding QI, while it could still use an omnibus account, it's much more prevalent that it will open a different kind of account—a withholding rate pool account. These would be accounts named for the rate of withholding tax to be applied to any assets held within that account. The most common types of rate pool account are:

0%	for tax-exempt assets
10%	NRA treaty rate
15%	NRA treaty rate
25%	NRA treaty rate
30%	NRA statutory rate

There could also be:

30%	FATCA rate pool account
0%	FATCA rate pool of US non-exempt payees and
24%	Backup withholding on US non-exempt payees

So, now I have set the scene. During the year, all parties in the chain, to the extent they are able, have documented their clients with Know-Your-Customer (KYC) and/or W-8 and W-9 documents. They have also documented themselves as intermediaries using the form W-8IMY.

The form W-8IMY is important here, because there are some parts of the form that have consequences for the way in which reporting is done and who is responsible for it.

The year progresses and, each time a payment is made, information flows up and down the chain so that the correct rate of tax is applied according to the rules.

As an aside, I often get challenged by people who believe that they have been 'over-withheld'. It actually transpires that, at the time the payment was made, their financial intermediary either did not have documentation to hand or was inadequate. As the rules apply, a 30% withholding on that date *is the correct withholding*. It may be mitigated later, but there was no technical 'over-withholding' at the time.

We now come to 31 December, the end of the US tax year, and proceed into the first two and half months of the next tax year. This time is frenetic for most intermediaries, as all levels in the chain prepare for reporting and try to gather and reconcile the previous 12 months of US-sourced FDAP income data across all their clients.

The US Withholding Agent

The US withholding agent's job is probably the easiest of all. In the model shown, it only has one QI as a customer. It files for extensions of time to file for both 1042 and 1042-S. The first important fact to know about forms 1042-S is that a financial intermediary must create one for each type of income received. For the most part and in the practical world, this consists of dividends and interest, although there are many more possible codes. So, typically, on 14 April, or before, the USWA will submit its 1042-S reports to the IRS and issue copies of these 1042-S forms to its QI customer.

The Qualified Intermediary

The QI has the same task, although it takes a slightly different approach. The QI will also probably file for extensions of time to file both the 1042 tax return and the 1042-S information reports.

The QI in this model has three customers, of which one is direct, is resident in a treaty country and has received only dividends, with the other two being intermediaries. There are three factors that differentiate how this QI must address its reporting obligations. They are:

1. Pooling
2. Downstream reporting
3. Disclosure

So, the first differentiator in 1042-S reporting is that the QI can protect the identity only of its non-US *direct* clients. All the income received by such clients can be 'pooled' onto one 1042-S report per income type, per upstream USWA, per exemption code pair.

The second differentiator is that the QI does not have to provide 1042-S reports to its customers. In one way this makes sense, since the reports filed to the IRS by the QI are not at the beneficial owner level, but are pooled. However, since the beneficial owner level 1042-S is a pre-requisite for being able to file a claim of over-withholding, the beneficial owner is now reliant on the QI to apply the correct withholding and if any adjustments are necessary, to make them within its QI mandate rather than placing its customer at a financial disadvantage. That said, the rules do state that if a client of a QI (that was subject to pooled reporting) specifically asks for a 1042-S, the QI cannot refuse.

The NQI customers of the QI cannot be pooled and must get their own 1042-S reports and equally be reported separately to the IRS. These 1042-S reports I am referencing are reports from the QI to its customer, the NQI as a financial institution.

The third differentiator is disclosure. When its customer, the NQI, documented itself on form W-8IMY, it will also have had a choice of whether or not to disclose its customers. If disclosure is indicated, the NQI is agreeing that it will provide all documentation of its customers to the QI, together with a withholding statement (which essentially provides allocation information relating to the income received by the underlying beneficial owner).

The act of disclosure, being both W-8s and a withholding statement, has the effect of transferring the reporting obligation for those disclosed clients of the NQI to the QI. These disclosed clients are referred to as 'indirect clients' of the QI.

If there are any recipients of US-sourced FDAP income that are not disclosed, this will result in a 1042-S form to the NQI itself on which the QI represents the payment and tax withheld as being made to an NQI with 'undisclosed recipients'.

Effectively, all NQIs must have all their recipients reported to the IRS. The only thing that changes is the 'who'. Disclosed indirect recipients are reported by the QI while undisclosed indirect recipients must be reported by the NQI.

This obviously creates enormous problems for everyone concerned, since it bifurcates the reporting obligations between two different financial institutions. I have seen a number of different approaches to this issue. The most common, presuming at least an awareness of IRC Chapter 3, is one of complete non- disclosure by the NQI.

I have devoted an entire chapter in this book to NQI issues, which includes further discussion of the reporting problems that they, and their upstream QIs, face.

Returning to Fig. 5.1, the QI in this model must therefore create its 1042-S package for the IRS, in which it will:

1. pool its direct accounts into 'pooled IRS reporting';
2. separately report each of its indirect accounts (e.g. NQIs)
3. separately report each beneficial owner of an NQI which ticked box 10b on its W-8IMY and provided a withholding statement and supporting documentation

Then, it will send out its 1042-S package downstream in which it will:

1. provide each indirect account holder with a copy of the 1042-S form sent to the IRS
2. to the extent required, send out copies of the 1042-S forms of the NQI's underlying customers either to the NQI for distribution or direct to the underlying beneficiary

That completes the first phase of the QI's reporting. Remember, it's better to file something on time than nothing.

I would note at this time a couple of other comments. First, that the method of filing is important. Reporting MUST be by electronic means and the IRS has a system by which this can be accomplished—the Filing Information Returns Electronically or 'FIRE' system.

In the next few weeks, any re-classifications that come through from upstream institutions will need to be integrated and reconciled to what was previously produced. Any errors found can also be reconciled at this stage. This continues until the time approaches for the QI to file its tax return on form 1042.

5 Information Reporting and Tax Returns

As noted before, the 1042 is a tax return, NOT an information report. QIs and NQIs should aim to get this return right first time. There are only two practical comments I'd make here:

First is that many QIs and NQIs will also send their final 'amended 1042-S' reports in at the same time as their 1042 tax return. Remember, there's no penalty for filing on time, then amending the report later—as long as everything is done by the time the tax return is filed. However, if any party makes a mistake and has to create a new 1042-S, that is, a data line in the report that is not an amendment of a previously existing line, then that will be treated as a new 1042-S and not an amendment and be subject to late-filing penalties.

Second, there is a difference in the way the 1042 is completed depending on whether the filer is a withholding QI or a non-withholding QI, as shown in Fig. 5.2.

If the filer is a withholding QI, then they will need to complete boxes 1–59 on the form, with the dates on which the tax liability arose during the year. This is effectively the pay date of the securities. If the filer is a non-withholding QI, this is not required and the filer merely puts the total for the year into December and replicates that in the total for the year.

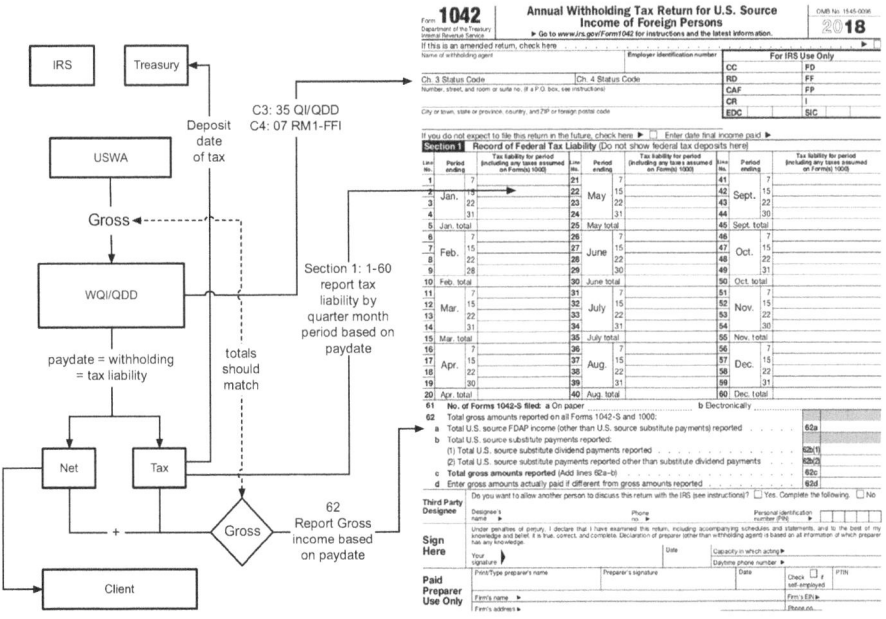

Fig. 5.2 Tax return completion for a withholding QI. Source: Author's own

Creating the Report Files

I mentioned that 1042-S reports to the IRS made by financial institutions must be in electronic form. The format of these files is prescribed in publication 1187 (for 1042-S) and publication 1220 (for forms 1099).

The file format for both 1042-S and 1099 is a basic American Standard Code for Information Exchange (ASCII) delimited format. Any half-way competent IT department can create these files. The challenge is in creating a file that not only meets the general format, but also contains the digital equivalent of the correct types of 1042-S. The following diagrams are intended to be a general explanation of this issue.

Figure 5.3 shows the general structure of the file. Each record must contain exactly 1020 characters. Most QIs will have one function extracting data from systems, another to package the data correctly and a third to convert the file into the ASCII format and test it before submitting it to the IRS. Generally, I see this data being extracted into spreadsheets so that it can easily be compared to upstream data (USWA 1042-S) and manipulated into pools and so on, as we shall see shortly. The problem with spreadsheets is that they do not pad data fields, they typically truncate them. So, where a data field in the 1042-S file may require five characters, a spreadsheet with only two characters will not 'pad' the field up to five. This is typically done by the IT department as part of file conversion.

Figure 5.4 shows how the data file is constructed based on the number of withholding agents above a QI and the structure and nature of recipients below it.

This may seem complex, but the preparation and understanding are key. If you are electing to do your own reporting, you will need to map out, in a similar diagram, your own firm in terms of the number of USWAs and the number and type of clients. These two factors drive the remainder of the diagram according to the instructions in Publication 1187.

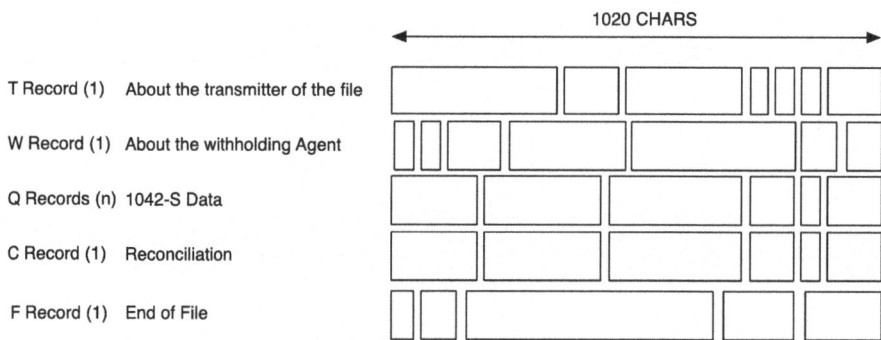

Fig. 5.3 General structure of 1042-S ASCII file. Source: Author's own

5 Information Reporting and Tax Returns   95

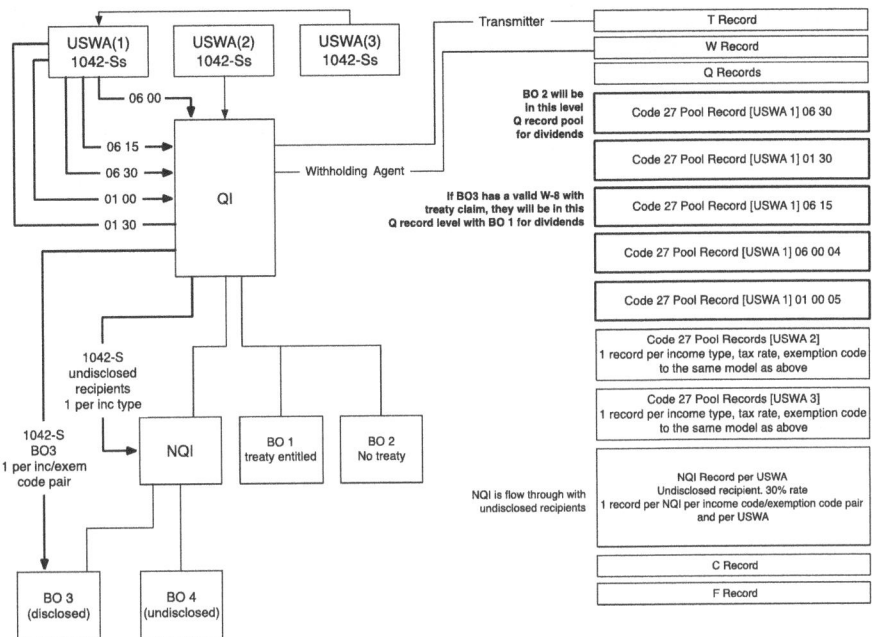

Fig. 5.4 Constructing the data for 1042-S reporting. Source: Author's own

There are third-party vendors who offer tax information reporting solutions that provide some level of relief from some of these issues. However, in all cases, the hard work is actually coding the income lines properly in the first place and preparing the correct pooling or not. No third-party provider will be able to code an income line for US tax purposes, so, for all intents and purposes, much of the work is down to the QI (or NQI) to prepare the source data for reporting, then code and sequence it correctly. Vendor solutions tend then to focus on receiving pre-formatted data and converting this into the required ASCII format.

Figure 5.5 shows another facet of the same reporting file construction. In this model, the QI has more than one upstream USWA. The message here is that you need to remember that 1042-S reporting is not just categorised by income type (code). It must also be categorised based on which USWA was the primary withholding agent. So this model describes a non-withholding QI with two upstream USWA counterparties. The packaging of the data is a combination of the upstream counterparties and their categorisation of income codes and exemption codes, together with the downstream categorisation of client types (direct, indirect, treaty, non-treaty, tax rate and exemption codes). The diagram is intended to show how certain boxes on the form should be completed, based on where the data in that line came from and

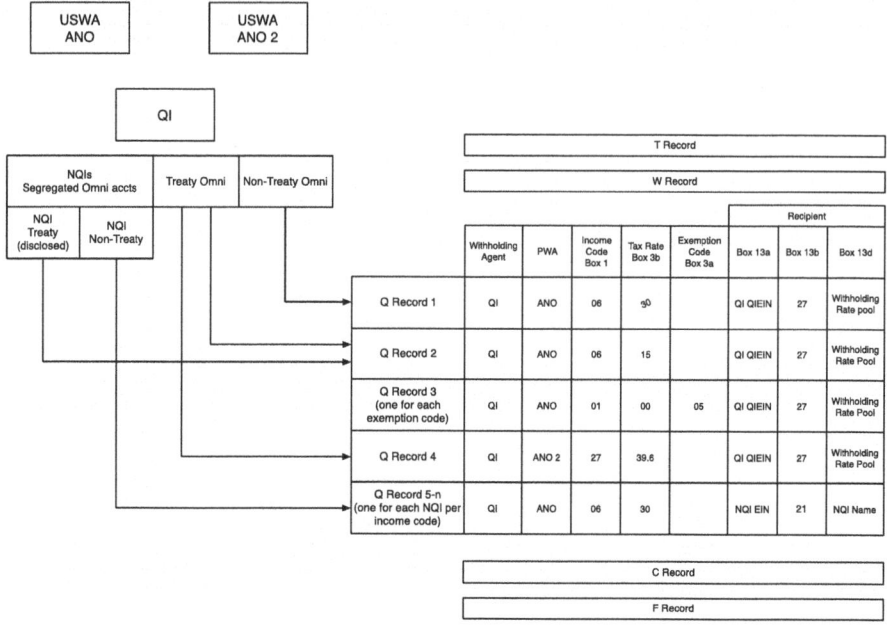

Fig. 5.5 Multiple withholding agents. Source: Author's own

what it represents. Again, third-party reporting vendors will not generally do this packaging or categorisation for you. The data is yours and the liability is yours.

For completeness, Fig. 5.6 shows the same format as applied to form 1099 reporting by publication 1220.

Now, all this data packaging and formatting leads to one end—the submission of the data on the IRS FIRE portal. Of all the IRS systems, this one is the most helpful in that, if the data submission has issues, the portal will generally spit the file out as a bad file and will also create a report that identifies the failures and the line number of the first occasion on which the failure occurred.

It is therefore sensible to do two things. First, once the data has been collated and converted to ASCII format (remembering to pad the data fields to the appropriate length), test the submission before it is entered into the portal. If there are failures in the file, these should be corrected and an additional line should be inserted in the pre-submission test so that following submissions are tested for that error. An example of a test harness for e-File submissions is below.

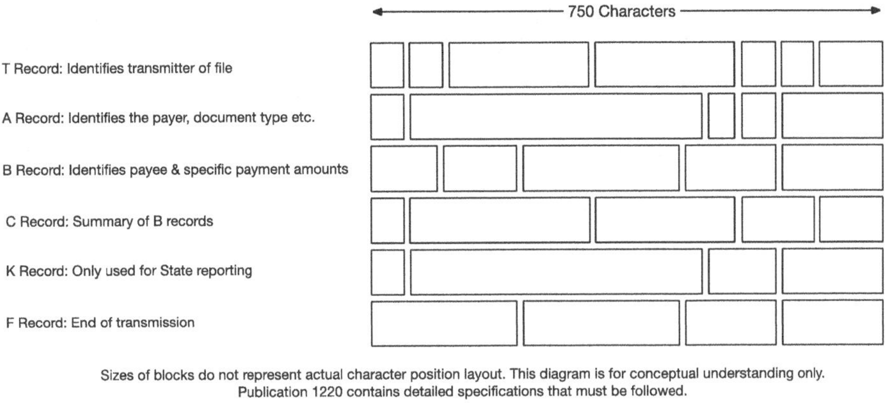

T Record: Identifies transmitter of file

A Record: Identifies the payer, document type etc.

B Record: Identifies payee & specific payment amounts

C Record: Summary of B records

K Record: Only used for State reporting

F Record: End of transmission

Sizes of blocks do not represent actual character position layout. This diagram is for conceptual understanding only. Publication 1220 contains detailed specifications that must be followed.

Fig. 5.6 Form 1099-X report data layout. Source: Author's own

Test Harness for 1042-S e-File

Purpose: To reduce or eliminate the risk of a bad file message from the IRS by checking that the main causes of errors in the production of the file are eliminated.

Sequence: Un-roll data from NQI (full disclosure NQIs only) for separate clients (individual Q record required). Obtain 1042-S from upstream. Once the 1042-S data has been compiled and submitted to IT, the following tests should be performed on the returned file prior to it being submitted to the IRS.

Constraints: The person performing these tests should not be associated with the original construction or interpretation of the file.

Notes: This test does NOT validate the contents of the original data file, that is, if the original data file contained content based errors, these tests will not identify them.

Version No.: X.X

1. Structure

    (a) T Record

    (i) Does the file have a T record?
    (ii) Is the T record 1020 characters long?
    (iii) Does the file have the correct tax year recorded?

    (b) W Records

- (i) Does the file have at least one W Record?
- (ii) Are the W records 1020 characters long?
- (iii) Does the number of W records equal the number of upstream agents that provided 1042-Ss?
- (iv) Does the W record have Chapter 3 status code?
- (v) Does the W record have Chapter 4 status code?
- (vi) Is the Chapter 3 status code valid and correct in the W record?
- (vii) Is the Chapter 4 status code valid and correct in the W record?
- (viii) Does the tax year in the W record match T record?

(c) Q Records

- (i) Does the file have Q Records?
- (ii) Are all the Q Records 1020 characters long?
- (iii) Does the Q record have Chapter 3 or Chapter 4 indicator for reporting purposes?
- (iv) Does the Q record have Chapter 3 and Chapter 4 exemption codes?
- (v) Does the Q record have Chapter 3 and Chapter 4 status codes (lines 12b/c, 13f/g and 15b/c as required)?
- (vi) Have the Chapter 3 and Chapter 4 status codes been checked?
- (vii) Are the correct columns completed?
- (viii) Does the Q record have valid country codes?
- (ix) Does the Q record have valid state/province codes (or blank)?

(d) C Record

- (i) Does the file contain a C record?
- (ii) Is the C record 1020 characters long?
- (iii) Does the total of Q records field in the C record match the number of Q records in the file?
- (iv) Does the total gross amount paid field in the C record match the sum of the gross amounts paid in the Q records?
- (v) Does the total withholding credit field in the C record match the sum of the withholding credits in the Q records?

(e) F Record

- (i) Does the file contain an F record?
- (ii) Is the F record 1020 characters long?

2. Formatting

(a) Do the fields in each line of the file have the correct lengths and data types?
(b) Has the padding of NUM data fields been correctly done?

(c) Has the padding of CHAR data fields been correctly done?
(d) Have all unexplained empty cells been reviewed and corrected?
(e) Does the file and relevant fields have valid characters?

3. Reconciliation

    (a) Do all the amounts in each W sub-block and associated Q records reconcile to the upstream 1042-S received from that withholding agent?
    (b) Where a Q record represents a 1042-S to an intermediary (i.e. indirect account holder), does the Q record contain the intermediary's EIN?

        (i) If yes, is the EIN in the Q record the same as the EIN of the W-8 form they supplied?

    (c) Have the GIINs been checked and tested?
    (d) Has the file been checked for duplicated information (same rate pool information—income code and tax rate)?
    (e) When a Q record represents a 1042-S for the underlying client of an NQI that has provided a withholding certificate has:

        (i) the information from the NQI been applied to the Q record correctly?
        (ii) the Chapter 3 code and Chapter 4 code been checked and confirmed?

If *any* of the answers to any of the above questions is NO, the test result is FAIL.

If ALL the answers to the above questions are YES, the test result is PASS.

Reporting is a high-visibility process that can be labour intensive. However, it is the final stage of the annual operational process that began with documentation, then withholding and depositing. Whether the reporting is correct, accurate and performed properly is dependent on the success of the preceding processes. Garbage in provides garbage out. It's also common for firms to focus on the period from January to April as the reporting season, but actually reporting is a process that takes up the whole year, including regular reconciliations with counterparties in order to avoid penalty notices. The biggest lesson to learn here, after understanding how reporting is structured, is that reporting is one of the two occasions when the IRS has a direct window into your operational processes. Therefore it's important to make sure it's right first time. Getting it wrong can absorb enormous amounts of time and energy in abatement of penalty notices and remediation of material failures or events of default related to reporting.

6

Control and Oversight

In any system as complex as IRC Chapter 3, there needs to be control and oversight to ensure that the system is being administered correctly. Under the previous QI Agreement, this was achieved by means of an independent Agreed Upon Procedure (AUP). However, while retaining many key aspects of the AUP, this model was replaced in 2017 with a more robust and wide-ranging system.

The control and oversight of the QI Agreement is in section 10 of the agreement.

The current system is based on several key principles shown below with citations to the specific clauses of the QI Agreement:

1. The requirement for QIs to appoint a Responsible Officer (RO) [Section 10.02];
2. The requirement for the RO to have a written compliance programme and adequate policies and procedures for training, systems and business monitoring (CP) [Section 10.02(A)(1)–(5)];
3. The requirement for the RO to conduct a triennial, independent Periodic Review of the compliance status of the firm [Section 10.02(A)(6)] unless the QI is eligible for a waiver of the Periodic Review; and
4. The requirement of the RO to make a triennial certification to the Internal Revenue Service (IRS) detailing its compliance status and, if not compliant, to provide a Remediation Plan and an attestation to assert that the plan will be implemented [Section 10.03].

Responsible Officers

This is a matter of some debate and confusion. In IRC Chapter 4 (Foreign Account Tax Compliance Act [FATCA]), firms that are in jurisdictions with an intergovernmental agreement (IGA) with the US have no requirement for a Responsible Officer (RO). Firms that are in jurisdictions that have no IGA with the US must sign an Foreign Financial Institution (FFI) Agreement to avoid non-participating FFI status. The FFI Agreement (Revenue Procedure 2017-16) does have the requirement for the firm to have an RO. The QI Agreement (Revenue Procedure 2017-15) also has a requirement for an RO.

Figure 6.1 hopefully explains two aspects of this. First, a QI in a non-IGA jurisdiction will require an RO under both FATCA and the QI Agreement. A QI in an IGA jurisdiction will need an RO under the QI Agreement even though they would not need one under the IGA. It's important to understand a related issue here which is also highlighted in Part II of this book. FATCA, for a financial institution, is about due diligence on _all_ financial accounts, reporting those that are (1) US, (2) recalcitrant and (3) non-participating FFIs and withholding a penalty where applicable. To that extent, when we speak of obligations of a QI under FATCA, we are referring to that subset of all accounts that receive US-sourced Fixed, Determinable, Annual or Periodic (FDAP) income and for which the QI is therefore acting in its capacity as a QI.

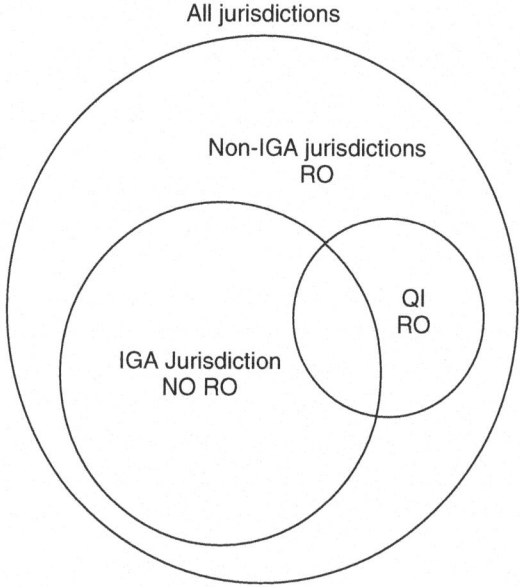

Fig. 6.1 The need for a responsible officer

The main requirement of a Responsible Officer is that they must be of sufficient seniority in the business to make changes in the business if required to meet the obligations of the agreement. Unfortunately, many firms, by accident or design, end up with ROs who are not sufficiently senior. The role goes to a department manager where it should really be going to a board member.

In being able to make changes necessary to meet the QI Agreement obligations, the RO must, of necessity, be able to straddle multiple functions across the firm. Again, this is rarely the case, because many financial institutions suffer from a silo effect. This can occur even at a board level, making it very difficult to find someone other than the CEO to have the requisite breadth of authority. Compliance and risk functions generally do have that cross-functional remit, but I rarely find the RO in these departments. The problem is usually therefore that if there is an RO with the requisite authority level, they are usually too high up to have a good enough understanding of the granular aspects of the business without relying on others. A team approach is the best approach.

Compliance Programmes

The primary role of the RO is to have, and maintain, a compliance programme (CP). The QI Agreement is very specific; the CP must be in writing and it must be implemented in a way that forces compliance to the obligations of the agreement. I always return to the base principle that the RO and CP are the US government's way of making sure that they have a representative inside the firm whose purpose and authority is to implement the QI Agreement.

Most CPs I see are not fit for purpose. Many, even when they do exist, are held at the operational level and do not have formal board approval (which they would need in order to be able to demonstrate that they have the appropriate control authority).

The CP should be the start and end point for compliance and the touchstone for everything in between. The first thing an RO should do when the firm obtains QI status (and in principle, long before that) is to map out the structure of the CP, based on what operational and commercial decisions the firm wants to take.

Policy decisions for accounts that receive US-sourced FDAP income (i.e. designated accounts) include:

1. Does the firm accept US clients?
2. Does the firm adopt primary withholding in IRC Chapters 3 and 4?

3. Does the firm adopt primary 1099 reporting and backup withholding responsibility?
4. Does the firm allow non-qualified intermediaries (NQIs) as clients?
5. Does the firm allow flow-through entities as clients?
6. Does the firm allow disclosure of indirect account holders?

Each of these policy decisions has implications for connected procedures. Some policies and procedures can be protective, that is, their purpose is to prevent some types of client or business access to the US market in order to remove certain compliance obligations from ever occurring. Other policies and procedures are designed to ensure correct processing of US business.

For example, many firms choose not to allow US clients and this has been a major issue for Americans with accounts overseas. Over-zealous financial firms off-boarded US clients and refused new ones because of a perceived risk and/or liability resulting from QI and FATCA regulation. The smart ones eventually figured out that American accounts are fine, provided the firm takes some simple precautions in the CP. This would include, for example, never allowing a US person to trade the US securities markets without a valid form W-9 on which the social security number (for individuals) or Tax Identification Number (TIN; for entities) has been validated against the IRS database. This simple procedure ensures that such clients will never be subject to backup withholding and the firm will never be subject to associated Form 945 reporting. Yes, the firm would need a 0% FATCA Rate Pool account if it is a non-withholding QI, but it will need a range of rate pool accounts anyway. Yes, the firm will have to do FATCA reporting—but it must do that anyway, whether or not it has US clients. It may have to do Form 1099 reporting, but in context to the value of such business and the complexity of reporting for non-US clients, that's usually not a material consideration.

A second example is worth describing. A decision is usually taken not to allow NQIs as clients, or if allowed, not to permit them to disclose their clients. While the regulations are based on the presumption that NQIs must disclose to QIs or USWAs, the reality of life is that the industry steps in with commercial policies that deflect the risk. After all, for a QI, an NQI represents an unknown. The QI will know its own direct client base in both scale and scope, so it can assess the resources needed to meet its QI obligations. However, a disclosing NQI is an unknown. If such an NQI has large numbers of indirect account holders (and perhaps even more NQI clients below them in the chain of custody), the QI will be receiving an unknown number of forms W-8 and W-9 that it will have to validate. It will be receiving withholding statements that it will have to match to the W-8s and finally, it will have to prepare a much more complex data file for 1042-S submission to the IRS and prepare physical 1042-S forms for each indirect account holder and deliver them within 30 days or face late-filing penalties. All this is cost and risk for the QI and the CP is the forum that triggers the discussion. Some QIs refuse to accept NQIs at all. Others accept NQIs but only if they do not disclose, so that all the W-8 validation and reporting goes away (for the QI). Others will allow disclosing NQIs but increasingly see this as a revenue stream where fees are levied on form validation, reconciliation and perform reporting to offset the resources the QI will have to deploy.

So, the CP is the place that these discussions take place, are agreed, then documented together with supporting protective procedures that can then be subjected to training policy and procedure.

Periodic Reviews (PRs)

The QI Agreement mandates that the RO must bring in an independent person to check the compliance status of the QI. There are several important things to understand about Periodic Reviews.

First, the Periodic Review is not the only compliance assessment that the RO needs to undertake.

Second, the PR is a highly prescribed, mechanical test of a number of accounts for which the QI acts as a QI (designated accounts). These accounts are selected by the Reviewer to a closely controlled sampling method (if the total number of accounts concerned receiving US-sourced FDAP is too large to review in total). The tests check documentation validity, withholding accuracy and reporting accuracy. That's it.

Third, the PR can be conducted by an external auditor, an internal auditor or a third-party consultant. In all cases, two things are paramount; independence—the Reviewer cannot have been involved in any aspect of developing or maintaining operational compliance of the QI; and competence—the Reviewer must be competent to make the assessments and run the tests.

As to the mechanics, the RO must choose a specific year out of the certification period. The Reviewer will then request data from the QI with respect to that year. The year that the RO selects also affects the date by which the final certification needs to be made.

Figure 6.2 explains how this works. A Reviewer has to review data for a given year out of the three-year certification period. That includes testing whether the reporting was accurate. However, the reporting on form 1042 for year 3 will not have been completed typically until September of year 4,

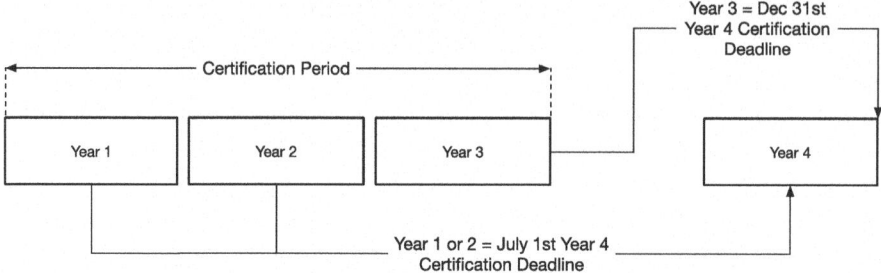

Fig. 6.2 Certification deadlines. Source: Author's own

assuming the QI obtained an extension. Thus, the deadline for certifications, if year 3 is selected as the review year, is 31 December of year 4. If either of the first two years of the certification period is chosen, then the deadline for the certification is 1 July of year 4, as in both cases the tax return form 1042 will have been completed by September of year 3.

In my experience, all QIs select year 3 of their certification period on which to conduct their PR, (a) because it gives them additional time and (b) because, out of the three-year period, the third year is the one most likely to get a positive result in analysis.

As I noted, the PR is a mechanical process. Unless the number of accounts is prohibitively large, all accounts that receive US-sourced FDAP income must be reviewed. The primary strata for the review are by bucketing these accounts into US and non-US with the proviso that certain types of clients, if they are present in the account population, must be in the analysis population, for example, FIs and flow-through entities. That said, the RO can mandate a more stringent set of strata if he or she wants. The deepest strata set for analysis would bucket accounts that received US-sourced FDAP income as follows:

1. Non-US individual treaty entitled
2. Non-US individual no treaty entitlement
3. Non-US entity treaty entitled
4. Non-US entity no treaty entitlement
5. Non-US FI (NQI)
6. Non-US FI (QI)
7. Non-US flow-through (partnership)
8. Non-US flow-through (trust)
9. US individual
10. US entity

This bucketing would be very complex to analyse, but from an RO perspective, would give a highly detailed picture of where any weaknesses, material failures or events of default are occurring in the QI-designated account population.

However, most QIs find the number of accounts for review too large as soon as they figure out that an external auditor will set their fees based on the size of the account population. This results in the use of a sampling methodology. The QI Agreement provides a safe harbour method in two steps. The first step is to determine the size of the sample based on the population size of the strata. The calculation is a statistical one and is the same one that is applied under the old AUP system.

The key thing to note about this statistical method is that, when used, the maximum size of any sample cannot be greater than 321 accounts.

The formula used is shown in Fig. 6.3. However, an easier way to look at this is by applying the several rules for sampling at the same time to a grouping of potential account populations (whether US or non-US or at the deeper level). This is shown in Table 6.1.

Table 6.1 takes account of three rules for determining sample size. First is that the sample must be the lesser of 25% of the population of a stratum and the number given by applying the formula in Fig. 6.3. However, for any stratum, the minimum sample size must be 60. For ROs, this table will give a quick estimate of the number of accounts that may be selected for analysis in a PR.

The Periodic Review itself is a process of three parts. First is the assessment of documentation by stratum. All accounts in the sample that fail the documentation test automatically go forward to the withholding test phase. If the number of fails at this stage is less than 60, the reviewer will go back to the documentation test phase and randomly select some of the passes and move these into the withholding test phase. This is repeated at each phase so that after the documentation testing phase, there will always be at least 60 accounts to test. Figure 6.4 shows how this works using the lightest strata of US versus non-US plus the mandatory inclusion of indirect accounts.

$$\text{Sample Size} = \frac{\frac{t^2 PQ}{d^2}}{1 + \frac{1}{N}\left(\frac{t^2 PQ}{d^2} - 1\right)}$$

Fig. 6.3 Formula for determining sample size in Periodic Reviews

Table 6.1 Application of multiple rules for determining sample size

Population N	25% Rule	Formula	Lesser of the two rule	MIN 60 rule
100	25	76	25	60
200	50	123	50	60
300	75	155	75	75
400	100	178	100	100
500	125	196	125	125
600	150	209	150	150
700	175	220	175	175
800	200	229	200	200
900	225	237	225	225
1000	250	243	243	243
1500	375	265	265	265
2000	500	277	277	277
2100	525	279	279	279
2200	550	280	280	280
2300	575	282	282	282
2400	600	283	283	283
2500	625	285	285	285
10000	2500	311	311	311
20000	5000	316	316	316
100000	25000	320	320	320

Source: Author's own

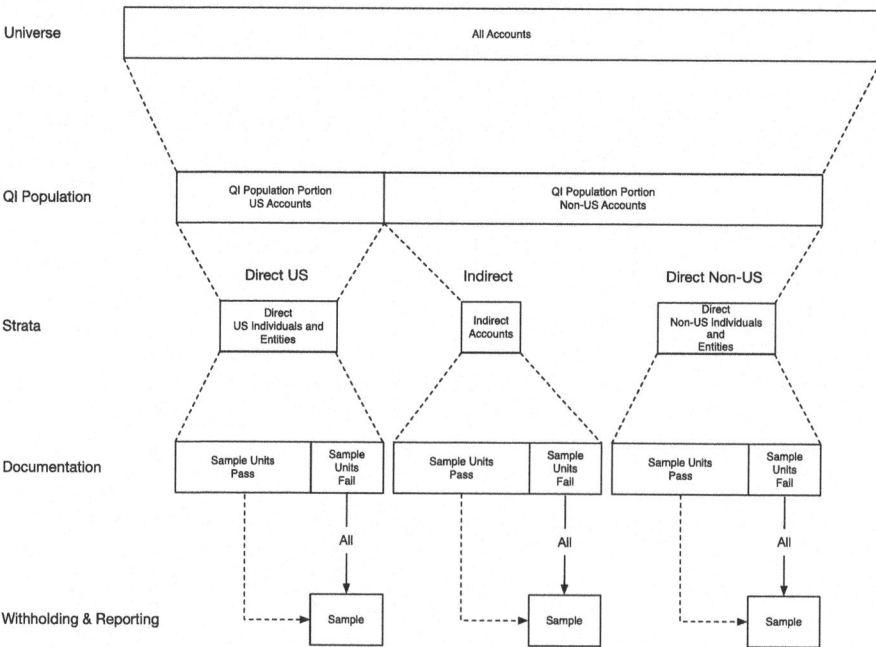

Fig. 6.4 Periodic Review assessment phases. Source: Author's own

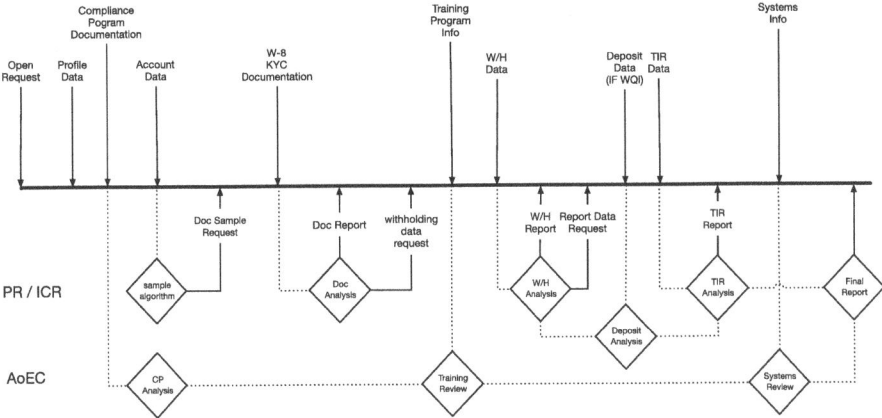

Fig. 6.5 Process flows for Periodic Review and assessment of controls. Source: Author's own

The output of all this activity will be a report. The coordination of this report with the certification is important as we will shortly see.

From a planning perspective, it's important for ROs that the teams involved in operational compliance understand the overall process by means of which the RO brings together the PR and other assessments ready for making a certification. Figure 6.5 shows this process.

As the reader can see, there are two strands to the process, each of which has discrete elements. Bear in mind that the people who will generally be preparing information for these strands, also have normal day jobs, much of which will be day-to-day operational tasks such as validating W-8s, moving assets in rate pool accounts or preparing reports and tax returns. It is therefore important to plan and prepare well in advance.

Certifications

Certification Periods

The framework within which these principles are packaged is the concept of a 'certification period'. The QI Agreement has a six-year term and within those six years there are two certification periods. Each certification period is three years and represents a full US tax year during which the QI held QI status. So, for example, a QI that has an effective date for its QI Agreement of 30 June 2019 will have a first certification period of 2020, 2021 and 2022.

From a technical and commercial perspective, all QIs must be fully compliant with the terms of the QI Agreement from _day one_. In practice this never, ever happens. Firms apply for QI status and generally have done some basic planning, but they do not implement any of those plans until they receive their Qualified Intermediary EIN (QIEIN).

Non-Periodic Review Matters

Figure 6.2 showed us the deadlines for certification by the RO on the IRS portal. However, it's important to understand that the certification is not just based on the Periodic Review. The RO must bring several strands of information together before deciding what kind of certification to make. While Section 10.02(A)(6) mandates the Periodic Review, sections 10.02(A)(1)–(5) are about those supporting activities that underpin effective controls. The certification itself is essentially a statement that the QI has effective internal controls. So, the QI Agreement mandates the PR to enable a mechanical test of documentation, withholding, depositing and reporting. The RO is, however, free to mandate any activity he or she wishes in order to determine if the firm also meets the requirements and standards expected in sections 10.02(A)(1)–(5). Those are about the compliance programme, training, systems and business change monitoring and determination of Qualified Derivatives Dealer (QDD) tax liabilities if the QI is also a QDD.

The reality is that if these supporting controls are not in place, or are in any way inadequate, it raises the risk that the Periodic Review will find either material failures, events of default or both. In other words, without adequate training or adequate W0-8 validation procedures or effective systems to manage withholding, it's very likely that things will go wrong operationally and that this will get picked up in the PR.

Factual Information

The QI Agreement essentially requires the RO to have the mandatory PR, but also use any other source of information at their disposal to assess the effectiveness of their internal controls. These two threads come together for the certification so it's important, from a timing and resource perspective, that the RO plan the certification at least a year in advance. It's also important in that planning to include the 'factual information' that will be required for that certification. Factual information is a requirement irrespective of which kind of certification is being made. These are data extracted by the RO, but, in my opinion, given the preparatory efforts, I usually expect to see the requirement in the PR mandate. That way, the RO will have someone else preparing the data required rather than scrambling at the last minute to get the information himself or herself.

The factual information requirements are laid out in the Appendices to the QI Agreement, so an RO has no excuse not to know what the requirement is.

Types of Certification

There are two types of certification—a 'certification of effective controls' and a qualified certification'.

The certification of effective controls means that, throughout the whole of the three-year certification period, the QI either had no material failures or had events of default or, if it did, it was identified and cured prior to the date of the certification.

In contrast, a qualified certification means that the QI, at the time of certification, has material failures or events of default that were uncured.

My firm has conducted eight reviews in the last 12 months and not one single QI has passed the reviews without some uncured failures.

The consequence of uncured material failures or events of default is that the IRS will require additional factual information at the time of certification, a Remediation Plan to show how those failures will be fixed and an attestation from the RO to the effect that they will be cured within a reasonable time.

The QI Agreement gives the IRS power to ask for more information, request a copy of the PR report, speak to the reviewer directly or meet directly with the RO, all depending on the number and severity of the failures. Ultimately the firm's QI status is at stake here.

Most firms do not take the whole QI cycle seriously enough. I have not yet seen, in the 18 years since the regulations came into force, a QI that has adequate resources or effective controls or that has planned properly for the certification. Yet, in every training course or workshop that I run, I make the point repeatedly that planning is fundamental and getting the documentation validation right is the principal activity that will drive good compliance.

Material Failures and Events of Default

I have mentioned material failures and events of default. These are defined terms in the QI Agreement. Material failures are defined in section 10.03(B) and events of default are defined in section 11.06.

There are a few things to note about these two issues.

Material failures are pretty much what they sound like. They are a failure of the QI to meet the requirements of the QI Agreement or its FATCA obligations. However, the agreement does provide limitations on what can be deemed to be a material failure. These are in subsections 10.03(B)(1)(i)–(iv).

Subsection (i) makes it an automatic material fail if a QI establishes a tax reserve or financial provision for a tax liability—they don't want you planning to fail.

Subsection (ii) makes it an automatic material fail if an RO fails to establish a CP—this is a fundamental control they want you to have.

Subsection (iii) makes it an automatic material fail if you have a criminal or civil sanction imposed with respect to Know-Your-Customer (KYC) or Anti-Money Laundering (AML)—QIs exist only in KYC-approved jurisdictions and these underpin the IRS' understanding that QIs will be regulated in their home state.

Subsection (iv) makes it a material failure if the RO becomes aware of the firm failing to withhold, provide sufficient or accurate information, allocate assets in a withholding statement, make deposits, report accurately or report on time.

However, of these four subsections, a failure in the fourth subsection is limited to being material only if it is either a deliberate act of an employee or attributable to a failure of the QI to implement effective internal controls.

Two things to note here. First, there is no such limitation for subsections (i), (ii) or (iii). Any failure in one of these subsections is automatically material. Second, while it may be problematic to assign a failure in subsection (iv) to a deliberate act of an employee, it will be much less onerous to conclude that a failure here was due to ineffective or inadequate controls.

Events of default look very similar to material failures, but one can assume that the IRS wants to add additional weight to some things more than others. Section 11.06 has 19 things that the IRS considers will be more than a material failure but a default of the QI Agreement. Paraphrased, these are:

1. Failure to implement adequate controls;
2. Under-withholding a material amount of tax (material is undefined here);
3. Making excessive refund claims;
4. Absent, incorrect or unreliable documentation of a significant number of direct account holders (significant is undefined here);
5. Filing materially incorrect forms 1042, 945, 1042-S, 1099 or 8966;
6. Failure to comply with FATCA obligations;
7. If QI is a sponsoring entity, failure to comply with sponsoring obligations;

8. For any accounts where QI does not act as QI (i.e. non-designated accounts), failure to comply with NQI obligations;
9. Failure to perform a Periodic Review when required;
10. Failure to cooperate with the IRS in a compliance review;
11. Failure to inform IRS of any change in KYC rules within 90 days;
12. Failure to inform the IRS of any significant change in business practices that affect its QI obligations;
13. Failure to inform the IRS of any Private Arrangement Intermediary (PAI) Agreement it operates;
14. Failure to cure a material failure identified in a qualified certification;
15. Making a fraudulent statement or misrepresentation of a material fact to the IRS, a withholding agent or a Reviewer;
16. A determination that the Reviewer is not sufficiently independent;
17. Default of an intermediary with whom the QI has a PAI Agreement and failure to terminate that agreement;
18. Default of a partnership or trust with whom the QI has an Agency agreement and failure to terminate that agreement;
19. Failure of a QDD, after 2017, to pay its QDD tax liability or fails to correct it.

What is curious about events of default is that, because of the way that section 11 is structured, only the IRS can issue a Notice of Event of Default. There is no provision or requirement for the QI to notify the IRS that an event of default has occurred, other than at the certification date. So, in theory, the QI could have been in serious default of its agreement with the IRS for nearly four years before it would be contractually required to notify the IRS via the certification.

In either case, it's important to understand that, irrespective of which type of certification is being made, the RO will have to disclose all material failures and events of default. The key is not whether there were any, it's whether they were spotted and cured, that is, did the control system work?

IRS Direct Action

While technically the IRS can get directly involved with a QI via either kind of certification, it's plainly more likely to occur if the QI submits a qualified certification. Usually one would expect that the IRS will review an RO's remediation plan together with the nature, scale and scope of the issues that caused the qualified certification. One may, at that stage, also take into account even the cured failures. If one is comfortable that the QI has good intent, that may be the end of it, with no further action. However, if one has unresolved concerns, there are mechanisms in the QI Agreement that allow for further steps to be taken.

The least onerous are a set of steps in which the IRS can ask for further information through a correspondence review outlined in section 10.08(C). If these too do not provide the IRS with enough comfort, they may direct the QI to undergo an additional review, outlined in section 10.08(D), under which it can direct the RO about what steps need to be taken to properly remediate problems. The QI Agreement also permits the IRS to speak with the original Reviewer and ask for copies of the original Periodic Review report and other materials that the RO relied on when making the certification. There is a specific clause in the QI Agreement that also ensures that a QI cannot contractually put a gag order on the Reviewer.

Consolidated Compliance Programmes (CCPs)

Of course there are QIs that are part of groups of one sort or another. That may be because there may be a single owner and a number of branches, or a group holding company with a number of commonly owned but independent firms:

PAIs, agency and so on.

For QIs that are members of a group under common ownership, the IRS allows a consolidated compliance programme in section 10.02(B). This means that firms that would otherwise have to have multiple compliance programmes, each independently constructed and monitored, can save costs by applying for the use of a consolidated programme. The benefits are that under a CCP, a group of QIs can operate under a uniform compliance programme document and share practices, procedures and systems. This also means that they can undergo a Consolidated Periodic Review (CPR). In order to achieve this, the group must appoint one of the QIs as a 'compliance QI' whose RO takes on the joint and several responsibilities for the obligations of all members of the group in the CCP. Again, the CCP is not automatic based on your structure. It has to be applied for and approved by the IRS.

Now this all seems good and large QI groups would naturally favour this model. However, there are some issues to consider before going down this route.

First is that most large QI groupings are going to exist because of geography, that is, they have QIs in multiple jurisdictions. For these groupings, not all members may be in jurisdictions where QI status is possible and even where it is possible, the member may not be a QI. The CCP applies to QIs, not NQIs.

Second, across multiple countries there will be differences of culture and language, even if, and where, the group operates common systems. These all provide barriers to an effective CCP. The larger the group, the bigger the problems. As Commander Montgomery Scott said in Star Trek II, the Search for Spock 'the more they overthink the plumbing, the easier it is to stop up the drain'. So it is with the additional risks involved in a CCP. I know of many QI groupings that have the ability to enter into a CCP, but have chosen not to, because the cost-benefit equation doesn't work for them.

Lastly, ROs already at most QIs are nervous about their responsibilities. You may recall that I said that it's common for ROs to be appointed at a level lower than that which the QI Agreement mandates. At these levels, the joint and several responsibilities are a significant concern.

Interim Compliance Reviews (ICRs)

As a matter of best practice, I often talk to QIs who are concerned with the costs of compliance, but who do not necessarily consider the cost of the alternative. In principle, the QI Agreement leaves QIs alone for nearly four years before anything needs to be done contractually from a control and oversight perspective. By the time the third year of the certification period comes around, the QI's operational compliance has been running for some time. The question is whether that compliance programme has been effective. The question I ask is simple. As an RO, do you really want to get nearly four years down the road, just to find that you were doing it wrong the whole time? Remember, the object of the control and oversight is to make sure that the firm can identify problems and fix them. The Periodic Review, at its heart, is simply trying to identify in an empirical way whether those controls have worked.

So, best practice is really to have an annual review of compliance controls to make sure that, when the formal Periodic Review is due, any failures have been identified and dealt with. These are called Interim Compliance Reviews (ICRs), often otherwise called compliance health checks. They are not formally mandated by the QI Agreement; they are however a common-sense, best-practice approach to avoid the serious financial and reputational risk that a qualified certification presents.

One of the other benefits of an annual ICR is that the firm is well prepared for the formal PR. Many firms that I have seen, even those familiar with audits, find the conduct of a PR difficult to manage. Documentation is often held in different places, payment and withholding records take time to extract from systems and data used for reporting is often not held in an easily analysable way. Those conducting a PR expect all of the above to be available in a short span of time and the firm's staff to respond in a timely and knowledgeable manner. This does not happen very often. An annual ICR means that staff get used to the sort of regimen that they will face in the formal PR and the kind of questioning they will receive.

I would also have to say that, in 18 years, I have not seen a single QI that has been compliant throughout its certification period. Many have multiple material failures and events of default and most of these have gone completely unrecognised until an ICR report brings it to their attention.

So, while I do not give advice, my strongly held opinion is that firms that approach a QI application, as well as those already in the programme, should budget for annual ICRs as an integral part of the compliance programme designed to give the RO another layer of information on which to base changes in policy and procedure, as well as mitigating the risk of a qualified certification at the end.

Waiver of Periodic Review

I speak to many QIs and NQIs about the compliance costs and resources needed to be an effective QI. One of the biggest problems is that, in general, neither the regulations nor the QI Agreement is written to accommodate different sizes of QI firms. However, one such area where size matters is the Periodic Review.

I have rarely seen the cost of a Periodic Review lower than $50,000 and, aside from other compliance costs such as training, business monitoring and systems, the cost of the Periodic Review alone can easily be larger than the reportable payments a QI receives, or the tax that may be withheld. So, it's very easy for some firms to conclude that the cost is more than it's worth.

However, the IRS does allow small QIs to have the requirement for a Periodic Review to be waived under certain conditions. It's important to understand that, even with a Periodic Review waiver, a QI will still need to make its certification in the normal way.

The main threshold for requesting a waiver is if the gross reportable amounts received by the QI in each year of the three-year certification period are less than US $5 million. In order to qualify beyond this stage, the QI must not also be acting as a QDD and cannot be part of a consolidated compliance programme. It must have properly and timely filed its tax return (1042), information returns (1042-S), FATCA reports (8966) and, if applicable, its US returns 1099 and/or 945. It must have also made all its required certifications and reviews both in QI and in FATCA.

The waiver is not automatic, but must be applied for. The application must also contain the factual information that would usually accompany a certification described in Appendix I of the QI Agreement. If the IRS does not approve the application, the QI is granted an automatic six-month extension of the time required to complete the Periodic Review.

So, as with many things, I see many QIs and particularly prospective QIs oversimplifying this issue down to just the value threshold of $5 million, not understanding that there are several hurdles they must jump before that waiver has meaning.

Conclusions

The new QI Agreement represented by Revenue Procedure 2017-15, together with the companion Revenue Procedures 2017-16 (the new FFI Agreement) and 2017-21 (the new Withholding Foreign Partnership and Withholding Foreign Trust Agreements), all focus on (1) an oversight by the IRS essentially outsourced to the Responsible Officer, (2) a triennial requirement for an independent and competently conducted Periodic Review and (3) a certification of adequate controls in the fourth year, based on a Periodic Review report and any other information that the RO has regarding the compliance status of the firm.

Some firms with limited US exposure that meet certain criteria can gain a waiver of the Periodic Review but not the certification requirement.

Certain larger QIs in commonly owned groups can benefit from a consolidated compliance programme.

Given the concerns of the IRS about tax evasion and the nature and complexity of the QI Agreement, ROs and QI boards of directors should not under-estimate or under-resource their compliance efforts. An annual review of compliance status is recommended as best practice and to help the QI team prepare for its formal Periodic Review.

7

Penalties

In addition to oversight and control mechanisms, IRC Chapter 3 and its associated QI Agreement have a system of penalties which are seen as a 'motivator' to compliance. Unlike many other jurisdictions, I have not seen the Internal Revenue Service (IRS) publicly announce the application of penalties, which would serve as an additional deterrent in the form of reputational damage.

Penalties: Key Facts

Application to QIs and NQIs

One of the most common, and I really mean very common, misconceptions by non-qualified intermediaries is that penalties don't apply to them because they haven't signed a QI Agreement. If they do understand this, it's also very common for non-qualified intermediaries (NQIs) to believe that the IRS has no way to calculate or apply such penalties.

Basis of Penalties

Penalties are assessed for a variety of reasons. Most financial institutions focus on reporting penalties, usually for late filing, but this is only one of several penalties the IRS can apply. These include:

- Late filing of forms;
- Failure to provide recipients with copies of reports (NQIs);
- Inaccurate information;
- Under-withholding on reports
- Incorrect method of submitting information reports;
- Incorrect timing of deposits to Treasury;
- perjury

Late-Filing Penalties

Penalties are reviewed regularly and, in recent years, have been seen to rise. The calculation of the penalty is based on when the intermediary eventually provides the filing, starting the clock from the due date, which is either 15 March each year in the absence of an extension, or 14 April if there is one. Remember that these penalties apply to information reports (i.e. 1042-S), not tax returns.

There are also caps on penalties in all but one scenario. Finally, the penalties vary depending on the size of the QI measured by the total gross receipts of US-sourced Fixed, Determinable, Annual or Periodic (FDAP) income.

1. Gross receipts greater than $5 million

   (a) Failure to file on due date: $270 per form, capped at $3,282,500
   (b) If corrected within 30 days: $50 per form, capped at $547,000
   (c) If corrected after 30 days but before 1 August: $100 per form, capped at $1,641,000

2. Gross receipts less than $5 million

   (a) Failure to file on due date: $270 per form, capped at $1,094,000
   (b) If corrected within 30 days: $50 per form, capped at $191,000
   (c) If corrected after 30 days but before 1 August: $100 per form, capped at $547,000

In addition to the above, there is a higher level penalty if the IRS considers that the QI or NQI has 'intentionally disregarded' its obligations. QIs and NQIs (mainly NQIs it has to be said) are subject to a penalty of $540 per form with no maximum upper limit on the penalty.

The above penalties apply to filings made from a QI or non-withholding qualified intermediary (NWQI) to the IRS. However, all NQIs and, to the extent that a QI has an indirect customer, the proper forms 1042-S must be provided to these customers within 30 days. The IRS assesses penalties here too (Fig. 7.1).

7 Penalties

Many QIs and NQIs do have US customers. To the extent that the institution has adopted primary backup withholding responsibility, the institution also has an obligation to file forms 1099 for which there are also penalties, both upstream to the IRS and, as with the 1042-S forms, downstream to US recipients. These penalties mirror the structure for 1042-S, being applied based on how late after the deadline (1 January), the forms are eventually submitted.

1. If the filing is submitted within 30 days, the penalty is $50 per form, subject to a maximum of $187,000 (small businesses) or $536,000 (large businesses);
2. If the filing is submitted after 30 day, but on or before 1 August, the penalty is $100 per form, subject to a maximum of $536,000 (small businesses) or $1,609,000 (large businesses);
3. If the filing is made after 1 August or the QI/NQI fails to file at all, the penalty is $260 per form, subject to a maximum of $1,072,500 (small businesses) or $3,218,500 (large businesses).

Again, the recipient is supposed to receive a copy of the form deposited with the IRS. The penalties are the same.

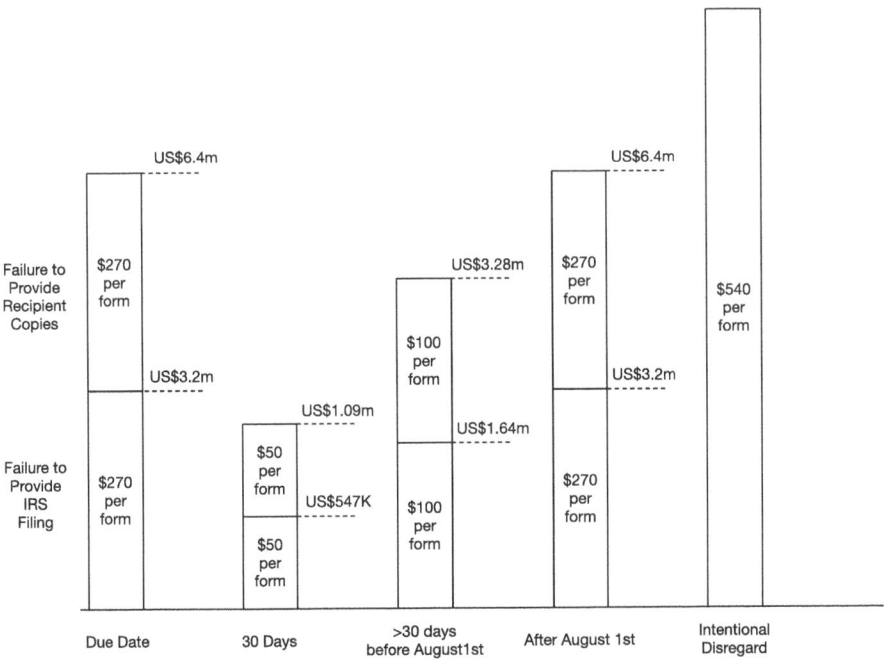

Fig. 7.1 Penalties for failure to file 1042-S (gross receipts > $5 m). Source: Author's own

So, in both cases, 1042-S and 1099-X, penalties are levied upstream and downstream. This exposes reporting NQIs to a much greater degree of risk than QIs.

The major flaw in this system that has been leveraged by many NQIs over the years is that, if you never file, you can't be penalised, because the IRS doesn't know the number of forms you would be liable to have filed.

Incorrect Timing of Deposits

The above penalties are all triggered by a late or incorrect report and tax return. Prior to this, in the processing cycle, US-sourced FDAP payments will have been assessed for withholding under one of the several possible tax rates—0, 10, 15, 20, 24, 25, 30 Non-Resident Alien (NRA), 30 FATCA and 39.4%. The consequence of the assessment is, of course, the depositing of tax to the US Treasury (remember the IRS gets reports and returns, Treasury gets the cash). This must be done by withholding QIs or US withholding agents in accordance with a formula shown in Fig. 4.4.

The current penalties are:

- 2% for payments 1–5 days late
- 5% for payments 6–15 days late
- 10% for payments more than 15 days late

Perjury

It would be remiss of me indeed not to mention that several of the IRS tax forms include text at the signature lines that remind the signor that the form they are executing is signed under penalties of perjury.

If convicted under federal law, the sentence can be up to five years in prison plus fines. If convicted under State laws, the sentences can vary, but are at least one year in prison plus fines.

Mitigation

If you are assessed for a penalty, you have three options:

- Ignore it and hope they go away (not recommended)
- Pay the penalty
- Request some mitigation

Clearly, the best way to mitigate penalties is to make sure that you're not subject to them in the first place. However, if you feel that there is a case to be made for a reduction or even removal, this is possible with a 'Reasonable Cause Defense' letter which a lawyer can help you draft. However, remember that 'ignorance is not bliss'. A reasonable cause defence letter that contains the phrase 'we did not realise' or similar is unlikely to succeed. Equally, such a letter should make some mention of what steps you intend to take to ensure that the reason for the failure does not occur again.

Practical Issues

Reconciliation

A common problem that generates penalties, particularly claims of under-withholding, occurs when a 1042 and/or 1042-S cannot be reconciled to an upstream report or return. This is usually due to the absence of an Employer Identification Number or EIN. QIs are given these when they sign their QI Agreement in the form of a QI EIN. However, since, with limited exceptions, all intermediary recipients of US-sourced income must file returns and reports to the IRS, in effect, all these intermediaries should have EINs. If an upstream QI or US withholding agent (USWA) is not provided with the EIN of its downstream counterparty (usually on a form W-8IMY), the effect is that when the upstream intermediary files its returns and reports, they will not have any identifying number on them to tie them to the returns and reports of the downstream intermediary. In the absence of the ability to reconcile one report to another, the IRS typically issues an under-withholding penalty notice on the downstream intermediary. This can be mitigated (1) with the use of a reasonable cause defence letter in which (2) the intermediary concerned identifies the lack of an EIN as the cause and obtains one. However, the intermediary may have to re-file its reports.

Incorrect Completion

Even when there is an EIN, many downstream intermediaries fall foul of one simple concept—every intermediary between a USWA and a beneficial owner is technically a 'withholding agent'. Many intermediaries assume that because someone else does the physical withholding (i.e. typically because they are a NWQI or an NQI), that they are not a withholding agent. Not only is this not technically true, it also leads to many incorrectly completed reports and returns where these firms enter numbers on the forms into the wrong boxes.

No Jurisdiction

Another common approach from NQIs is to assume that the IRS can't get to them and, even if they could, if they've never filed a report, how would the IRS know how many forms had not been submitted. This is usually expressed as a concern over extraterritoriality, that is, the application of a penalty by a foreign government in a country where it has no jurisdiction. The second of the two arguments is perhaps the most logical. If an NQI does not tick box 17b on its W-8IMY and subsequently refuses to disclose its customers, the upstream entity can only report at the NQI level (its customer) and then only that there are 'undisclosed recipients'. To that extent, the IRS is unable, as is the upstream QI or USWA, to find out how many forms are supposed to have been filed—ergo no 'per form' penalty can be assessed. This is the situation that many NQIs find themselves in. Equally, the NQIs who take this view are also generally the ones who have never filed a report since 2001. One could argue that, if found, this would be pretty good evidence of 'intentional disregard'.

IRS Resource

All the above are factual statements, true as far as I'm able to ascertain. However, the practical question that arises is—has the IRS ever actually applied any of these penalties? On the one hand, one would have to assume so, although, as noted, the IRS does not publicise this. On the other hand, I have anecdotal experience that, particularly with respect to historical failures to file, the IRS does not really appear that interested. With respect to the current year, I have seen penalties applied. That said, my view has always been that, just because the IRS may or may not apply any of these penalties, does not mean that they can't, or won't in the future. I believe it may be a simple matter of resource for the IRS. From an operational viewpoint, filing all these reports has absolutely no benefit to a QI or NQI—it's simply a cost of doing business in the US equity markets. It's understandable therefore that, if the IRS is not taking a public and strong position on the imposition of penalties, that, particularly NQIs believe that it's a reasonable strategy to ignore the issue. From their viewpoint, this year's current filing is next year's historic filing, so, every year they get away with it, becomes another year that the IRS is unlikely to pursue.

The other side of this coin is not operational; it's compliance and reputational damage. If you ask an operations person, they would clearly prefer not to have to do all the work associated with something that doesn't benefit their company. If you ask a compliance person the same question, well, to them it's not even a question, especially when the market concerned happens to be the largest capital market on the planet. One of the most interesting types of conversation I have is with institutions which have relatively small reportable amounts of US-sourced income each year. For them, the cost of compliance can easily be higher than the reportable amounts they are receiving. I've even spoken with one brokerage firm where the cost of producing their 1042-S filings each year amounts to almost half their entire profit margin for that year. For these smaller institutions, the cost of becoming and being a QI is simply out of the question. Their only other options are either to withdraw from the US market (not a good competitive strategy), take the risk of being found out (as opposed to 'stepping up to the plate') or pass on some of the compliance cost in higher client fees.

This latter is becoming much more common. I see fees being applied by QIs to NQI customers at the rate of $35 for validating a disclosed W-8 form and $80 for producing a beneficial owner level 1042-S. This is not unsurprising and will probably continue to become more widespread. It not only remunerates the upstream entity for the work it must do consequent on disclosure, but it also means that, if penalised, it has some funds from which to pay the penalty.

In conclusion, penalties are, of course, best avoided. The object of this book is to help QIs and NQI perform intelligently and compliantly so that penalties are avoided. However, many circumstances occur, some of which are beyond the control of the firm, that lead to penalty notices. Where possible these should be abated. Firms should however understand that 'penalties' should be broadly interpreted to include not just fiscal penalties but also reputational damage, residual risk damage and loss of business, turnover or profits arising from general failures to either take QI status seriously or, more commonly, apply insufficient focus or resource.

8

Issues for Non-qualified Intermediaries

Awareness

Non-qualified intermediaries (NQIs) are by far the most common type of financial institutions receiving US-sourced income. There are only about 5000 qualified intermediaries (QIs); every other financial institution is an NQI. NQIs are also deemed by the US to be facilitators of tax evasion, which means that they are subject to more rigorous disclosure obligations and risk of higher penalties for non-compliance. This chapter explains the most common issues faced by NQIs and also by QIs with NQI clients.

One of the most common misconceptions about IRC Chapter 3 is that it only applies to QIs. This is false. The persistence of this issue is not helped by the fact that most people use the term 'QI regulations' as a short name. This is not only untrue, it's very misleading.

As noted, an NQI or non-qualified intermediary is any financial institution located *outside* the US, which has *not* signed a QI Agreement with the Internal Revenue Service (IRS).

NQIs fall into two general categories. Those that are located in Know-Your-Customer (KYC)-approved jurisdictions and those which are not. The latter have no choice but to be NQIs, since the IRS does not approve the KYC rules in that jurisdiction; they will not be permitted to sign a QI Agreement. The former, those NQIs in jurisdictions with approved KYC rules, have this default status either (1) because they've taken a positive decision not to contract with the IRS or, more likely, (2) because they're not aware of, or have misunderstood, the regulations. Over 18 years after these regulations came into force, a large proportion of my time in consulting is spent explaining the regulations, their existence and their impact to NQIs whose knowledge, on a scale of 1 to 10, is between 1 and 3. In fact, there is a substantial minority that hold the view that they are not covered by IRC Chapter 3, because they haven't signed any agreement with the IRS. Again, this is untrue.

At the time of writing, there are estimated, according to an informed source, to be just over 5000 QIs in total. The IRS does not yet publish lists or numbers of QIs. Clearly, on a global scale, the number of financial institutions that have an exposure to the US equity and debt markets is much larger than 5000. It's estimated that the number could be in the region of 50,000. Whatever the actual numbers, most financial intermediaries, by number, that receive US-sourced income are NQIs.

The IRC Chapter 3 rules are essentially a cascade structure, so while the number of NQIs may be large in comparison to the number of QIs, the nature of the asset servicing chain is that a large proportion of the assets that generate US-sourced income is held through QIs at some point in the chain. This is usually at the level immediately below a US withholding agent (USWA). USWAs have become very averse to having direct relationships with NQIs due to the nature of the obligations that I will describe in this chapter and the way that the US government views these NQIs.

In 2009, then President Barrack Obama and Secretary Geithner said that the default view of the US government towards NQIs was that they were 'presumed to be facilitating tax evasion'. To be precise, the Press Room cites in TG-119 on 4 May 2009:

> This proposal requires foreign financial institutions that have dealings with the United States to sign an agreement with the IRS to become a 'Qualified Intermediary' and share as much information about their U.S. customers as U.S. financial institutions do, or else face the presumption that they may be facilitating tax evasion and have taxes withheld on payments to their customers. In addition, it would shut down loopholes that allow QIs to claim they are complying with the law even as they help wealthy U.S. citizens avoid paying their fair share of taxes.

Key Principles for NQIs

Non-qualified intermediaries face a tough time, even when we only look at them through the lens of Chapter 3. As IRC Chapter 4 of the Code deploys, their situation will become more and more complex.

Awareness

As I began to explain at the outset of this chapter, many of an NQI's problems start with awareness. There are very common myths in the NQI community and, I have to say that neither the QI community nor the IRS has been particularly effective at dispelling these myths, or even at engaging with NQIs to educate them. Four typical examples are:

- 'We're not subject to US tax regulations because we haven't signed a contract with the IRS.'
- 'We don't have to send reports to the IRS because 30% tax was withheld on our accounts.'
- 'The IRS can't impose penalties on us because they have no jurisdiction over us.'
- 'Anyway, how would they find us even if they did?'.

All four of these positions are false.

NQIs are subject to IRC Chapter 3 regulations if they have received US-sourced income. It has nothing to do with whether they have, or have not, signed an agreement with the IRS.

The US Treasury handles tax dollars. The IRS handles reports. It's also immaterial what the level of tax deposits were, those tax deposits must be reported, even if the amount withheld was 30%.

The penalties are set by the US Treasury and receipt of US-sourced income places the NQI under the terms of the regulations. Again, it has nothing to do with whether there's a contract in place. How will they find these NQIs? They don't need to 'find' them. In the cascade reporting system, the upstream institution where the NQI has its accounts will report it as a recipient and, if appropriate, show it with 'undisclosed recipients'—red flag time.

It must also be said that there are occasions where an NQI does not hold this status out of choice and therefore it's unreasonable to tar all NQIs with some sort of 'bad' badge. The IRS rules provide that an institution can only sign a QI Agreement if the KYC rules of that institution's residency jurisdiction have been approved by the IRS. Since not all countries' KYC rules have been approved, there are a number of places in the world where financial institutions are incapable of being anything other than NQIs.

However, apart from awareness, there are other issues that cause NQIs difficulties and these issues do not stand alone. They are connected.

Account Structures

In the custody and brokerage world, having an account costs money. Therefore, there are several models an institution can adopt when opening accounts that allow them to trade in any given market. These are 'omnibus' or 'rate pool' accounts (accounts that co-mingle assets of more than one underlying client but where the tax rate applicable to all those assets is the same), 'proprietary accounts' (accounts holding non-client assets) and 'segregated accounts' (accounts holding only one underlying client's assets) and all three are shown in Fig. 8.1.

There are hybrids that deal in tax issues to an extent, for example, 'segregated omnibus' accounts, otherwise known as pooled accounts. From a practical perspective, an institution usually wants to open the smallest number of accounts consistent with it being able to do business, in order to keep costs low. For this purpose an omnibus account allows an NQI to have one account at an upstream institution (USWA or QI) in which it places all of its customers' assets, irrespective of who the customers are, their tax entitlements or their residencies. The alternative would be to open segregated accounts, that is, one upstream account reflecting each account held downstream with an underlying recipient. The latter creates more work for the NQI in managing assets in multiple accounts and also more cost as each account costs money to open and run. The hybrid solution is to open a few accounts which are omnibus in nature, that is, each account holds the assets of more than one underlying recipient, but there is a common-

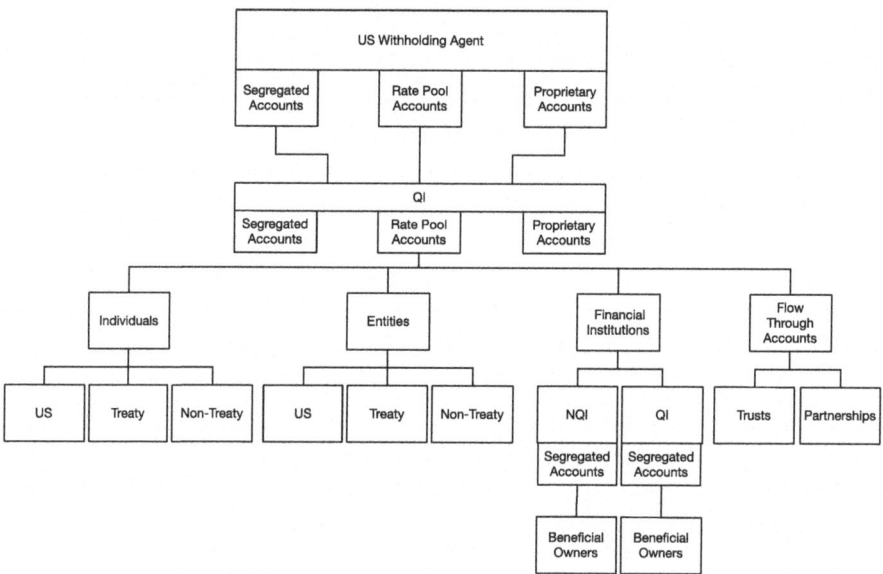

Fig. 8.1 Account structures. Source: Author's own

ality in that each account will only hold the assets of recipients who are entitled to the same rate of tax. So an NQI might have several segregated omnibus accounts called 0, 10, 15, 20, 25 and 30, these being the number of possible tax rates that could apply to US-sourced income. There are a couple more but it's quite rare for income to be received in these brackets (e.g. 39.4%) but often a USWA can identify these kinds of assets within another rate pool account. That's a much smaller number of accounts to pay for and maintain BUT this issue now connects with the disclosure issue. When both are considered together, in practice, most NQIs elect to have single omnibus accounts.

Disclosure

The main objective of the IRC Chapter 3 regulations is to support the US as a relief at source tax jurisdiction. In the relief at source framework, the only entity types that can apply relief at source are US withholding agents, withholding QIs, withholding foreign partnerships and withholding foreign trusts—not NQIs.

Equally, in a competitive world, many investors are not best pleased to see all their US dividends and portfolio interest taxed at 30%. On the former, if there's a treaty available, they should be taxed at that lower treaty rate when the dividend is distributed. If they receive portfolio interest, this shouldn't be taxed at all, irrespective of whether there's a treaty or not. However, the NQI is not in a position to provide relief at source and must rely on one of the other entities upstream in the chain to do this for them. This can't happen unless there is disclosure. In other words, an institution capable of providing relief at source will only do so if it has 'valid documentation on hand on pay date evidencing a lower rate of tax'.

This means that an NQI would have to provide documentation, that is, W-8s for each of its underlying recipients, proving their entitlement to a treaty rate of tax, or a portfolio interest exemption together with a withholding statement. A withholding statement is often a spreadsheet, but basically contains data that allocates any payment to the disclosed beneficial owners so that the receiving institution can validate the W-8s and apply relevant tax rates. 'Disclosure' per se means both the documentation and the withholding statement. One without the other is not disclosure.

Clearly this is both an onerous task for any NQI with a significant customer base and a commercially sensitive issue since the entity they would be sending these documents to would, in essence, be a potential competitor. The base model is that the disclosure takes place prior to each payment; however, this is commercially unrealistic.

There is an 'Alternative Procedure' which allows an NQI to provide this breakdown information and documentation just once a year, by 31 January at latest with respect to the prior US tax year—but the disclosure at the beneficial owner level must take place one way or another. This means that an NQI can operate tax rate pool accounts at a QI or USWA and move assets between them based on the applicable tax rate as long as, by 31 January of the next year, it provides a full withholding statement allocating the payments made throughout that prior year. To use the alternative procedure, the QI or the USWA must agree to use the procedure and this must be documented in its compliance programme and with the NQI concerned.

This is notwithstanding any data protection issues that might apply from the movement of personal information across borders. That said, the US regulations are written with this disclosure model as the base assumption. An NQI, under the regulations, has a presumed obligation to provide a W-8IMY, with which it documents itself to its upstream counterparty (USWA or QI) plus a Full Withholding Statement (FWS) and all documentation of their underlying customers. As I've said, for the reasons given, this rarely happens.

By the way, do not confuse a Full Withholding Statement (FWS)—which is a disclosure of beneficial owners and their assets, with a withholding rate pool statement (WRPS), which is how a QI instructs a USWA to withhold on a given income event without disclosing its direct customers.

The Perfect Storm

So, now these three issues mix to create the perfect storm. For cost reasons, most NQIs only operate omnibus accounts at USWAs and QIs. For competitive and privacy reasons, most NQIs do not provide full disclosure (anything less than full disclosure is non-disclosure in practical terms). Any USWA or withholding qualified intermediary (WQI) faced with a customer who is an NQI in these circumstances cannot provide relief at source on any US-sourced income and *must* withhold 30% from all such payments. On the pay date, since there has been no documentary disclosure, the QI cannot assess which recipients are entitled to which rate of tax. Even if it did, operating an omnibus account for the NQI, the USWA/QI has no way to know what portion of the payment is allocable to which underlying recipient.

FATCA Rate Pool Statement

That 30% would need to be categorised. Under a clarification made by the IRS in December 2018, an NQI must provide a Foreign Account Tax Compliance Act (FATCA) rate pool statement to indicate whether any portion of a payment must be taxed at 30% in FATCA. This is a nil reporting situation, that is, if there is no FATCA penalty to apply, the FATCA rate pool statement must still be produced (saying nothing to withhold). In the absence of a FATCA Rate Pool statement, a QI or USWA must treat its client as a non-participating foreign financial institution (FFI) in FATCA, even if it has a W-8IMY with a Global Intermediary Identification Number (GIIN) on it. Remember that payments must be assessed under IRC Chapter 4 first, then IRC Chapter 3. This prioritisation means that an NQI that does not disclose may be caught by IRC Chapter 4 before the payments are assessed in IRC Chapter 3. It may think it is compliant with FATCA, but even if it is, if it fails to provide a FATCA Rate Pool Statement, it must be presumed to be an NP-FFI and thus subject to IRC Chapter 4 penalty 30% and not IRC Chapter 3 30% Non-Resident Alien (NRA) tax.

Cost is not just an issue for the NQI in this model. If an NQI were to provide a Full Withholding Statement and all the documentation required under the regulations, a USWA or QI could then provide relief at source on the NQI's accounts. In order to do that, in addition to the workload associated with its own direct clients, it would also have to perform all the due diligence and analyses on the documents and data associated with the customers of its client. If the number of such customers is significant, this task would be both onerous and very costly and may even outweigh the benefit of the relief gained for the customers.

Of course there are exceptions to every rule and, for completeness I have to say that I have come across instances where full disclosure has taken place and the IRS model works. But these are very rare in my experience.

So, despite the intent of the IRS and despite the objective of relief at source, most NQIs still operate omnibus accounts today, do not disclose and their customers pay 30% tax on all US-sourced income. Many will find out from 2019 onwards that, if they fail to provide that FATCA Rate Pool Statement, they will also have their income taxed at 30% in FATCA.

That, unfortunately, is only one half of the problem.

Information Reporting and Tax Returns

I mentioned three myths at the beginning of this chapter. There is a fourth. Actually there's a fifth, sixth and many more, which I'll deal with as we go along. But the fourth myth is that the only US government entity involved here is the IRS. While they are both part of the one arm of the US government, the US Treasury and the IRS work very differently and have different objectives. Treasury has the role of collecting the tax. It operates structures such as the Electronic Federal Tax Payment System (EFTPS) which allows USWAs and WQIs to deposit tax dollars. On the other hand, the IRS' role is to receive and analyse information returns. These returns are expected each year by 15 March from all institutions in the payment chain, including NQIs.

Now, remember that the basic assumption in the way the regulations are written is that all NQIs will disclose all their customers to their QI or USWA and provide a full withholding statement or operate segregated accounts. Based on this assumption, the regulations require the QI or USWA, since both are under direct control of the IRS via QI Agreement and US domestic regulation respectively, to create and file their tax return 1042 and information reports 1042-S. They have this obligation for their own direct clients although to the extent possible they are able to 'pool' these clients and thus make their reporting obligations less onerous. However, the regulations are clear. It's the job of the QI or the USWA, to the extent that there is full disclosure, to file information reports 1042-S on behalf of the NQI's customers. Because there is an NQI involved, the information returns are required at the beneficial owner level and cannot be pooled.

To the extent that there is partial or non-disclosure, a USWA or QI clearly does not have enough information to create these reports. However, the obligation to report at the beneficial owner level does not just evaporate in this circumstance, it flows to the NQI. If the NQI is unaware of this flow of obligation, they will be in breach of the regulations and subject to all the penalties associated with failure to file information returns.

This can create a major connectivity problem. Consider that a form 1042 is a tax return, not an information report. As such, a 1042 tax return can only be completed by the NQI. Let me explain further. Consider an NQI with two USWAs. At one, the NQI maintains an undisclosed omnibus account. At the other, it maintains an omnibus account but provides a W-8IMY with box 17b ticked, a Full Withholding Statement and associated W-8BENs. The first USWA can only file a 1042-S at the NQI level (sending a copy to the NQI). The second USWA has had full disclosure so provides a 1042-S to his NQI client, together with 1042-S reports for each of the NQI's underlying customers. The only thing left to do is for the NQI to file its tax return on form 1042 on which it will have to aggregate the US-sourced income and tax withheld by *both* USWAs. It should become immediately clear that neither of the USWAs can help the NQI produce or file its tax return since they each lack information about the income and tax paid to the NQI by the other. It's very common for NQIs (and often QIs) to misunderstand the difference between a tax return and an information report in terms of who is able to do what. Some disclosing NQIs are not compliant simply because they think the job is done when the 1042-S forms go out to the IRS and customers, forgetting that they still have an outstanding obligation at their level to file the 1042 tax return.

One final comment with regard to reporting. In December 2018, the IRS issued a Notice of Proposed Rulemaking in which it clarified the requirement for an NQI to provide a FATCA Rate Pool Statement. This was discussed earlier in this chapter. The net result of course would be that when an NQI affected by this rule received its 1042-Ss from its upstream counterparty, all the tax applied would be a penalty, not a tax per se. That would mean that when the NQI produces its recipient copies, those forms would reflect a penalty and not a tax. The IRS Notice clarified that NQIs in these circumstances can re-categorise their upstream FATCA 1042-S into a downstream NRA 1042-S. The reasoning being that this will allow the beneficial owners to more easily claim a deduction of the amounts from their domestic tax authorities.

Figure 8.2 shows two different operating models for an NQI. The solid lines represent documentation flows. The chain link lines represent payments of US-sourced income and the dotted lines represent reporting.

The left hand diagram shows an NQI that does not disclose its clients. It presents a W-8IMY to a QI with box 17b unchecked. It has also failed to present a FATCA Rate Pool Statement. The QI in this case will treat the NQI as a Non-Participating FFI in IRC Chapter 4, so when the payment is made, assessment under IRC Chapter 4 comes first and the payment is taxed at 30%

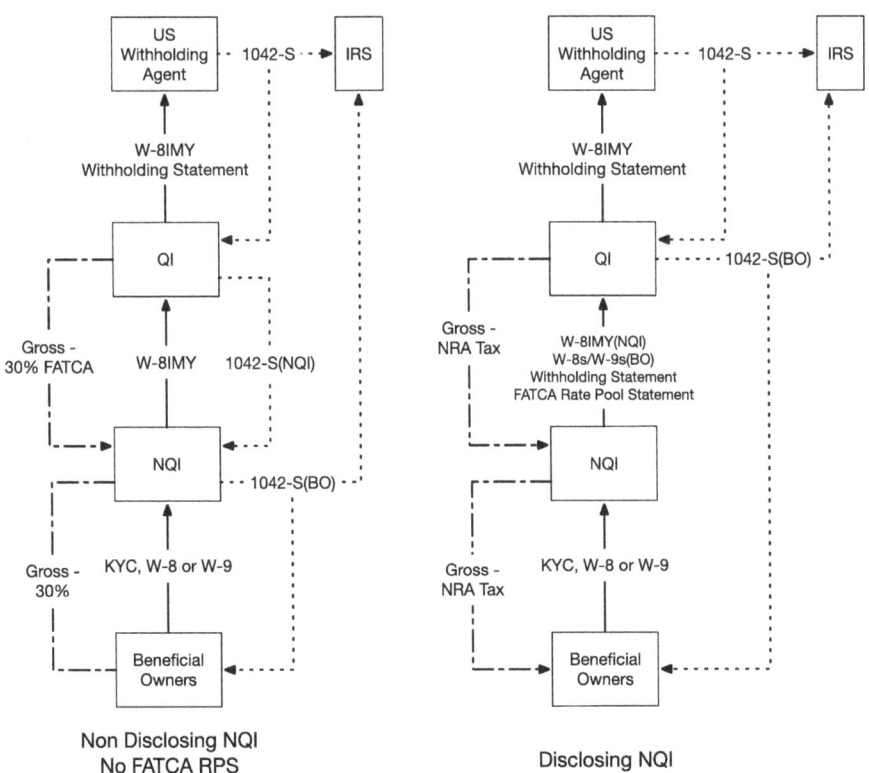

Fig. 8.2 Effects of disclosure on payments and reporting for NQIs. Source: Author's own

and categorised as a FATCA penalty. Because there was no disclosure, the NQI only requires a single omnibus account at the QI as all income will be taxed at the same rate. This client will also be reported on the QI's FATCA report on form 8966. When it comes to reporting the income and tax withheld, because there was no disclosure, the QI reports the NQI on form 1042-S coded for FATCA withholding and with 'undisclosed recipients'. Under the Notice of Proposed Rulemaking, the NQI can create recipient forms 1042-S, but represent the payments as being made under NRA IRC Chapter 3 rules and not as FATCA penalties.

The right hand diagram shows an NQI that does disclose its clients. It presents to its QI counterparty—a W-8IMY with box 17b checked. It may adopt either the standard or the alternative procedure for disclosure, but in either case this means that the QI also receives W-8s of the indirect account holders and a full withholding statement. The NQI also presents a FATCA Rate Pool Statement (or includes the FATCA element in its normal withholding statement). This disclosure opens the possibility of using tax rate pool accounts with the QI so that the NQI can place assets of its clients into relevant rate pool accounts and gain the benefit of treaty rates if claimed. When it comes to reporting, because of the disclosure, the NQI is not reported at all by the QI since all the income can be allocated (via the withholding statement) to the indirect account holders. The 1042-S filing to the IRS contains beneficial owner level 1042-S data lines (where its own direct clients are pooled). The QI must now produce and distribute recipient copies of the 1042-S forms to the underlying indirect account holders.

For most QIs and NQIs this form of operational and procedural mapping is fundamental to understanding what's going on, who has to do what and when.

Practical Compliance

In this section, I will expand on some of the principles established in the preceding section with a particular emphasis on the real practicalities. Last year, I travelled 186,300 miles and visited 28 countries. What I found was virtually every possible permutation of business model being operated by US withholding agents, QIs and NQIs. By far the most common, as I noted, is the use of omnibus accounts, for cost reasons; non-disclosure for competitive and privacy reasons; leading to a 30% tax on customer accounts and generally no knowledge that information reporting even existed. Where it was known of, it was assumed that, because 30% tax had been withheld, no reporting was required. This is clearly very far from the model envisaged by the regulations.

I found myself, on several occasions, having to explain these issues to NQIs to be faced with shock, followed by 'why did no-one tell us?'. The latter is usually directed at their QI or USWA or the IRS.

As I hope I've demonstrated, if this were just about regulation, it might, just might, be a bit simpler. However all these institutions, USWAs and QIs, are large, complex businesses. The regulations themselves, in the way they are written, make assumptions about the way the industry works that just don't always stand up. There are cost and resource issues both at the QI and at the NQI level and other things to think about. There are also privacy and domestic compliance concerns as well as structural issues. So, it's perhaps not surprising that everyone in the chain is somewhat self-focused and concerned to contain cost and risk. In this world we are into the art of the minimal. What's the minimum we need to do to comply for ourselves. After all, there is no financial benefit to these regulations for the financial institutions concerned. Their customers may get relief at source, but the regulatory load on the institutions is enormous and much of it has nothing to do with the benefit gained by an investor. So let's start at the beginning. Knowing what to do and why is a case of assessing several variables in a sort of compliance equation. This is not like IF x THEN DO y. Each of the variables has an effect of its own, but can also combine with other variables to change the operational compliance requirements. Figure 8.2 was and is a good example.

Documentation

The first variable in the compliance equation is documentation. Most NQIs do not understand the documentation requirements of IRC Chapter 3 nor its consequences.

Basically an NQI is an intermediary, and therefore it's not a beneficial owner. It would thus typically document itself to an upstream QI or US withholding agent using form W-8IMY. Equally, little guidance is given to NQIs of the consequences of the way in which these forms are completed. The biggest issue is the way in which question 17 is answered on form W-8IMY. Ticking box 17a is mandatory for an NQI since this is a statement of fact. Ticking box 17b, however, has a different impact. Box 17b is where the NQI establishes whether it is going to disclose all of its underlying beneficial owners to its QI or upstream USWA. This is critical because it will establish (1) the rate of withholding that's applied and also (2) who does the information reporting at year end. There is a connection between these two issues that we'll explore later in this chapter.

Incidentally, an issue that I also come up against in the documentation area is that of proprietary trading.

The issue can be described as follows: If an NQI has two accounts at an upstream QI and one of them represents the assets of its underlying customers, while the other represents its own proprietary assets, it should be providing two forms W-8, not one to its upstream counterparty. A W-8IMY would represent the fact that for one account NQI acts as an intermediary and not a beneficial owner. The second form expected would be a W-8BEN-E where it is representing the fact that the assets in the other account relate to its own proprietary trading book—where it is the beneficial owner (and by definition not an NQI but a corporation). Most QIs and USWAs do not really explain this well to NQIs and NQIs themselves, for the most part, are completely unaware of the issue, even when it applies. The chances are that the NQI would just submit a form W-8IMY since this is its main focus. In the event of no disclosure of beneficial owners in the intermediary account, it's likely that the NQI would be over-withheld on its proprietary assets, presuming a treaty exists between their residence jurisdiction and the US.

Account Structures

The second variable that really affects NQIs is the structure of the accounts they operate with QIs and USWAs. Since most financial institutions charge fees per account opened, it's relatively rare to find an NQI maintaining segregated accounts—one for each of its customers. The most common structure used is an omnibus account, that is, a single account in which the assets of all its customers are comingled. There are account types in between which have some characteristics of both types, for example, segregated rate pool accounts, that is, multiple accounts in which the assets of the underlying beneficial owners are comingled based on the tax rate applicable to the income. However, to understand the import of these account types we must remember that the US government doesn't like NQIs. Therefore, its position is that an NQI must disclose its customers to someone with whom it does have a higher level of control. That would be a QI, by reason of its contract with the IRS, or a US withholding agent, by reason of its location within the borders of the US. We should also remember that one of the two objectives of the US system is to provide for relief at source on US Fixed, Determinable, Annual or Periodic (FDAP) income for those who are entitled to it by reason of a treaty or exemption. So, if an NQI has an omnibus account, of whatever flavour, while it may be a cheaper operational method of doing business, from the US perspective it means that additional work would have to be done in order that relief at source on the income could be achieved. This is because any account structure short of segregated by beneficial owner means that the upstream QI or USWA does not have the first part of 'disclosure' necessary to provide relief at source tax rates. That first part is income data. By having segregated accounts at the beneficial owner level, the QI or USWA will automatically have access to all the data about income paid to each account of each customer of an NQI. If the second part of disclosure is provided (see below), the QI or USWA would be able to provide the NQI's customers with relief at source tax rates. However, as I mentioned, it's very uncommon to see this type of account being used. Omnibus is by far the most prevalent and with it, the high likelihood that all of an NQI's customers would be taxed at 30% on US-sourced FDAP income, because the upstream QI or USWA has not been provided with enough information by its customer to do its job.

Disclosure

As I noted above, the types of account that NQIs typically operate, place them at a disadvantage almost immediately and before any other issues are addressed. I also noted that there are two halves to the operational aspects of disclosure before we even think about legal and privacy issues.

That second issue also provides us with the third variable in the compliance equation. Even if the NQI uses segregated accounts or provides its QI or USWA, with a beneficial owner level breakdown of income paid to an omnibus account (of any flavour), without documentary disclosure, the accounts will still be taxed at 30%. To understand this we must, again, remind ourselves that the US government does not trust NQIs. They structured the regulations to dis-incentivise NQIs from having, or keeping, this status on the grounds that the US believes that NQIs are the primary route through which American tax evaders are managing to maintain hidden accounts and assets outside the US. So the basic rule is that NQIs must disclose their customers at the beneficial owner level. In the regulations, this takes the form of providing not just income data, but also documentation. The principle is that once this level of disclosure has taken place, it's the QI or USWA's job to assess the documentation and data, to make sure that (1) there are no US persons in the NQI's account structure, (2) that any withholding is appropriate to the entitlements of the underlying beneficiaries and (3) that appropriate reporting to the IRS at the underlying beneficial owner level is achieved. Again, in practice, this is even rarer than data disclosure. For the NQI this is burdensome, even when it doesn't trigger data privacy risks. Equally, most QIs and USWAs have little, or no, interest in assessing someone else's documentation. They have enough problems assessing their own.

Apart from the practical aspects of disclosure that cause NQIs and QIs problems, many also face issues around data privacy. Whether this is an issue depends, to a certain extent, on whether the NQI is in a jurisdiction with data privacy and/or banking secrecy laws. Most jurisdictions have one or the other at some level.

One of the most common questions I get from NQIs is 'my customer doesn't want me to send a report to the IRS and is claiming data privacy. What do I do?'

Well, the obligation to report at the beneficial owner level was triggered by the status of the customer's financial institution—the NQI. So, to some extent, the explanation to a customer can be a little difficult. It doesn't matter whether the NQI has disclosed or not to its upstream QI or USWA—the end-of-year reporting, whoever it's done by, must be at beneficial owner level and is the obligation of the institution.

On the one hand, this can cause a conflict where the NQI would need to breach its own domestic laws in order to comply with the US regulations. Ignorance is no defence. In principle, the NQI is supposed to know what obligations it will be subject to when it accesses any given market, particularly the US.

Withholding

Withholding is probably the simplest issue for NQIs to understand. Generally speaking, the default statutory rate of 30% is what most customers of NQIs pay on their US-sourced income. This is because any one of the variables discussed in this chapter, not addressed correctly, will result in that rate being applied. No disclosure—30%. Omnibus account—30%. No FATCA withholding statement—30%. The withholding itself is performed by an upstream financial institution. This will be either a USWA or a QI. From a practical perspective, this does give NQIs a relationship management problem downstream. Investors receiving US-sourced income taxed at 30% are usually not happy. Basic research tells them that if they are resident in a country that has a treaty with the US, they should be taxed at only 10%, 15%, 20% or 25% depending on their country of residence. It tells all their customers that if they are holding bonds, they should be receiving coupon payments without any withholding tax deduction, portfolio interest being exempt. The NQI's problem is that the reason its customers are subject to 30% tax, is often due to its business decisions or policies. That explanation doesn't usually go down well with customers and so the regulations get blamed, or the US government gets blamed. But the regulations do provide options—become a QI, disclose and so on, which would ultimately mean that NQI customers could get relief.

Reporting

All NQIs who receive US-sourced FDAP income must send reports to the IRS, either directly or indirectly. This is not based on the QI Agreement; it's based on the regulations. Apart from documentation, it's the single largest misunderstanding and compliance failure I see.

The reporting required is not like a QI's reporting. The general rule is that QIs can pool for the purpose of withholding and reporting while NQIs can only pool for the purpose of withholding. An NQI must therefore report each of its customers individually, and by type of income, directly to the IRS. The way that the regulations are written, the presumption is that NQIs will disclose their customers to an upstream QI or USWA. Therefore, the regulations provide that when this happens, it's the QI or USWA's job to file the reports, both to the IRS and also with copies of each report, to the NQI's underlying customers.

In practice, this disclosure rarely happens.

So, the upstream QI or USWA is not in a position to file these reports because it doesn't know who the NQI's customers are. However, the reporting obligation doesn't just evaporate, it moves down the chain to the NQI. This is the simple fact that most NQIs are either unaware of or fail to act on. Much of this is, of course, down to a lack of education and information available.

I mentioned customer reports, known in the vernacular as recipient copies. This is another difference between QI reporting and NQI reporting. A QI does not need to provide its direct customers with copies of forms 1042-S. Remember that for many customers, their US-sourced income will have been pooled into a tax rate band for the purpose of reporting to the IRS. There is, therefore, no one-to-one relationship between IRS reporting and downstream reporting. The situation is different for an NQI. Every 1042-S form it is required to send to the IRS, must have a copy sent to its customer. The IRS establishes penalties for failure to file to them and also for failure to file copies to customers. The size of that penalty increases dependent on how long after the deadline of 15 March, the NQI submits its reports. NQIs can use the same system as QIs to give themselves some extra time to file. This is done with form 7004 for the 6-month extension to file the 1042 return and form 8809 for a 30-day extension to file.

So, let's take a typical example. An NQI has an omnibus account with a US withholding agent. He provides the withholding agent with a form W-8IMY on which he represents that he is an NQI, but he fails to tick box 17b of the form and also fails to provide a withholding statement or any of the underlying documentation of his customers. Quite often, upstream QIs and USWAs don't provide enough information about the different options available to NQIs. This is sometimes because they don't want to have the additional work to do of receiving withholding statements and documentation of another institution's customers. Equally NQIs are usually very reticent about providing such information about their customers. Let's presume that this NQI has 2500 customers, each of whom received US-sourced dividends and portfolio interest during the year.

Because the NQI failed to disclose, the upstream institutions can't fulfil the requirement to report the NQI's customers individually and by income type. The obligation thus flows to the NQI. The upstream institution will send its 'customer', the NQI, two forms 1042-S, one for the dividend income and one for the interest. On each of these forms, the upstream institution will identify its customer, the NQI, as an NQI and also that it has 'undisclosed recipients'. It's this latter statement that essentially creates the flow of reporting obligation. What's more important is that the NQI needs to understand that a copy of the report that they receive, will be sent to the IRS. So, the IRS has all the information it needs to know that the NQI exists and has a reporting obligation.

On 15 March, as a direct result of their exposure to the US markets, this NQI must file a tax return form 1042 and 5000 information reports 1042-S to the IRS. At the same time, the NQI must send 5000 copies of these 1042-S reports to each of its customers.

If the NQI does not apply for an extension and fails to file these reports, it becomes exposed to the risk of penalties which increase with time. If the NQI filed its reports after 1 August for example, the penalty would, just for the 1042-S forms, be 5000 × $270 (failure to file to the IRS) + 5000 × $270 (failure to file copies to customers). A total of $2.7 million. There would be additional penalties for failing to file the form 1042 and also a penalty for failing to file using the correct (electronic) method. As you can see, you don't need many customers as an NQI to be exposed to penalties of over a million dollars.

Now, the practicalities of reporting are not as simple as they may sound either. The NQI must file its reports to the IRS electronically. To do this, it will need a 'Transmitter Control Code' or TCC and an Employer Identification Number or EIN. As with all things IRS, there is an application form for each of these.

8 Issues for Non-qualified Intermediaries

So, NQIs face some tough challenges complying with IRC Chapter 3. Awareness is obviously critical and this, to a large extent, is exacerbated by distance, language and culture. Remember, most financial institutions are NQIs.

I would point out here that life is rarely as simple as some of these diagrams show.

Figure 8.3 shows how easily the chain of custody can get complex. This figure is a generalisation of a real life scenario, in which there are five NQIs in a chain of custody between a USWA and a final beneficial owner. NQI 5 and NQI 1, for different reasons choose not to disclose their clients. NQIs 2, 3 and 4 choose to disclose. The USWA only knows its customer, NQI 1, and therefore reports its customer on forms 1042-S with 'undisclosed recipients'. However, NQI 2 discloses its clients including NQI 3. Equally, NQI 3 has disclosed its client NQI4 and NQI 4 has disclosed its client NQI 5. Each has provided a withholding statement showing what was paid to each level. As a result, NQI 2, 3 and 4, do not receive any 1042-S from their counterparties,

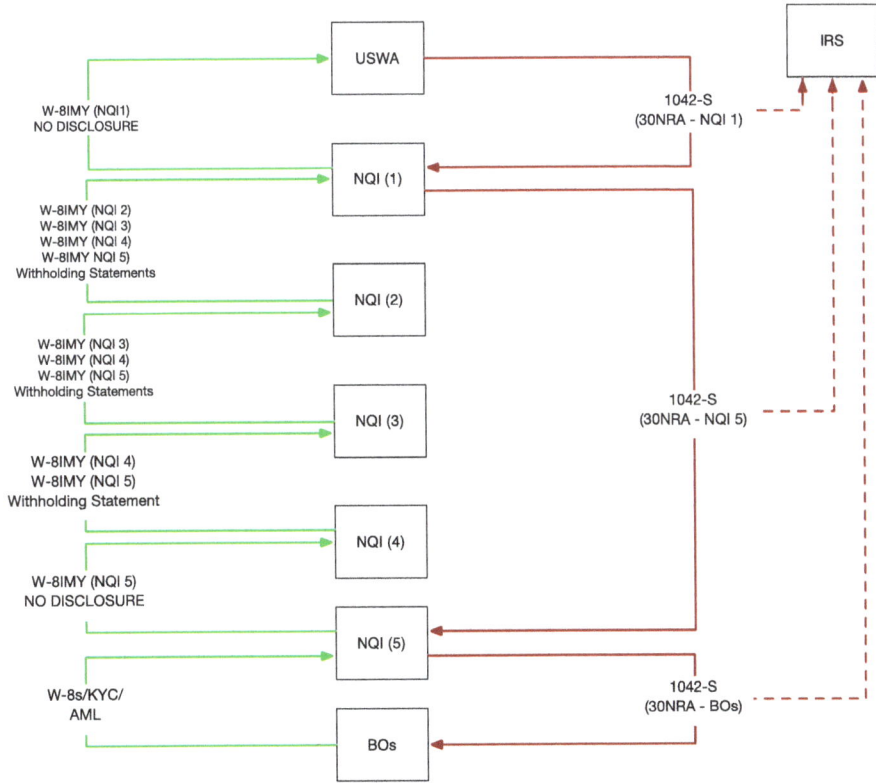

Fig. 8.3 Nested NQI chains of custody. Source: Author's own

because they were all disclosed. Ultimately, NQI can trace the payment via the withholding statements and W-8IMYs down to NQI 5. Hence NQI 2 reports only NQI 5 on form 1042-S with 'undisclosed recipients. NQI 5 must now file a tax return and forms 1042-S to the IRS and recipients. Each counterparty operated a single omnibus account upstream and hence was withheld at 30% NRA, because the withholding statement included a Chapter 4 status for their NQI client.

This diagram hopefully shows how it's important not just to have a narrow view of your immediate counterparties, but also a wide view of the custody chain ecosystem in which you operate, in order to understand who is doing what and what the implication is for your firm.

Conclusion

In conclusion to this chapter, we must remember that NQIs still represent the largest proportion by number of financial institutions receiving US-sourced FDAP income. Their status, however, is deemed to be facilitators of tax evasion and so, most USWAs and QIs are trending towards forcing NQIs to be QIs, or ceasing to do business with them.

The regulations are written on the presumption that all NQIs will disclose their clients to a USWA or QI and, on that basis, the role of reporting at beneficial owner level, shifts to the USWA or QI. That disclosure also allows the QI or USWA to apply tax treaty benefits to the indirect account holder clients of its customer, the NQI. Hence disclosure is a win-win.

However, for both historical and awareness reasons, NQIs typically do not disclose their clients. As a result, they cannot access tax treaty benefits and, without a FATCA Rate Pool Statement, they will be treated as a non-participating FFI, even though they may have a GIIN and be otherwise FATCA compliant. The lack of disclosure also means that reporting obligations, at beneficial owner level, stay with the NQI, who is thus more financially exposed to penalties by reason of the fact that the number of forms involved in reporting is higher for NQIs than it is for QIs.

9

871(m) and QDD

I mentioned in the introduction to this book that much of the discussion would be about IRC Chapters 3 and 4. However, I also said that the QI Agreement brought together several other IRC Chapters that take effect in different ways as soon as US-sourced income is received. One of those is IRC Chapter 1 and in particular Section 871(m).

Section 871(m) refers to the US regulations governing the taxation of dividend equivalent payments (DEP).

Qualified Derivative Dealer (QDD) status is an option available to qualified intermediaries that trade in instruments that create DEPs. The QI Agreement provides a set of rules designed to mitigate cascading withholding on DEPs in certain derivatives transactions.

Key Points

- The 871(m) regulations are implemented in IRC Chapter 1, Section 871-15
- 871(m) relates to the taxation of certain dividend equivalent payments (DEPs)
- 871(m) applies to payments made to non-US persons holding derivative positions on US equities, sale-repurchase and securities-lending transactions
- 871(m) specifies:
  - The type and scope of financial instruments involved
  - The threshold after which taxation is required
  - How to calculate any withholding required

The What, Why and How

Section 871(m) is the section of the US Internal Revenue Code that specifies how financial institutions should treat in scope dividend equivalent payments that reference (i.e. are contingent upon or determined by) dividend-paying US equities, as actual US-sourced dividends for the purposes of withholding.

Section 871(m) is designed to prevent tax avoidance schemes that use derivatives, by preventing non-US persons using yield enhancement strategies, where the non-US person transfers stock to a lower tax jurisdiction bank before the ex-dividend date and receives a 'dividend equivalent' payment. Section 871(m) also applies to similar arrangements using swaps.

IRC Chapters 3 and 4 specify how these transactions should be handled with respect to withholding and reporting. Essentially, 'in scope' transactions, as defined in Section 871(m), should be withheld and reported under normal IRC Chapters 3 and 4 rules.

Financial institutions that have opted to become qualified intermediaries could benefit from the introduction of qualified derivatives dealer (QDD) status in the 2017 QI Agreement, which provides additional rules to help QDDs manage Section 871(m) transactions.

Section 871(m) applies to Dividend Equivalent Payments (DEPs), also known as substitute dividends or synthetic dividends. These are usually:

- Equity derivatives
- Securities-lending transactions
- Sale-repurchase transactions

Dividend equivalents can be cash **or** stock distributions that are derived from the value of an actual dividend. The dividend equivalent amount is calculated on the earlier of:

- the underlying dividend record date; or
- the day prior to the ex-dividend date.

Several types of DEP transaction can be classified as 'potential 871(m) transactions'. These include:

1. **Equity-linked instruments (ELI)** if they:
   (a) reference an underlying US security
   (b) include forwards, futures, options

2. **Notional principal contracts (NPC)**, that is:

    (a) Swaps in which the fixed leg is pegged to a US security

3. **Securities-lending transactions**, when:

    (a) stock is lent to a party so they can short sell (usually to hedge) and
    (b) the short party pays the stock lender a dividend equivalent payment

4. **Sale-repurchase transactions**, when:

    (a) a security is sold by a party with an obligation to repurchase on a future date and
    (b) dividend equivalent payments are made to the seller if an actual dividend occurs while the buyer holds the security.

Some examples of products that could result in potential 871(m) transactions include:

- Equity options
- Stock futures
- Index futures and options on index futures
- Structured and exchange traded notes (debt securities)
- CFD contracts
- Securities-lending transactions
- Equity REPOs
- Derivatives on custom baskets
- Warrants

Due to the complexity of derivatives contracts, a number of steps (tests) must be undertaken to ascertain whether a potential Section 871(m) transaction is withholdable, and if so, by whom. The steps that need to be taken are:

1. Determine which party has responsibility for running the following tests and withholding
2. Determine whether it is a simple or complex contract
3. Calculate the delta
4. Perform the Substantial Equivalence Test (SET)

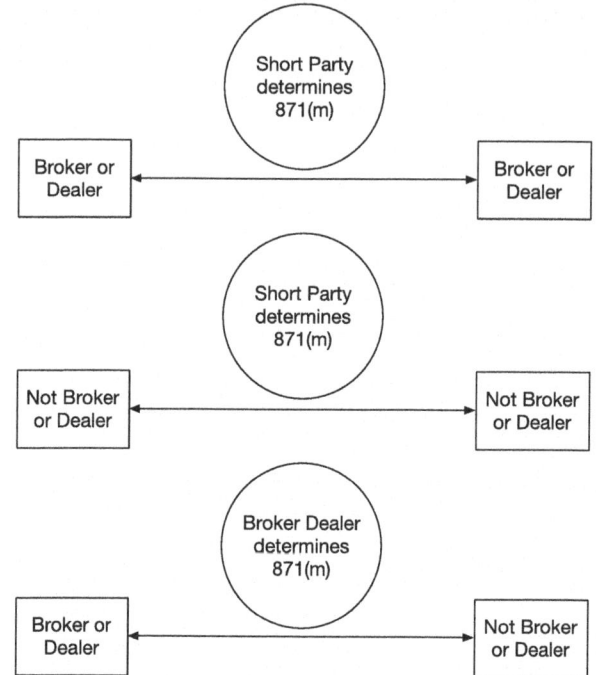

Fig. 9.1 Who determines if a transaction is 871(m)? Source: Author's own

Determining Section 871(m) Responsibility

Figure 9.1 explains which party has responsibility for running the 871(m) tests and subsequent withholding. The short party is generally the payor of dividend equivalent payments.

Simple and Complex Contracts

Section 871(m) provides rules to establish whether a contract is either 'simple' or 'complex'. The regulations also establish different methodologies for treatment of transactions in each of these two categories.

A simple contract is an NPC or ELI for which the amounts that reference an underlying security are calculated by reference to a single, fixed, number of shares of the underlying security. The number of shares must be ascertained at the calculation time for the contract and there must be a single maturity or exercise date to which all amounts are calculated with respect to the underlying security.

A potential Section 871(m) transaction that is a simple contract must undergo the Delta test to determine whether withholding is required.

A complex contract is any NPC or ELI that is not a simple contract.

A potential Section 871(m) transaction that is a complex contract must undergo the Substantial Equivalence Test (SET) to determine whether withholding is required.

Delta Test

The Delta test is performed to determine whether a potential Section 871(m) transaction that is a simple contract is withholdable, and is carried out at the earlier of:

- When the transaction is priced
- When the transaction is issued

If the pricing date is more than 14 days before issue, then use the issue date.

At the calculation time, if the transaction Δ is 0.8 or greater, it is considered a Section 871(m) transaction and must be withheld upon.

Substantial Equivalence Test (SET)

The Substantial Equivalence Test (SET) is performed to determine whether a potential Section 871(m) transaction that is a complex contract is withholdable.

The test assesses whether a complex contract replicates the economic performance of the underlying security by comparing the difference between:

- the expected changes in value of the complex contract and its initial hedge and;
- the expected changes in value of a benchmark simple contract and its initial hedge

The contract is an 871(m) transaction if the expected change in value is less than or equal to the benchmark.

The inputs for the SET must be determined in a 'commercially reasonable manner'.

If the SET can't be applied to a complex contract, the taxpayer must use the 'principles of the SET' to 'reasonably determine' whether it is a Section 871(m) transaction.

Withholding

The long party is liable for tax on any DEP only while the long party is party to the transaction. The amount for any DEP is determined as follows:

- **Securities-lending and sale-repurchase transactions:**
  - Per share actual dividend paid × Number of shares
- **Simple contracts:**
  - Per share actual dividend amount × Number of shares × Δ
- **Complex contracts:**
  - Per share dividend amount × Initial hedge of the underlying security

871(m) Workflow

Figure 9.2 provides an overview of the workflow for determining if a transaction should be classified as an 871(m) transaction:

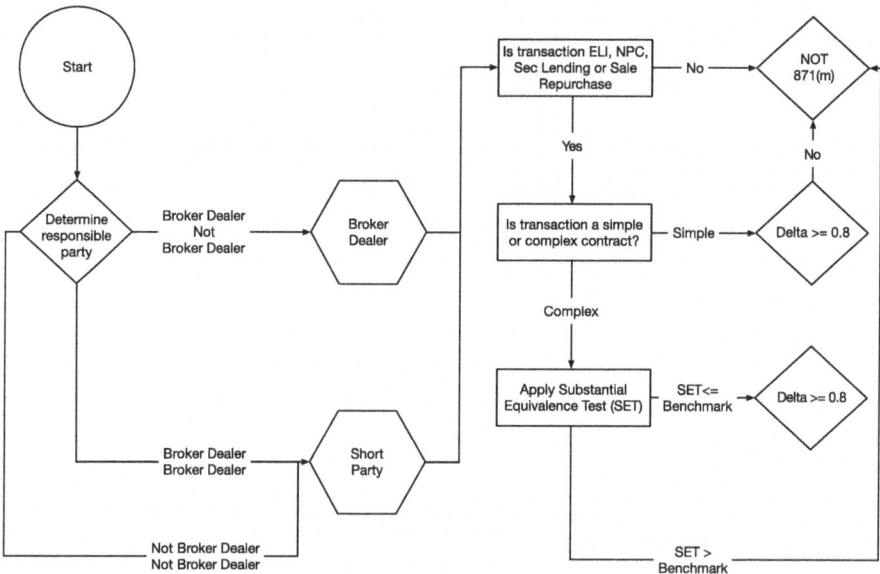

Fig. 9.2 871(m) Determination workflow. Source: Author's own

Qualified Derivatives Dealer Status (QDD)

If a QI has assumed QDD status, they must:

- assume primary Chapter 3 and Chapter 4 withholding for potential 871(m) transactions
- assume primary 1099 reporting and backup withholding for potential 871(m) transactions
- calculate your 'QDD tax liability'

The 2017 QI Agreement imposes prescriptive systems requirements. QIs acting as a QDD must also:

- Maintain a reconciliation schedule for their Section 871(m) amounts.
- Make quarterly QDD tax liability estimates
- Have appropriate systems to:
    - Calculate QDD tax liability
    - Identify potential Section 871(m) transactions
    - Calculate and record its net Δ
    - Record its long and short positions, 871(m) amount, QDD tax liability
    - Calculate and record DEPs made by the QDD
    - Record dividends received in its equity derivatives dealer capacity
    - Calculate Δ delta
    - Perform Substantial Equivalence Test (SET)
    - Record and calculate combined transactions

QDD status has a number of benefits, including:

- Preventing cascaded (or multiple) withholding on dividend equivalent payments
- Dividend equivalent payments made to QDDs acting as equities dealers are not withheld.

The two components of taxation that QDDs need to proceduralise are the withholding and reporting of tax on dividend equivalent payments.

1. **Withholding on dividend equivalent payments**
   (a) Withhold tax from payments made to non-US recipients of in scope dividend equivalent payments
   (b) Withhold tax on ELI, NPC, securities-lending or sale-repurchase contracts. Transactions from these instruments are classed as 'Potential 871(m)'
   (c) Perform the Delta and Substantial Equivalence tests
2. **Reporting of QDD tax liability**
   (a) QDDs must calculate the total amount of tax to be paid to the Treasury on the QDD's portion of each transaction
   (b) The QDD tax liability must be added to QI's tax liability on its 1042 filing
   (c) To calculate the QDD tax liability, the QDD should calculate their net Δ exposure and Section 871(m) amount, taking into account-related prop trades:
      (i) The net Δ exposure is calculated using the overall position in a security, by taking into account the dealer's long and short positions.
      (ii) The net Δ exposure is used to calculate the Section 871(m) amount, by multiplying it by the dividend amount per share.
   (d) The QDD tax liability is calculated on the earlier of:
      (i) The underlying dividend record date; and
      (ii) The day prior to the ex-dividend date

Net Δ Exposure Calculation

871(m) Amount

Continuing the example from Fig. 9.3 (Fig. 9.4).

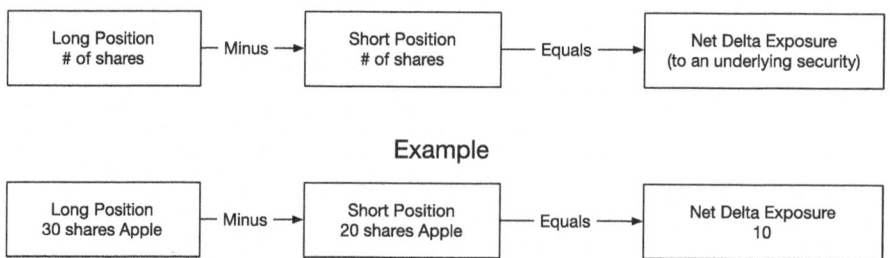

Fig. 9.3 How to calculate the net Δ exposure? Source: Author's own

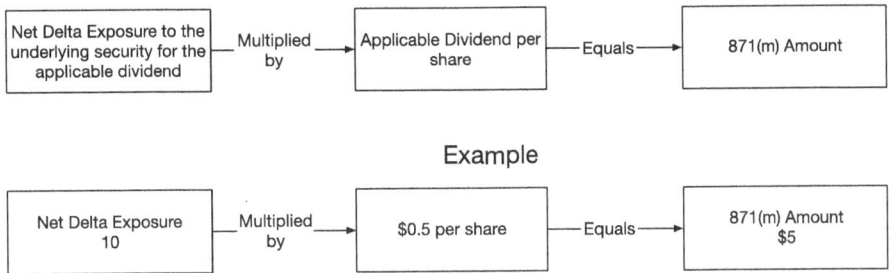

Fig. 9.4 How to calculate the 871(m) amount? Source: Author's own

QDD Tax Liability

Phased Implementation

In 2018, the Internal Revenue Service (IRS) issued Notice 2018-72 providing clarification for Qualified Derivatives Dealers concerned about the phased implementation of the QI Agreement for 871(m) transactions (Fig. 9.5). Key points included:

- The 'good faith efforts' period for withholding and reporting on delta-one transactions was extended through 2020
- The 'good faith efforts' period for QDDs was extended through 2020
- Withholding and reporting is required for non-delta-one transactions from 1 January 2021, with a 'good faith efforts' period applicable throughout 2021
- Custodians and brokers are not required to withhold on dividends paid to validly documented QDD accounts before 2021
- Qualified Securities Lender (QSL) accounts are still permitted until at least 2021
- Regular combination rule should be applied from 1 January 2021
- Withholding and reporting is still required for delta-one transactions, and the simplified combination rule should continue to be applied to over-the-counter transactions only. There have been no changes to the rules in these areas.

The QDD rules are some of the most contentious rules in the QI space at present and there is a great deal of confusion and much less in the way of good faith efforts being made. More firms are 'bending' existing systems to

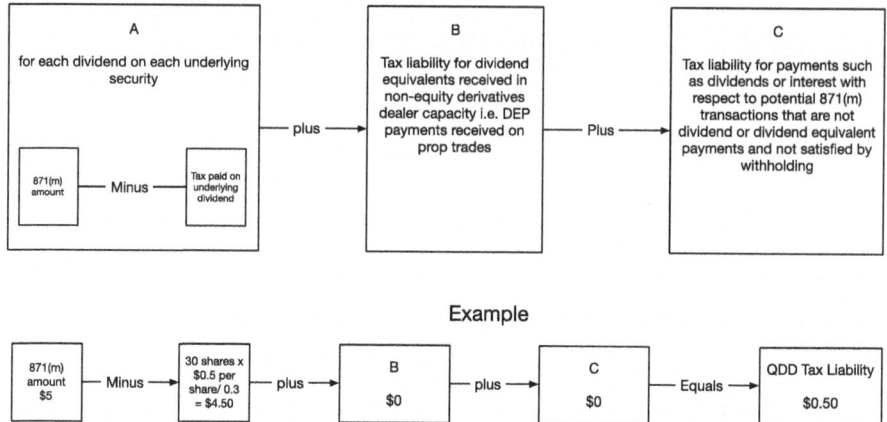

Fig. 9.5 How to calculate QDD tax liability? Source: Author's own

catch some of the information. It has to be said that prior transitionary arrangements and delays in implementations have made most firms very wary of spending too much on compliance until the IRS issues definitive rulings.

Part II

FATCA

10

An Introduction to FATCA

Introduction

In this part of this book, we will look at the second major thread to US withholding tax—Foreign Account Tax Compliance Act (FATCA). The qualified intermediary regulations are all about the proper taxation of US-sourced income through a chain of financial intermediaries. FATCA, on the other hand, is all about the reporting of all income by US persons and, in parallel, the reporting of global income to the foreign (non-US) financial accounts of US persons as part of the USA's anti-tax evasion framework.

In Part I, we looked at IRC Chapter 3, more commonly called the QI regulations, although the regulations apply to both QIs and NQIs. IRC Chapter 3 deals with US-sourced income paid to recipients outside the US. Technically, IRC Chapter 4, on the other hand, deals with *any* income paid to a US person outside the US.

The term FATCA is an acronym for the Foreign Account Tax Compliance Act. There is actually no such Act on the US statute books. The term is a misnomer that has entered into the general vernacular, even at the Internal Revenue Service (IRS), and originates from 2008 with the House of Representative's Bill HR3933 which went by that name but was never passed.

The basic text of what we now call FATCA was sequentially moved, from HR3933, to HR4213, the Tax Extender's Bill of 2009 and finally to HR2847—as Title V of the Hiring Incentives to Restore Employment (HIRE) Act which passed into law in March 2010.

So, whilst tax technically incorrect, I will, grudgingly, follow the general trend today and refer to the content and intent of Title V of the HIRE Act as FATCA.

Purpose of FATCA

FATCA is an anti-tax evasion framework. Its purpose is to provide the IRS with the tools and information necessary to identify US persons potentially evading US taxes on their global income.

While the US is regarded by some as itself a de facto tax haven, the incremental tax rates applicable to wealthy Americans, even in the Trump era, are such that there is a significant motivation for these Americans to move and hold their wealth outside the US, typically in complex entity structures that hide their true ownership or control and can access lower tax rates on income than would otherwise apply.

In order to address this, FATCA, as a US statute, has two structural elements.

First, it inserts a new IRC Chapter into the Revenue Code—Chapter 4. This IRC Chapter is designed to force non-US financial institutions to collect information on all financial account holders, identify those who are US individuals or entities that are either substantially owned or effectively controlled by US persons and report them annually to the IRS.

Second, it inserts a new section—6038D to IRC Chapter 61 Part III Subpart A. This is what forces US persons to disclose financial accounts held outside the US and certain information about the assets in those accounts, subject to a penalty of $10,000 for failure to disclose and a further $10,000 for each 30-day period during which non-disclosure continues, capped at $50,000.

This section also increases the penalty for underpaying taxes, if they are attributable to a failure to disclose foreign assets, from 20% of the underpayment to 40% of the underpayment. This section also sets the statute of limitations with respect to these failures to disclose at six years.

The idea is simple, as shown in Fig. 10.1. FATCA forces US persons to report their foreign financial accounts to the IRS and it simultaneously, but separately, forces the financial institutions that operate those accounts to report them to the IRS.

In this way, the IRS gets information that it can match and reconcile to make sure that its taxpayers are correctly disclosing their foreign accounts and paying the correct taxes on their global income.

For obvious reasons, the financial community outside the US tends only to focus on the part of FATCA that directly affects them, IRC Chapter 4.

It's important to understand the larger context of FATCA because, as we'll see, the current enforcement of FATCA by the IRS in either of these two structural elements can be extremely serious. Cases are arising in 2019 that show clearly that US law enforcement agencies are prepared to engage in covert sting operations outside the US to identify financial institutions

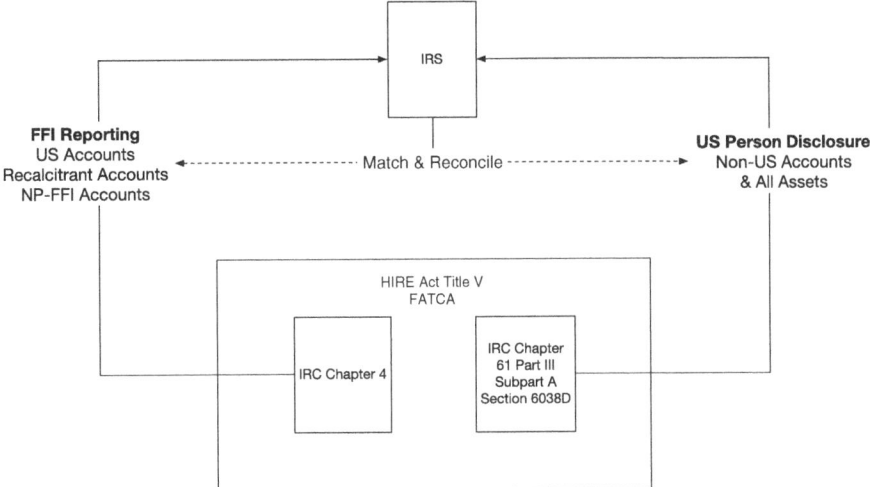

Fig. 10.1 Structural elements of FATCA. Source: Author's own

effectively facilitating tax evasion. Other cases are showing that FATCA is being used directly in court cases in the US to prosecute Americans failing to meet FATCA reporting obligations.

FATCA is effectively a pincer movement by the IRS that will trap the American that evades their disclosure obligations and/or the financial institution that facilitates, deliberately or through lack of effective controls, to properly report such accounts. As we shall see, it can also unfortunately trap Americans not evading tax who have concerns over their privacy rights under US law and the US Constitution and also accidental Americans who did not even realise they had US citizenship.

FATCA Legal Framework

The core of FATCA is the HIRE Act (2010) as passed by Congress. To that extent, the legal structure is extraterritorial inasmuch as non-US financial institutions are subject to it by the use of a couple of methodologies.

Intergovernmental Agreements

The reporting element of FATCA also brought about issues of data protection that would, unresolved, have led to financial firms breaking their domestic data protection laws in order to meet the extraterritorial element of US FATCA law.

The US therefore created the concept of an intergovernmental agreement (IGA) to circumvent this issue. Any jurisdiction that entered into an IGA would gain certain benefits for its financial institutions, in addition to which, reporting would be structured so that data would be sent, not directly to the IRS, but to a domestic regulator. The domestic regulator would then, under the IGA, and also leveraging authority under other pre-existing legal agreements such as Double Tax Treaties (DTTs) and/or Tax Information Exchange Agreements (TIEAs) aggregate this data and send it to the IRS.

The end result being that the data ends up with the IRS but does not create a legal problem for IGA resident reporting financial institutions.

The Evolution of IGAs

There are several complicating factors related to IGAs. I will go into these in more detail in later chapters; however, for the moment, I will explain at high level using Fig. 10.2.

The IGAs represent variations of Title V of the HIRE Act that have been agreed bilaterally between the US and certain jurisdictions.

The world's tax jurisdictions, according to FATCA, are one of three types—jurisdictions that have signed an IGA, those that have not and those that have agreed in principle to sign an IGA but have not yet done so ('In Substance').

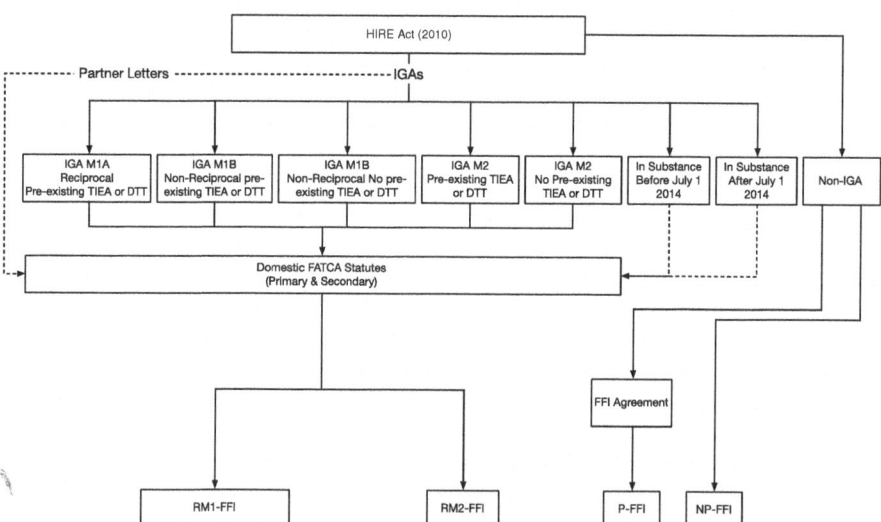

Fig. 10.2 Legal structures for FATCA. Source: Author's own

Models 1 and 2 IGAs

Where a jurisdiction has signed an IGA, there are two types—Model 1 and Model 2. For each model there are sub-variations in the IGA text, dependent on whether the jurisdiction already has a pre-existing TIEA or DTT and whether the IGA is reciprocal or not. In other words, not only will the jurisdiction share information with the IRS about US accounts, the IRS will, in theory, share information with the jurisdiction about that jurisdiction's account holders with US financial firms.

This leads to a number of different types of IGA and, for each, the requirement is that the IGA be translated into domestic law, in order that it can have effective force on that jurisdiction's financial institutions. One of the complaints about the extraterritorial nature of FATCA was that a non-US financial institution could not be subject to US law directly. The IGAs removed this issue, provided the jurisdiction concerned enacts domestic law to close the loop.

'In Substance' IGAs

In the second category, the jurisdiction has indicated that it will sign an IGA but has not yet done so. These jurisdictions are deemed to have an 'in substance' agreement, that is, they can act as if there is a signed agreement. The problem was (and is) that this type of intergovernmental negotiation can take years and the IRS wants to see evidence of intent. In substance, jurisdictions fall into two sub-categories, those that were in substance prior to July 2014 and those that have become in substance since July 2014. In both cases, the evidence that the IRS is looking for is some legal basis domestically that the jurisdiction is preparing for FATCA.

Non-IGA Jurisdictions

The third category is non-IGA jurisdictions. Financial institutions in non-IGA jurisdictions have two choices. Either sign an foreign financial institution (FFI) Agreement directly with the IRS so that the HIRE Act (2010) applies directly through the contractual agreement, or remain a 'non-participating foreign financial institution' (NP-FFI).

Partner Letters

In Fig. 10.2, the reader will note a dotted line from IGAs labelled 'Partner Letters'. As if the legal structure weren't complicated enough, as the bilateral discussions forming the base of the FATCA landscape evolved, some jurisdictions negotiated better terms than others. Rather than dealing with ever-increasing complexity from diverging bilateral agreements, the US inserted 'most favoured nation' clauses into its IGAs so that any better terms negotiated with one jurisdiction were automatically applicable to other jurisdictions of the same type. These changes are communicated through Partner Letters. The reason they are significant here is because those changes, if and when they occur, change the basis of the IGA and therefore trigger a need to review and potentially update domestic legislation by domestic law makes and similar operations and compliance review by the financial firms once any changes are made.

If you are a single financial institution operating in just one jurisdiction, you will only need to know the rules as they apply to you. So, much of this structural complexity will go away. However, if you are an adviser or a financial institution operating in multiple jurisdictions, the map of the whole will be much more relevant and have significant operational impacts.

There are 113 jurisdictions with IGAs signed, or in substance, out of a possible total of 193.

Documenting FATCA Status

The fundamental precursor to FATCA reporting is the conclusion of and acquisition of FATCA statuses for all account holders, including the levels of due diligence required, based on how high a risk an account represents for tax evasion in the view of the US. We will see just how complex this can be in the following chapters.

Reporting

For firms that are subject to FATCA, the primary objective is to complete due diligence on all financial account holders, in order to determine if the account is reportable, then report. For firms in IGA jurisdictions this will typically be to their domestic regulator, who will then use IDES (International Data Exchange System) to submit their data. Firms in non-IGA jurisdictions will be submitting their data directly to IDES. In all cases, the format for reporting is standardised and uses the Extended Mark-up Language (xml) Schema.

Penalties

One of the elements of FATCA, as it applies to FFIs, that is confusing are the penalties and that's just it, they are penalties. They are assessed based on the failure either of an account holder to provide an adequate IRC Chapter 4 status to an FFI or on the FFIs failure to meet its FATCA obligations. The problem is that they are applied and reported via the same withholding tax system used for IRC Chapter 3. However, the reader must remember that a FATCA penalty is imposed using US-sourced Fixed, Determinable, Annual or Periodic (FDAP) income as the withholdable source. So, there is an overlap between IRC Chapter 3 that determines the treatment of US-sourced FDAP income and IRC Chapter 4, where there is potential for a penalty to be applied prior to the assessment of IRC Chapter 3.

At the end of 2018, the IRS also confused matters more by allowing firms that receive information returns showing the application of a FATCA penalty, to change the classification of the penalty to an IRC Chapter 3 amount on their information returns.

Now the logic of the system is that if a firm does have an IRC Chapter 4 status for all its clients, reports correctly and fully and has no NP-FFIs in its custody chain, there will be no penalties.

So, in concluding this introductory chapter, we have learned about the purpose and legal structure of FATCA, as well as some tantalising insights into how the apparently simple purpose of these regulations becomes far more complex at the operational level.

11

Principles of FATCA

In this chapter we will discuss the main principles and effects of Foreign Account Tax Compliance Act (FATCA), leaving the more detailed aspects of the regulations to subsequent chapters. This will be a good chapter to read for those otherwise unfamiliar with FATCA. There are two constituencies for FATCA.

For an 'American', FATCA is all about reporting your non-US accounts and assets to the Internal Revenue Service (IRS) or otherwise be subject to financial and potentially legal sanctions under the Hiring Incentives to Restore Employment (HIRE) Act (2010).

For a non-US financial institution (broadly interpreted), FATCA is about conducting due diligence on all account holders to determine their FATCA status, reporting those that are US, recalcitrant (in the case of individuals or entities) or non-participating (in the case of financial institutions) to the IRS (directly or indirectly) and, in some circumstances, applying a FATCA penalty to any US-sourced Fixed, Determinable, Annual or Periodic (FDAP) income which those accounts receive.

The principles underpinning the objectives of FATCA can thus be summarised as:

1. Registration and management
2. Due diligence;
3. Reporting;
4. Penalty withholding.

How Tax Evasion Happens

Before we get to the principles themselves, I want to re-state some issues surrounding the basic purpose of FATCA as a US-centric, bilateral anti-tax evasion framework, so that all further observations have some context.

We must take as our starting point that there are Americans who have decided to deliberately evade some, or all, of their US taxes, by putting their assets into non-US financial accounts. That might typically be a simple bank or brokerage account held at a non-US financial institution. The account could be depository in nature, that is, cash, or a securities custodial account containing equities, bonds or other financial instruments.

What's happening here is that the Americans may be relying on weak policies and procedures or corruptible officials. They used to rely also on domestic secrecy laws to prevent any information being revealed to the IRS. However, the scope of FATCA compliance and intergovernmental agreements (IGAs) is now so widespread, that this is a closing window of opportunity. Also, evasion tends not to take place simply by opening a bank or custody account. Those evading taxes (not just Americans) will usually choose a more 'furtive' method and hide their assets through one or more investment vehicles in which their assets are pooled, or comingled, with others. Other methods would include setting up chains of shell companies or other vehicles in various jurisdictions in order to make it more difficult for the American to be identified. The reason for this is that these Americans have figured out that FATCA, in its simplest form, will catch them and so they move on to more complex investment structures, in the hope that the complexity itself provides a means to hide assets.

What is usually happening here is that an advisor has identified a mechanism by which current regulation, usually Know-Your-Customer (KYC) or Anti-Money Laundering (AML), can be circumvented at worst or, at best, where a weakness in the system of checks and balances can be found and leveraged.

The object, of course, is preparatory to tax evasion and not evasion in itself. There's nothing inherently wrong (morally or legally) with these investment strategies. There are many thousands of Americans who have legitimate bank accounts overseas. The US expats have been significantly affected by FATCA even before the regulations came into effect. The mere threat of FATCA caused several major banks to either close all accounts of Americans or move their accounts to a US branch.

The point at which having an account or investments overseas becomes evasion is when the American fails to disclose these assets to the IRS and pay tax on the income generated from them. This contravenes the HIRE Act (2010).

There, as we saw, FATCA has two structural elements. The first explicitly requires Americans to declare their non-US assets and income. The second requires the financial institutions where those accounts are held to report those accounts to the IRS (ref. Fig. 10.2).

FATCA leverages the fact that, in order to evade tax, there is one common component necessary to the act—a financial account through which, directly or indirectly, the income is held and funnelled. Thus FATCA is essentially a system, designed to be extraterritorial in nature and to force the industry to find and report the income of Americans.

The logical consequence of this is, presumably, that the US will hope that Americans will begin to voluntarily disclose their foreign assets, rather than be reported by their financial institution first. The US has also geared up to penalise all those Americans who appear on reports and for whom the IRS has no reconciling Report of Foreign Bank and Financial Accounts (FBAR) report. There have already been indictments in the US using FATCA as the legal basis.

Accidental Americans

It's worthwhile at this stage, to mention at least one of the unintended consequences of FATCA that has caused, and continues to cause, much angst—the so-called accidental Americans.

This occurs because financial institutions have an obligation to perform due diligence on ALL their account holders to determine their IRC Chapter 4 status. The level of due diligence can vary depending on a number of factors (mainly the aggregated value of accounts), but the search is designed to separate out reportable accounts (i.e. those of Americans, from non-reportable accounts—which would include non-Americans and also non-financial accounts and some exempted products). In that search, they are looking for 'US indicia', that is, indicators on an account record (or even a transcript of a conversation) that means the account 'might' be an American.

The result of finding US indicia is triggering a 'cure process'. In other words, 'Might be an American' is not good enough, and more work needs to be done by the financial institution to cure the indicia.

Some of those indicia are pretty clear—US Passport, US address or unambiguous US citizenship. Any account holders who have these indicia are not really 'accidental' Americans. The only thing perhaps accidental is that they may not have realised that they had to take some remedial action. They must prove not only that they have citizenship of another country (not the US) but that they have also revoked their US citizenship. The accepted evidence for this is a Certificate of Loss of Nationality (CLN).

Some indicia are less obvious (to the account holder). This includes US place of birth, which makes the account holder technically an American citizen for the purpose of FATCA. This becomes more obvious given that most financial institutions will collect 'place of birth' as part of their account-opening procedures. There is a significant minority cohort of account holders who fall into these categories. In the US, for example, it's common that when parents have children, they register the birth and at the same time apply for a social security number (SSN) for their child. This means that the child, at birth, has both citizenship and evidence of having a presence in the US tax system. However, there are cases where the birth is registered, but the parents removed the child from the US and thus never obtained an SSN. The child, of course, lives its life probably never encountering any nexus to the US—until they open up a financial account and provide their place of birth. They are technically American, but will have no easy means of curing this since they will not have realised they are American, let alone have obtained a CLN.

Some indicia will only become apparent through 'enhanced due diligence', usually conducted when the value of assets of an account holder exceeds $1 million, and are less obvious. These include the parental test, the substantial presence test and the green card test.

If either of your parents was born in the US (Winston Churchill is a good example). If you ever held a green card and have never revoked it. If you've been physically present in the US for over 183 days aggregated over the last three years. If you 'pass' any of these tests, you will have a tax return liability to the US and thus, technically, be a reportable person.

So, first, if you have no US indicia and you're not an American—no problem.

Second, if you know you're an American, you should (and are expected to) know, understand and meet the obligations to which you are subject under the US domestic tax system. In this respect, FATCA should be immaterial. If you are properly disclosing your offshore accounts and income and paying tax on them, then whether your financial institution files a separate report to the IRS about those accounts, should be of no consequence to you, since you've done nothing wrong and there will be no other impact.

Third, if you are an American and actually conducting tax evasion, clearly FATCA is a concern, although, on the basis that the criminals are always a step ahead of the cops, there appear to be enough loopholes and inefficiencies in FATCA to cause the sophisticated tax evader no more than a passing annoyance—they'll figure out another way. In fact, they probably already have.

Fourth, if you are an accidental American, you may encounter problems. Whether and how those problems can be cured depends mainly on the FATCA policies of the financial institution that finds these indicia.

Principles

FATCA is based on nine principles.

1. Application and management
2. Status
3. Structure
4. Global versus local
5. Identification
6. Reporting
7. Withholding
8. Intergovernmental agreements & reciprocity
9. Convergence to IRC Chapter 3

Application and Management

The IRS has set up a portal for the management of FATCA. It is at this portal that foreign financial institutions (FFIs) must register for a Global Intermediary Identification Number (GIIN). The portal allows for registration of the FFI and management of many of the aspects of compliance such as certifications and messaging.

The IRS has a separate portal, the International Data Exchange System (IDES), for submission of reports.

Many of the aspects of FATCA, and indeed QI, that were manual or had thresholds below which manual processing was permitted, have now gone and, for the most part, QI and FATCA are essentially automated and standardised.

Status

Everyone outside the US falls broadly into just three categories:

1. Individual
2. Non-financial foreign entity (NFFE)
3. Foreign financial institution (FFI)

The object of these status types is to allow for different due diligence and reporting processes to be applied, since the way and degree to which tax evasion might take place, that is, risk, will vary depending on this status.

However, there is recognition in FATCA through 'carve-outs', exemptions and exceptions that:

1. not all accounts are suitable for tax evasion—hence only defined financial accounts are within scope;
2. not all financial products provide a feasible mechanism for tax evasion—hence most IGAs define exempt or excluded products whose value does not count towards due diligence thresholds;
3. not all accounts are of a value that would make tax evasion efficient—hence de-minimis thresholds, below which reporting is not required;
4. not all types of account holder are high risk for tax evasion—hence some account status types (e.g. Passive NFFEs) are subject to more scrutiny and reporting, while others (e.g. Local FFIs) can be deemed to be compliant, because they predominantly service domestic market banking needs.

So, while FATCA may sound simple in terms of identifying the status of an account holder, the nature of the industry and its innate complexities, means that the status of an account holder can make a big difference.

In other areas, even at the sub-category level there may be little or no choice. NFFEs, for example, have two sub-categories—'Active' and 'Passive'. Which sub-category an NFFE fits into is definitional not optional, but may be variable. What is important to understand is that these definitional categories apply to everyone outside the US—for the purpose of determining the application of FATCA.

It's this unilateralism that has caused so much anger outside the US. The approach is effectively a 'negative proof' system requiring everyone and all firms, to be categorised under a US definition in order to determine the risk that Americans will be there evading tax.

The reason for this scale of categorisation is that the US claims the right to tax the global income of its taxpayers, not just US-sourced income. So this is about really substantial amounts of tax. For a US person suffering non-US tax on a portfolio for example, they can usually only take a domestic deduction for that portion of the foreign (non-US) tax that was not recoverable under a double tax treaty. So, the effect of global income taxation can be substantial even when double tax treaties are taken into account and the IRS is looking at substantial tax revenue deficits when all is added up.

It was rather ironic when the European Union (EU) originally proposed the EU Financial Transactions Tax (EU-FTT) which would be applied to any transaction, anywhere in the world, including the US, where the securities involved in the transactions were sourced in EU Member States, irrespective of where the parties to the transaction were located. The US responded vigorously to this proposal, citing extraterritoriality and the unacceptability of the EU applying a tax that would impact its citizens. Many observers outside the US commented that the US should look to its own extraterritorial tax rules before it complained about others adopting the same strategy.

There is one more very important point I want to make here and it goes to the way in which the IRS has changed the definition of 'financial institution' and also that of 'financial account'. In the regulations, the definition of an FFI is very clear, but it contains a widening of what most people would determine to be a financial institution. This has major implications because, from a practical viewpoint, those firms that are traditional financial institutions already have many of the policies, procedures and systems that are the foundation of compliance for FATCA. For them, FATCA is a regulatory change of degree not kind. However, in their hunt for tax evaders, the IRS added, paraphrasing 'everyone else that's involved in the investment chain' and particularly collective investment vehicles (CIVs) into the definition of foreign financial institution. This was so that these investment vehicles, classic places for tax evaders to hide, could be caught up in the regulatory requirement to go find those Americans.

In the absence of this widening of the definition, it would have been left to the traditional institutions to do this. However, the problem in this section of the definition is that these firms have not thought of themselves as financial firms before in quite this way. They have varying degrees of compliant systems and policies and procedures which are both legacy (i.e. old) and highly and narrowly specific to their market segment. The burden of FATCA compliance falls very hard on these firms unless they fall into one of the areas of carve-out.

Structure

Most financial firms outside the US operate in single jurisdictions. For them FATCA tends to be relatively simple because they are having to operationalise just one dimension of FATCA based on their jurisdiction's status. For international and multinational firms, FATCA is far more complex.

Structurally, one way of looking at the FATCA world is based on whether the jurisdiction has an IGA or not. In this view, FATCA's operational variances within IGA jurisdictions (including 'in substance') depend on:

1. what each country has negotiated with the US in terms of exceptions and exemptions to reporting (based on types of account and types of product or distribution mechanism);
2. whether the jurisdiction has a Double Tax Treaty (DTT) or Tax Information Exchange Agreement (TIEA) in place with the US—which determines the particular variant of the IGA model used; and
3. whether reporting is direct to the IRS or via a domestic regulator.

Outside of IGA jurisdictions, FATCA variances depend on:

1. whether an FFI has signed an FFI Agreement or not

Another way to look at operationalising FATCA is based on whether an account holder receives US-sourced FDAP income or not and, if so, whether the financial institution is acting as a qualified intermediary (QI) or non-qualified intermediary (NQI) in IRC Chapter 3, with respect to that account. In this respect, if the financial institution is a QI, then its QI Agreement provides contractual obligations with respect to FATCA, in addition to the legal obligations it will be subject to via the domestic implementation of an IGA.

Figure 11.1 attempts to show this. In this diagram, A and B represent the total of all accounts held by the financial institution. A represents those

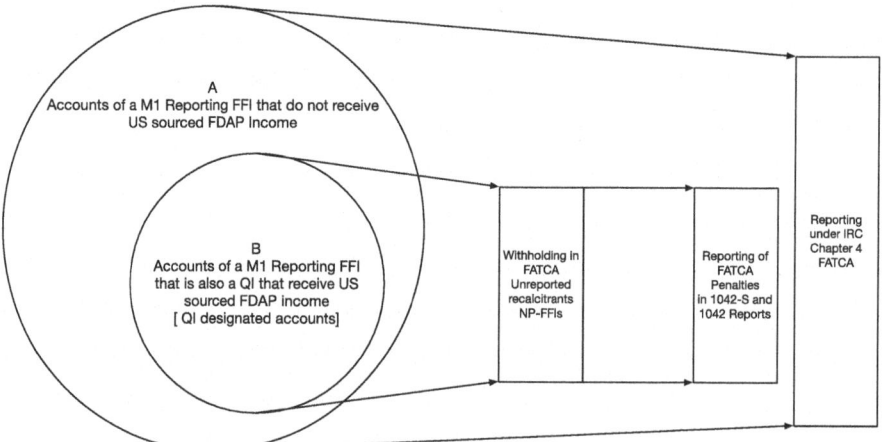

Fig. 11.1 Effect of QI status on FATCA

accounts that do not receive US-sourced FDAP income, for example, depository accounts or non-financial accounts. These accounts would be subject either to reporting under domestic law via an IGA, or to reporting under an FFI Agreement in a non-IGA market. That reporting would be the generally accepted FATCA reporting of US, recalcitrant and NP-FFI accounts.

There is however a second set of accounts: those that do receive US FDAP income. These accounts would also be reported in the normal FATCA way, if the due diligence and FATCA status require it. However, a financial institution with these types of accounts will also have to report whether a FATCA penalty was applied and this would be done in what is normally considered IRC Chapter 3 reporting, that is, using forms 1042-S and 1042. That's because, while FATCA withholding is a penalty, the penalty is applied via the withholding tax system. So, when we talk about FATCA reporting, we must remember that there are two aspects to FATCA reporting—that which is mandated by an IGA or FFI Agreement to the IRS of US persons and so on, plus, if necessary, the reporting of the application of FATCA penalties.

So, for example, any given FFI may have US accounts, recalcitrant accounts and NP-FFI accounts, that it may need to report in FATCA (via form 8966 or via an electronic portal). However, if a FATCA penalty has been applied to any account, by definition that means that those accounts must have received US-sourced FDAP income and income and penalty will be reported on forms 1042-S and 1042.

In the same way that IRC Chapter 3 is a cascade system, IRC Chapter 4 is also cascade, both in its identification concepts as well as reporting and withholding. It recognises that there can be a long chain of ownership between a source country income distribution and the final recipient. There may be financial institutions, FFIs, in between with different statuses and equally, in tax evasion strategies, there may also be layers of NFFEs within those structures. FATCA tries to determine the processes that are necessary, given any permutation found in the chain. These include searches of databases for US indicia which might not get caught in KYC or AML, certification processes between layers, for example, between FFIs, FFIs and US withholding agents and so on, and between the IRS and everyone in the chain.

Global Versus Local

In final regulations, IRS recognised that there would be significant pushback from those parts of the world and industry which believed that the impact of FATCA would be disproportionate to the likely population of tax evaders.

The IRS thus established the general principle of global versus local, recognising that many firms' activities were so focused on their own local market, that the opportunity for tax evasion is very low.

There are parts of the regulations that essentially codify this different approach. Of particular note for later discussion are the concepts of 'Local FFIs' and certain types of deemed compliant FFIs.

On the converse side, IRS recognises that there are global players in the field and those with regional or multi-branch, multi-jurisdictional coverage. In this area, the IRS has the concept of an expanded affiliate group, or Expanded Affiliate Group (EAG), which it uses to try to ensure that account holders cannot evade detection by entering at one point in the financial chain and having their account moved to a different part of the same group where lower compliance thresholds apply. This addresses one of the flaws in the IRC Chapter 3 regulations, where Americans could, relatively easily, open an account at a QI and have that account moved to a branch that is a non-disclosing NQI, thus evading the disclosure rules.

Equally, where an FFI in IRC Chapter 4 also happens to be a QI in IRC Chapter 3, the regulations allow for larger FFIs that exist in groups, to adopt a 'consolidated compliance programme' (CCP) in which control over IRC Chapter 3—and to the extent that they are subject to IRC Chapter 4, contractual obligations can be managed centrally, subject to approval by the IRS.

Identification

The IRS has, in regulation, identified a number of areas where it believes either directly or as a result of lobbying, that tax evasion is low risk. These are called 'carve-outs', more technically—exemptions and exceptions. In the absence of a carve-out, the burden falls on FFIs to follow FATCA rules to establish whether, and to what extent, there are Americans in their account base.

The issue here, as I've said many times, is actually not the expat or the American individual who declares him or herself as such at account opening. The difficulty lies in identifying tax evaders, who will be much more covert in their activities.

This is also the most complex part of FATCA, because there are so many variables that need to be considered. There are three main variables that determine the identification processes required:

1. When the account was opened;
2. The value of the account;
3. The documented status of the account;

A word on when the account was opened: In the first edition of this book, I spoke at length about the fact that the IRS understood that, at any point in time when the regulations took effect, there would be two classes of accounts at financial institutions—new accounts and those accounts that already existed when the regulations came into effect. The so-called pre-existing accounts.

The regulations, when released, therefore provided rules for identification of account holders that are new accounts, since this would be the accepted norm going forward. However, they also gave a grace period during which financial institutions could go back and determine the FATCA status of all their pre-existing accounts. So, by the end of the grace period, the idea was (and is) that a financial institution will have adopted policy and procedure to capture FATCA status of all new account holders at onboarding and that all pre-existing accounts had been successfully documented. The final grace period ended on 31 December 2018, when many FFIs had to submit a certification to the IRS—a certificate of Completion of due diligence on Pre-existing Accounts (COPA). That was the theory. While many FFIs have indeed completed their pre-existing due diligence, it is an unfortunate fact of life that many have still not done this. So, while following a technical route, this book should not need to deal with pre-existing accounts at all, I have chosen to include reference to it, to help those firms that either aren't aware of the obligation or are and need my reference as a wake-up call.

As a result of the identification process, three further processes or 'outputs' are basic to the principles of FATCA. These are:

1. Do Nothing;
2. Withholding;
3. Reporting.

Do Nothing

If, following the relevant due diligence, the account holder is determined to be (1) not American if an individual or entity, (2) not recalcitrant, that is, has provided all requested information and (3) not a non-participating FFI ('NP-FFI) if an FFI—then you're done. There is no further action required under FATCA.

Withholding

There is only one penalty withholding rate in FATCA—30% and it can only be applied to US-sourced FDAP income paid to certain kinds of account holder.

There are therefore two requirements for any withholding to take place in FATCA. They are

1. that the account holder must have received US-sourced FDAP income (in order for there to be income on which to withhold) and
2. the account holder must be either recalcitrant (if an individual or an entity) or a non-participating FFI (if an FFI). This specifically includes accounts that are Passive NFFEs (P-NFFEs) which have not provided details of US substantial owners.

Whilst this may sound relatively simple, there are a number of situations when withholding must take place but does not and this leads to a problem for the FFI concerned, inasmuch as they will be under-withholding and inaccurately reporting. Here are two examples of how this can get complex very quickly.

Example 1. All the IGA models contain a clause that provides a suspension of withholding on recalcitrant accounts. So, in theory, there should never be withholding on recalcitrant account holders when the FFI concerned is in an IGA jurisdiction. However, the suspension is conditional on the FFI reporting said recalcitrant account in its FATCA report. If it fails to do this (individually or at pooled level), then the suspension does not apply and FATCA penalty withholding must be applied. Many FFIs approach compliance to FATCA in a siloed way, so the people doing the due diligence may not be the same people doing the reporting and the people who are trying to join the two together with policy and procedure may be a different group again.

Example 2. An FFI that has a client that is a reporting IGA FFI in IRC Chapter 4, but an NQI in IRC Chapter 3, must receive a Chapter 4 withholding rate pool statement from its client prior to 31 January, to ensure that the FFI has knowledge that none of the underlying indirect account holders are subject to a FATCA penalty. If it does not do so, then the FFI must apply the IRC Chapter 4 presumption rules and, even though it has a valid form W-8IMY from its client with a GIIN, the lack of the withholding statement means that it must treat its client as a non-participating FFI and withhold at 30% FATCA and report in the same way.

It's vital for financial firms to remember that any payment made must have IRC Chapter 4 rules applied first and, if there is no penalty, then apply IRC Chapter 3 rules, subject to the principle of no duplicative taxation.

It's also worth noting, because many forget, that there is another set of teeth that FATCA has and those are the sanctions that the IRS can take against FFIs themselves. Where recalcitrant withholding is reserved for account holders, the IRS has the ability to terminate FFI Agreements and take similar countermeasures as are in IRC Chapter 3, which may have significant reputational effects while the US remains the largest capital market.

Reporting

Reporting is the main objective of FATCA. The IRS has on several occasions noted that while the stick, in terms of financial non-compliance penalties, is very large, it is not the [stated] intent to use the system for penalties. They would prefer reporting compliance.

The reporting of Americans to the IRS should not trouble any American who is not evading tax, for example, expats, unless of course they've 'forgotten' to declare their accounts on their FBAR reports, or forgotten to file their FBAR reports or if they are accidental Americans.

The reporting itself, in terms of what goes into the reports each year, was phased in over the period 2015–2017.

1. Name, address, US Tax Identification Number (TIN) of US accounts or non-US entity accounts with US owners;
2. Account number;
3. Name and GIIN of the reporting institution
4. Account balance or value
5. For custodial accounts

    (a) Total gross interest, gross dividends and total gross 'other income' paid or credited during the year
    (b) Total gross proceeds

6. For depository accounts

    (a) Total gross interest

7. For other types of accounts (not custodial or depository)

    (a) Total gross paid to the account

Reporting data required can vary each year and by jurisdiction, so this is only a guide to the types of data that are required.

Reporting *only* applies to those occasions where there are accounts which are either definitively US (e.g. the account of an American) or (1) substantially owned by, or (2) effectively controlled by, Americans. This is an important point. Given that the data-set required by the IRS is relatively simple, the actual act of filing these reports should be easy, at least for those FFIs that were traditional financial institutions before.

FFIs that are in Model 1 jurisdictions will be reporting to their domestic tax authorities, while FFIs in non-IGA jurisdictions will be reporting direct to the IRS at their International Data Exchange System portals (IDES). All reporting is packaged in xml (extended mark-up language) and the IRS frequently updates this standard at its portal.

Intergovernmental Agreements, Reciprocity and GIINs

I reference FATCA Partner Countries and IGAs above. This refers to the results of a major backlash against the US in 2012, where several industry groups and governments complained, both directly and via their financial institutions and industry associations, that two of the main planks of FATCA would cause legal problems. These were: data privacy laws and account closure. The problem is created by the concept of reporting within the regulations for those who are deemed, under FATCA, to be US, and closure of long-term recalcitrant accounts.

The base presumption is that an FFI will file reports directly to the IRS, identifying those of its customers who are, in the eyes of FATCA, US (including here the concepts of substantial ownership and effective control). The problem is that these account holders do have some protection of the domestic jurisdiction where the account is maintained, not least because the KYC and AML tests applied at account opening would not typically have resulted in US status for many of these account holders. To that extent, the account holder, as far as the domestic institution is concerned, is not US. Many jurisdictions have banking secrecy laws and their equivalents, as well as data protection concepts which would then make it illegal for them to file these reports to the IRS.

Equally, FATCA contains the concept of withholding on recalcitrant accounts and then closure of the account if the account holder does not subsequently comply with information requests. This also poses legal issues for some financial institutions where domestic law prohibits the closure of some types of accounts especially where there is a fiduciary duty.

The response to this backlash was the concept of a FATCA Partner Country. The US essentially agreed to negotiate bilateral intergovernmental agreements with these FATCA Partner Countries to get round the legal problems that FATCA causes for those jurisdictions.

The principle characteristics of IGAs are that they

1. simplify the identification and documentation rules;
2. replace reporting to the IRS with reporting to domestic regulators and;
3. suspend the requirement to withhold on, and remove the requirement to close, recalcitrant accounts.

Clearly, the rest of the world was thinking ahead when the IRS started discussing IGAs. The US is not the only country with people evading tax and it was not long before the discussion of IGAs led to discussion of reciprocity. Other governments are keen to have US financial institutions disclose details of their own taxpayers with US accounts, so that they can make sure that their tax revenues are optimised. The concept of a reciprocal IGA thus emerged. While the US, as a government, may engage in reciprocal IGAs, US financial institutions, like their non-US counterparts, are not in favour of the implications of such reciprocity. It's also likely that, even with the concept of reciprocity enshrined in an IGA, there will need to be changes to US law to allow for this information flow and several years before US institutions are able, and/or willing, to submit to the reporting obligations this would imply.

The net result is that today we have three primary types of IGA available: Model 1A (reciprocal), Model 1B (non-reciprocal) and Model 2. Model 1A is provided in Appendix V for ease of reference.

The impact of FATCA was originally uniform across the world. The same, very complex rules and penalties, applied to everyone. The emergence of IGAs has significantly altered that landscape.

If a firm falls into the definition of FFI, the first and biggest question is whether they and/or any subsidiaries, affiliates and so on fall within any one or more IGA jurisdictions. Those that do, face much simplified and much easier compliance. Those that don't, face the full force of the regulations.

This is analogous to the situation the industry already faces with IRC Chapter 3. In IRC Chapter 3, we have regulation as one stratum. Below that, we have QI Agreements as a secondary stratum that modifies the regulations to provide specified benefits through contracts with the US government.

There are two issues that make the IGA landscape more complex today. First are Partner Letters and the second is 'in substance'.

Partner Letters represent special conditions negotiated by specific countries with the US. However, because all IGAs have a 'favoured nations' clause, this means that any term specially negotiated by one country must be available to all the others. Partner Letters are the IRS' way of communicating those changes and represent an important issue for change management within financial institutions, as these changes must often also be translated into domestic law before they can be applied.

Many countries want to have an IGA but take time to put them in place. The IRS has agreed to allow some countries to act as if they have an IGA in place, even though the instrument has not been signed—the so-called in substance IGAs. However, on the one hand, the structure of FATCA means that, even in an in substance jurisdiction, the application of the rules would require translation of in substance terms into domestic law, before they could be deemed to apply to a financial institution. Second, there are several in substance jurisdictions that obtained that status many years ago and have still not signed the instrument. The IRS is painfully aware that 'in substance' should not be a long-term status and some jurisdictions are actively under scrutiny for their failure to make reasonable progress.

Finally, in this section, the IRS has a unique identifier for any FFI that registers—a Global Intermediary Identification Number or GIIN. While not all FFIs require a GIIN, many do and, in any event, such was the confusion when they were first launched, that there are undoubtedly firms out there with GIINs that do not technically need them. For many FFIs, these GIINs are basically identifiers that tell them that their client is compliant with FATCA and therefore does not need to be reported and that they themselves will be taking on the responsibility for reporting US, recalcitrant and downstream NP-FFIs.

GIINs are semi-intelligent codes. You can tell certain things about the holder based on the structure. In particular, the last three digits are the ISO country code for the FFI and the preceding two characters tell you the type of FFI, for example, whether the FFI is a Lead FFI, a single FFI, a Branch FF and so forth. You can search for an FFI's GIIN to verify it and download a complete list of published GIINs at: https://apps.irs.gov/app/fatcaFfiList/flu.jsf.

Convergence

The final principle of FATCA is convergence. In 2010–2013, many commentators and professionals were very concerned that the complexity of IRC Chapter 3 would be duplicated in IRC Chapter 4. Their fears were well founded and FATCA in some ways is more complex than 'QI'. However, between guidance in 2010 and 2011 and final regulations in 2013, several major simplifications took place. I have already alluded to one such, being the IGAs. The other is the convergence of IRC Chapter 3 and IRC Chapter 4 in certain operational respects. In particular, convergence means:

1. reliance on KYC and AML (also an IRC Chapter 3 principle) instead of enhanced due diligence (an IRC Chapter 4 concept);
2. the use in FATCA of US tax forms W-8 (or substitutes) and W-9 which are prevalent in IRC Chapter 3 and
3. use of IRC Chapter 3 reporting forms 1042, 1042-S and 1099.

This convergence is both welcome and unwelcome at the same time. It's welcome in that, in principle, it offers a route to simplicity so that firms don't have two entirely separate sets of policy and procedure to deal with one tax jurisdiction. On the other hand, it's unwelcome in that the route I reference has to change the IRC Chapter 3 system, in order to be able to encompass both IRC Chapters. This causes enormous practical problems.

We see that, for FATCA to work, the non-US financial services industry must:

1. decide which of the applicable **STATUS**, that is, FFI, NFFE, individual apply to them and assess whether they are subject to any of each of the sub-statuses that exist which might mitigate their compliance load;
2. understand to what extent IGAs affect their compliance obligations and, based on this;
3. understand the **STRUCTURE** of their counterparties, accounts and account holders and where they sit in the financial chain with respect to others in order to understand their obligations, operational processes, interfaces and the risks;
4. assess their structure in FATCA to focus on the **GLOBAL versus the LOCAL** which may alter those policies and procedures, both from a regulatory and from a commercial viewpoint;
5. design new processes and procedures to meet the intent of FATCA to **IDENTIFY** Americans in account structures;
6. **REPORT** all those Americans together with information about their accounts, income and tax withholdings, as well as information about recalcitrant accounts;
7. Penalise any account holders that receive US-sourced FDAP income and are unreported recalcitrant IGA, recalcitrant non-IGA or NP-FFI, with a 30% **WITHHOLDING** on FDAP income, and finally;
8. Understand the complexities and risks associated with the **CONVERGENCE** of IRC Chapters 3 and 4, particularly with regard to documentation and reporting.

Most firms I speak to think that FATCA is pretty much a done deal. A 2014 project that is sorted out. Many have now moved on to replicate operating procedure into Automatic Exchange of Information (AEoI)/Common Reporting Standard (CRS). Nothing that I have seen in the market supports the view that FATCA is a done deal. Tier 1 institutions certainly seem to have a good grasp, but even here I have seen some substantial problems caused mainly by a lack of corporate memory. In all tiers, the expertise and knowledge is in the heads of a few people and is rarely translated into good policy and procedure. In addition, there has been a massive blind spot in the due diligence requirements on pre-existing accounts and I know many firms that have, for one reason or another, either not realised their obligation or not prioritised it within the backlog of regulation they all have to deal with. In addition, there have been operational process failures that have led to over-withholding, under-withholding and inaccurate reporting—all caused by not properly connecting IRC Chapter 4 processes with IRC Chapter 3 processes. Many of these failures will go unnoticed for many years especially of such accounts don't happen to get picked up in a Periodic Review sample.

FATCA is not over.

12

Due Diligence

Solicitation and Validation

Of all the activities envisioned in Foreign Account Tax Compliance Act (FATCA), identification and documentation, collectively 'due diligence', lies at the heart of the system and is, by far, the most complex and challenging. This applies, as in IRC Chapter 3, to both the financial intermediaries in the chain and the financial account holders. I would remind readers at this juncture that this book is not about a line-by-line explanation of the regulations—because a line-by-line explanation would of necessity be longer than the original regulation and all the intervening transition arrangements and new agreements and I suspect most readers would have lost the will to live well before that. My intention, as stated in the introduction, is to provide the reader with an interpretation of key areas of the regulations—those which will provide the greatest operational challenges.

The purpose of due diligence is to identify accounts that are reportable. That's it!

FATCA is essentially a reporting framework with rules determining who has reporting obligations and how and when those reports are submitted.

Accounts become reportable based on a number of factors. However, most firms acquire information at onboarding using a combination of Know-Your-Customer (KYC), Anti-Money Laundering (AML) and either the W-8 forms (or substitutes) or W-9.

Solicitation

The effort at onboarding is mainly to make sure that every account is properly documented and every document is valid for its purpose.

KYC and AML are of course the foundations of both FATCA and QI because the Internal Revenue Service (IRS) knows that financial forms are already required to collect this information under domestic statutes.

The problem with the solicitation process is that it's often the blind leading the blind. Unless using an automated system, the people interfacing with clients at onboarding generally have a mountain of paperwork to go through with the client of which the tax forms are just one part. Lack of training also leads to high error rates even when the forms are collected. However the main problem is that the client usually has little interest and/or no knowledge of why the form is being requested and often asks for help. The onboarding staff, unable and unlicensed to give tax advice, usually are not able, trained or willing to help the client. This means that if the client does complete the form and it is subsequently failed in validation, the form ends up in a negative loop with the client—'I asked you for help, you couldn't help, now I've given the form and you don't accept it—you should have helped!'.

FATCA rules are also often misinterpreted by onboarding staff and management to imply that the staff must somehow be Sherlock Holmes and question every statement made by clients on these tax forms. This is not the case and FATCA uses the same principle of 'reason to know' and 'reasonableness' for staff looking at forms, as we will see in a moment.

Substitute Forms

The advent of Automatic Exchange of Information (AEoI)/Common Reporting Standard (CRS) has meant that many firms now also choose to combine their CRS solicitation obligation with their FATCA solicitation obligation. This is often done by combining the data requirements of FATCA and CRS into one new form (or series of forms for individuals and entities). While this might simplify processing for the receiving department, it usually makes for a far more complex form for the client and thus more questions. This makes the use of clear guidelines and explanations very important and the clear explanations of the many acronyms used. If these forms are used for both CRS and FATCA, the primary question being asked is not whether the client is an American; it is whether the client has any tax residencies or tax citizenships other than a domestic one.

Another type of substitute form is an automated form in which an IT system, often deployed online, is used to make it easier for clients to provide the required information in an easier way. These automated systems can more easily provide culturally and linguistically appropriate interfaces and also group data requests into a much simpler form so that the client does not see a 12-page complex form, but a small number of screens with simple questions behind which sit the complex business rules that will help catch any 'impossible' combinations of data or worse, US indicia.

These automated systems can also exploit changes to IRS rules that allow not only electronic forms instead of paper and 'wet signature' originals, but also electronic signatures. The IRS, up until early 2019, also offered an e-W8 Memorandum of Understanding or 'MoU'. Provided a firm could demonstrate that its system ensured that it was able to meet its due diligence and validation obligations, such a system would effectively be certified by the IRS as adequate. There are other automated systems for W-8s that don't require an MoU, particularly those that ultimately generate a paper form that then needs to be validated by hand. In 2019, the MoU offering was suspended, I believe due to President Trump's views on the legality and enforceability (or otherwise) of MoUs generally. Whatever the reason, as I write, the IRS is not taking on any new requests for MoUs. That said, the MoU is not a pre-requisite for an automated system, as the regulations themselves specifically allow for a withholding agent to use any method it chooses, including electronically, provided it meets the obligations in the regulations.

In any of the above cases, it's important to remember that recording of these data is critical to the success of subsequent processes. So systems need to be robust and capture a great deal of data in addition to the core data flags that determine reportability.

Entities

I would like to say a few words here about solicitation with regard to entities. Entities are viewed as a high risk for use as tax evasion and so there are some additional requirements in FATCA that effectively mean that there is an interest in piercing the entity to find underlying controllers or owners. Many foreign financial institutions (FFIs) get quite worked up about this and representatives of entities also get tied up (depending on the nature of the entity).

For FFIs, provided the rules are followed, the certifications sought from account holders are 'self-certifications' and generally absolve the FFI from liability. However, there are some nuances to consider. The largest one is the penalty of perjury issue. The original W-8 form provides for absolution from liability on the basis that the form is signed under penalty of perjury under US law (and provided validation was conducted correctly). If the data on this form is used in a substitute form, that penalty of perjury clause must also be used on or in the substitute form or system in order for the liability to remain with the certifier. This does not always happen, sometimes because the country concerned has no equivalent to US perjury laws and/or the FFI is concerned not to confuse a domestic account holder with legal terms of a foreign government. In these cases, FFIs must be careful to understand their exposure.

In particular, as a self-certification, the certifier of an entity, particularly a passive non-financial foreign entity (NFFE), has an obligation to disclose any US controllers or substantial owners. It is not for the FFI, unless there is reason to know, to become a detective.

Equally, entities in particular, but all certifiers in general, must be aware that solicitation is only one half of the equation. The FFI has an obligation to solicit a FATCA status, but the certifier also has an obligation to be aware of that status and whether it is variable or not. If it is variable, it must have an adequate tracking mechanism and re-certify to its FFI(s) within 30 days if it becomes aware of a material change in circumstance. 'Material' is defined here as anything that would change the FATCA status of the certifier. As many entities have found to their cost, there are a number of FATCA statuses that can be variable over time. For example, if an Active NFFE's (A-NFFE) circumstances change such that the proportion of their income derived from active trading falls below 50% of their gross, they may become a Passive NFFE (P-NFFE).

The same thing can be said about some types of registered and deemed compliant FFI. A Local FFI (L-FFI) can cease to be eligible for its deemed compliant status if, for example, it acquires an FFI with a substantial non-domestic client base meaning that it no longer meets the criteria for deemed compliance. In these circumstances, it is quite normal for those conducting mergers and acquisitions, even with a regulatory gap analysis, to miss the fact that their eligibility changed. If the matter is public record, it would also be an obligation of the FFI to have reason to know that a change would be likely to have occurred.

So, if anyone tells you that FATCA is 'a done deal' even in 2019 and is pretty much over, I would seek to disagree, especially based on what I see in the market.

In the validation section below, I also mention re-solicitation. This occurs if the form and data have time limited validity—usually three years from the end of the year signed for the W-8 series. FFIs use a number of tactics to make sure that they always have a valid FATCA status on record. This is because the lack of such status, uncorrected within 30 days, means the firm must apply IRC Chapter 4 presumption rules. This is not only costly and complex, but once cured, means that retrospective data and reporting fixes need to be applied. Long story short, FFIs don't want to get into that presumptive situation, so great efforts are (and should be) applied to make sure that re-solicitation, when needed, is applied well in advance. This typically means potential multiple outreaches to clients starting three months in advance of year end.

Validation

Where solicitation is the act of acquiring data from an account holder, validation is a separate process in which that data or form(s) are taken through prescribed procedures to make sure that the statements made by account holders are complete and reliable. This applies as much in FATCA as it does in QI matters. However, while KYC and AML underpin FATCA and can, to a limited extent, be used to presume FATCA status, this is not always the case and, in any event, means that the FFI concerned retains liability.

Firms use one of two strategies with respect to the additional data required for FATCA status. If a firm is using the W-8 series forms _solely_ to collect FATCA status, then the forms so collected are valid indefinitely or until there is a change in circumstances. However, if the forms are being used for IRC Chapter 4 and IRC Chapter 3 (and in particular a claim of treaty benefits), then the form is only valid for three years from the end of the year in which it is signed. This of course occurs if an account is custodial in nature and the account receives US-sourced Fixed, Determinable, Annual or Periodic (FDAP) income.

Most firms, and certainly the ones that retain us, use flow charts to map out procedures. Figure 12.1 is an example of the validation process for the W-8BEN form in FATCA and QI. Similar charts can be produced for the other forms in the series and can also be produced for substitute forms and forms that aggregate FATCA with QI and CRS.

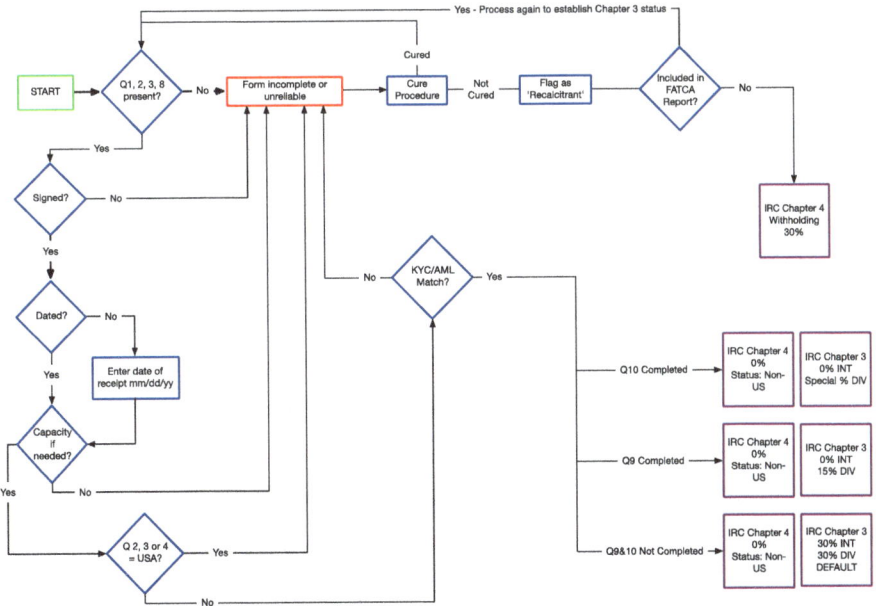

Fig. 12.1 W-8 validation for W-8 in FATCA and QI indicia strategies. Source: Author's own

Fundamentally, the edge cases of validation of data are that the account is definitively US or definitively non-US. In between lies the morass of US indicia.

First, as with IRC Chapter 3, the procedure that finding US indicia triggers is called a 'cure procedure'. Finding US indicia does not mean the account is US. It means you have to do extra work to come to a decision. The actual cure process used depends on the type of US indicia found. Figure 12.2 takes you through the cure procedures for all US indicia including those for accidental Americans.

In the absence of a cure, the IRC Chapter 4 presumption rules mean that you must treat the account holder as a US non-exempt recipient (form individuals or entities) or as a NP-FFI for financial institutions.

Pre-existing Accounts

I note here that, as mentioned in the last chapter, all financial firms should have completed due diligence on pre-existing accounts by 31 December 2018. As such, all non-US FFIs must now have a validated FATCA status for ALL their financial account holders. While there is little written about the consequences of not having completed this due diligence in terms of penalties or other consequences, it would seem logical that, given the five years in which this process is meant to have been completed (including extensions), the IRS would not consider this to be a 'minor or administrative' error but a substantial error worthy of the intervention by competent authorities. So, if, in 2019, you have any accounts without a valid IRC Chapter 4 status—you are in trouble.

That said, the principles of the due diligence on pre-existing accounts are pretty much the same as those of new accounts. While a FATCA status is gained at onboarding for new accounts, the regulations (and as translated into domestic law for intergovernmental agreement [IGA] FFIs and the FFI Agreement for non-IGA FFIs) recognise that circumstances change over time and that the FATCA status of any given account holder may change and therefore their reportability.

Intermediaries

The intermediaries in the financial chain, typically banks, brokers, custodians, depositaries, depositories and the like, have an obligation to identify themselves and their FATCA status to their counterparties. This is achieved between counterparties through the use of the W-8IMY which is eight pages

12 Due Diligence 189

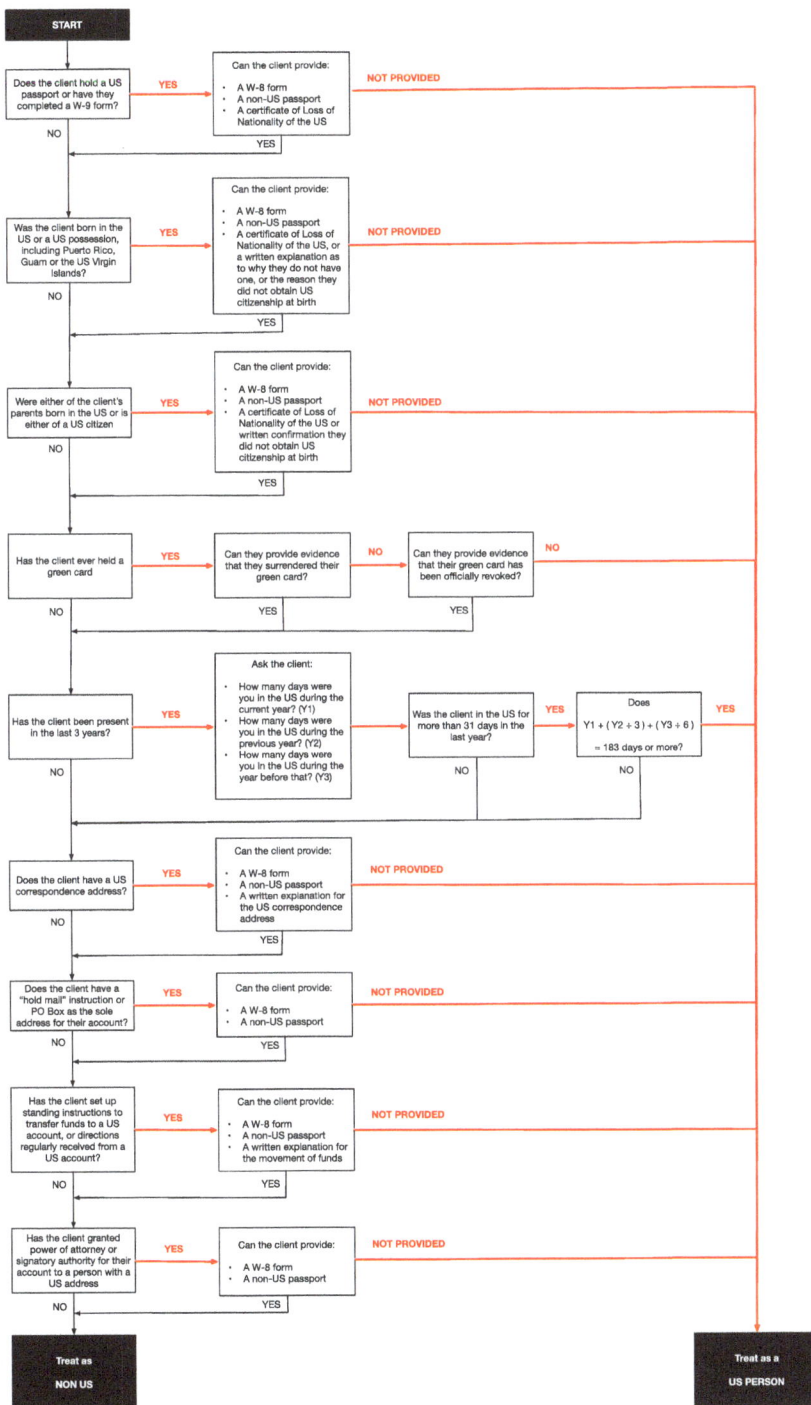

Fig. 12.2 Is your client an American? Source: Author's own

long in the current July 2017 revision and is in 29 sections to encompass the different types of foreign intermediary that exist within FATCA regulation. This is the first place that there is clear convergence between IRC Chapter 3 and IRC Chapter 4.

The question is—what is an intermediary? And for this purpose, there is divergence. Based on the objective of the US government in IRC Chapter 4, to identify and report US persons with assets outside the US that may be evading tax, it's clear that the traditional financial institutions constitute 'intermediaries'. However, collective investment vehicles offer an alternative route for the budding tax evader and so, in IRC Chapter 4, we see the new concept of a 'foreign financial institution' or FFI. This concept includes both the traditional financial services intermediaries, but also now includes the wider concept of collective investment vehicles (Fig. 12.3).

Most traditional financial intermediaries (banks brokers etc.) have resources and experience (legal, compliance, operations, tax) to be able to assess and comply efficiently, even with an expanded self-certification like the W-8IMY. The problem is going to come from those firms that have not traditionally viewed themselves as financial institutions. The largest single sector thus affected is the collective investment vehicles. While these firms do have regulatory oversight for the most part, these are not in the same category as the traditional institutions. Two other factors to take account of here are (1) language and (2) culture. These problems have already been identified as major contributors to many of the failures and flaws of the IRC Chapter 3 regulations.

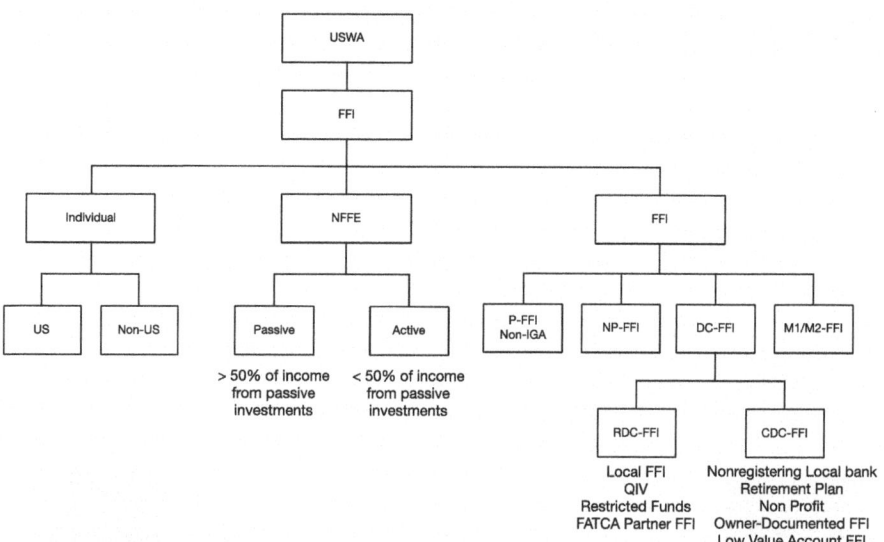

Fig. 12.3 Types of account holders under FATCA. Source: Author's own

If you draw a line from Washington DC eastwards, the degree of understanding (and therefore compliance) drops almost in an inverse square relationship. Not only are the forms becoming much more complex in terms of their length, they are written in tax technical American, not English. Communicating the intent and requirements of these documents, even to traditional financial institutions, is a challenge at best. When you arrive as far as Asia, cultural differences start to pop up which compound the problem. Signatures, to take one small example, in that part of the world are frequently 'chops' or graphical representations rather than what an IRS agent might normally view as a 'signature'.

I also mentioned that the W-8IMY's at eight pages is based on the IRS trying to shoe-horn all possible states in which an FFI might exist. Many of these states are created due to carve-outs granted by the IRS under lobbying pressure, for example, participating, non-participating, registered deemed compliance and certified deemed compliance. My biggest concern here, particularly bearing in mind the linguistic and cultural issues, is whether any given FFI has the awareness or real knowledge to be able to complete one of these forms intelligently. They will be 'relied upon' by upstream FFIs and USWAs, but without a serious programme of education from both the IRS and industry as a whole, the lack of a Responsible Officer concept in FATCA in IGA jurisdictions leaves the field open for everyone to assume that everyone else knows what they are doing. And we know where that got the financial services industry.

When one drops below the level of FFI to NFFEs and Individuals, the use of KYC and AML documentation is encouraged by the IRS but the W-8 series has undergone significant change over the years and the IRS continues to add data elements even in the most recent 2017 revisions. These self-certifications suffer the same linguistic and cultural issues as their forerunners and so, it's to be expected that, even though these forms will be used in their millions, the proportion actually fit for purpose will be quite low.

As a result of due diligence, all FFIs should have a valid FATCA status for all account holders.

Annual Due Diligence

So far, we have spoken mainly about due diligence that should have been conducted on pre-existing accounts and due diligence performed at onboarding. However, due diligence also needs to be performed annually so that any accounts not reportable historically or at onboarding can be re-assessed for whether they have become reportable during the year.

In essence this allows an FFI to take into consideration any material changes notified by account holders as well as reportability based on levels of search criteria.

The most relevant criterion for the IRS as far as potential tax evasion is concerned is the value of the account or accounts as aggregated. So, as we will find in later chapters, the reporting in FATCA is based on a prior annual assessment of due diligence that uses aggregated account value as its trigger.

The effect is that the IRS publishes a spot FX rate on 31 December each year, which FFIs use to convert local account values into US dollars. All accounts that are connected with a beneficial owner have their values aggregated. That aggregated value then determines an end-of-year due diligence process which is either:

1. No due diligence (and no reporting)
2. Search of electronic indicia
3. Search of electronic indicia, paper records and relationship management enquiries

These additional searches, triggered by account value fluctuations, are designed to make sure, at an annual level, that there are no US indicia that were not observed at onboarding or found in the due diligence on pre-existing accounts, but that may be visible on subsequent searches.

If you recall, this book is about practical impacts, not about line-by-line explanation of the rules. So, while the actual thresholds and methods of application might be of interest, they can be found easily enough in the IGAs and country-by-country guidance. My concern here is to discuss what's not in those documents—the impacts of these control structures.

The idea of this annual due diligence is clearly to spot a dynamic change in accounts that might represent the use of the account for tax evasion and thus the account becomes reportable. While the levers for these procedures are quite blunt, their effect on financial institutions can be substantial.

The main issue is the interpretation of the rules so that the aggregation is accurate and that the subsequent due diligence is properly compartmentalised and performed based on the aggregate value.

Election Not to Apply Thresholds

The IRS does give FFIs an ability to not apply thresholds, which often allows FFIs to apply a single level of due diligence to all accounts irrespective of account value. However, this is an election that must be made at the FATCA portal and it's rare that operational staff are aware of the potential for the election, let alone its consequences. A blanket due diligence process may be more homogeneous to apply but it will undoubtedly bring many more accounts into review than are strictly necessary.

Spot FX Rate

The idea of a spot FX rate may sound simple, but in practice any given FFI may be operating multiple currency accounts and have products whose calculator is not as simple as the value of cash or equities, for example, insurance contracts. Larger FFIs or EAGs will have even more difficulty. The timing of this also raises many problems for non-US firms, not least of which is the fact that 31 December is not an ideal operational moment and many will have other priorities including the beginning of preparations for the upcoming US tax reporting season in both QI and FATCA and similar preparations under CRS. All of this activity is very similar but will include various drill-downs and slices and dices of data and administrative activities such as applying for extensions of time to file. Whoever the team is that deals with anti-tax evasion regulations and/or QI matters needs to have their wits about them at this time.

Searchable Databases

The IRS expects FFIs to connect beneficial owners across accounts that may be direct cash or equity accounts but also across entities where the beneficial owner may be a substantial owner. While the IRS does not expect FFIs to build searchable databases or develop systems for making connections where those connective flags do not exist, the fact is that their urge to find tax evasion and vendors' efforts to build functionality into their systems puts pressure on core banking systems to be able to identify, across a bank or a group, all the accounts with which any beneficial owner has a connection. Realistically, given all the other regulations facing financial firms, this will be a logistical and operational challenge to get right.

Paper Records and Relationship Management

Depending on the number of accounts that fall into high-risk 'enhanced due diligence' based on their value, the easy bit will be the electronic search especially if data has been well and properly flagged. Many firms hold legacy systems and also have data on multiple sometimes interconnected systems. While data mining is supposed to be an advanced tool, many banks are challenged simply to get historic income data for one client out of their systems in a coherent and consistent way because the beneficial owner and/or account holder may be represented slightly differently in different systems whether by accident or design.

However, paper searches will be arduous, repetitive and boring even when those records are easily available. These documents may be in different geographical locations and some banks don't even have the concept of a customer record, bizarre as that might seem to an outsider.

Relationship management enquiries will also be a challenge. Reason to know rules mean that these enquiries could possibly delve into conversations between RMs and clients and, if the financial institution is subject to European Market Infrastructure Regulation (EMIR), it may even mean access to recordings of telephone conversations given that the data and analysis would exist. Notwithstanding that rather extreme example, RMs are going to need training on these matters and the likelihood is that rather than produce results, it will create an unwillingness to speak of certain areas for fear of triggering such disclosures. These will all be challenges for FFIs.

CIVs

I've titled this section 'CIVs' but what I want to include here is really any type of institution, firm or other legal entity which is not a traditional financial institution like a bank or broker.

These firms face enormous problems because their basic operating model is different from that of a traditional financial institution. To adapt to a FATCA landscape, there will therefore need to be a much higher level of awareness as a precursor to operational compliance. In the funds industry for example, the principle of 'fund distributors' has to be integrated into the FATCA model. As far as the US is concerned, it's just trying to make sure that funds distributed outside the US are not used for the purpose of tax evasion. The regulations therefore expect fund managers to ensure that appropriate changes are made to fund distribution agreements in order that US persons are excluded and, where they are found (e.g. by historical due diligence) they are either expelled from the fund or their assets transferred out. My point here is that the IRS has gone to some lengths to identify the high-risk areas and, in an effort to show willingness to mitigate the full effects of FATCA, and only require action to be taken where those high-risk areas are. The problem as I see it is that this is not fundamentally how the industry works. So while laudable, all these due diligence 'carve-outs' serve to achieve is to create more complexity, more cost and more risk—and that's for those who make the effort to comply. For those who take a similar attitude to that which they evidenced with IRC Chapter 3, there may be a significant level of non-compliance which goes almost wholly unnoticed.

NFFEs

I've spoken a great deal about the firms that fall into the definition of a 'financial institution', the so-called FFIs and below I will discuss some of the issues facing individuals. In between the two are account holders who are neither individuals nor FFIs. These are called Non-Financial Foreign Entities or NFFEs. From the identification and documentation perspective, most FFIs would expect to receive a form W-8BENE from these customers since they are clearly not financial institutions. However, the IRS has indicated that some types of NFFE could be used as vehicles for tax evasion. Hence it has described two sub-categories of NFFE—'passive' and 'active'. I try to explain these concepts by considering a corporation which makes widgets. Its main business activity is making and selling widgets. It's so successful that it builds up a pile of cash. Such business entities may well develop a Treasury function to make good use of that pile of cash, through investments. As long as the proportion of their income derived from such investments is less than 50%, they are considered 'active NFFEs', that is, they actively make widgets. However, let's say that this company suffers a sharp decline in sales. Now, if the proportion of the invested funds exceeds 50% of the income, they will be considered 'passive NFFEs', that is, the act of making widgets has become somewhat secondary to the act of receiving investment income. Of course the second type of passive NFFE would be a corporation set-up originally with the intent of having more than 50% of its income from passive (i.e. non-widget making) activities. For FFIs this category clearly presents its own challenges. Not least is the frequency and method by which an FFI can interact with its NFFE customer base to find out what the latest 'proportion' is. The net result of the calculation itself is mainly to determine the additional due diligence needed for passive NFFEs which would determine if they are US, effectively controlled by or substantially owned by US persons for the purpose of FATCA. The natural answer would be by reference to the balance sheet or regular financial statements made by these entities. However, across the world, there is no set standard for the frequency of such reporting nor any automated method by which the information could easily be extracted.

Effective Control and Substantial Ownership

When it comes to indirect vehicles such as funds, the issue of being a US person becomes a slightly different question—one of 'effective control' or 'substantial ownership'. In both cases there are rules defining what triggers additional due diligence and/or reporting. Effective control essentially means that an FFI has to identify whether the account has any associated instructions that would mean that a US person or persons had effective control over the account. That would typically mean a power of attorney at the account level or a standing instruction on the account record to transfer assets and/or cash to another account that is again either a US person or is in turn effectively controlled or substantially owned by a US person or persons. You can see how quickly this can become completely un-manageable.

Substantial ownership suffers similar practical issues. While there may be some mechanism by which an FFI could determine with its customer whether, irrespective of the view of the customer, the facts indicate that the non-US customer is in fact substantially a US entity, the fact is that the initial interpretation could change with time. In other words, an account holder who discloses the proportion of its members that are US will need to indicate whether that proportion is liable to change and, if it does, over what period and to what degree. This information in turn will need to be used by the account holder to decide what frequency of repeat internal due diligence is necessary to maintain the accuracy of its certification to its financial counterparties. Remember, the irony is that this work needs to be done, even if the result is that the account holder is not substantially US owned. FATCA remains very much a negative proof system.

The difficulty for any FFI (or NFFE) is that, for the most part, the types of documentation available to identify these issues, as mentioned earlier, are not in electronic form, they are in paper form. This means that, for most FFIs, there will be a gruelling analysis of account set-up information and associated documents which will be both slow and costly.

Actual Knowledge and Reason to Know

The difficulties that FATCA presents so far have been in how certain facts can be identified typically in account records. Some, such as the address, as discussed, are relatively simple. Others such as telephone number in the US are more subtle. More subtle still are the concepts of actual knowledge and reason to know. Both these concepts are described elsewhere in this book. However, my point in mentioning them in this chapter is both for completeness and also to highlight the practical difficulties that the concepts would present to an FFI. The biggest issue for firms that use relationship managers as the interface between the operational function and the account holder is finding a way to address the reason to know and actual knowledge concepts. On the one hand, in a perfect world, there would need to be some mechanism for translating what could be deemed to be 'gossip' or 'hearsay' into a record on the account holder's record. On the other, one can imagine a world where relationship managers begin every conversation with something like 'don't talk to me about any of the following … just in case'.

What we end up with is an identification and documentation system that is very, very complex. At its simplest, the 'financial institutions' in the chain must document themselves to their counterparties in the chain. But this will be with more complex documents and be less familiar to those who have not heretofore considered themselves to be financial institutions at all. These institutions will have to review the regulations, as well as what will be constantly changing 'triggers and thresholds', in order to figure out which account holders should be subject to which kinds of due diligence. The process can then proceed apace—presuming everyone understands the documentation and its interpretation.

In concluding this chapter, I would say the following. In the framework of anti-tax evasion, documentation of account holders is becoming more onerous because it's no longer just about knowing your customer enough to allow them to operate a financial account. Due diligence is the precursor to a number of different processes that will in all probability be undertaken by different people in different parts of the bank. As that precursor it is by far the most important to get right. If you get it right, the rest will be much easier to handle. If you get it wrong, you will be in for a world of pain.

From a FATCA perspective, make sure that, if you haven't already done so, get your due diligence on pre-existing accounts completed. Then make sure that your onboarding policies and procedures are robust, well documented and effectively trained into staff. That means understanding the purpose of the due diligence and its importance in the overall process. It means making sure there are clear guidelines for what is a US account holder, if you're in an IGA market, know the domestic statute and local guidance with respect to any accounts, products and so on that may be exempt from due diligence or subject to lower requirements, that is, make intelligent informed choices about what operational procedures you adopt. A one-size-fits-all approach may be easier but may also be costlier. Then make sure you train and cross-train at all levels. I see so much inefficiency because of a siloed operational approach horizontally (i.e. departmentally) combined with a lack of knowledge vertically (i.e. up the management chain). This is the worst of compliance worlds, yet it's also the most common.

13

Simplifying FATCA

In this chapter, we will look at some of the ways in which the burdens of Foreign Account Tax Compliance Act (FATCA) can be reduced.

For the most part, as I have indicated, FATCA affects individuals, entities and foreign financial institutions (FFIs). Individuals and entities are mainly the object of FATCA, while FFIs are usually the subject of FATCA.

In many cases, unfortunately, 'it is what it is'. If you're an individual or an entity, the obligations of FATCA are fixed by what you are. By the time FATCA comes around, all you can do is be informed so that if there any unexpected nexus points to the US, you are prepared to respond to your financial institution.

Individuals

To that extent individuals have a relatively easy job already. They aren't really expected to know much about FATCA since they have no real choice in the matter and, when they are asked for their FATCA status, it will usually be via an FFI requesting a self-certification form.

As FATCA is a negative proof system, small cash account holders will be affected to exactly the same extent as more sophisticated account holders. However, from a practical viewpoint, the only individuals for whom there is a possibility of simplifying FATCA are accidental Americans. To do that, you must know at outset what the possible triggers are—substantial presence, green card, parents and birth place.

Substantial presence really affects only frequent travellers. I myself maintain a spreadsheet of my visits to the US so that if the formula appears to be getting me close to the threshold (183 days over three years), I can at least be aware of the consequences and take preventative action.

For those tripping over (or realising that they are in) the green card, parental or birth place risk area, there are different approaches. First, if you expect to have less than $50,000 aggregated in your accounts at any one FFI, there's really nothing to worry about since your account is below the threshold for review, due diligence and reporting. That said, be careful that your financial institution has not elected not to apply the FATCA thresholds because then it will matter. If you are going to have accounts worth more than $50,000 and/or you are going to trade in US securities (and thereby receive US-sourced Fixed, Determinable, Annual or Periodic [FDAP] income), you are going to be affected because you will be found to have US indicia. The way to get ahead of this issue is one of two strategies. First, the tax technical strategy is to obtain a Certificate of Loss of Nationality (CLN). Your FFI will ask for this together with a non-US form of governmental ID and a self-certification.

There are some edge cases where this can be difficult. If you do not have a US Social Security Number (SSN), in order to revoke your US citizenship (which you may have acquired without your knowledge), you'll need to apply for one as an adult (they are usually applied for and assigned at birth), then go through the revocation process, which includes, amongst other things, providing three years of US tax returns. If you can't get a CLN, then your financial institution can still treat you as a non-US person if you can provide a reasonable explanation. In the circumstances I see quite often, that's not difficult, because the time and expense required for an accidental American to get a SSN, then a CLN is, in the view of most FFIs, prohibitive and, if there are no other US nexus points, it's often taken as a reasonable explanation.

Simplifying FATCA for individuals is also easy simply by paying attention to the certification forms. Most individuals I speak to have received no guidance or help from their FFI and have little understanding of the purpose or consequences of filling the form incorrectly. So, pay attention is the message and think carefully about what you are being asked and make sure the form is complete and accurate before handing it back.

Entities

Life gets a bit more complex for entities because these are the most commonly used vehicles for tax evasion and therefore there is more attention given to their structure, location and controlling persons. Historically advisors have constructed some extremely complex combinations of entities in various structures often not with the direct purpose of evading tax. The problem is that these structures often either have an inadvertent effect of reducing tax liability or just look like they might. If I see diagrams with networks of corporate structures that include certain well-known jurisdictions and investment vehicle types, they just scream 'tax evasion'. The problem is that this affects even those structures that aren't evading tax because the rules are set the same for everyone.

Clearly, the most obvious ways to simplify FATCA for entities is to make sure that either (i) you have no US person in any position of substantial ownership or effective control, that is, be careful who you give powers of attorney to and don't set up standing orders to US banks. However, if you do have US exposure in your structure, get some professional tax advice quickly, not least because many FFIs have standing policies to off-board accounts that show up with US exposure.

Entities of course come in a variety of types. The most common are straightforward corporates, then trusts, then collective investment vehicles such as Société d'investissement à Capital Variable (SICAVs) and Société d'Investissement à Capital Fixe (SICAFs). Again, for depository and low-value accounts, FATCA is simplified by structural relaxation of the due diligence rules. For custodial accounts held by these types of entity, exposure to the US may take the form, not just of US persons in the structure via ownership of control, but also by having an exposure to the US capital markets as part of an investment strategy. This in turn opens up the possibility that if you do not respond to requests for information from a financial institution, you may be subject to a FATCA penalty. This takes the form of a 30% withholding on any US-sourced FDAP income.

For entities there is a little more freedom since these structures are artificial legal creations and can therefore be adjusted or planned for. This is not to say that simplification of FATCA should mean the planned removal of US individuals from non-US entities. FATCA being a negative proof system, such a strategy would not be effective. However, the simplification does come from avoiding the consequences of US persons present in non-US entities.

The first of these is to make sure that those responsible for making certifications on behalf of entities understand what they are doing.

The forms W-8BENE and W-8IMY are complex when it comes to FATCA. In particular some of the rules for determining risk are variable. As we have seen, an Active non-financial foreign entity (NFFE) and a Passive NFFE have very different risk profiles when it comes to FATCA, so before 'ticking the box' for A-NFFE, the directors should have some controls in place to monitor that status and be ready to change it if circumstances change.

The area of trusts is particularly fraught. Many factors affect the way in which trustees complete self-certifications of FATCA status. Most non-US trusts have structures that are affected by domestic law. However, the US tax regulations are built on the US definitions—simple, complex and grantor. This matter is made even more complex because the US recognises that the US treatment may be different from the non-US in the area of transparency. Hence FATCA certifications for trusts contain the concepts of hybrid and reverse-hybrid entities to describe situations where a vehicle of a give type, for example trust, can be transparent in the US but not in its domestic setting and vice versa.

There really is no substitute for knowledge and awareness in this space. You may know that you are not evading any tax, but the application of the rules and your lack of knowledge of how this system works could easily trip you up.

FFIs

Where individuals and entities can be viewed as the object of FATCA, FFIs are really the subject of FATCA.

Both individuals and entities must know their FATCA status, but that, in most cases, should be a relatively simple matter to understand and address. The rest becomes a case of making sure the certification is done correctly, that any disclosures are made properly and, if your FATCA status is inherently variable, making sure you have monitoring processes in place. Other than that, it's important that if there are US persons in positions of substantial ownership or effective control, that they are aware of the impact of FATCA on them—any accounts with which they can be connected will likely be reportable to the Internal Revenue Service (IRS). If those people have not disclosed those accounts domestically in the US, then they face potential legal action under FATCA. From a reputational standpoint, it's worth noting that if any of this occurs, the entity itself may be exposed to reputational damage by connection.

FFIs on the other hand are the subject of FATCA, that is, the target. It is through FFIs that individuals and entities operate financial accounts. So, FFIs in FATCA are the ones responsible for due diligence, documentation, penalty withholding and ultimately reporting. The opportunities for simplification are therefore greatest for FFIs. It has to be said that the opportunities to get it wrong are also highest in this area.

Simplification comes in a couple of ways.

Reputational Risk Factors

Many firms assess their clients based on risk. Normally, that risk does not include regulatory risk exposure, but smart firms are now including this factor, that is, what is the risk of being associated with a client who is actually evading tax. That's a multiple point line which has, for the FFI, the risk that their policies and control procedures are ineffective or that their employees are vulnerable to corrupt practices either deliberately or inadvertently. The fact that the US person got caught evading tax will not be the primary concern. The method by which they achieved it, if it becomes public domain, will be a concern.

So, one strategy, that was adopted to great publicity in the early days of FATCA, was to do the relevant due diligence and off-board any clients that were either US or had US indicia (cured or not). Since those days, many firms have come to understand what I said in the first edition of this book—that such a strategy, while it may reduce or remove reputational risk by taking away the possibility of having a US account holder ergo a potential tax evader, it was not going to simplify FATCA in operational terms because of the negative proof nature of the system.

For FFIs, the indirect reputational risk is enough to force a policy of not accepting Americans at all. This can be nuanced in various ways by selectively permitting US clients but restricting the services or products they are able to access. In simple terms for example, this may include permitting US clients to open depository accounts but not custodial accounts. Of course, where the account is disclosed at onboarding as US, we are not talking about 'curing US indicia' because the account is self-certified as US. The constraints on accessible products merely make certain aspects of compliance less complex to meet. In the case of a US account for example, if it is able to trade US securities, the FFI will need a 0% FATCA rate pool account (because US persons are not subject to IRC Chapter 3 for their withholding obligations, but to IRC Chapters 31 and 61).

The second group of US accounts are those that are presented as non-US, but have US indicia that is not cured. These are aggravating for FFIs because they involve extra work, for no benefit to the firm. The IRC Chapter 4 and IRC Chapter 3 presumption rules are complex. Therefore most firms when structuring cure procedures for US indicia become very robust. While the regulations allow 90 days for curing these indicia, most firms jump on these 'recalcitrant' account holders as fast as possible. So, in terms of simplifying FATCA, it's a question of having very robust policies and fast acting procedures. In fact, in our opinion, we observe that one of the most robust policies is to make the curing of US indicia a conditional rule for account opening, that is, the best way to avoid injecting risk into the business is to preclude it before it gets that far and have account opening be fully conditional on the account having no uncured US indicia.

The third aspect to this reputational risk reduction strategy is to have a robust procedure to handle changes in circumstances (CiC). If we assume that all pre-existing due diligence is complete and new account-opening procedures preclude the possibility of recalcitrant accounts, then we are left with what happens over time. I will discuss some of these issues from a different perspective later in this chapter. However, at this stage, the issue is that anything that affects the tax status of an account holder is a matter of concern in FATCA. For individuals, this would be adopting US citizenship. For entities the issues can be much more complex, as explained for Active and Passive NFFEs. Of course, both individuals and entities have an obligation to be aware of their FATCA status and to re-certify within 30 days if there is a material change in circumstances. For the most part, FFIs rely on this obligation. However, the 'reason to know' rules do have an impact here as well as the principles of reasonableness. This means that, even if the account holder does not re-certify, there are situations in which the FFI could 'reasonably have been expected to know' that its client may have suffered a change in circumstances. This is most common with entities and other financial institution clients where changes may be public knowledge (e.g. information at public exchanges or at their web site). In these circumstances, the FFI may not be able to avoid liability. Therefore, simplifying FATCA (or a consequence of FATCA) means ensuring that monitoring policies and procedures are effective. This usually means some level of cross-departmental communication (difficult for most forms at the best of times). This may be as simple as selecting any account with value over $1 million and annually checking their web site and any relevant public exchange for any information that looks like it might have an effect. This is typically a merger or acquisition where the secondary entity's profile, when merged or acquired by the FFI's account holder, effectively changes the tax profile of the whole (including the FFI's account holder). Some firms also specifically ask certain high-risk clients (by value or type) to re-check their status. This is not a request for re-certification. It's more to remind the client and thus provide an evidence trail for the FFI to show they did everything they could 'reasonably be expected to do'. This is, after all is said and done, about risk exposure.

In summary, having no US persons reduces reputational risk but does not remove operational costs. Having US persons with restricted product access can preclude reputational risk and also reduce operational costs. Not allowing accounts with US indicia to be opened (let along trade US securities markets) again reduces both reputational risk and operational cost. Managing changes in circumstances reduces reputational risk but does involve some additional operational costs. It's viewing the regulations in this multi-layered way that is most effective for most businesses.

There are a couple of structural aspects of FATCA that have been designed to allow larger firms to simplify FATCA. These are expanded affiliate groups (EAGs) and consolidated compliance groups (CCGs).

Expanded Affiliate Groups

If you are a large FFI that is part of a group of FFIs with a common parent, then you have the option of applying to be treated as an expanded affiliate group (EAG) sometimes known also as an FFI Group.

There are rules that apply to EAGs. An EAG will naturally have one member that is a Lead FFI, one that is a Point of Contact FFI (that can also be the lead), a Compliance FFI and of course a Member FFI.

It's estimated that in Europe alone the average spend on FATCA by tier 1 financial institutions, that is, those most likely to benefit from an EAG, is at least $25 million per year.

Whether an EAG actually simplifies FATCA or not is debatable. My own opinion is that it's a marginal call. Typically, the benefits to be gained are often offset by additional organisational costs of setting up the various types of FFI in the group. Ultimately it's a matter of culture. There are EAGs that are more like commercial franchises in which the local FFI has much operational independence from the group because of domestic cultural differences. Even when there is strict central control in an EAG, many benefits are lost if the jurisdictions in the EAG include non-intergovernmental agreement (non-IGA) and IGA.

So, EAGs may be relevant for some tier 1 FFIs, but not all. In general, as soon as you drop to tier 2 and below, the value of EAGs diminishes very quickly.

Consolidated Compliance

Also the option to adopt a consolidated compliance programme (CCP) in which, as the name suggests, you can adopt a single centralised control mechanism. Again, mainly a benefit for tier 1 FFI groups that already have substantial centralised control mechanisms in place. My experience of such things is that you spend almost as much time managing the various differences and exception reports through language and culture as you save by standardising policy and procedure.

Carve-Outs

Now, apart from structural issues that would really affect only large FFIs, we can look at ways to minimise effort when considering review of accounts. These rules apply irrespective of whether you are a large FFI or a small FFI or part of a group of FFIs. The way to view these 'carve-outs' is to consider them from two directions. Like having US accounts, some of these carve-outs may present opportunities to allow certain kinds of account at onboarding while precluding others in an attempt to increase the overall proportion of accounts that may be subject to a carve-out and therefore reduce the operational workload and cost. The second way to look at these is purely based on workload. However, in a highly mixed account environment be careful not to spend more time evaluating the strata than you save by having the strata in the first place.

Accounts Exempt from Review

Low-Value Accounts

The main, and possibly the most practical argument of many that oppose FATCA, is that many Americans outside the US are not actually evading tax. It's a popular thought that if someone has an account outside their country of residence, they must be avoiding tax at best and actively evading it at worst. This has already caused major problems for the many thousands of Americans who live and work outside the US. They have found it increasingly difficult to open and maintain simple banking facilities. In the first Guidance Notices issued by the IRS, the model adopted was to have stringent documentation procedures on all FFIs with particular focus on certain types of account that were felt to be particular targets of tax evaders. This was changed in the draft and final regulations. In fact, it was the largest change I've seen in the IRS' position between guidance and regulation. Rather than target types of account, the regulations create the concept of an 'aggregated value of accounts'. Below this aggregated value, the hypothesis is that the account holder is probably not evading tax, that is, there is a low risk. This model, like its 'account type' predecessor, has practical problems—how and when do you value non-US dollar denominated accounts? How do you value securities in accounts as opposed to simple cash in depository accounts? How do you aggregate this data (many FFIs do not have systemic capability to aggregate these data)? For example, a customer may have a financial account with an institution but also be a substantial owner in another account. Many firms operate different types of account on different systems and platforms that do not always 'talk' to each other. So, firms face a challenge where an account holder has both depository and custodial accounts as well as also being a substantial owner in other types of account. To some degree, the IRS has been lenient in its guidance, indicating that it does not expect firms to develop new systems to enable such granular aggregation. Aggregation need only be done to the extent that an FFI's systems are capable of aggregating the data. Of course, time will tell, but tax evaders are likely to be quite clever at identifying and exploiting loopholes in complex tax systems. It may be therefore that identifying FFIs with whom to open accounts, based on their systems capabilities, may become a focus for tax evasion activities, in the same way that data privacy laws achieved the same objective in prior years.

Then, there is the obvious—how would that system track an evader who simply opened up multiple accounts at multiple unrelated institutions such that no one institution had accounts that triggered the due diligence tests?

Deemed Compliance

Types of Deemed Compliance

The main object of deemed compliance is to allow the IRS to shift its FATCA focus away from the truly local, where evasion is 'unlikely', to the truly global, where they feel it's more likely that opportunities to structure hidden assets will exist.

Deemed compliance is essentially a way in which the IRS can identify certain types of account or investment strategy that, in their opinion, pose a low risk. The idea of deemed compliance merely means that the FFI concerned may not have to enter into an FFI Agreement because it is already 'deemed' to be in compliance simply by reason of the way in which it exists in the financial services framework. This may be that the rules under which accounts are opened clearly preclude US persons or that the scope of the FFI's activities is so local that US persons are unlikely to target them as a method for evading tax.

The IRS has defined two types of Deemed Compliance—Registered Deemed Compliance and Certified Deemed Compliance. The concept of deemed compliance was first established in IRS guidance Notice 2011-34 and draft and final regulations merely expanded on this concept.

The important thing to note about both of these categories is (1) FFIs do not get the chance to debate whether or not they can be deemed compliant. The regulations define, for each category, the types of FFI that can fall into the definition; (2) even if your firm falls into the definitional aspect of a deemed compliant FFI, this does not mean that you are automatically deemed compliant. For each category, each type of firm must meet certain criteria to be compliant. In other words, even though, for example, a qualified investment vehicle (QIV) is one of the types of FFI that can be deemed compliant, they will only actually be capable of certifying that status if they meet certain criteria. Ergo, there will be some firms that, don't meet the sub-level criteria and thus, even though they could theoretically be deemed complaint, they fail the detail level tests to do so.

We should also be clear as to what the result of deemed compliance is. The carve-out is on the withholding aspect of FATCA. Remember, the three aspects of FATCA are documentation, reporting and withholding. Deemed compliant status merely means that the withholding aspects of FATCA do not apply. Documentation and reporting obligations are still active.

Registered Deemed Compliance

In this model, an FFI that meets the relevant criteria can register directly with the IRS to declare their status. They must, as inferred above, make a formal attestation that they meet the procedural requirements of FATCA.

Types of FFI that are permitted to register this status are:

- Local FFIs
- Non-reporting members of P-FFI groups
- Qualified investment vehicles (QIVs) and
- Restricted funds

As noted above, simply meeting the definitional aspect is not enough. The following shows how this works.

Local FFIs

To meet registered deemed complaint status a local FFI must:

1. Meet certain licencing and regulation requirements
2. Have no fixed place of business outside their country of organisation
3. Not solicit account holders outside their country of organisation
4. More than 98% of account holders must be residents of the FFI's country of organisation
5. The FFI must be subject to withholding and reporting obligations in their own country of organisation
6. The FFI must have policies and procedures in place to preclude US persons who are not residents of the country of FFI's organisation

There are a couple of interesting things in this list worth noting. First, IRS has already signalled that, as far as the European Union (EU) is concerned, for the purpose of the definition of local FFI, the EU is essentially one country. This means that, as far as 3 and 4 go, FFIs in the EU can solicit customers in any other EU Member State and have less than 98% of customers in their own jurisdiction—and still be considered to be eligible for deemed compliant status.

Non-reporting Members of a P-FFI Group

This category of registered deemed compliance applies only to firms that are part of a group and where one or more members of that group are participating FFIs (P-FFIs). The issue here is that there are many firms that are groups where one or more members of the group face difficulty meeting the requirements of FATCA. The most obvious is where one member of the group is organised in a country which does not allow a financial firm to send data about its customers to a foreign government in the form of a report. Clearly, this creates a problem for those members of the group that want to, and are capable of being fully fledged P-FFIs. So, the rules here are relatively simple. To be able to register as deemed compliant, you must:

1. Ensure that there is at least one P-FFI in your group;
2. Transfer all pre-existing US accounts to that P-FFI
3. Within 90 days of any new US account being opened, transfer the account to the P-FFI

It's also important to understand that the single country and non-solicitation criteria that apply for local FFIs do not apply in this circumstance.

Qualified Investment Vehicles

This category of registered deemed compliance is reserved for those investment vehicles that:

1. Are regulated as collective investment schemes and where
2. All direct interest holders in the QIV are:

    (a) P-FFIs
    (b) Deemed compliant FFIs or
    (c) Exempt beneficial owners

Restricted Funds

The final type of FFI that can apply for registered deemed compliant status is restricted funds. There are a number of criteria that need to be met before a fund can satisfy this requirement.

1. The fund must be regulated as an investment fund by its country of organisation
2. Each distributor of the fund must be one of the following:

    (a) A P-FFI
    (b) A registered deemed compliant FFI
    (c) A non-registering local bank
    (d) A restricted distributor

3. All distribution agreements must prohibit sales to US persons, N-P-FFIs and passive NFFEs
4. Prospectuses for these funds must also reflect the distribution agreements in terms of their restrictions.

Certified Deemed Compliance

If, as an FFI, you do not fall into one of the categories that permit registering for deemed compliant status, all is not lost. You may be able to meet the criteria for certified deemed compliance. Certified deemed compliance is open to the following types of FFI:

- Non-registering local banks
- Retirement plans
- Non-profit organisations
- Owner documented FFIs
- FFIs with low-value accounts

The difference between registered deemed compliance and certified deemed compliance is that registered status is by registration with the IRS. Certified DC status is obtained by making a certification to a withholding agent. There is no communication to the IRS. Equally, it is therefore theoretically possible that an FFI that meets the criteria may certify DC status to one withholding agent, but not another. The certification itself is via the revised form W-8. SAs in the previous section, we will review the criteria necessary for an FFI to meet certified DC status.

Non-registering Local Banks

To meet the criteria to be a Certified Deemed-Compliant FFI (C-DCFFI), a non-registering local bank must:

1. Offer only basic banking services;
2. Operate only in their country of organisation;
3. Have balance sheet assets of less than $175 million and, if they are part of an expanded affiliate group, their total group balance sheet assets must be less than $500 million.

It's easy to see both here and in registered deemed compliant status how the criteria have been developed to isolate truly local financial firms from the more global.

Retirement Plans

In the last two years one of the most vociferous interest groups pushing back on FATCA was the pension industry and not least because the definition of a retirement plan in the US is different from the definition of a pension plan. That discrepancy led to some concerns. In the regulations, this has to some extent been mitigated by defining retirement plans (including pension plans) as capable of certified deemed compliant status. However, of all the types of firm able to have C-DCFFI status, retirement plans have the most complex criteria to fulfil. They are:

1. The plan must be organised as a pension plan or retirement plan in its country of establishment or operation;
2. Contributions to the plan must:

    (a) Be limited by reference to earned income and be sourced only from one or more of—the employer, employee or government
    (b) Be excluded from 'income' of the beneficiary and/or taxation of the attributable income must be deferred
    (c) Be sourced at least 50% from employer or government

3. No single beneficiary can be entitled to more than 5% of the assets of the plan.

Non-profits

Another class of C-DCFFI are non-profits. To be eligible for this status, the FFI must:

1. Be established and maintained in its country of residence
2. Have exclusive purposes, for example, religious, charitable, artistic, scientific and cultural
3. Have no shareholders or members with proprietary interests and
4. Be subject to restrictions on private inurement of assets or income.

Low-Value FFIs

One of the main thrusts of these carve-out provisions is to remove from the equation, any account types that either represent a low risk of tax evasion or where the amounts involved are so de-minimis that it's more effort than it's worth to pursue. The final type of certified deemed compliance is for those FFIs that only have low-value accounts.

To qualify for this type of deemed compliance, the FFI must:

1. Have no financial account with a balance of more than $50,000 and, if the FFI is also part of an expanded affiliate group,
2. The EAG must have less than $50 million in assets on its balance sheet.

As a final remark on these two broad categories of deemed compliance, I would remind the reader that the mitigation of the regulations is only with respect to withholding.

NFFEs

Most of the carve-outs that IRS has given are to FFIs. The population of FFIs will far exceed the population of NFFEs—non-financial foreign entities. However, both for FFIs that have to document them and for the NFFEs themselves, there is one 'carve-out' of note.

The IRS has defined two types of NFFE—Passive and Active. Every time I describe the difference I get the same quizzical look, because the difference is not intuitive. Consider a firm that makes widgets. It may be very successful at making widgets and accrues large cash balances. It would be natural for such a firm to make the most of its cash balances and invest the money. So, this firm's income is made up of revenue from widget sales and revenue from investments. There's a second element to the calculation here. We must now also look at the assets of the company and ensure that less than 50% of the assets produce 'passive' income. In this case, as long as both these conditions are met, the NFFE is 'active' (A-NFFE). I like to phrase it as—it 'actively' makes widgets as its reason for existence. The converse would be any firm that derives more than 50% of its income from investments. These firms are 'passive' NFFEs. It's passive NFFEs that cause the main risk of tax evasion.

Practical Issues

All these carve-outs are all well and good. However, they do create their own problems in a very practical way.

Deemed Compliant FFIs

The most obvious problem is for the entities that supposedly fall into these categories. It's important to remember that being, for example, a QIV does not automatically mean that the fund is deemed compliant. There are a number of steps:

1. Each entity must know that it falls into the definition of an FFI
2. It must know that it falls within a deemed compliance category.
3. It must know what the criteria are for the particular type of deemed compliance.
4. It must apply those criteria to its status to determine whether it meets those criteria

5. If it does meet the criteria, it must apply the rules to gain that status:

    (a) provide a certification to its withholding agent(s) if it is of a type for certified deemed compliance or
    (b) register with the IRS if it is of a type for registered deemed compliance

6. if the criteria for any given status can change with time, it must put in place controls to monitor how these changes could affect its deemed compliant status and finally,
7. if it does not meet the criteria for deemed compliant status, it must decide whether to 'participate' and sign an FFI Agreement with the IRS or become a non-participating FFI by default

I have expounded this process in some detail because it makes it that much clearer that there continues to be a need for a process of education or research by means of which the FFI understands that it even has this problem.

So the main practical issue here is one of awareness. Certainly, the traditional financial institutions at which these type 3 entities would have accounts will create some downward awareness, since they will need to know the status of their customer under IRC Chapter 4 also.

FFIs

In this context, an FFI would be the traditional financial institutions at which a deemed compliant FFI would have accounts. The deemed compliant concept can cause problems here too.

The most obvious is systemic. In order to truly 'know' and manage their customer accounts, types 1 and 2 FFIs will need to have technology systems capable of assigning deemed compliant status to their customers. This will be difficult enough. However, as noted, some of the criteria for this status can change with time or other factors. A type 1 or 2 FFI will therefore need to have systems which can manage changes in deemed compliant status together with the changes in processing, reporting and withholding that these might entail.

And so we see that while deemed compliant status may remove workload and risk, its very structure creates workload and risk in other areas.

Intergovernmental Agreements (IGAs)

The IGAs were originally heralded as a massive simplification of FATCA. That said, the reason for IGAs was not simplification. It was the US' response to a backlash over data privacy concerns by many governments and the EU.

Most of the text of the IGAs provides no benefit over non-IGA markets in terms of the core requirements to perform due diligence, have a FATCA status and report. There are however some noteworthy observations.

Suspension of Withholding

The precursor to this section is to remind readers that FATCA withholding is imposed only on US-sourced FDAP income and then only on recalcitrant account holders or non-participating FFIs. So, while there is an IRC Chapter 4 impact in that recalcitrants and NP-FFIs must be reported in FATCA, there is an overlap to the QI regulations because the application of the penalties is reported via the forms 1042-S and 1042 as part of the reporting obligations of a qualified intermediary (QI) or non-qualified intermediary (NQI). With that in mind, the following represents one of those strategies that look like they may simplify FATCA but in actual fact, they just increase risk.

Most IGAs contain a clause that provides a suspension of FATCA penalties applicable to recalcitrant account holders (i.e. recalcitrant individuals and entities). It's important to understand the contingent nature of this clause. On the one hand, the existence of a suspension on penalties is a good thing because it offers the chance to simplify FATCA for those accounts where the FFI in IRC Chapter 4 also acts as a QI in IRC Chapter 3. In other words, you'd normally expect an operational response to preclude ever having recalcitrant accounts in order to avoid having to have a 30% FATCA rate pool account at a US withholding agent and the consequent increase in 1042-S reports.

To some extent therefore, some FFIs consider that the suspension removes the need for this robust policy. However, many of these same FFIs miss the fact that the suspension is contingent on those recalcitrant account holders being reported as such in FATCA (whether individually or as part of a recalcitrant pool).

If you have recalcitrant account holders (because you think there's no withholding problem) but you fail to report them in FATCA, then the criterion for the suspension on withholding is not met and FATCA penalties must be applied. So, it's important, in any event, that those people who extract data and prepare FATCA reports ensure that any recalcitrants are included. If not, the result would be that there could be under-withholding and inaccurate reporting, both of which attract penalties and are material failures under IRC Chapter 3 as well as demonstrating a lack of effective controls for a Responsible Officer.

Reporting

The IGAs for the most part make efforts through defining timing, method and responsible parties for reporting to be conducted to domestic Competent Authorities (usually the tax authority) so that an FFI is not breaking domestic law by passing reportable client information to its own tax authority. While this is helpful in the overall scheme of things, it provides little or no operational benefit to any FFI mainly because the format and encryption of the data tends to be the same wherever the data is going.

Guidance

The IGAs do provide one opportunity where simplification, if not easier understanding, is the benefit. As a result of IGAs, jurisdictions have had to take the IGA text (as between governments) and translate this into domestic statute so that their financial institutions are directly subject to its force.

In non-IGA jurisdictions the relationship is a contractual one directly between the P-FFI and the IRS.

So, in an IGA jurisdiction 'US FATCA' does not apply. What applies is the domestic statute that replicates FATCA becoming effectively 'Domestic FATCA'. In these jurisdictions it is common for the tax authorities to take a more active role in providing guidance notes to domestic FFIs on how the domestic FATCA should be interpreted. That means that, often, FATCA is being explained within a domestic context so cultural and linguistic issues are, for the most part, removed.

In concluding this chapter, I observe that 'simplifying FATCA' is in itself something of an oversimplification. Tier 1 large FFIs and EAGs will always have the most complex exposure to FATCA because of their nature as cross-border operational entities with highly complex client structures in multi-cultural and multi-lingual environments. The single brand identities of these large groups do not mean equivalent simplification of regulation. At the other end of the spectrum tier 3 FFIs that are single jurisdiction with little exposure to either the US securities markets or to US investors should be able to slide into relatively simple levels of FATCA provided by many of the carve-outs mentioned in this chapter. In between, for tier 2 financial institutions, FATCA is most complex because even a small exposure to a risk category carries the full weight of the regulatory controls, that is, there is no real 'FATCA-Lite'. The best you can do, in all circumstances, is spend time and effort being aware of the structure of FATCA, keep track of how it's changing and make intelligent, informed decisions that reduce your exposure to either risk, operational cost or both.

14

FATCA Withholding

In this chapter we will look at the main 'stick' that the US government has to enforce Foreign Account Tax Compliance Act (FATCA).

FATCA withholding is reserved for two types of account holder—recalcitrant and non-participating foreign financial institutions (NP-FFIs).

Recalcitrance

This is defined term in the regulations, but effectively means an account holder that has not given an FFI the information it reasonably requested in order to determine the account holder's IRC Chapter 4 status. By definition recalcitrant is a term reserved for account holders that are either individuals or entities. Financial institutions cannot be recalcitrant. They can only be NP-FFI for the purpose of FATCA withholding.

NP-FFI

The moniker of NP-FFI can apply in more than one circumstance, which will be described here, but FATCA withholding applies to NP-FFIs by default.

An NP-FFI is most common as a financial institution, resident in a non-intergovernmental agreement (IGA) jurisdiction that has not signed an FFI Agreement with the Internal Revenue Service (IRS). In effect, by adopting this status, they are saying that they do not accept any of the obligations to find and report US persons to the IRS. Therefore, the US position is simple and 30% FATCA withholding must apply to US-sourced Fixed, Determinable, Annual or Periodic (FDAP) income paid to any NP-FFI.

However, there are also circumstances in which an FFI in an IGA jurisdiction can end up being 'presumed' to be an NP-FFI if it fails to meet its FFI obligations. The most common of these is the provision of an IRC Chapter 4 withholding statement to an upstream FFI. This most commonly occurs when the financial institution concerned is an non-qualified intermediary (NQI) in IRC Chapter 3 but a P-FFI in IRC Chapter 4. As such, the regulations provide that the NQI must disclose its underlying beneficial owners and importantly, part of that requirement includes a Chapter 4 withholding rate pool. If the financial institution fails, in its NQI obligations, to provide an IRC Chapter 4 withholding statement, then the upstream financial institution, using the rule of applying IRC Chapter 4 first then IRC Chapter 3, must presume their client to be an NP-FFI in IRC Chapter 4 (even if they have a W-8IMY with a Global Intermediary Identification Number [GIIN]) and apply a 30% FATCA penalty before proceeding to IRC Chapter 3 (where there would be nothing to do under the principle of non-duplicative taxation).

As you might expect, operationally, the larger organisations are certainly adopting policies to preclude, as far as possible, any recalcitrance or the presence of NP-FFIs. This is happening at lower levels in the chain too, but at these lower levels, it is much more difficult. This is because, at the higher levels in the chain, US withholding agents and large FFIs (e.g. expanded affiliate groups) are much more likely only to have other FFIs as customers. At lower levels, the proportion of an FFI's customer base, presuming them to also be traditional FIs (e.g. banks and brokers), is more likely to include a large proportion of direct customers that might be non-financial foreign entities (NFFEs) or individuals. If the FFIs down the chain are not traditional FIs, then the point in the chain that this workload (and risk) occurs is much higher up.

So, at some point there is likely to be documentation going on where the information available to an FFI is insufficient or, where there are US indicia, the explanation for these indicia is insufficient. At this point FATCA withholding must take place.

So, it's ironic that while the US position is that it would want all financial institutions signed up to its anti-tax evasion strategy, it's actually achieving this indirectly via the top echelons of the financial institutions not being willing to do business with other financial firms if they are either (1) an NQI in IRC Chapter 3 and/or (2) a P-FFI in IRC Chapter 4.

Purpose

The point of FATCA withholding is to penalise recalcitrant account holders and NP-FFIs and essentially incentivise them to provide required information or adopt P-FFI status respectively. In the IRC Chapter 3 world of QIs and NQIs, you may remember that I pointed out that most wealthy Americans would view the 30% withholding tax on FDAP income as a 'good deal' because, if they were to invest in the US and declare their income, they'd be more likely to suffer a tax rate between 40% and 50% or more even in current US administration's tax reduction strategy. In the world of IRC Chapter 4 (FATCA) the 30% withholding still applies, but it's only the starting point, not the ending point. While it's a personal viewpoint and is challenged by some of the accounting firms, I remain of the firm belief that it's important to understand that FATCA withholding is *not* a tax. It's a penalty applied for failure to comply with documentation procedures. The penalty is, it's true, applied via the tax system, but this is not a tax on income based on the taxability of that income. Now, the opponents to this view point out that one could probably take the position that you would have to presume, as a default, that a recalcitrant account holder is *probably* an American engaged in tax evasion. In which case, the IRS is missing out on tax from this person and that, therefore, the FATCA withholding on this account is in lieu of domestic US tax that the IRS would expect to receive. There is some logic to this, since the regulations also say that FATCA withholding can be 'reclaimed', but only as an offset to a US tax liability. This latter of course presumes that the account holder who was penalised has a US tax liability in the first place. The converse of this rule is of course that any recalcitrant account holder who is not US will be unable to reclaim any FATCA withholding that was applied.

The IRS has gone to some pains to point out that it does not seek the revenue from penalties as a goal of FATCA; it would prefer to have compliance to the core principles of the regulations. This further distances FATCA withholding from a true tax. That said, if one reviews the US Treasury estimates of the amount of money expected to be received by the US from FATCA withholding, the number is a significant number of billions of dollars. At a time of financial crisis and a debt of over $22 trillion (as at March 2019), it would be easy to see why some commentators would have difficulty accepting the IRS position.

FDAP

In IRC Chapter 3, we came across the concept of FDAP income. This is an acronym that stands for any income that is Fixed, Determinable, Annual or Periodic. For the purposes of most investors, this equates to dividends and bond interest, although the IRS has over 20 different income codes that fall into the FDAP category. Importantly 'gross proceeds' are not included in the definition of FDAP and prior attempts by the IRS to impose FATCA penalties to gross proceeds have now been abandoned.

This means that, if an account holder is recalcitrant or an NP-FFI, an FFI will have to calculate and withhold 30% on future payments of dividends and interest (FDAP).

Systems Issues

As one might imagine, all of FATCA poses problems of a varying scale and scope depending on your status and position in the chain of accounts. Therefore the types of systems issue that might flow from FATCA withholding depend on where you are in that chain and what your status is.

FATCA Withholding Not a Tax

One of the most difficult systems issues is that the tax being withheld is (1) not a tax and (2) must be applied with the non-duplicative rules (see later). This has importance because many of the tax-related data elements in most institutions' books of record are also connected to domestic reporting requirements. It's therefore important to ensure that there is no contamination between deductions from income resulting from tax as opposed to a penalty.

This is made more complex for institutions higher up the chain because of the many types of exemption and exception being granted—the so-called deemed compliance. While this provides some relief from withholding complexities, it does mean that larger organisations must have better ways of documenting this deemed compliance among the population of their clients so that they know which accounts can be withheld and which do not need to be withheld.

In similar vein, the matrix of system flags also becomes complex because FFIs higher up the chain will also be more likely to come across clients who are not only deemed compliant but also may be resident in FATCA Partner countries.

Of course, traditional financial institutions will have basic banking or brokerage systems in place from which these types of system issues can be resolved through development. Software and outsource vendors are also very active in understanding these challenges to provide solutions to these firms. The real challenges are in the lower level FFI population.

Non-duplicative Taxation

There is a connection between IRC Chapter 3 and IRC Chapter 4. In fact, as time goes by, it's clear that the number of points where IRC Chapter 3 and IRC Chapter 4 converge is increasing. However, in cash terms, there is a principle underlying IRC Chapter 3 and IRC Chapter 4 called the principle of non-duplicative taxation. I find this rather incongruous since FATCA withholding is a penalty not a tax, whereas the tax withheld in IRC Chapter 3 is a true tax. Nevertheless, in principle, if an account holder is subject to a 30% tax in IRC Chapter 4 (by being recalcitrant or NP-FFI), then there is no further taxation imposed by reason of IRC Chapter 3. This makes sure that an income payment cannot be taxed at 60% by applying a penalty under one IRC Chapter, then adding the tax in the other IRC Chapter.

Reporting

While withholding in IRC Chapter 4 is a penalty, that penalty is applied via the withholding tax system that otherwise applies to IRC Chapter 3, that is, via 1042-S and 1042.

In its clarifications in December 2018, the IRS responded to concerns that NP-FFIs that were penalised in FATCA were receiving forms 1042-S that reported the withholding as a penalty. This, in turn, when reported similarly by the FFI to its clients meant that those underlying clients could not offset the penalty against their domestic taxes. It's interesting to note here a difference between recalcitrant withholding and NP-FFI withholding. FATCA penalties on recalcitrant account holders, when applied, are the result of the actions (or lack thereof) of the account holder that is being penalised. On the other hand, the FATCA penalty applied to NP-FFIs is applied to institution itself without regard to the actions of that institution's clients (who may well be properly documented). In other words, the NP-FFIs are penalised simply because of their status, however, the entity does not pay the penalty, it's the underlying clients of the NP-FFI that pay the cost.

The IRS clarification allows an NP-FFI receiving a 1042-S that categorises payments as withheld in IRC Chapter 4, to issue 1042-S forms to its clients that effectively re-categorise the penalty into an IRC Chapter 3 withholding.

So, in concluding this chapter, we have learned that:

1. FATCA withholding is a penalty and is applied at one rate—30%
2. FATCA withholding only affects recalcitrant accounts and NP-FFIs;
3. Most IGAs provide a suspension on FATCA penalties on recalcitrant accounts (but not NP-FFIs);
4. The IGA suspension is contingent on recalcitrants being reported in FATCA;
5. Any penalties applied are reported on forms 1042-S and 1042
6. NP-FFIs that receive such forms can re-categorise the penalty to an IRC Chapter 3 withholding for their direct clients.

Overall, FATCA penalties, while they started out being a big stick, have reduced in importance over the years as the industry has increasingly adopted anti-risk measures so that FATCA penalties are now much rarer than they were. That's because of the IGA suspension that has removed most recalcitrants from the penalty population, because most firms in IGA jurisdictions do not want to offer accounts to NP-FFIs and finally, the number of non-IGA jurisdictions is relatively small (when considered in context to the US exposure of those jurisdictions).

15

Reporting

Reporting is the fundamental objective of IRC Chapter 4.

Reporting in Foreign Account Tax Compliance Act (FATCA) is the last stage after due diligence, aggregation of financial accounts and application of thresholds following which data extraction takes place of those accounts required to be reported (Fig. 15.1).

The data extracted must then be consolidated and converted into an .xml file that can be sent to the Internal Revenue Service (IRS). In an intergovernmental agreement (IGA) market that will be via a domestic tax authority. In a non-IGA market that will be directly to the IRS' International Data Exchange System (IDES).

The actual data in the reports has changed over the years, increasing each year.

The data reportable is as follows. This is important not just for the issue of data collectability but also for the cyber risk it presents as I will discuss in the next section. Here is a paraphrased summary of the data required.

1. the name, address and US Tax Identification Number (TIN) of each specified US person that is an Account Holder of such account and, in the case of a non-US entity that, after application of the due diligence procedures, is identified as having one or more controlling persons that is a specified US person, the name, address and US TIN (if any) of such entity and each such specified US person;
2. the account number (or functional equivalent in the absence of an account number);
3. the name and identifying number of the Reporting Financial Institution;

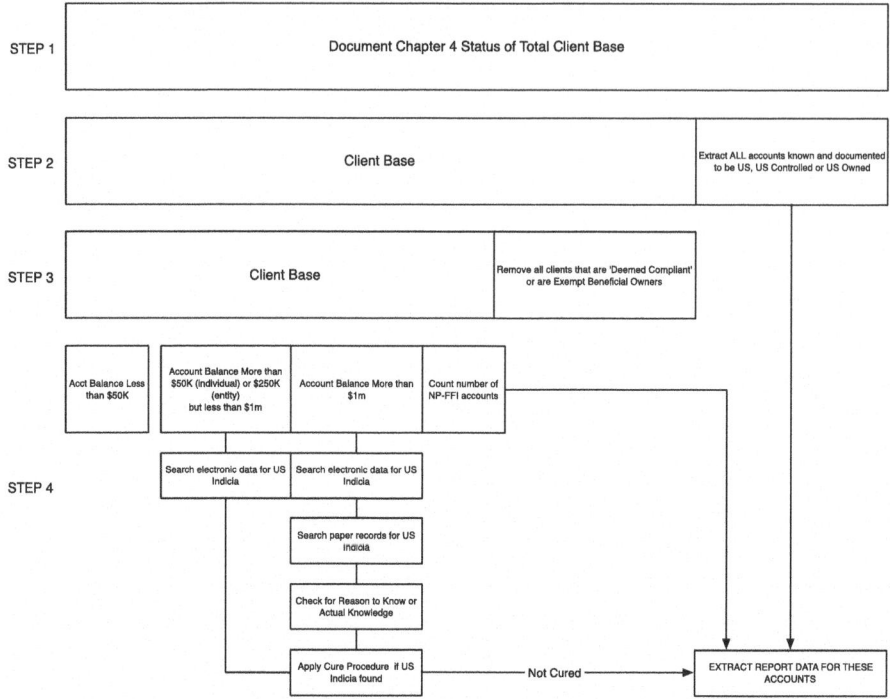

Fig. 15.1 Selection of accounts for FATCA reporting. Source: Author's own

4. the account balance or value (including, in the case of a Cash Value Insurance Contract or Annuity Contract, the Cash Value or surrender value) as of the end of the relevant calendar year or other appropriate reporting period or, if the account was closed during such year, immediately before closure;
5. in the case of any custodial account:

    (a) the total gross amount of interest, the total gross amount of dividends and the total gross amount of other income generated with respect to the assets held in the account, in each case paid or credited to the account (or with respect to the account) during the calendar year or other appropriate reporting period; and

    (b) the total gross proceeds from the sale or redemption of property paid or credited to the account during the calendar year or other appropriate reporting period with respect to which the Reporting Financial Institution acted as a custodian, broker, nominee or otherwise as an agent for the Account Holder;

6. in the case of any Depository Account, the total gross amount of interest paid or credited to the account during the calendar year or other appropriate reporting period; and
7. in the case of any account not described elsewhere, the total gross amount paid or credited to the Account Holder with respect to the account during the calendar year or other appropriate reporting period with respect to which the Reporting Financial Institution is the obligor or debtor, including the aggregate amount of any redemption payments made to the Account Holder during the calendar year or other appropriate reporting period.

All this gets wrapped up in an xml data schema that is too long, too complex and not pertinent to the purpose of this book, to include here. However, it can be found at the IRS website and is updated from time to time and is also now converged with the Organisation for Economic Co-operation and Development (OECD) xml schema for Common Reporting Standard (CRS) reporting.

Issues

The practical issues, which are what this book is concerned with, include:

- Resources
- Timing
- Cyber risk
- Phased implementation

Resources

Most firms are still siloed and by number most firms do not have enough resources to meet most of these reporting requirements. Firms are having to make decisions about how they use their resources.

For example QI, FATCA and CRS all have commonalities. However, FATCA and CRS have commonality of purpose—both being anti-tax evasion frameworks with similar due diligence and reporting models, while QI and FATCA share the commonality of being US centric and use the same withholding and reporting framework for penalties.

In reality, all three should be handled operationally by one function, but this is rarely the case. The result is usually that.

Timing

Reporting in FATCA is usually due around 15 April. This is the same as CRS reporting and also the deadline for QI reporting assuming that financial firms obtained the required extension for the 1042-S reporting. This has two effects.

First is that everyone assumes that reporting is a discrete activity that somehow magically happens on or around the deadline. Nothing could be further from the truth. As we have seen FATCA reporting cycle will start in January with account aggregation and conversion using the spot FX rate published by the IRS. Due diligence at onboarding and via CiC will be ongoing. So the actual report submission will have some feverish level of activity from January through April as firms gather, check and re-check their data, convert for submission and test.

This is exacerbated by the parallel activities going on in the QI and CRS worlds. CRS is probably most easily included within the same project timelines as FATCA. However, if an foreign financial institution (FFI) has accounts to report in FATCA that also had FATCA penalties applied, then the FATCA project has a contingent line of activity going into the 1042-S and 1042 reporting that they will be conducting as either a qualified intermediary (QI) or non-qualified intermediary (NQI). This then becomes logarithmically more complex if the institution is a Qualified Derivatives Dealer (QDD) and has 871(m) exposure. While there is no cascade in pure FATCA reporting, there is a cascade in the reporting of FATCA penalties and in that vertical all the financial institutions in the chain have the same deadline. So, timing is an issue not just to understand for planning purposes, it also has a major impact on resource allocation and budgeting.

Cyber Risk

It's worth considering cyber risk for a moment both at the framework level and at the reporting FFI level. Experience every day in financial services proves that you can't assume that there is a zero risk. So, here, I will comment on the cyber risk associated with the concept of reporting in FATCA.

Figure 15.2 is designed to show cyber risks based on the way in which both FATCA and CRS have been structured. There are three players—the reporting financial institutions, the domestic (HCTA) or host country tax authorities

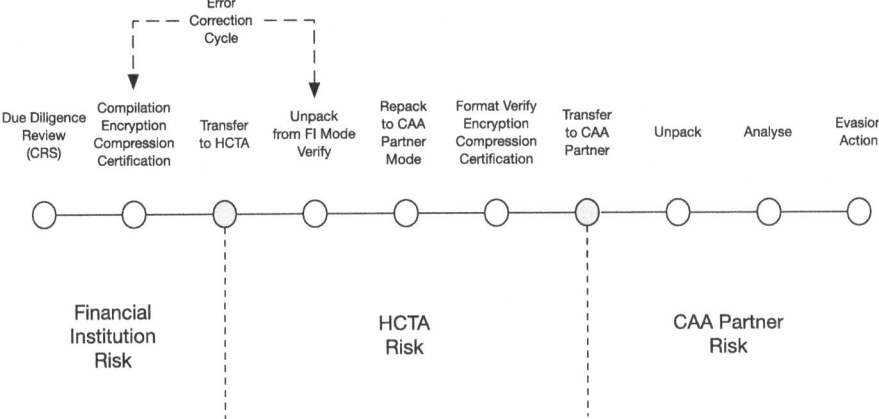

Fig. 15.2 Cyber risk. Source: Author's own

(local tax authorities in a FATCA IGA jurisdiction) and the Competent Authority Partner that would be the US in FATCA and any partner jurisdiction in CRS.

The nature of risk that is created evolves from the fact that data being shared has value to a cybercriminal. The type of risk flows from the number and types of counterparty that are sending and receiving the data.

With respect to the former, I direct the reader to the data that is being shared mentioned earlier in the chapter. The purpose of FATCA is to report US account holders in the expectation that some may be evading tax. Ergo, the data being collected is generally focused on high value accounts of US persons. It includes information that would facilitate many types of criminal activity from basic identity theft to actual theft of assets.

With respect to the latter, we should not fall into the trap where we assume that just because a government agency is a counterparty or that they are defining the data sharing methodology or that they are providing the transfer mechanism itself, that this means that the risk is somehow mitigated or removed.

Overall, the diagram is meant to highlight that in both FATCA and CRS there are many steps at each stage where sensitive data is being collected, aggregated, collated, packed up, compressed, encrypted, tested, submitted, de-crypted, unpacked, re-packaged and analysed before anyone actually looks at the data for the purpose it was collected. At every stage there is risk from every type of cybercriminal and it would be foolish to think that, given the publicity given to FATCA and CRS, the cyber criminals won't figure out the potential value of such data (far greater than retail credit card data) and build strategies to attack that data at one or more points in its travels.

It will be a reputational risk for financial institutions even if they are not the target. A cyber breach at a HCTA or the IRS will inevitably mention who the original aggregator of the data was.

Phased Implementation

In efforts to assuage the financial services community, various aspects of the IRC Chapter 4 regulations have been 'phased in'. This applies not just to reporting, but also to the preceding activity of documentation and the subsequent activity of withholding. As is usual in such matters, while the phasing-in process gave financial institutions some respite from major systems builds and structural re-organisation, phased implementation did bring its own problems with it. It meant that some processes, policies and procedures needed to be changed over time. In terms of reporting, the change is essentially the data detail included in the reports. The latest of these was the abandonment of the withholding on gross proceeds addition to FATCA penalties. While everyone accepts that this is a good thing, the industry spent almost two years preparing for the implementation of the passthru payments method of calculating and applying withholding on gross proceeds which was then removed at the last minute in December 2018. This kind of last minute change does no one any favours. All the efforts to prepare have effectively been wasted. It's interesting that the same efforts are now being made with respect to implementation of 871(m) with a phase in period and 'good faith efforts' requirement. Rather rich (sic) given the passthru payments scenario. Many people believe that 871(m) will continue to undergo change and new transitionary arrangements.

Standards and Automation

I mentioned earlier that FATCA reporting is expressed and delivered in xml, the extended mark-up language. That defines how everyone must communicate and that is based on a standardised taxonomy or dictionary that defines the terms used in the language. The IRS has created an online portal, the International Data Exchange System (IDES), where report files, written in xml using the proper taxonomies, can be delivered. The requirement is also for such data files to be both encrypted and compressed before submission according to defined rules. Incidentally, most IGA tax authorities have adopted identical methodologies so that what they get from their reporting financial institutions is in the same format as the IRS requires of them—which minimises workload. Many tax authorities have also combined this idea for CRS reporting so that you end up with tax authorities having tax reporting portals that receive both CRS and FATCA reports so that they can handle them appropriately, sending FATCA reports to IDES and CRS reports (after unpack, repack and re-encrypt) to their partner jurisdictions.

So, it's clear that a lot of work has gone on to provide automation tools and standards tools to allow these frameworks to operate effectively. In the expectation of good governance, we should hopefully expect either some data from the US and OECD to show how much evaded tax has been caught by these frameworks or a cost-benefit analysis from financial institutions to show on average what the cost increase per account is resulting from all the various aspects of FATCA being included as an operating cost, given that there is no benefit to the institution.

Part III

Related Global Tax Initiatives

16

International Context

In this chapter, I will review, compare and contrast other tax initiatives that have similar elements to the US tax landscape and therefore should be considered as a look into the future of how this industry is likely to evolve in the next few years.

There are two main initiatives I want to consider:

- The OECD TRACE Project and;
- The European Union Withholding Tax Code of Conduct (WTCC).

Of these the Organisation for Economic Co-operation and Development (OECD) project is probably viewed as the more advanced since it has not only established concepts for simplification but also gone some way to showing how the concepts could be delivered in a practical environment through the Tax Relief and Compliance Enhancement (TRACE) Implementation Protocol or 'IP'. It also has the benefit of having been formally adopted by at least one country—Finland in 2019.

Over the last few years, the European Union has had several projects looking at simplifying the withholding tax landscape in and between the Member States. There is a degree of overlap between the Member States and the OECD markets both in terms of countries included and in terms of how the two blocs have approached this thorny issue.

The EU perspective started with the work of Alberto Giovannini who defined the 'barriers to the free movement of capital' within the EU. Subsequent groups were set up to look at different aspects of these 'hurdles', one of which was the Fiscal Compliance group or 'FISCO'.

FISCO's report in 2009 made a series of top-level recommendations which were then picked up by a group called the Tax Barriers Business Advisory Group (T-BAG), of which the author was a contributory member and editor of the final report. T-BAG reported to the European Commission in February 2013 with more detailed analysis of the ways in which a simplified approach to withholding tax could be adopted by Member States. The ideas and concepts and principles of these various groups were ultimately recommended for implementation via either an EU Directive or a Voluntary Adoption Programme.

In 2017, the EU Commission issued a Code of Conduct for withholding tax that is a non-binding document calling on EU Member States to 'consider' adopting the Code which, by the EU's own admission, is a 'compilation of approaches' designed to improve the efficiency of withholding tax procedures.

The 2013 report and subsequent Code of Conduct are important in the context of this book for two reasons. First, there are clear similarities between the results and recommendations of the T-BAG Report and the existing framework of the US' IRC Chapters 3 and 4. Second, the nature of the way in which the US, the OECD and the EU are converging these frameworks is to include the concepts of tax withholding on income (which would have its own reporting regime) and that of detection of tax evasion through reporting by foreign intermediaries.

The overall impact I want to get over here is that the majority of this book is talking about the US tax system and how it's changing more rapidly than ever before. It's perhaps an unintended consequence, but other markets have taken a long hard look at both the IRC Chapter 3 and IRC Chapter 4 rules and adopted many of the principles into withholding tax concepts which will fundamentally affect the way that withholding tax is handled in the major markets over the next five to ten years.

To the extent that this is already happening, I have included both the EU and OECD initiative as separate chapters so that the reader has a grasp of the US scenario and is also able to compare and contrast this with the other initiatives currently 'in play'.

In Table 16.1, I have tried to reduce these initiatives down to their 'key elements' for simple comparison.

In addition to the table, I think it's also useful to have an enumerated summary of the key elements of the OECD and EU models. Each of these is further explained in more detail in the following sections.

Table 16.1 Comparison of TRACE IP, FATCA, QI and code of conduct

	US	US	OECD	EU
Market(s)				
Project name	IRC Chapter 3	IRC Chapter 4	TRACE IP	T-BAG Code of Conduct
Stage	In force (2001)	In force (2013)	Approved January 2013	2017
Markets	1	1	34	27
Primary today	Relief at source	Deter tax evasion	Combination withholding	Combination withholding
Intended	Relief at source	Deter tax evasion	Relief at source	Relief at source or refund
Projects commenced	2001	2009	2006	2009
Structure	Qualified intermediary	Participating foreign financial intermediary	Authorised intermediary	Authorised intermediary or BO claims
Legal form	Commercial contract between IRS and financial institution	Domestic statute (IGA markets) Commercial contract between IRS and financial institution (non-IGA markets)	Contract with source country	Contract with a Member State
Qualifiers	KYC rules must be approved	Jurisdiction must have a DTT or TIEA with US	KYC rules must be approved	None
Documentation	KYC and self-certification	Due diligence to identify US financial accounts	Investor self-declaration	TIN, KYC, self-certification and PoAs
Transmission	Electronic	Electronic	Electronic	Electronic
Standard	Proprietary	Proprietary	ISO20022	Any
Withholding	By QI as a tax	By P-FFI as a penalty	By AI as a tax agent	By AI as a tax agent

(continued)

Table 16.1 (continued)

Reporting	Tax return + Information reports To source country Annual Some pooling Mixture of paper & electronic Proprietary standard	US persons plus numbers of recalcitrant accounts Domestic routing in IGA markets. Direct to IRS elsewhere. Electronic reporting XML standard	Information reports To source country or via domestic regulator Annual	None
Control and Oversight	Periodic Review and triennial certification	None	AUP	None
Reclaims	Not encouraged other than as a collective refund by QIs on 1042 Manual 3–8 months repayment	Only in limited circumstances	Standardised Electronic 6 months repayment	Standardised Electronic 6 months repayment

Source: Author's own

OECD TRACE IP

Let's get the obvious out of the way first. What is TRACE? TRACE is an acronym of Tax Relief and Compliance Enhancement. 'IP' is the Implementation Protocol which details how the TRACE Group believes the industry can move from acceptance of the principles of simplification, standardisation and automation into a real business environment.

What follows in this chapter is an edited extract from the OECD TRACE IP document showing the work that this group has done and proposes to do in regard to withholding tax simplification across the OECD Member States.

Background

In 2006, the Committee on Fiscal Affairs (CFA) and the Business and Industry Advisory Committee (BIAC) agreed to pursue work on improving the process by which portfolio investors could claim treaty benefits. To this end, an Informal Consultative Group (ICG) made up of government representatives and experts from the business community was created. The initial two-year mandate of the ICG had two aspects: (1) legal and policy issues, primarily relating to the extent to which either collective investment vehicles (CIVs) or their investors are entitled to treaty benefits; and (2) procedural aspects regarding claims for treaty benefits when assets are held indirectly, whether through CIVs or through nominees and custodians.

The ICG prepared two reports. The first report (Granting of Treaty Benefits with respect to the Income of Collective Investment Vehicles), which addresses the technical issues relating to treaty qualification of income earned by CIVs, made a series of concrete recommendations regarding the technical issues relating to the treaty eligibility of collective investment vehicles. This work was pursued by Working Party No. 1 of the CFA, which deals with tax treaty issues. The ICG also concluded that the approaches recommended in that report, several of which would allow a CIV to make claims for benefits on behalf of its investors, would depend on the development of practical and reliable procedures for determining ownership of interests in CIVs and of securities held through other intermediated structures. The second report (Possible Improvements to Procedures for Tax Relief for Cross-Border Investors) discusses the procedural problems in claiming treaty benefits faced by portfolio investors more generally and included a number of recommendations regarding best practices regarding procedures for making and granting claims for treaty benefits for intermediated structures. The objective of the work on best practices is two-fold:

1. to develop systems that are as efficient as possible, in order to minimise administrative costs and allocate the costs to the appropriate parties; and
2. to identify solutions that do not threaten, and that ideally enhance, countries' abilities to ensure proper compliance with tax obligations, from the perspective of both source and residence countries.

The ICG recommended that further work be undertaken to promote substantial uniformity across source countries in terms of the format used for reporting to multiple source countries, procedures to be followed by the intermediary to confirm the identity and treaty eligibility of their clients, and other compliance procedures, including liability issues. The basis for the proposed work was to develop these documents on the basis of the best practices as recommended in the second ICG Report, while taking account of any difficulties concerning the feasibility of the proposals in the report. In January 2009, the CFA approved the formation of a Pilot Group made up of government delegates and business representatives to pursue this work. In December 2009, the Pilot Group produced a draft of the Implementation Package in fulfilment of its mandate.

In January 2010 the CFA decided to release the Pilot Group's draft for public consultation and established a dedicated TRACE Group, made up of government delegates, to further develop the Pilot Group's draft Implementation Package in close consultation with a standing Advisory Group of business representatives.

This revised version of the Implementation Package takes into account the comments received on the Pilot Group's draft; it was approved by the TRACE Group in December 2012 and by the CFA in January 2013.

Outline of the IP

The system produced by the adoption of the Implementation Package would allow authorised intermediaries to claim exemptions or reduced rates of withholding tax—pursuant to tax treaties or domestic law on a pooled basis on behalf of their customers that are portfolio investors. One of the major benefits to intermediaries of such a system is that information regarding the beneficial owner of the income may be maintained by the intermediary with the most direct account relationship with the beneficial owner, rather than being passed up the chain of intermediaries. Accordingly, intermediaries in the chain can facilitate withholding tax relief claims for their customers, without passing proprietary customer information to potential competitors (i.e. the other intermediaries). Investors would be able to indicate their entitlement to exemptions or reduced rates of withholding tax by providing a standardised investor self-declaration to the intermediary with respect to which they have a customer relationship, without procuring a certificate of residence. Improving automatic exchange of information could replace any lingering source country requirements for certificates of residence by providing a more robust process for checking eligibility to withholding tax relief, thereby reducing administrative costs for source countries, residence countries, investors and intermediaries. Accordingly, the system also eliminates the time and expense of handling large amounts of paper. By reducing inefficiencies, the system would make it more likely that investors will in fact obtain withholding tax relief in a timely manner.

The Implementation Package is designed so that the system can be used for claiming withholding tax relief offered under tax treaties and domestic law of the source countries. However, there may be circumstances in which countries consider it more appropriate for certain types of domestic law relief to be provided through some other mechanism (e.g., where the conditions for relief are complex and would be difficult to verify by the Authorised Intermediary). The Implementation Package allows for this, although countries are encouraged to apply the system to as many forms of relief as possible in order to promote the efficiencies the system is designed to promote.

The Implementation Package requires an intermediary that wants to claim benefits on a pooled basis to provide to the source country tax administrators (on an annual basis, not at the time of payment) investor-specific information regarding the beneficial owners of the income. The information to be provided to the source country would include details of the income received, name and address of the beneficial owner, and, where the investor's residence country issues taxpayer identification numbers, that Tax Identification Number (TIN), or such other identifying information as the residence country uses to identify individual taxpayers. Where appropriate arrangements are in place and where the source country and the AI's country agree, it is contemplated that a source country may allow an AI to fulfil its reporting obligations to the source country by reporting the required information to the tax authority of the AI's country, which would then exchange the information on an automatic basis with the source country. Once that information is received by the source country government, it is expected that the source country will provide it to the government of the investor's residence country through automatic exchange of information programmes. Ideally, the latter country, to the extent it receives the information in a timely fashion, will inform the source country soon thereafter if the investor who purports to be a resident thereof in fact is not. Governments adopting the system are encouraged to agree on the timing and modalities of such exchange of information by entering into a Memorandum of Understanding, based on a model developed by the OECD. This way the Implementation Package would provide a robust process by which both source and residence countries could determine whether income for which withholding tax relief is being claimed is in fact eligible for such relief and also whether it is being taken into account by the investor when it prepares its residence country tax returns. Countries that have received such investor-specific information would have the tools necessary to focus their further inquiries on the specific taxpayers that may present issues. Compliance by the authorised intermediaries with their obligations under their arrangement with the source country would be verified by an independent reviewer, in accordance with agreed procedures.

The source country would, of course, control which intermediaries could act as authorised intermediaries. A financial intermediary wishing to act as an authorised intermediary would make an application to the source country, which would then approve or deny it. An intermediary would have to represent that it is subject to Know-Your-Customer rules that are consistent with specified Anti-Money Laundering principles (though not necessarily identical to those principles) and an authorised intermediary can only operate through offices that are subject to such rules and that are located in countries that have been approved by the source country. An authorised intermediary would also have to agree to be subject to an independent review of its compliance with its obligations to the source country. An intermediary that does not become an authorised intermediary would be allowed to make claims for benefits through an authorised intermediary, but would have to provide customer information to the authorised intermediary in order to do so. Moreover, the source country could, in certain circumstances, prohibit an intermediary from making claims where the intermediary's past conduct has demonstrated that information provided by the intermediary is unreliable.

Although the primary means by which reduced withholding would be claimed would be through relief at source, situations will remain in which an investor will be subject to full withholding at the time of payment and will need to make a claim for refund. The Implementation Package therefore also provides standardised procedures for the authorised intermediaries to make claims on behalf of their account holders. Governments would endeavour to process the claim and make payment as soon as possible but should not delay payment beyond six months after the request for refund, and all necessary information from the account holder and the authorised intermediary have been received, except in unusual circumstances.

The ICG Report notes that, although it is possible for a source country to adopt some, but not all, of the best practices, in many cases the practices are inter-related. This is especially true with respect to the Implementation Package. For example, certain procedures, such as the procedures for independent review, are appropriate and work correctly only against the backdrop of the safeguards provided by information reporting to the source country. Accordingly, while there are some modifications that are relatively easy to make, countries should be cautious in picking and choosing pieces of the Implementation Package, particularly if intending to delete a requirement. One exception to this general rule relates to the model mutual agreements regarding the treatment of collective investment vehicles. These model mutual agreements provide procedures for determining the ownership of collective investment vehicles that are compatible with, but not dependent on, adoption of the procedures set out in the Implementation Package. That is, a source country could adopt the relief at source system provided in the Implementation Package without entering into any mutual agreements relating to the treatment of collective investment vehicles (although questions could arise in that case about the proper treatment of collective investment vehicles, as discussed below). Conversely, a source country could enter into mutual agreements, or new treaties that utilise the procedures in the model mutual agreements, without implementing the relief at source system first.

Contents of the IP

The ICG Report concluded that the most efficient way for the best practices to be implemented was through individual source countries entering into contracts with financial intermediaries. The Implementation Package consists of a self-contained set of all the agreements and forms that would pass between a source country and the financial intermediaries and investors participating in the system.

The following documents make up the Implementation Package:

- An application to be completed by a financial intermediary requesting authorisation from a particular source country to act as an authorised intermediary and providing certain information about the financial intermediary that the source country government will need in order to decide whether to enter into an agreement with the financial intermediary;
- The contract between the source country and the financial intermediary;

- Agreed procedures that the authorised intermediary would follow in implementing the system, including rules on the extent of the authorised intermediary's liability for any under-withholding of tax;
- The forms to be used under the system, including:
    - Separate investor self-declarations for individuals and for entities;
    - Intermediary declarations to be provided by authorised intermediaries, which may pass on pooled information, and by other intermediaries, which can make claims only by passing on their customers' investor self-declarations;
    - Forms to be used for annual information reporting with respect to investors and with respect to other authorised intermediaries;
    - A year-end summary to be filed at the same time as the annual information reports, aggregating the information contained in those reports;
    - Forms to be used for claiming refunds when it has not been possible to claim relief at source and for notifying the authorised intermediary that a refund has been made (or has been denied);
    - A description of the procedures to be followed by the independent reviewer;
    - Additional procedures to be followed by an authorised intermediary that has also taken on primary withholding responsibilities; and
    - Model mutual agreements providing procedures applicable to CIVs. The documents are drafted so as to minimise the amount of material that will be customised from country to country. Accordingly, the agreement between the authorised intermediary and the source country government is relatively short, containing primarily that information that is specific to individual authorised intermediaries (such as their mailing addresses and name of independent reviewer) or to specific source countries (such as rules regarding the geographic scope of the arrangements and statutes of limitations). The longest document, on procedures to be followed by an authorised intermediary, should be the same from source country to source country, except for the insertion of the name of the relevant source country. To that end, the procedures deal with the simplest case, with options that create complications (e.g., taking on primary withholding responsibility) found in annexes and appendices. It is acceptable and expected for intermediaries to conform the formatting and presentation of the forms to other documents presented to their customers, particularly other documents completed as part of an account-opening package, as long as all the information in the form is included in the same order.

Adoption of the IP

While the documents in the Implementation Package are self-contained, in many circumstances the source country will need to modify its domestic law in order to adopt the system. Some countries have indicated that they would have to change their domestic law in order to allow the contractual agreements contemplated by the Implementation Package.

Others have indicated that they would implement the system by incorporating the procedures into their domestic law or regulations. In that case, there would not be a contract between the source country and the financial intermediary but financial intermediaries would apply to the source country and would be approved to act as authorised intermediaries. It appears that the documents in the Implementation Package could be adapted relatively readily by a country pursuing such an administrative approach. In that case, the application to become an authorised intermediary would likely be quite similar to the one provided in the Implementation Package. The other concepts addressed by the Implementation Package, including those in the agreement, would be reflected in the source country's domestic law or regulation. Irrespective of the legal means by which the Implementation Package is implemented, it is clear that national law of the source country and relevant treaties would apply to any matter which is not addressed in the Implementation Package (such as for instance penalties and interest that may apply in case of late payment).

The Implementation Package provides that an authorised intermediary will be liable for under-withholding if that under-withholding relates to an investor who has an account directly with the authorised intermediary, or if the investor holds securities through one or more intermediaries that are not authorised intermediaries. In these cases, the authorised intermediary will be liable even if it has complied with the procedures set out in the Implementation Package. Those procedures are intended to reduce the risk of under-withholding, but not the authorised intermediary's liability, as described above, if such under-withholding in fact occurs.

Some countries may be content with a contractual claim against the authorised intermediary, particularly if the domestic law already provides for a claim for under-withholding against a domestic withholding agent and the investor. Other countries believe that, for the approach to operate as intended, they will need to change their domestic law so that each intermediary in the chain would be potentially liable for under-withholding. Each source country therefore will need to consider how best to achieve that result in the context of its own legal framework. For example, some countries may need to provide that the annual reporting forms constitute a—tax return under the source country's domestic law.

In considering how to implement these procedures, countries will want to consider the effect that the introduction of these procedures will have with respect to their domestic withholding agents and to coordinate that treatment with the treatment of any authorised intermediary that has taken on primary withholding responsibilities. For example, the Implementation Package provides that an authorised intermediary may be liable for under-withholding even if it has complied with the procedures set out therein. At least in part, this—strict liability standard recognises that the intermediary that has the most direct account relationship with the investor has access to information about the investor beyond what is provided on the investor self-declaration. A country may decide, however, that a domestic withholding agent, such as the company paying the dividend, should not be held strictly liable for any under-withholding. Such a company may be reluctant to take on the risk of under-withholding because it must rely on information provided by others, including many with which it has no relationship, contractual or otherwise. Unless this problem is addressed, the company may be reluctant to participate in the relief at source system, and may insist on withholding tax at the statutory rate, forcing investors to request refunds and undermining the system. Various approaches have evolved to address this problem. In some countries, it is common for the issuer of securities to require indemnification against its potential liability; providing such indemnifications may require adjustments to current contractual relationships, or the creation of new ones. Another approach is taken by countries that do not hold a withholding agent or other intermediary liable (or will not collect against it, even if it is still technically liable for the tax) if the withholding agent or intermediary has taken reasonable measures to collect the correct tax or has operated in good faith. A reasonable measures or good faith standard may be left to circumstances or to requirements spelled out in detail by the source country (e.g. requiring the domestic withholding agent to collect the identification numbers assigned to authorised intermediaries that have received the dividend and to check them against a list of those intermediaries that have been designated by the source country as ineligible to make claims for relief at source on behalf of their customers). If such a standard is adopted, it should be applied in a non-discriminatory manner, so that any difference in treatment between a domestic withholding agent and a foreign intermediary is based on relevant differences in their circumstances (such as their relationship to the investor or access to information) rather than the mere fact of their residence in different countries.

Under the Implementation Package, there may be circumstances in which an upper-tier withholding agent is required to pay a tax that has been under-withheld and which the source country tax authorities have been unable to collect from the authorised intermediary that is nearest to the investor. In that case, if the government simply identified for the upper-tier withholding agent the investor with respect to which there was under-withholding, or even the investor and the authorised intermediary that reported the payment to the source country, the information might not be helpful to an upper-tier entity seeking to enforce an indemnification. The entity would need to have information regarding the payment that it made that eventually was passed on through the chain to that authorised intermediary on behalf of that investor. The more information regarding the chain of intermediaries that the government can provide, consistent with its rules regarding confidentiality of taxpayer information, the more likely it is that the indemnifications will in fact result in the costs of under-withholding being imposed on the person best in a position to prevent under-withholding in the future.

Further Development of the IP

While the Implementation Package provides a framework for the system of relief at source, there are a number of technology issues that need to be addressed before it can be adopted.

For example, the system assumes a certain level of automatic exchange of information between the tax authorities of the source country and of the residence country. Countries may want to assure themselves that they can achieve that level of exchange before adopting the system. A related issue is the format and communications channel for information to be reported by authorised intermediaries to the source countries. In order to achieve a level of standardisation that will make the system economically feasible for intermediaries, government and business are working together to develop information technology systems that will provide a seamless process for information that is reported by the authorised intermediaries to be exchanged with the residence countries and used by the residence countries in their computerised matching programmes.

In addition, the introduction of any new system requires governments to consider how they will review taxpayers' compliance with the system. While the Implementation Package addresses compliance issues, and includes reporting forms that would be used in that regard, these are necessarily based on a few countries' experience with similar systems. Because the system that would be adopted through the Implementation Package is not identical to any existing system, it is likely that both governments and business will want to continue to review these procedures during the process of implementation to ensure that they provide governments with the information that they need to review intermediaries' compliance without being more burdensome than is necessary.

As I noted at the start, the TRACE IP is a much more fully developed concept than, say, the EU T-BAG Report. However, there are differences in approach in several areas, some of which may be substantive barriers to one or other models. It should also be very clear to the reader by now that there are a large number of very close analogies between the TRACE IP and the US withholding tax system, particularly IRC Chapter 3. It is almost impossible not to come to the conclusion that the world of withholding tax is on the brink of changing from a disorganised and fragmented model, to a more consistent model. That doesn't mean that it's a better system, just that it's more likely to be consistently applied and therefore offer more opportunities for automation and standardisation in the industry, which should reduce costs and risk while providing a much larger population of investors with correct levels of taxation in real time.

European Union

In this section, I will look specifically at the European Union's work to simplify withholding tax as an example of how the principles of the US system in both IRC Chapter 3 and IRC Chapter 4 can clearly be seen to be emerging into a more global context.

Much of this section draws first on the work of the T-BAG Group that effectively took the work of prior committees that established the nature, scale and scope of the issues involved and attempted to construct a consistent holistic approach to how such issues could be resolved to meet the needs and constraints of both government tax administrations and of the financial institutions that are the interface between beneficial owners and the tax administrations. Also included is a section of the EU Code of Conduct that was published in 2017, three years after the T-BAG Report which attempts to encode a voluntary adoption principle (which was one of the two implementation methods suggested in T-BAG).

The Code of Conduct has come in for much criticism, some of which I will reference in this chapter, but the, in the final accounting, results are what will determine if the voluntary approach and Code of Conduct are deemed to have been successful.

Current Problems

Member States currently adopt a variety of different approaches to the issue of withholding tax, which has been described in previous reports and the work of Alberto Giovannini. These problems can be broadly categorised as follows:

1. Concerns over the legal basis under which cross-border tax simplification could be implemented
2. Lack of adequate or consistent interpretive guidance from Member States
3. Lack of a consistent tax relief model between Member States
4. A plethora of procedures, forms and information requirements from Member States
5. Lack of a mandate for the use of automation and standards.

The T-BAG Group reviewed those issues in context to the different withholding tax systems currently operated by Member States in detail and its recommendations for specific issues to facilitate Member States adopting a simplified approach.

As part of its review, and in context to the FISCO recommendations, the T-BAG Group also reviewed the remedial tax reclaim processes of Member States and makes recommendations here for the provision of an EU-wide standardised tax reclaim which would lend itself to the transition by Member States from paper-based reclaim processing, to electronic and thus contribute to achieving the removal of some of the tax barriers laid out by Professor Alberto Giovannini.

International Context

A comparative analysis to the US system (US Revenue Code Chapters 3 and 4) allowed the T-BAG Group to provide suggestions on those aspects of the US system which would work effectively in a European context, notwithstanding that at least one European Member State has already implemented a similar, albeit simplified system (i.e. Ireland). This applies particularly to the procedural aspects of contracts, documentation, withholding, information reporting and audits.

A comparative analysis in the T-BAG Report to the work of the OECD also allowed the T-BAG Group to recommend several areas where there are common elements of an Authorised Intermediary system on which significant granular work has already been completed, for example, self-certifications of residency, standardised messaging and from which both business and Member States could benefit in terms of both reduced development and implementation costs in a European context.

2013–2015

In normal circumstances Member States and the T-BAG Group itself would have had ample time to weigh considerations and recommendations on its mandate. However, in the period following the publication of the first edition of this book, the rate of change in the international environment both inside the EU and outside it increased rapidly. Some of those changes were outside the direct mandate of the T-BAG Group. Others, albeit in principle within the mandate, only subsequently became substantive and the Group did not have sufficient time to analyse them in detail nor make recommendations. Notwithstanding this, the T-BAG Group urged the Commission and Member States to take cognisance of this amplified rate of change which, they believe, increases the need for an integrated approach to short- and long-term planning. Some of the issues which were not analysed in detail in the report but which were recommended to be included in further work were:

1. Effects of the widespread implementation of a Financial Transaction Tax (FTT)
2. Use of Legal Entity Identifiers (LEIs) as an additional beneficial owner identification tool;
3. Effects of Target 2 Securities (T2S) regulation

The Group recommended an explicit support for many of the elements of the TRACE Implementation Protocol (IP) for short-term solutions since many aspects of the IP (1) are congruous to the Group's recommendations and (2) already have substantive implementation detail associated with them from which Member States could benefit.

Summary of Previous FISCO Reports

The EU Clearing and Settlement Fiscal Compliance Experts' Group (FISCO) that was created in March 2005 following the Communication 'Clearing and Settlement in the European Union—The Way Forward'[1] had as one of its key objectives the resolution of Giovannini Barriers 11 and 12.

---

[1] COM(2004) 312 final.

The FISCO Group published two reports—The FISCO Fact Finding Study 2006[2] and the FISCO Second Report on Solutions to fiscal compliance barriers related to post-trading within the EU 2007.[3] The two reports described as a serious problem the fact that withholding tax collection and relief procedures vary considerably between Member States and that different procedures often apply even to different classes of securities within the same Member State. Many Member States restrict withholding responsibilities to entities established within their own jurisdiction. As a consequence, foreign intermediaries are often disadvantaged in their capacity to offer relief at source from withholding tax due to the significant extra cost of using a local agent or local representative in the discharge of their withholding obligations. The reports also pointed out that Member States' current relief procedures do not take sufficient account of the multi-tiered holding environment and often put tax collection responsibilities on an entity that is not connected to the beneficial owner/final investor. These procedures therefore assume that the market will organise itself to transfer information and (paper-form) documentation on the beneficial owner up through the chain of intermediaries. In reality, however, this is costly and inefficient and may also create confidentiality and data privacy issues. The FISCO Group concluded that the present fiscal compliance procedures hinder the functioning of capital markets and increase the cost of cross-border settlement. It said that the complexity and administrative costs resulting from the present procedures may lead investors to forego the relief to which they are entitled and may, for the same reason, discourage cross-border investment.

The FISCO Group proposed solutions aimed at improved, standardised, simplified and modernised withholding tax relief procedures that would be adapted to the way financial markets operate today. The present procedures are both costly and inefficient. The FISCO Group was of the opinion that:

- *At-source relief procedures* are the best method to improve the present situation because of the optimised cash flow they offer to investors;
- In order to make relief procedures simpler, a paper-form certificate of residence should be replaced by alternative means to prove the investors' entitlement to tax relief, such as *self-certification and Know-Your-Customer (KYC) rules*. Furthermore intermediaries should be allowed to make use of modern technology to pass on investors' information to the withholding agents *in electronic format*.

---

[2] http://ec.europa.eu/internal_market/financial-markets/docs/compliance/ff_study_en.pdf.
[3] http://ec.europa.eu/internal_market/financial-markets/docs/compliance/report_en.pdf.

- Many of the existing problems could be solved by *shifting withholding responsibilities* to intermediaries, that is, by allowing all intermediaries in the custody chain either to assume full withholding responsibilities or to take responsibility for granting withholding tax relief by passing on pooled withholding tax rate information to the upstream intermediary. Avoiding the need for intermediaries to pass detailed information on beneficiaries up the chain would overcome data protection and client confidentiality concerns.
- Even though relief at source is the preferred relief method, there is a clear need also for *efficient refund procedures*. A supplementary standard and quick refund procedure should be implemented within the Member States by using similar formats for applications, by centralising refund procedures in each Member State to one tax authority or tax office only and by introducing a time limit for making the refunds. The reclaim process should also be capable of electronic adaptation in order to optimise efficiency.

Summary of the Proposed Solution Framework

The solution recommended by the T-BAG Group had the following major characteristics.

1. Member States agree a common standardised 'Authorised Intermediary' Agreement (AIA) which may be entered into between a financial intermediary and a Member State.
2. AI Agreements would provide rules for the conducts of (1) documentation of beneficial owners, (2) application of relief at source on payments, (3) withholding, (4) information reporting and (5) control and oversight;
3. Member States agree a common form and distribution mechanism (e.g. web site) for Guidance on the application of treaty benefits to different types of beneficial owner on which an AI may rely, subject to the understanding that such guidance does not overrule a Member State's ability to question any specific case for a claim of treaty entitlement. It is envisaged that existing mechanisms for clarification of individual cases would still be available;
4. The identification of beneficial owners to be permitted by AIs through the mechanism of (1) TINs issued by the beneficial owner's home State, (2) application of the KYC rules of the AI's home State, to the extent that the source State accepts the degree to which, in its view, KYC rules establish beneficial ownership and (3) agreement by Member States to the development and use of a common and electronically transmissible self-

certification of residency ('Investor Self-Declaration' or ISD). To the extent possible, the system should permit the use of Powers of Attorney (PoA) to allow AIs and authorised third parties to facilitate any additionally required documentation;

5. Provided the documentation and identification rules are met, AIs would be permitted to make (or instruct) payments to eligible beneficial owners net of the appropriate treaty rate of withholding tax on pay date.
6. Liability for under-withholding and/or incorrect documentation of beneficial owners should lie (1) with the beneficial owner (for incorrect or fraudulent representations), (2) the AI for processing errors and (3) the Source Member State for technical issues related to treaty eligibility, the latter being minimised through the clear Guidance proposal.
7. AIs servicing beneficial owners directly would provide annual information reports (1) to the source State at beneficial owner level of disclosure and (2) upstream at pooled level (by withholding rate applied) to other AIs in the payment chain. Such reports to be electronic and to a format standardised between Member States, for example, XML;
8. Where a source country receives information reports from an AI and wishes to query the eligibility of any beneficial owner, Exchange of Information rules would be applied to permit the source country to apply directly to the home country using the TIN of the beneficial owner;
9. Under the terms of an AI agreement, AIs would be subject to a choice of internal review, certified by a Responsible Officer and subject to appropriate penalties, or external oversight by an approved independent third party by means of an 'Agreed Upon Procedure' (AUP) whose report would be available to the Source Member State. Governments would retain the right to undertake spot checks in both cases.
10. For those beneficial owners who were unable to meet the relevant documentation standards prior to pay date, but where they can still prove eligibility under a treaty, Member States agree to develop a standardised, machine readable tax reclaim form capable of being delivered electronically.

Overarching Principles

The overarching principles that drove business in researching, discussing and making these proposals to Member States are the need for both governments and business to reduce costs and make the withholding tax system more efficient, reliable and accessible for all those involved in it. The core principles needed to achieve this, wherever possible, were defined in the report and include: (1) agreement to common simplified approaches, (2) standards and (3) automation. So, while the conclusions of the report go into some granular detail about the different elements of an efficient withholding tax system, for example, documentation, liability, exchange of information, reporting and tax reclaims and so on, a common thread in many proposals is the development and use of voluntarily agreed standards between Member States and wherever possible for information to be transmitted securely in electronic form.

The T-BAG Group reviewed both FISCO reports, together with an analysis of the US withholding tax system and projects in hand by the OECD to establish, from experience, some of the best practices that could be incorporated into an EU withholding tax system.

The prior FISCO reports concluded that the most effective system for the EU would be an 'Authorised Intermediary' type system in which relief at source would be the base model with optional post pay date tax reclaims available in all Member States. The framework solution proposed takes this principle and addresses some of the challenges that this concept produces at an intermediate level of granularity. If Member States approve this proposal, at this level of granularity, further work will need to be conducted to produce the finalised framework.

Code of Conduct

The Code of Conduct, published in 2017, takes some but not all the recommendations from prior reports and essentially simplifies that work into a series of suggestions from which EU tax administrations can pick or choose (or not choose). Each suggestion is designed to address certain 'problems' and, importantly, each suggestion contains a range of possible methods by means of which tax administrations can solve those problems. The basic principles of the Code of Conduct are below.

1. **Claiming entitlements**: Member States can choose to allow beneficial owners, non-resident financial institutions and other representatives to submit refund claims or apply for relief. This is in order to address low participation rates in low-value claims, avoidance of problems caused by chains of intermediaries and different rules between them and different costs applied in processing.

(a) **Claiming entitlements**: Member States can choose to allow beneficial owners, non-resident financial institutions and other representatives to submit refund claims or apply for relief. This is in order to address low participation rates in low-value claims, avoidance of problems caused by chains of intermediaries and different rules between them and different costs applied in processing;
(b) **User-friendly procedures**: Member States can choose to use digital technology to automate and/or standardise the tax reclaim process to address high compliance costs, unnecessary manual interventions and delays due to manual processing;
(c) Member States tax administrations can use IT systems to reduce the burden of paper processing, reduce delays from manual inefficient processing and to allow for automated controls to reduce the risk of fraud;
(d) **Speed of processing**. Member States can adopt procedures to formalise a six-month standard for the provision of refunds or relief;
(e) **User-friendly forms**. Member States can adopt more user-friendly forms for use by beneficial owners and their agents to address difficulties with language or complex tax rules;
(f) **Documentation**. Member States can provide clearer requirements about supporting documentation required to substantiate claims, include via more efficient communication methods, to address costs for claimants and their agents flowing from lack of clarity;
(g) **Point of contact**. Member States should appoint a single point of contact available at the tax administration's web site;
(h) **Relief at source**. Member States can adopt a relief at source process or a refund process depending on what they think is most effective for them.

For reference, this Code is in stark contrast to the original ten principles recommended by the T-BAG Group, which in turn was the result of the Giovannini committee's work followed by FISCO.

Implementation

In context for the T-BAG Report and the Code of Conduct, the T-BAG Group did suggest in its report that voluntary adoption by Member States would be the most effective way to implement the report's recommendations and that there were self-evident economic benefits to government, investors and business. The alternative method of a Directive would probably take seven to ten years to accomplish (cf. European Savings Directive) and would result in more complexity and cost for governments and the industry in the interim. Some Member States (e.g. Slovenia, Ireland) are already adopting their own variations of an AI model.

A Directive would only need to be envisioned if it transpired that certain Member States had not taken any voluntary action to adopt the recommendations in a phased approach. The measure of Member State adoption should be proportionate to the economic benefits/costs. However, the T-BAG Group believed that the degree of cost saving and efficiencies gained by early adopters will be a compelling driver for other Member States.

In total, the implementation of the recommendations will, it's believed, achieve the objectives of the Commission and Member States, to improve the efficiency of the markets by removing the barriers to the free flow of capital resulting from the current inconsistent, fragmented and inefficient relief mechanisms.

As can immediately be seen, again there are many areas where the EU Report is similar to, if not identical to, aspects of both IRC Chapter 3 and IRC Chapter 4.

The Future

The difference between the OECD and the EU is of course that the OECD cannot mandate change within its membership, it can only recommend, support and suggest. The EU on the other hand can take its report and, ultimately if it believes it supports the will of the Member States, mandate the model in the form of an EU Directive which would force the Member States to change their domestic laws to fall in line. The downside is that directives are usually contentious and administratively burdensome and long winded. A more rapid implementation can be sought by means of 'voluntary adoption', although this could easily lead to another fragmented model.

I'm often asked, when looking into the future of such initiatives, not just whether this will happen, but if so, when. This is a vexed question. On the one hand, the models are well researched and have had some of the brightest business people apply themselves to a scenario that is not starting as a clean sheet of paper. On the other hand the proposed model (and I speak here of both the OECD and EU models) not only has to have a technically achievable end point but also has to be able to *look* achievable when viewed from the perspective of government. 'Business' tends to take a very pragmatic approach while government may want to have that style, but is usually embedded in political considerations which business often minimises.

That said, I think that what is important in the current scenario is that three different and very large 'bodies of thought'—the US, OECD and EU have all had many years thinking and developing models and, almost at the same time, all three have come up with principles and a model which are almost coincident if not convergent. This should give us all some hope that the speed of adoption should be faster than in the past since the areas of disagreement are already substantially lower than they otherwise might be.

The big question is whether, having mandated the research, governments, which, in the main, currently have non-standardised, paper-based, fragmented and inefficient systems (which probably reflect the approaches of the people in them), will be willing to take up the recommendations with equal fervour. I find it rather amusing, although not surprising, that the OECD and EU tax models have taken nearly 20 years to get to this fulcrum point or recommendation, while the financial transaction tax took just a few months to go from a concept to a full-fledged and adopted (albeit imperfect) system. Money it seems (particularly the lack thereof) is still the motivator it always has been.

The driver for the OECD and EU initiatives, and to a large extent the US system too, is based on trying to make the tax system more efficient. While this is a good and laudable objective, the tax revenue itself is a secondary consideration, at least in the minds of those who are constructing these models. Most do not even consider that the overall effect of an efficient cross-border tax system will be to encourage cross-border investment—which is exactly what the world needs to be able to extract itself from its current doldrums. However, as the models are all converging and reaching a state of maturity, I believe that the focus can rise above the detail of whether it's this AI system or that data transmission standard, to a level where the bigger picture can be grasped more easily. I think that over the next two to three years, these models will have been discussed in depth and their 'big picture' advantages will start to become obvious to governments and tax authorities, who will then start to make the investments needed to complete the picture.

Finland: First Adopter

One final thought. It is interesting to see that the snowball has at least been formed—with the adoption of the OECD TRACE IP by Finland in June 2019.

As Finland starts to move forward, other countries will be looking carefully at the implementation experience and benefits that Finland obtains. The key aspects of this first stage of TRACE implementation in Finland is characterised by the following aspects:

1. Finland re-iterates that its new TRACE process is intended to be a tax relief at source basis with exceptional procedures where relief at source is not possible;
2. Implementation only applies to shares registered in nominee form;
3. The foreign custodian register is abolished and replaced with a Register of Authorised Intermediaries due to open in July 2020 with guidance expected by the end of 2019 and publication of the register in January 2021;
4. The previous Finnish 'simplified procedure' for tax benefits will be abolished but treaty benefits at source will still be permitted under a different process due to start in January 2021 with the tax administration's decision on the use of ISDs and associated guidance expected by the end of 2019;
5. Annual information returns will be replaced with TRACE reports to the TRACE xml schema that will begin on 31 January 2022 with respect to dividends paid in 2021. Technical testing of the xml schema is expected by Spring 2021;
6. Liability for withholding resides with the Finnish Issuer but the Issuer can rely on an AI's pooled information when withholding. If there is no AI in the chain, the Issuer has all the liability and must collect beneficial owner information (or apply the relevant statutory rates). Note however that while pooled information is sufficient for withholding, TRACE reports will not be pooled but must be at beneficial owner level.
7. The Finnish quick refund procedure remains, but TRACE reports will need to reflect adjustments made during the year to account for 'quick refunds';
8. Firms that choose not to become Finnish AIs can become Contractual Intermediaries (CIs). This concept is similar to the idea of QI and NQI in the US model;
9. Finland has decided not to adopt the principle of an independent review.

Finland may be the first to adopt the TRACE IP but it certainly won't be the last and, in any event, joins the US, Ireland and Japan in having a similar framework for withholding tax.

In context, some of the eastern European countries have much higher proportions of young people in their workforce and many of these markets have just become members of the EU. So they are already in a state of rapid change. The more traditional EU markets still show signs of morbidity and lack of political inertia when it comes to adopting change, unlike, for example, the Scandinavian countries which have more in common in this respect with their eastern EU neighbours. It will also be interesting to see how some of the emerging markets react to the structural changes being described here. These markets are again more used to rapid change in the current world and therefore may be in a better position to not only recognise a good idea but also implement it. So, ironically, while the ideas described in this book from the US OECD and EU perspectives are being developed over an extended period of time by slower moving economies naturally slow at implementing change, I think that, having defined the new paradigm, it's the newer markets that will perhaps create and dictate the speed of change.

17

Conclusions

First, I'd like to apologise to the reader—and thank you for getting this far. Trying to write a book about tax that doesn't drown the reader in technical details is difficult. I received many letters after the first edition of this book with comments like 'this is my "go to" book' and 'this book is always on my desk'. These are either very welcome accolades or signs of some very disturbed people out there!

In order to provide the practical observations I have, it has been necessary to some extent to explain the nature of these frameworks in some detail. As mentioned at the outset, a technical explanation doesn't get you too far when you need to interpret the rules into one, perhaps more jurisdictional, cultural and linguistic environments, let alone into a commercial structure.

Results

One of the obvious questions for a conclusion is—has either qualified intermediary (QI) or Foreign Account Tax Compliance Act (FATCA) actually worked?

There are two ways to look at this question. First by looking at how well the frameworks have been adopted and second by looking at whether the expected results have been delivered.

In QI, assessing results is very difficult, mainly because the Internal Revenue Service (IRS) does not publish numbers of QIs nor any statistics on the proportion of US-sourced Fixed, Determinable, Annual or Periodic (FDAP) that flows to direct clients of those QIs. However, sources in a position to know indicate that the number of QIs today is just over 5000 globally. I estimate that the number of firms that would be eligible to be a QI, by reason of their location in a Know-Your-Customer (KYC)-approved jurisdiction and exposure to the US securities markets, is over 50,000. That, if a reasonable estimate, means that only 10% of eligible firms have obtained QI status. For a programme that has been running since 2001, that does not seem to represent a very good conversion rate and certainly, to my knowledge, that number has not changed significantly in over ten years (i.e. terminations and signings must have matched). That said, from my own experience, the impact of FATCA over the last five years has increased the rate of QI applications. It is also certainly likely that the perceived cost-benefit analysis of QI status may not be compelling enough for many smaller firms because the framework does not provide enough opportunities for cost and risk reduction for smaller firms. In terms of taxation the statistics published by the IRS, mainly the data associated with 1042-S submissions, is not granular enough to make any statements about the role of QIs in the payment and taxation chain by value of assets or even tax withheld.

In FATCA the number of firms that have adopted a compliant approach to FATCA can be estimated by looking at the number of Global Intermediary Identification Numbers (GIINs) issued. As not all compliant firms need to have a GIIN, this is not an absolute guide, but it is, I believe, a good indicator.

We can learn two things from Table 17.1. First, over 50% of all the GIINs have been issued in just six jurisdictions—Cayman, the UK, Brazil, Japan, Luxembourg and the British Virgin Islands (BVI). In other words, roughly 50% of the GIINs come from just 2.5% of the jurisdictions. It has been estimated that the number of firms that potentially could apply for a GIIN is over a million worldwide which, if a reasonable estimate, would put adoption at around 30%. Either way, the GIIN population is highly skewed to six jurisdictions which would not seem to be a logical conclusion for the likely spread of tax evasion activity.

In terms of results in FATCA, the most obvious measure is the amount of evaded tax that was repatriated to the US. Here too, information is scarce and difficult to interpret. At a Congressional Hearing in 2018 witnesses were referring to returns being in the millions of dollars, until someone pointed out that those figures represented FATCA penalties and not repatriated tax. The most high-profile FATCA issues are currently the result of covert sting operations, alluded to in earlier chapters in which extraditions and indictments have taken place, but again the spotlight is on the Responsible Officer of the foreign financial institution (FFI) in question allowing a US person to open an account and hide the fact in FATCA reporting. As a sting operation that

Table 17.1 FATCA GIIN issuance by jurisdiction

Cayman Islands	63,364
UK	32,208
Brazil	24,280
Japan	21,367
Luxembourg	14,193
Virgin Islands (British)	11,891
Canada	11,696
Guernsey	7856
Jersey	7640
France	7064
Ireland	6987
Hong Kong	6957
Australia	6632
Switzerland	6570
Netherlands	5689
Germany	5150
Mauritius	4820
New Zealand	4772
Bermuda	3952
Thailand	3921
Singapore	3773
Spain	3700
Italy	3405
Austria	2735
India	2595
Mexico	2356
China	2199
Israel	2022
Taiwan	1916
Panama	1862
South Africa	1766
Finland	1720
Bahamas	1684
Malaysia	1630
Sweden	1594
Poland	1528
Isle of Man	1490
Russian Federation	1484
US	1410
Argentina	1394
Chile	1389
Malta	1360
Cyprus	1311
Liechtenstein	1295
Korea, Republic of	1250
Norway	1180
Indonesia	1067
Peru	894

(*continued*)

Table 17.1 (continued)

Gibraltar	864
United Arab Emirates	774
Denmark	761
Turkey	662
Colombia	652
Ukraine	639
Other	609
Hungary	536
Saint Kitts and Nevis	517
Morocco	494
Belize	492
Curacao	424
Czech Republic	417
Saint Vincent and the Grenadines	414
Belgium	408
Greece	402
Pakistan	399
Portugal	387
Saudi Arabia	387
Seychelles	335
Marshall Islands	308
Philippines	307
Bulgaria	305
Anguilla	302
Egypt	279
Bahrain	266
Kuwait	255
Romania	249
Uruguay	248
Barbados	219
Andorra	216
Viet Nam	212
Cook Islands	209
Lebanon	192
Monaco	189
Tunisia	176
Slovakia	172
Slovenia	170
Croatia	167
Ecuador	161
Costa Rica	157
El Salvador	151
Lithuania	149
Dominican Republic	145
Cambodia	126
Kazakhstan	119
Turks and Caicos Islands	114
Kenya	112

(*continued*)

Table 17.1 (continued)

Saint Lucia	107
Trinidad and Tobago	95
Samoa	94
Macao	93
Jordan	92
Bosnia and Herzegovina	87
Estonia	86
Vanuatu	86
Nigeria	84
Qatar	83
Guatemala	82
Namibia	80
Venezuela, Bolivarian Republic of	79
Iraq	78
Bangladesh	77
Jamaica	77
Angola	74
Azerbaijan	73
Belarus	73
Bolivia, Plurinational State of	72
Serbia	66
Georgia	65
Latvia	65
Sri Lanka	64
Côte d'Ivoire	62
Haiti	62
Ghana	61
Oman	58
Liberia	57
Antigua and Barbuda	51
Iceland	50
Honduras	49
Algeria	47
Paraguay	45
Tanzania, United Republic of	44
Armenia	43
Macedonia, The Former Yugoslav Republic of	43
Grenada	42
Zambia	39
Myanmar	38
Uganda	37
Dominica	36
Lao People's Democratic Republic	35
Sudan	35
Botswana	34
Senegal	34
Nepal	32
Uzbekistan	31

(*continued*)

Table 17.1 (continued)

Zimbabwe	31
Cameroon	30
Kyrgyzstan	30
Tajikistan	29
Brunei Darussalam	28
Libya	28
San Marino	28
West Bank and Gaza	27
Nicaragua	26
Albania	25
Aruba	25
Montenegro	24
Mongolia	23
British Indian Ocean Territory	22
Moldova, Republic of	22
Congo, Democratic Republic of the	21
Guyana	21
Mozambique	21
Sint Maarten (Dutch Part)	21
Togo	21
Rwanda	20
Ethiopia	19
Guinea	19
Yemen	19
Mali	18
Swaziland	18
Afghanistan	17
Benin	17
Burkina Faso	17
Mauritania	17
Gambia	15
Cape Verde	14
Congo	14
Bonaire, Sint Eustatius and Saba	13
Comoros	13
Kosovo	13
Niger	13
Turkmenistan	13
Gabon	12
Montserrat	12
Djibouti	11
Malawi	11
Suriname	11
United States Minor Outlying Islands	11
Chad	10
Fiji	10
Madagascar	10
Lesotho	9

(*continued*)

Table 17.1 (continued)

Papua New Guinea	9
Sierra Leone	9
South Sudan	9
Maldives	8
Syrian Arab Republic	8
Burundi	6
Equatorial Guinea	6
Solomon Islands	6
Central African Republic	5
Greenland	5
Guam	5
New Caledonia	5
Sao Tome and Principe	5
Timor-Leste	5
Tonga	5
Virgin Islands (U.S.)	5
French Polynesia	4
Somalia	4
Guinea-Bissau	3
Micronesia, Federated States of	3
Bouvet Island	2
Christmas Island	2
Holy See (Vatican City State)	2
Puerto Rico	2
Saint Martin (French Part)	2
Saint Pierre and Miquelon	2
Aland Islands	1
Bhutan	1
Eritrea	1
Falkland Islands	1
Faroe Islands	1
French Guyana	1
Kiribati	1
Martinique	1
Mayotte	1
Northern Mariana Islands	1
Palau	1
Reunion	1
Saint Barthelemy	1
Wallis and Futuna	1
Grand total	329,303

Source: www.irs.gov

tells us nothing about amounts of evaded tax, it tells us more about how far the US is prepared to go to impose its regulatory framework. Across all of this, there is no information, to my knowledge, that clearly shows a connection between the amounts spent on FATCA (whether by the IRS in implementing it or by FFIs complying with it) and the amount of evaded tax recovered as a result of it.

So, perhaps ironically, there is little or no transparency in terms of numbers or results from the US concerning a set of regulations whose objective is to force transparency and disclosure from others.

Clarity and Consistency

Given that QI and FATCA are overseen by the same US agency, it still remains a mystery as to why these two frameworks are so convoluted and complex. Given that they have different purposes and that they were promulgated over a decade apart, we should perhaps, in the vernacular, cut them some slack. It seems however that as new situations arise, these are handled as exception extensions in each case. While this gives some short-term benefits because firms with established methodologies can just 'add new procedures', after a time, the number and complexity of the changes make the frameworks almost unworkable.

As an example, while there may be a very good reason for it, take IRC Chapter 4 penalties as an example and the fact that recalcitrants and NP-FFIs must be reported in FATCA, any penalties they are subject to are reported under the QI framework on forms 1042-S and 1042. Now, the argument that the penalties result from the receipt of US-sourced income is valid, but misses the point that it is more logical to report in FATCA both the accounts that are recalcitrant and NP-FFI as well as the penalties they received as a result. The so-called convergence of FATCA with QI is more to do with connecting two systems used for different purposes because it was easier to use the taxation system to apply penalties than create a separate penalty system.

However, this chapter is not intended to muse over what should be or might have been if a more workable framework had existed capable of absorbing change in an effective way. The complexity of this convergence between FATCA and QI stems from the fact that FATCA penalties are applied via US-sourced FDAP income. The result is a framework of documentation (W-8s, W-9s, substitutes, withholding statements) and reports (1042-S and 1042) that manages to mix up the two dialects of the US tax language that most English-speaking QIs struggle with, let alone the non-English speakers.

From a financial institution's perspective the issue is a complex one of the right resources in the right place at the right time. Most FIs are historically siloed both in operations and in management. QI may be handled separately to FATCA, not least because one is a taxation system, thus involving onboarding and income processing primarily. FATCA on the other hand involves onboarding but only peripherally income processing (if there are penalties to apply). FATCA reporting of course also requires annual aggregation of accounts and subsequent due diligence and cure processes that before the advent of Automatic Exchange of Information (AEoI)/Common Reporting Standard (CRS) were activities that had no natural home. If you place them with onboarding teams, you divert resource away from their core role. If you set up a separate group, you add cost to a non-revenue generating activities thus hurting your own bottom line.

Figure 17.1 allows me to make two observations that flow from the siloed approach and how to deal with it. The diagram shows a financial institution with two business lines accessing the US securities market. One business line is a custodial business with three upstream US withholding agents and relevant rate pool accounts at each that allow it to operate as a non-withholding QI. The second is a prime execution services business line of the same legal entity in which it is acting as a withholding QI and Qualified Derivatives Dealer (QDD). Both business lines have completely separate management structures, although both business lines have a common element of their downstream client base delivered via affiliates in five countries. While this is clearly not a simple scenario, at country or even regional level it is not uncommon.

So, in a chapter about conclusions, what does this tell us? My first message is—make sure that before you take one step, you should map out your firm's exposure to key factors of QI and FATCA. Identify your actual exposure to the US in financial, competitive and reputational terms. Financial, in terms of the value of US assets. Competitive in terms of whether you can actually afford not to have a US exposure without losing business (US and non-US) to competitors and finally reputational in terms of whether non-qualified intermediary (NQI) status is something you are prepared to accept in view of the position taken publicly by the US government.

Then map business structure, legal entities, types of clients and start to identify areas where commonalities exist or where particular procedures can be leveraged.

The business in Fig. 17.1 for example would be a candidate for an expanded affiliate group (EAG) in FATCA and even potentially a consolidated compliance programme in QI, although its business culture will determine whether the benefits outweigh the costs. Equally, noting that the five affiliates are mainly NQIs in IRC Chapter 3 leads to the use of the Alternative Procedure that makes life easier for NQIs and the QI itself. Adding numbers to this type of diagram also starts to create hot spots where the volumes mean that expenditure in these areas could save both cost and risk.

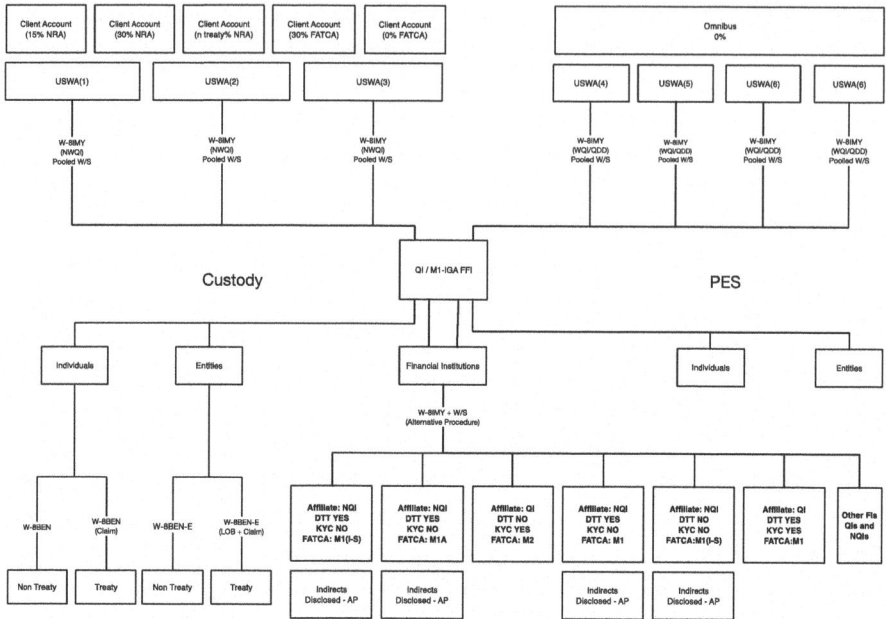

Fig. 17.1 Operational structure map (OSM). Source: Author's own

This type of diagram also helps to identify risk points, such as onboarding which, in this circumstance, was performed in two separate functions. Finding someone high enough up in the management food chain is also difficult when these operational structures are complex, not least because the knowledge and authority don't usually exist in the same person.

Standardisation and Automation

This book has tried to address just two out of many regulatory frameworks. However, there are some commonalities not just between FATCA and QI but with other tax frameworks. These include standardisation and digitisation.

The financial services industry has made great strides towards complete automation and digitisation of the financial ecosystem. This has been led by the payments industry and latterly in the securities space. However where payments, especially at retail level, have sufficient volume to warrant removal of manual processing, the securities industry—which is where most non-property-related tax evasion takes place—has lagged behind significantly.

This lag creates a difficult operating environment for QI and FATCA. Resources are not sufficient, budgets are hard to justify and long lead times in the replacement of legacy computer systems means that efficiencies, while available, are not deliverable in a consistent manner.

Equally, from a 'hearts and minds' perspective, the extraterritorial nature of QI and particularly FATCA means that generally the financial institutions must bear the cost without any perceivable benefit and so compliance is grudging at best. That said, the IRS is increasingly adopting automated systems to acquire data, although this is a mix of proprietary and international standards. It has recently ceased its use of the MoU for the development of automated and standardised systems for solicitation of W-8 forms (or their substitutes). The overall picture for QI and FATCA is a patchwork of what is allowed, what is not allowed, what has an internationally acceptable standard involved and what is US or IRS proprietary. In addition to the structural map diagram in Table 17.1, we usually recommend a digital compliance map (DCM) which is usually a bit of a misnomer as many aspects of the map are typically manual. It does however, as shown in Fig. 17.1, start to create a compliance environment that converges the business operating model with the compliance obligations.

The use of the DCM together with the OSM begins a process that identifies major cost and risk savings. There are a number of opportunities that such analyses offer. Not least of these is that of integrating different systemic approaches that are separately permitted by the IRS but not inherently connected other than structurally within the compliance framework. One example, as shown in Fig. 17.2, might start out with a strategy to

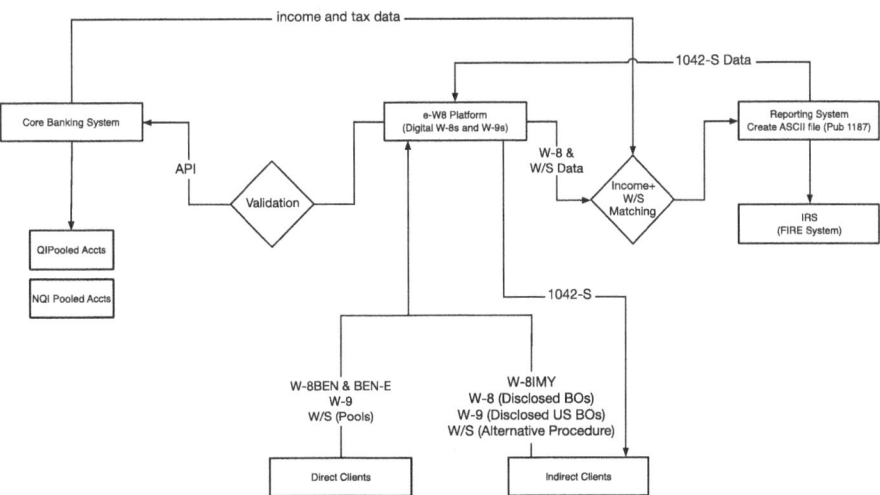

Fig. 17.2 Digital compliance map (DCM). Source: Author's own

automate and standardise document solicitation and validation using an e-W8 system in which no physical W-8 or W-9 exists and data is held digitally. However, this is only one element of a digital ecosystem plan for QI and FATCA. The natural second step would be to automate and standardise the delivery of withholding statements which are currently a mix of manual and proprietary formats with no digital standard. Withholding statements are required between downstream and upstream FIs and may be at beneficial owner level (for NQIs) or pooled (for QIs) and may include both IRC Chapter 4 and IRC Chapter 3 code determinations. This then allows for, as an example, an Application Programming Interface (API) approach to a core banking system receiving the digital output of the document validation system (e-W8). As the core banking system is used to manage income, this would allow assets to be moved via sub-routine, into relevant pooled accounts. Assuming a robust 'change in circumstance' procedure at the e-W8 portal, assets can be moved automatically based on a rules engine behind the scenes. Finally, the income output from the core banking system can be output to whatever method is used for reporting. Some firms use third-party providers which would indicate flat file transfers, but since the IRS accepts flat files anyway, many other firms do their own reporting directly to the IRS Filing Information Returns Electronically (FIRE) Portal. Copies of those forms can then be delivered via the same documentation portal used to upload the original trigger data for collection by the client (or if a client portal already exists, then to there).

This begins to sound like an automated ecosystem because we have encapsulated three elements of the annual process. Making the systems bi-directional, that is, a delivery as well as a receipt portal means that a QI *receiving* W-8s, W-9s and withholding statements could also use the same system to *deliver* reports 1042-S. many firms spend an enormous amount of effort printing 1042-S forms or delivering 1042-S forms in PDF format by email neither of which is intelligent or secure. An ecosystem approach also allows for much faster and robust matching and reconciliation that can be reinforced with an API-based approach to importing payment data from core banking systems.

This is not meant to be a template for such an ecosystem (although it has been used for at least one). It is meant to show that, while the level of standardisation and permitted automation may be fragmented at best, with a little innovation, most financial institutions could substantially reduce risk and cost.

The Future

QI now lives in a world with other QI style regimes already in existence (e.g. Ireland, Japan) and others in a development process (e.g. OECD TRACE IP, EU WTCC). So, the general model seems to have been accepted. However, the rate of adoption of the US QI programme has been somewhat inexplicably low and the EU framework has undoubtedly been weakened by lack of political will to push a single solution. The OECD framework has also not changed since 2013 perhaps signalling a lack of driving force to make anything happen or alternatively a reflection of the glacial speed with which tax matters typically progress at international level. This is a shame because a lot of very smart people have spent a lot of time and effort analysing the historical problems and figuring out a system that would work for everyone and deliver benefits to tax administrations around the world.

FATCA of course now lives in a world alongside the OECD AEoI/CRS framework. Perhaps understandably, given that the purpose is anti-tax evasion, these frameworks, collectively called 'GATCA' or Global Account Tax Compliance Activities, have seen a much more rapid adoption rate. I assume that people think that GATCA would bring about some substantial increase in tax receipts and that this was the driver for that adoption rate. Unfortunately, if it has been successful, no one is telling anyone about it, so the industry continues to take a position that it is the one paying the price either in operational and compliance costs or in penalties for non-compliance and getting absolutely nothing in return.

I do see a general trend towards more automation and standardisation, but unfortunately this is not a directed effort. It's more that tax administrations are moving in that direction anyway and, at some points in the operational cycle, the efforts of financial institutions to automate and standardise happen to coincide with the efforts of tax administrations to facilitate it. Hence we see much more effort in the digitisation of documentation now that IRS allows it and OECD and EU are in principle in favour of it.

I see little in the way of movement by tax administrations to recognise that compliance should be proportional.

The big questions: Will QI principles become the de facto framework for cross-border investment taxation? Yes, eventually, but the process remains on a long and glacially slow road and the speed is determined by the slowest adopters—the tax administrations. Will US tax evasion be stopped by FATCA? No. Both FATCA and its global counterpart, AEoI/CRS, have too many flaws and loopholes that one could drive the proverbial truck through. It is and will however continue to be a significant deterrent in that it makes those with a desire to evade tax take more precautions to avoid the mainstream institutions. FATCA and AEoI also continue to suffer from project complexity creep in that the frameworks were not designed to be flexible and so we have multiple transitionary arrangements, carve-outs, Partner Letters and such. Every time one of these 'fixes' happens, the system globally creaks under the weight of extra cost to collate information, understand the change, adapt policy and procedure, implement then monitor the new system—before the next change happens.

I have tried in this book to explain the almost unexplainable and offer some insights into the ways in which efficiencies can be extracted from processes that generally provide no business benefit to the institutions affected. As a driver for that approach, I take the view that the best way to approach the subject is to stop thinking of it as a task and start thinking about it as a product. If I have to leave the reader with just one thought that will provide maximum value, it's not any observation about any particular part of either QI or FATCA. It's to change the way you think about these frameworks. Tax is a product not a task. If you look at it in that way, you start to look for automation and efficiencies because they reduce costs. You look to QI status because it's a marketing badge of acceptance that can make you more competitive or protect your client's identities better than your NQI counterparts. Knowledge and training (requirements of the QI Agreement) become career advancement opportunities that expand your corporate culture and make you 'best in class'. Better designed onboarding and client outreach, triggered by QI and FATCA requirements, should make your market offering better, smoother and present fewer obstacles to clients signing up with you. The opportunities go on and on, but only if you see compliance in different way.

18

Further Reading

Appendix 1: Useful Terms and Definitions

Useful terms

Term	Definition
Beneficial owner	Beneficial owner refers to anyone who enjoys the benefits of ownership of a security or property without necessarily being on the record as being the owner. Webster's defines a beneficial owner as "one who enjoys the benefit of a property of which another is the legal owner". The legal owner (i.e., the owner on the record) may be described as the registered owner and if they are not the beneficial owner they may be described as a "nominee".
Distribution	A distribution is a company or fund's payment of stock, cash or physical products to its shareholders, or a payment of interest, principal or dividend by the issuer of a security to shareholders.
Financial institution (FI)	A financial institution generally means an entity that is a depository institution, custodial institution, investment entity or an insurance company (or holding company of an insurance company) that issues cash value insurance or annuity contracts.
FIN (FATCA identification number)	Certain entities do not need to have a GIIN. These entities instead provide a FIN to be used in place of a GIIN for FATCA reporting. Examples of entities that may provide a FIN include U.S. withholding agents, territory financial institutions, third-party preparers or commercial software vendors.

(continued)

(continued)

Term	Definition
FDAP	Fixed, determinable, annual or periodic income. FDAP income normally includes income that is:
	• fixed or for which the amounts to be paid are known ahead of time;
	• is determinable or there is a basis for figuring the amount to be paid;
	• is annual or paid yearly; or
	• is periodic or paid from time to time not specifically in regular intervals.
	FDAP income is defined very broadly and generally includes all U.S.-sourced income except gains derived from the sale of real or personal property and income specifically excluded from gross income such as tax-exempt interest and qualified scholarship income.
	Examples of types of income generally considered FDAP income include dividends, certain interest, original issue discount, pensions and annuities, alimony, rents, royalties, scholarships and fellowship grants, prizes, awards, purses for boxing, compensation for personal services, sales commissions paid monthly, commissions paid for a single transaction, distributable estate or trust non-ECI income, and distributed partnership non-ECI income
GIIN (Global Intermediary Identification Number)	The IRS approves certain types of institutions and entities and assigns a GIIN, which they can use to identify themselves to withholding agents and tax administrators for FATCA reporting purposes.
	A GIIN is a 19-character identification number made up of several identifiers. It will be formatted as XXXXXX.XXXXX.XX.XXX. These characters will never contain the letter 'O'.
Professional trustee	An entity that is regulated or licensed as a trustee by their country's financial services authority.

Nationality, domicile, residency and citizenship

Term	Definition
Nationality	Nationality, often used as a synonym for citizenship, is the state of being part of a nation whether by birth or naturalization or ties to a specific nation.
Domicile	Domicile is the country that a person treats as their permanent home, or lives in and has a substantial connection with. However, domicile is, in common law jurisdictions, a different legal concept to residence, though the two may often lead to the same result.
Residency	Residency can refer to domicile and is the act of establishing or maintaining a residence in a given country despite not necessarily having citizenship.
Citizenship	Citizenship is the status of a person recognized under the custom or law as being a legal member of a sovereign state or belonging to a nation. In some countries, for example, the United States and United Kingdom, nationality and citizenship can have different meanings.

(continued)

(continued)

Term	Definition
Residency for tax purposes	Residency for tax purposes can vary considerably from jurisdiction to jurisdiction, and 'residence' can be different for other, non-tax purposes. For individuals, physical presence in a jurisdiction is the main test. Some jurisdictions also determine residency of an individual by reference to a variety of other factors, such as the ownership of a home or availability of accommodation, family and financial interests.

IRC chapter 3 status definitions

Term	Definition
Corporation	A legal entity that is recognized as separate from its owners. Owners are issued stock. The owners are not liable personally for the corporation's debts.
Disregarded entity	A legal entity that is separate from its owner, but elects to be treated as part of its owner for U.S. tax purposes.
Partnership	The relationship between two or more persons who join to carry on a business.
Simple trust	A trust which must distribute all of its income currently and none of its income may be devoted to charity.
Grantor trust	A type of trust in which the person who created the trust (the grantor) retains powers over the trust that make its income taxable to the grantor.
Complex trust	A complex trust is any trust that is not a simple trust or a grantor trust.
Estate	An estate that holds the assets of a deceased person until distribution to the heirs.
Government	A political governing body at the federal, state or local level.
Central Bank of Issue	The institution in a country that issues the currency.
Tax-exempt organization	Organizations that qualify for exemption from federal income tax. A complete list is available on the IRS website here.
Private foundation	Any nonprofit organization in the federal law of the United States that is one of 29 types of nonprofit organizations exempt from some federal income taxes, that does not fall into one of the categories specifically excluded from the definition of that term.
International organization	An organization that is composed primarily of foreign governments or recognized as an intergovernmental or supranational organization under a foreign law similar to the U.S. International Organizations Immunities Act.

Chapter 4 status definitions

Chapter 4 status	Definition	GIIN required
Nonparticipating FFI	A foreign (non-U.S.) financial institution that is does not comply with FATCA. In IGA countries, the intergovernmental agreement will define a level of 'significant non-compliance' that would lead to a financial institution being labelled as 'nonparticipating'.	No
Participating FFI	A foreign (non-U.S.) financial institution that has entered into an agreement with the IRS to comply with its FATCA obligations.	Yes
Reporting Model 1 FFI	A foreign (non-U.S.) financial institution or a branch of an FFI that is treated as a reporting financial institution in a Model 1 IGA jurisdiction.	Yes
Reporting Model 2 FFI	A foreign (non-U.S.) financial institution or branch of an FFI that is treated as a reporting financial institution in a Model 2 IGA jurisdiction and that has entered into an agreement with the IRS to comply with its FATCA obligations.	Yes
Registered deemed-compliant FFI	An FFI that has registered to confirm that it meets the requirements to be treated as a local FFI, nonreporting member FI of a PFFI group, qualified collective investment vehicle, restricted fund, qualified credit card issuer, or sponsored investment entity or controlled foreign corporation **OR** A reporting FI under a Model 1 IGA that is registering to obtain a GIIN **OR** An FFI that is treated as a nonreporting FI under a Model 1 or 2 IGA and that is registering pursuant to the applicable Model 1 or 2 IGA.	Yes
Sponsored FFI	A foreign (non-U.S.) financial institution who's FATCA obligations are carried out by a sponsoring entity. A sponsoring entity must be registered with the IRS and agrees to perform FATCA compliance on behalf of one or more sponsored entities. A sponsored FFI will provide the GIIN of their sponsoring entity.	Yes[a]

(continued)

(continued)

Chapter 4 status	Definition	GIIN required
Certified deemed-compliant non-registering local bank	A company that operates and is licensed solely as a bank or credit union in its country of incorporation or organization. A certified deemed-compliant non-registering local bank will: • Engage primarily in the business of receiving deposits from and making loans to retail customers or credit union/cooperative members; • Not solicit account holders outside its country of organization; • Have no fixed place of business outside of its country of organization; • Have no more than $175 million in assets on its balance sheet (Note: If it is a member of an expanded affiliated group, the group will have no more than $500 million in total assets on its consolidated or combined balance sheets).	No
Certified deemed-compliant FFI with only low value accounts	A foreign (non-U.S.) financial institution which is not engaged in investing, reinvesting or trading in securities, partnership interests, commodities, notional principal contracts, insurance or annuity contracts. • No account maintained by the FFI or any member of its expanded affiliated group has a balance or value in excess of $50,000. • Neither the FFI nor its entire expanded affiliated group has more than $50 million in assets on its consolidated or combined balance sheet as of the end of its most recent accounting year.	No
Certified deemed-compliant sponsored, closely held investment vehicle	A financial institution that is an investment entity (NOT a U.S. qualified intermediary, withholding foreign partnership or withholding foreign trust), and has a contractual arrangement with a sponsoring entity that is registered with the IRS as a sponsoring entity and is a participating financial institution, reporting Model 1 financial institution or U.S. financial institution. The sponsoring entity should be that is authorized to manage the financial institution and enter into contracts on its behalf under which the sponsoring entity agrees to all due diligence, withholding and reporting responsibilities that the financial institution would have if it were a reporting financial institution. The sponsored vehicle does not hold itself out as an investment vehicle for unrelated parties and has 20 or fewer individuals that own its debt and equity interests.	No

(continued)

(continued)

Chapter 4 status	Definition	GIIN required
Certified deemed-compliant limited life debt investment entity	A limited life debt investment entity that is deemed-compliant because an FFI is the beneficial owner of the payment and that FFI meets certain requirements described in the regulations. The entity should have been in existence as of January 17, 2013 and have issued all classes of its debt or equity interests to investors on or before January 17, 2013.	No
Certain investment entities that do not maintain financial accounts	Investment advisors and managers. These entities must be in the business of providing investment advice and/or managing investments for clients.	No
Owner-documented FFI	Closely held passive investment vehicles that are investment entities, where meeting the obligations under the agreement would be onerous given the size of the entity. An owner-documented FI must not: • Maintain a financial account for any nonparticipating financial institution; • Be owned by—or be a member of a group of related entities with—any financial institution that is a depository institution, custodial institution or specified insurance company.	No
Restricted distributor	An entity that operates as a distributor that holds debt or equity interests in a restricted fund as a nominee. Certain conditions must be met.	No
Nonreporting IGA FFI	An FFI that is identified as a nonreporting financial institution in a Model 1 or Model 2 IGA jurisdiction, but is NOT a registered deemed-compliant FFI.	NO
Foreign government, government of a U.S. possession or foreign central bank of issue	A non-U.S. government, government of a U.S. possession or a non-U.S. central bank of issue that is not engaged in commercial financial activities of a type engaged in by an insurance company, custodial institution or depository institution.	No
International organization	An organization that is comprised primarily of foreign governments or recognized as an intergovernmental or supranational organization under a foreign law similar to the U.S. International Organizations Immunities Act. The benefit of the organization's income should not inure to any private person; The organization should be the beneficial owner of the payment and not engage in commercial financial activities of a type engaged in by an insurance company, custodial institution or depository institution with respect to the payments and accounts.	No

(continued)

(continued)

Chapter 4 status	Definition	GIIN required
Exempt retirement plans	A Broad Participation Retirement Fund or a Narrow Participation Retirement Fund or a Pension Fund of a Governmental Entity, International Organization or Central Bank	No
Entity wholly owned by exempt beneficial owners	An investment entity where each direct holder of an equity interest in the investment entity is an exempt beneficial owner and each direct holder of a debt interest in the investment entity is either a depository institution or an exempt beneficial owner. The entity should provide an owner reporting statement that contains the name, address, TIN (if any), Chapter 4 status and a description of the type of documentation provided to the withholding agent for every person that owns a debt interest or direct equity interest in the entity; it should also provide documentation establishing that every owner of the entity is an entity.	No
Territory financial institution	A financial institution (other than an investment entity) that is incorporated or organized under the laws of a possession of the United States.	Yes[b]
Excepted non-financial group entity	A non-U.S. entity that is a member of a non-financial group where: • the entity is not a depository institution or custodial institution • the entity is a holding company, treasury center or captive finance company • the entity does not hold itself out as an arrangement or investment vehicle that is a private equity fund, venture capital fund, leveraged buyout fund or any similar investment vehicle established with an investment strategy to acquire or fund companies and to treat the interests in those companies as capital assets held for investment purposes and • the entity is not a specified insurance company.	No
Excepted non-financial start-up company	A non-U.S. entity that is investing capital in assets with the intent to operate a new business or line of business other than that of a financial institution or passive NFFE for a period of 24 months.	No
Excepted non-financial entity in liquidation or bankruptcy	A non-U.S. entity that was not a financial institution or passive NFFE at any time during the past five years and that is in the process of liquidating its assets or reorganizing with the intent to continue or recommence operations as a non-financial entity.	No

(continued)

(continued)

Chapter 4 status	Definition	GIIN required
501(c) organization	A nonprofit organization in the federal law of the United States that is one of 29 types of nonprofit organizations exempt from some federal income taxes.	No
Nonprofit organization	An entity that is established and maintained in its country of residence exclusively for religious, charitable, scientific, artistic, cultural or educational purposes. The entity will be: • Exempt from income tax in its country of residence; • Have no shareholders or members who have a proprietary or beneficial interest in its income or assets; • Not permitted to distribute any income or assets to a private person or non-charitable entity other than pursuant to the conduct of the entity's charitable activities • Required to, upon the entity's liquidation or dissolution, distribute all of its assets to an entity that is a foreign government, an integral part of a foreign government or a controlled entity of a foreign government.	No
Publicly traded NFFE or NFFE affiliate of a publicly traded corporation	A foreign corporation that is not a financial institution, with stock that is regularly traded on one or more established securities market or is a member of the same expanded affiliated group as an entity the stock of which is regularly traded on an established securities market.	No
Excepted territory NFFE	Entities excluded from the FFI definition and not subject to withholding including: • Corporation with stock traded on established securities market • Affiliated group of those corporations • Entity organized in U.S. Territory and owned by its residents • Foreign government • International organization • Foreign Central Bank of Issue • Any other specifically identified class, including those posing a low risk of tax evasion, as determined by the IRS.	No

(continued)

(continued)

Chapter 4 status	Definition	GIIN required
Active NFFE	A non-financial foreign (non-U.S.) entity that operates an active trade or business other than that of a financial business. • Less than 50% of the entity's gross income for the preceding calendar year is passive income. • Less than 50% of the assets held by the entity are assets that produce or are held for the production of passive income.	No
Passive NFFE	A non-U.S. entity, organization or company that is in receipt of passive income or holds passive assets and do not fall under any of the other FATCA classifications. These entities do not carry on the business of a financial institution.	No
Excepted inter-affiliate FFI	A non-U.S. entity that is a member of a participating FFI group where: • the entity does not maintain financial accounts • the entity does not hold an account with or receive payments from any withholding agent other than a member of its expanded affiliated group; • the entity does not make withholdable payments to any person other than to members of its expanded affiliated group • the entity has not agreed to report or otherwise act as an agent for Chapter 4 purposes on behalf of any financial institution	No
Direct reporting NFFE	A non-financial foreign (non-U.S.) entity that elects to report information about its direct or indirect substantial U.S. owners to the IRS.	Yes
Sponsored direct reporting NFFE	A non-financial foreign (non-U.S.) entity that is a direct reporting NFFE with another entity, other than a nonparticipating FFI, that has agreed with the NFFE to act as its sponsoring entity.	Yes[a]
Account that is not a financial account	An account that is not maintained by a financial institution, including depository accounts and custodial accounts.	No

[a] Will provide GIIN belonging to sponsoring entity
[b] GIIN is replaced with FIN (FATCA Identification Number)

LOB definitions

LOB option	Definition
Government	A foreign (non-U.S.) government.
Tax-exempt pension trust or pension fund	A pension trust or fund where more than half of the beneficiaries or participants are residents of the country of residence of the trust or fund itself.
Other tax-exempt organization	Organizations that qualify for exemption from federal income tax.
Publicly traded corporation	A corporation with a principal class of shares that is primarily and regularly traded on a recognized stock exchange in its country of residence.
Subsidiary of a publicly traded corporation	A company where more than 50% of the shares are owned, directly or indirectly, by five or fewer companies that are publicly traded corporations.
Company that meets the ownership and base erosion test	A company where more than 50% of the company is owned by individuals or entities that are resident in the company's country of incorporation, and less than 50% of the company's gross income is accrued or paid to persons who are outside of the country of incorporation.
Company that meets the derivative benefits test	A company where more than 90% of the aggregate votes and value of the company's shares be owned, directly or indirectly, by seven or fewer equivalent beneficiaries **AND** where less than 50% of the company's gross income is paid or accrued, directly or indirectly, to persons who would not be equivalent beneficiaries. An equivalent beneficiary is an ultimate owner who is resident in an EU, EEA or NAFTA country and is entitled to identical benefits under their own treaty with the U.S. under one of the ownership tests included within the LOB article (other than the ownership and base erosion test).
Company with an item of income that meets active trade or business test	A company that is engaged in an active trade or business in its country of residence, with activities in that country that are substantial in relation to its U.S. activities, receiving payment from a payer is a related party, and the income be derived in connection to or incidental to that trade or business.
Favorable discretionary determination by the U.S. competent authority received	A company with a favorable determination granting benefits from the U.S. competent authority stating that, despite the company's failure to meet a specific objective LOB test in the applicable treaty, it may nonetheless claim the requested benefits.

Appendix 2: Useful Terms and Definitions

Abbreviations

General

AML	Anti-Money Laundering
CiC	Change in Circumstances
CIV	Collective Investment Vehicle
DCM	Digital Compliance Map
EU	European Union
IRC	Internal Revenue Code
IRS	Internal Revenue Service
KYC	Know-Your-Customer
OECD	Organisation for Economic Co-operation and Development
OSM	Operational Structure Map
OTC	Over the Counter
REIT	Real Estate Investment Trust
SaaS	Software as a Service
SWIFT	Society for Worldwide Interbank Financial Telecommunications
TIN	Tax Identification Number

IRC Chapter 3

EFTPS	Electronic Federal Tax Payment System
EIN	Employer Identification Number
FDAP	Fixed, Determinable, Annual or Periodic income
FIRE	Filing Information Returns Electronically
FWS	Full Withholding Statement
IRC	Internal Revenue Code
ITIN	Individual Taxpayer Identification Number
LoB	Limitation of Benefits
MoU	Memorandum of Understanding (*for the eW-8 Program*)
NQI	Non-Qualified Intermediary
NRA	Non-Resident Alien
NWFP	Non-Withholding Foreign Partnership
NWQI	Non-Withholding Qualified Intermediary
PAI	Private Arrangement Intermediary

QI   Qualified Intermediary
QDD   Qualified Derivatives Dealer
QIEIN   Qualified Intermediary EIN
QSL   Qualified Securities Lender
SSN   Social Security Number
SSNA   Social Security Numbering Agency
TCC   Transmitter Control Code
TIN   Tax Identification Number
USWA   United States Withholding Agent
WFP   Withholding Foreign Partnership
WFT   Withholding Foreign Trust
WQI   Withholding Qualified Intermediary
WRPS   Withholding Rate Pool Statement

IRC Chapter 4, OECD and EU

AEoI   Automatic Exchange of Information
BIAC   Business Industry Advisory Committee
CCP   Common Compliance Program
CCG   Consolidated Compliance Group
C-DCFFI   Certified Deemed-Compliant FFI
CFA   Committee on Fiscal Affairs
CLN   Certificate of Loss of Nationality
DCFFI   Deemed-Compliant FFI
EAG   Expanded Affiliate Group
EEA   European Economic Area
EoI   Exchange of Information
FATCA   Foreign Account Tax Compliance Act *(misnomer)*
FFEIN   FFI Employer Identification Number
FFI   Foreign Financial Institution
FISCO   Fiscal Compliance Experts Group
HIRE   Hiring Incentives to Restore Employment Act (2010)
ICG   Informal Consultative Group
IP   Implementation Protocol
NFFE   Non-Financial Foreign Entity
NP-FFI   Non-Participating FFI
PFFI   Participating FFI
R-DCFFI   Registered Deemed-Compliant FFI
RM[n]-FFI Reporting Model n FFI (n = 1 or 2)

OECD	Organisation for Economic Co-operation and Development
T-BAG	Tax Barriers Business Advisory Group
TRACE	Tax Relief and Compliance Enhancement
WTCC	Withholding Tax Code of Conduct

Appendix 3: The QI Agreement

I have included here the original text of the current QI Agreement for reference. This is Revenue Procedure 2017–15. Due to space considerations, the Appendices to the QI Agreement are not included here. Please also note that a backup withholding rate of 24% is mentioned in the QI Agreement. This has since been changed to 24%.

THIS AGREEMENT is made under and in pursuance of sections 1441, 1442, 1471, and 1472 and §§1.1441-1(e)(5) and 1.1441-1(e)(6):

WHEREAS, QI has submitted an application in accordance with Revenue Procedure 2017–15 to be a qualified intermediary;

WHEREAS, QI and the IRS desire to enter into an agreement to establish QI's rights and obligations regarding documentation, withholding, information reporting, tax return filing, deposit, and refund procedures under sections 1441, 1442, 1443, 1461, 1471, 1472, 1474, 3406, 6041, 6042, 6045, 6049, 6050N, 6302, 6402, and 6414, and tax liability under sections 871(a) and 881 for a QI that is acting as a qualified derivatives dealer (QDD), with respect to certain types of payments;

WHEREAS, QI represents that there are no legal restrictions that prohibit it from complying with the requirements of this Agreement; and

WHEREAS, if QI is a foreign financial institution (FFI), QI represents that, as of the effective date of this Agreement, it has agreed to comply with the requirements of the FFI agreement, in the case of a participating FFI (including a reporting Model 2 FFI); §1.1471-5(f)(1) or the applicable Model 2 IGA, in the case of a registered deemed-compliant FFI (other than a reporting Model 1 FFI); or the applicable Model 1 IGA, in the case of a reporting Model 1 FFI or a registered deemed-compliant Model 1 IGA FFI;

NOW, THEREFORE, in consideration of the following terms, representations, and conditions, the parties agree as follows:

Section 1. Purpose and Scope

Sec. 1.01. General Obligations. When the IRS enters into a QI Agreement with a foreign person or a foreign branch of a U.S. person, that foreign person (or foreign branch) becomes a QI. QI is a withholding agent under chapters 3

and 4, and a payor under chapter 61 and section 3406, for amounts that it pays to its account holders.

If QI is an FFI, the requirements QI has agreed to as a participating FFI, registered deemed-compliant FFI, or registered deemed-compliant Model 1 IGA FFI apply in addition to the requirements under this Agreement. If QI acts as a QI with respect to an account, this Agreement will reference QI's chapter 4 obligations when necessary to facilitate coordination with the QI's obligations under chapters 3, 4, and 61 and section 3406 with respect to such account holders. A participating FFI's (including a reporting Model 2 FFI) obligations are provided in the FFI agreement, a registered deemed-compliant FFI's (other than a reporting Model 1 FFI) obligations are provided in §1.1471-5(f)(1) or the applicable Model 2 IGA, and the obligations of a reporting Model 1 FFI or a registered deemed-compliant Model 1 IGA FFI are provided in the applicable Model 1 IGA. For purposes of chapter 4, QI must comply with its FATCA requirements as a participating FFI, registered deemed-compliant FFI, or registered deemed-compliant Model 1 IGA FFI (as applicable) in order to maintain its required chapter 4 status, as well as the requirements of a withholding agent for any payee that is a nonparticipating FFI or NFFE that is not an account holder. If QI is an FFI, QI must also, pursuant to this Agreement, assume primary reporting responsibility for purposes of section 1472, for certain indirect account holders for which it acts as a QI. If QI is an NFFE acting on behalf of persons other than its shareholders, QI must assume primary reporting responsibility for purposes of section 1472 for any person for which it acts as a QI.

If QI acts as a sponsoring entity on behalf of a sponsored FFI (as defined in §1.1471-1(b)(121)) or sponsored direct reporting NFFE (as defined in §1.1471-1(b)(123)), it must comply with the due diligence, withholding, reporting, and compliance requirements of a sponsoring entity in addition to its requirements under this Agreement.

For purposes of chapters 3 and 61 and section 3406, QI must act in its capacity as a QI pursuant to this Agreement for those accounts that QI holds with a withholding agent and that QI has identified as accounts for which it acts as a QI. QI is not required to act as a QI for all accounts that it holds with a withholding agent. However, QI must, as part of its QI Agreement, materially comply with the requirements of a withholding agent or payor, as applicable to a nonqualified intermediary (NQI) under chapters 3 and 61 and section 3406, for any account for which it does not (or cannot) act as a QI and for any payee that is not an account holder. If QI identifies an account as one for which it will act as a QI, it must act as a QI for all payments made to that account and obtain the documentation required under section 5 of this Agreement for such account.

When QI acts as a QI for an account and assumes primary chapter 3 withholding responsibility for payments to the account, QI must also assume primary withholding responsibility for withholdable payments made to such account for chapter 4 purposes.

If QI acts as a QI with respect to payments of substitute interest, as described in section 3.03(A) of this Agreement, it must act as a QI and assume primary withholding responsibility for all such payments of substitute interest.

If QI acts as a qualified securities lender (QSL) with respect to substitute dividend payments (as defined in §1.861-3(a)(6)), QI is required to act as a QSL and assume primary withholding responsibility for all substitute dividends received and paid by QI when acting as an intermediary or dealer with respect to securities lending and similar transactions. A QI that acts as a QDD may not act as a QSL, except with respect to a payment on a securities lending or sale-repurchase transaction for which the QI has determined that it is acting as an intermediary for the payment.

The home office (as defined in section 2.43 of this Agreement) and each branch of a foreign person that intends to act as a QDD must each separately qualify and be approved for QDD status, as provided in section 1.02 of this Agreement. A foreign branch of a U.S. financial institution may also apply for QI and QDD status provided it separately qualifies as an eligible entity. If QI acts as a QDD with respect to the home office or branch, the home office or branch, as applicable, must act as a QDD for all payments made as a principal with respect to potential section 871(m) transactions and all payments received as a principal with respect to potential section 871(m) transactions and underlying securities, excluding any payments made or received by the QDD to the extent the payment is treated as effectively connected with the conduct of a trade or business within the United States within the meaning of section 864. For purposes of this Agreement, any securities lending or sale-repurchase transaction (as defined in §1.871-15(a)(13)) QI enters into that is a section 871(m) transaction is treated as entered into by QI as a principal unless QI determines that it is acting as an intermediary with respect to that transaction. A QI may not act as a QDD when it receives or makes payments as an intermediary and must act as either a QI or NQI for the payment. A QI acting as a QDD must assume primary chapter 3 and chapter 4 withholding responsibility and primary Form 1099 reporting and backup withholding responsibility under section 3406 for payments made as a QDD with respect to any potential section 871(m) transaction provided the amount paid is an amount subject to chapter 3 or 4 withholding or a reportable payment under chapter 61. A QI acting as a QDD (other than a QDD that is a foreign branch of a U.S. financial institution) also must satisfy its QDD tax liability as determined under section 3.09 of this Agreement. The QDD (other than a QDD that is a foreign branch of a U.S. financial institution) must report its withholding tax liability under chapters 3 and 4 on Form 1042 and must report its QDD tax liability on the appropriate U.S. tax return (as prescribed by the IRS). A U.S. financial institution with a foreign branch that acts as a QDD must file the appropriate U.S. income tax return (e.g., Form 1120, *U.S. Corporation Income Tax Return*) for the tax year covered by this Agreement to report and pay its tax liability under chapter 1 and would not have a separate QDD tax liability.

A dividend or dividend equivalent is treated as received by a QDD acting in its non-equity derivatives dealer capacity if the dividend or dividend equivalent is received by a QDD acting as a proprietary trader. Transactions properly reflected in a QDD's equity derivatives dealer book are presumed to be held by a dealer in its equity derivatives dealer capacity for purposes of determining the QDD tax liability. In addition, for purposes of determining whether a dealer is acting in its equity derivatives dealer capacity, only the dealer's activities as an equity derivatives dealer are taken into account.

Sec. 1.02. Parties to the Agreement. This Agreement applies to:

(A) QI; and

(B) The Internal Revenue Service.

If QI is an FFI, QI can only act as a QI for an account if the branch of QI that holds the account operates in a KYC jurisdiction identified on the IRS's Approved KYC List. QI may add any jurisdiction in which it operates a branch that is not initially included in its QI application without prior IRS approval if the jurisdiction is identified on the IRS's Approved KYC List and QI updates its information on the QI/WP/WT Application and Accounts Management System with respect to such branch prior to treating such branch as a QI. Notwithstanding the preceding sentence, a QI may not add a branch that will act as a QDD through the QI/WP/WT Application and Accounts Management System. Instead, the branch must separately qualify and be approved for QDD status in accordance with the procedures to be prescribed by the IRS. A branch of a QI that is not subject to the provisions of this Agreement remains subject to the rules of chapters 3, 4, and 61 and section 3406, as provided in section 1.01 of this Agreement.

Section 2. Definitions

For purposes of this Agreement, except as otherwise provided in this Agreement, the terms listed below are defined as follows:

Sec. 2.01. Account. 'Account' or 'Financial Account' has the meaning given to that term in §1.1471-1(b) with respect to QI's obligations for chapter 4 purposes. For other purposes under this Agreement, 'account' or 'financial account' means any account for which QI acts as a QI. With respect to a QI acting as a QDD, 'account' means any potential section 871(m) transaction or underlying security where QDD receives payments as a principal and any potential section 871(m) transaction where QDD makes payments as a principal.

Sec. 2.02. Account Holder. If QI is an FFI, an 'account holder' means any person that is a direct account holder or an indirect account holder of an account that QI has identified to a withholding agent as an account for which it is acting as a QI and also includes any person that receives a U.S. source substitute dividend payment from a QI that is a QSL for the payment. 'Account holder' also means any person that enters into or holds a potential section 871(m) transaction with a QI acting as a QDD. If QI is an NFFE acting as a QI on behalf of persons other than its shareholders, an 'account holder' means any person for whom QI is acting as an intermediary with respect to a reportable payment or withholdable payment. With respect to a QI that assumes primary withholding responsibility for a substitute interest payment as described in section 3.03(A) of this Agreement, an 'account holder' includes any person that receives such a payment from the QI.

(A) Direct Account Holder. A direct account holder is any account holder who has a direct relationship with QI. In the case of an NFFE acting as a QI on behalf of persons other than its shareholders, a direct account holder is any person for whom QI is acting with respect to a reportable payment regardless of whether such person is the beneficial owner.

(B) Indirect Account Holder. An indirect account holder is any account holder who does not have a direct relationship with QI. For example, a person that holds an account with a foreign intermediary or an interest in a foreign flow-through entity which, in turn, has a direct relationship with QI is an indirect account holder of QI. A person is an indirect account holder even if there are multiple tiers of intermediaries or flow-through entities between the person and QI.

Sec. 2.03. Agreement. 'Agreement' means this Agreement, the Appendices to this Agreement, and QI's application to become a QI. The Appendices and QI's application are incorporated into this Agreement by reference.

Sec. 2.04. Amount Subject to Chapter 3 Withholding. An 'amount subject to chapter 3 withholding' is an amount described in §1.1441-2(a) regardless of whether such amount is withheld upon.

Sec. 2.05. Amount Subject to Chapter 4 Withholding. An 'amount subject to chapter 4 withholding' is a withholdable payment (as defined in §1.1473-1(a)) for which withholding is required under chapter 4 or an amount for which withholding was otherwise applied under chapter 4.

Sec. 2.06. Assuming Primary Withholding Responsibility. 'Assuming primary withholding responsibility' refers to when a QI assumes primary chapters 3 and 4 withholding responsibility with respect to payments of U.S. source FDAP income or assumes primary Form 1099 reporting and backup withholding responsibility. A QI that assumes primary withholding responsibility assumes the primary responsibility for deducting, withholding, and depositing the appropriate amount from a payment. Generally, a QI assuming primary chapters 3 and 4 withholding responsibility or assuming primary backup withholding responsibility relieves the person who makes a payment to the QI from the responsibility to withhold. Notwithstanding the preceding sentence, a QI acting as a QDD (that assumes primary withholding responsibility as required by section 3 of this Agreement) remains liable for the tax under section 881 and therefore remains subject to withholding on all U.S. source FDAP payments with respect to underlying securities, other than dividend equivalents; however, with respect to dividends (including deemed dividends), a QDD will not be subject to withholding on those payments until January 1, 2018.

Sec. 2.07. Backup Withholding. 'Backup withholding' means the withholding required under section 3406.

Sec. 2.08. Beneficial Owner. A 'beneficial owner' has the meaning given to that term in §1.1441-1(c)(6).

Sec. 2.09. Broker Proceeds. 'Broker proceeds' means gross proceeds (as defined in §1.6045-1(d)(5)) from a sale that is reportable under §1.6045-1(c).

Sec. 2.10. Chapter 3. Any reference to 'chapter 3' means sections 1441, 1442, 1443, 1461, 1463, and 1464.

Sec. 2.11. Chapter 3 Reporting Pool. A 'chapter 3 reporting pool' means a reporting pool described in section 8.03(B) of this Agreement.

Sec. 2.12. Chapter 4. Any reference to 'chapter 4' means sections 1471, 1472, 1473, and 1474.

Sec. 2.13. Chapter 4 Reporting Pool. A 'chapter 4 reporting pool' means a reporting pool described in section 8.03(A) of this Agreement.

Sec. 2.14. Chapter 4 Status. 'Chapter 4 status' means the status of a person as a U.S. person, a specified U.S. person, an individual that is a foreign person, a participating FFI, a deemed-compliant FFI, a restricted distributor, an exempt beneficial owner, a nonparticipating FFI, a territory financial institution, an excepted NFFE, or a passive NFFE.

Sec. 2.15. Chapter 61. Any reference to 'chapter 61' means sections 6041, 6042, 6045, 6049, and 6050N.

Sec. 2.16. Dealer. A 'dealer' has the meaning given to the term dealer in §1.871-15(a)(2) (i.e., a dealer in securities within the meaning of section 475(c)(1)).

Sec. 2.17. Deemed-Compliant FFI. 'Deemed-compliant FFI' means an FFI that is treated, pursuant to section 1471(b)(2) and §1.1471-5(f), as meeting the requirements of section 1471(b).

(A) Certified Deemed-Compliant FFI. 'Certified deemed-compliant FFI' means an FFI described in §1.1471-5(f)(2) and includes a nonreporting IGA FFI but excludes a nonreporting Model 2 FFI that is treated as a registered deemed-compliant FFI.

(B) Registered Deemed-Compliant FFI. 'Registered deemed-compliant FFI' means an FFI described in §1.1471-5(f)(1) and includes a reporting Model 1 FFI and a nonreporting Model 2 FFI that is treated as registered deemed-compliant FFI. For purposes of this Agreement, a reference to a registered deemed-compliant FFI that is providing a chapter 4 withholding rate pool of U.S. payees includes a registered deemed-compliant Model 1 IGA FFI.

(C) Registered Deemed-Compliant Model 1 IGA FFI. 'Registered deemed-compliant Model 1 IGA FFI' means an FFI treated as a deemed-compliant FFI under an applicable Model 1 IGA that is subject to similar due diligence and reporting requirements with respect to U.S. accounts as those applicable to a registered deemed-compliant FFI under §1.1471-5(f)(1), including the requirement to register with the IRS.

Sec. 2.18. Deposit Interest. 'Deposit interest' means interest described in section 871(i)(2)(A).

Sec. 2.19. Dividend Equivalent. A 'dividend equivalent' has the meaning given to that term in §1.871-15(c).

Sec. 2.20. Documentary Evidence. 'Documentary evidence' means any documentation obtained under the appropriate know-your-customer rules, any documentary evidence described in §1.1441-6 sufficient to establish entitlement to a reduced rate of withholding under an income tax treaty, or any documentary evidence described in §1.6049-5(c) sufficient to establish an account holder's status as a foreign person for purposes of chapter 61. Documentary evidence does not include a Form W-8 or Form W-9 (or an acceptable substitute Form W-8 or Form W-9).

Sec. 2.21. Documentation. 'Documentation' means any valid Form W-8, Form W-9 (or an acceptable substitute Form W-8 or Form W-9), or documentary evidence as defined in section 2.20 of this Agreement, including all statements or other information required to be associated with the form or documentary evidence.

Sec. 2.22. Effective Date. For a prospective QI that applies to be a QI on or before to March 31 of a given calendar year, the effective date of this Agreement will be January 1 of that year. For a prospective QI that applies after March 31 of a given calendar year and that has not received any reportable payments prior to the date the application is submitted, the effective date of this Agreement will be January 1 of that year. For a prospective QI that applies after March 31 of a given calendar year and that has received a reportable payment in the calendar year prior to the date the application is submitted, the effective date of this Agreement will be the first of the month in which the QI application is complete and the QI has received its QI-EIN.

Sec. 2.23. Eligible Entity. 'Eligible entity' for QDD status means a home office or branch that is a QI and that is—

(A) An equity derivatives dealer subject to regulatory supervision as a dealer by a governmental authority in the jurisdiction in which it was organized or operates;

(B) A bank or bank holding company subject to regulatory supervision as a bank or bank holding company, as applicable, by a governmental authority in the jurisdiction in which it was organized or operates and that, in its equity derivatives dealer capacity, (1) issues potential section 871(m) transactions to customers, and (2) receives dividends with respect to stock or dividend equivalent payments pursuant to potential section 871(m) transactions that hedge potential section 871(m) transactions that it issued;

(C) An entity that is wholly owned (directly or indirectly) by a bank or bank holding company subject to regulatory supervision as a bank or bank holding company, as applicable, by a governmental authority in the jurisdiction in which the bank or bank holding company was organized or operates and that, in its equity derivatives dealer capacity, (1) issues potential section 871(m) transactions to customers, and (2) receives dividends with respect to stock or dividend equivalent payments pursuant to potential section 871(m) transactions that hedge potential section 871(m) transactions that it issued; or

(D) A foreign branch of a U.S. financial institution, if the foreign branch would meet the requirements of paragraph (A), (B), or (C), if it were a separate entity.

The home office or any branch that wants to be a QDD must separately meet the requirements of paragraph (A), (B), or (C) as if it were a separate entity.

Sec. 2.24. Excepted NFFE. 'Excepted NFFE' means a person described in §1.1471-1(b)(41).

Sec. 2.25. Exempt Beneficial Owner. 'Exempt beneficial owner' means a person described in §1.1471-1(b)(42) and includes any person that is treated as an exempt beneficial owner under an applicable Model 1 or Model 2 IGA.

Sec. 2.26. Exempt Recipient. For purposes of Form 1099 reporting and backup withholding, an 'exempt recipient' means a person described in §1.6049-4(c)(1)(ii) (for interest, dividends, and royalties), a person described in §1.6045-2(b)(2)(i) (for broker proceeds), and a person described in §1.6041-3(q) (for rents, amounts paid on notional principal contracts, and other fixed or determinable income), for which no Form 1099 reporting is required. Exempt recipients are not exempt from reporting or withholding under chapter 3 or 4.

Sec. 2.27. FATCA Requirements as a Participating FFI, Registered Deemed-Compliant FFI, or Registered Deemed-Compliant Model 1 IGA FFI. 'FATCA requirements as a participating FFI, registered deemed-compliant FFI, or registered deemed-compliant Model 1 IGA FFI' means—

(A) For a participating FFI or an FFI that agrees to be treated as a participating FFI, the requirements set forth in the FFI agreement;

(B) For a registered deemed-compliant FFI (other than a reporting Model 1 FFI) or an FFI that agrees to be treated as a registered deemed-compliant FFI, the requirements under §1.1471-5(f)(1) or an applicable Model 2 IGA; or

(C) For a registered deemed-compliant Model 1 IGA FFI, reporting Model 1 FFI, or an FFI that agrees to be treated as a registered deemed-compliant Model 1 IGA FFI or reporting Model 1 FFI, the requirements under an applicable Model 1 IGA.

Sec. 2.28. Financial Institution (FI). 'Financial institution' or 'FI' is defined in §1.1471-5(d) and includes a financial institution as defined under an applicable Model 1 or Model 2 IGA.

Sec. 2.29. Foreign Financial Institution (FFI). 'Foreign Financial Institution' or 'FFI' means a foreign entity (as defined in §1.1473-1(e)) that is a financial institution.

Sec. 2.30. FFI Agreement. 'FFI Agreement' means an agreement described in §1.1471-4(a) and provided in Rev. Proc. 2014-3, 2014-3 I.R.B. 419, as revised by Rev. Proc. 2014-38, 2014-29 I.R.B. 131 (and any superseding revenue procedure).

Sec. 2.31. Flow-Through Entity. A flow-through entity is a foreign partnership described in §301.7701-2 or 3 (other than a withholding foreign partnership), a foreign trust (other than a withholding foreign trust) that is described in section 651(a), or a foreign trust if all or a portion of such trust is treated as owned by the grantor or other person under sections 671 through 679. For an item of income for which a treaty benefit is claimed, an entity is also a flow-through entity to the extent it is treated as fiscally transparent under section 894 and the regulations thereunder.

Sec. 2.32. Foreign Person. A 'foreign person' is any person that is not a 'United States person' and includes a 'non-resident alien individual', a 'foreign corporation', a 'foreign partnership', a 'foreign trust', and a 'foreign estate', as those terms are defined in section 7701. For purposes of chapters 3 and 4, the term foreign person also means, with respect to a payment by a withholding agent, a foreign branch (including a foreign disregarded entity) of a U.S. person that provides a valid Form W-8IMY on which it represents that it is a QI. A foreign branch of a U.S. person that is a QI is, however, a U.S. payor for purposes of chapter 61 and section 3406.

Sec. 2.33. Foreign TIN. A 'foreign TIN' is a taxpayer identification number issued by a foreign person's country of residence.

Sec. 2.34. Form W-8. 'Form W-8' means IRS Form W-8BEN, *Certificate of Foreign Status of Beneficial Owner for United States Tax Withholding (Individuals)*; IRS Form W-8BEN-E, *Certificate of Status of Beneficial Owner for United States Tax Withholding and Reporting (Entities)*; IRS Form W-8ECI, *Certificate of Foreign Person's Claim That Income is Effectively Connected With the Conduct of a Trade or Business in the United States*; IRS Form W-8EXP, *Certificate of Foreign Government or Other Foreign Organization for United States Tax Withholding and Reporting*; and IRS Form W-8IMY, *Certificate of Foreign Intermediary, Foreign Flow-Through Entity, or Certain U.S. Branches for United States Tax Withholding and Reporting*, as appropriate. It also includes any acceptable substitute Form W-8.

Sec. 2.35. Form W-9. 'Form W-9' means IRS Form W-9, *Request for Taxpayer Identification Number and Certification*, or any acceptable substitute Form W-9.

Sec. 2.36. Form 945. 'Form 945' means IRS Form 945, *Annual Return of Withheld Federal Income Tax*.

Sec. 2.37. Form 1042. 'Form 1042' means IRS Form 1042, *Annual Withholding Tax Return for U.S. Source Income of Foreign Persons*.

Sec. 2.38. Form 1042-S. 'Form 1042-S' means IRS Form 1042-S, *Foreign Person's U.S. Source Income Subject to Withholding*.

Sec. 2.39. Form 1099. 'Form 1099' means IRS Form 1099-B, *Proceeds From Broker and Barter Exchange Transactions*; IRS Form 1099-DIV, *Dividends and Distributions*; IRS Form 1099-INT, *Interest Income*; IRS Form 1099-MISC, *Miscellaneous Income*; IRS Form 1099-OID, *Original Issue Discount*;

and any other form in the IRS Form 1099 series appropriate to the type of payment required to be reported.

Sec. 2.40. Form 8966. 'Form 8966' means IRS Form 8966, *FATCA Report*.

Sec. 2.41. Form 1099 Reporting. 'Form 1099 reporting' means the reporting required on Form 1099.

Sec. 2.42. Global Intermediary Identification Number (GIIN). 'Global intermediary identification number' or 'GIIN' means the identification number that is assigned to a participating FFI, registered deemed-compliant FFI, direct reporting NFFE, or sponsoring entity of a direct reporting NFFE. The term also includes the identification number assigned to a reporting Model 1 FFI or registered deemed-compliant Model 1 IGA FFI that is a QI for the purpose of identifying itself to withholding agents.

Sec. 2.43. Home Office. 'Home office' means a foreign person, excluding any branches of the foreign person, that applies for QDD status.

Sec. 2.44. Intermediary. An 'intermediary' means any person that acts on behalf of another person such as a custodian, broker, nominee, or other agent or a person that acts as a QSL with respect to a substitute dividend payment.

Sec. 2.45. Know-Your-Customer Rules. 'Know-your-customer rules' refers to the applicable laws, regulations, rules, and administrative practices and procedures governing the requirements of QI to obtain documentation confirming the identity of QI's account holders.

Sec. 2.46. Marketable Securities. For purposes of this Agreement, the term 'marketable securities' means those securities described in §1.1441-6 for which a U.S. TIN (or foreign TIN) is not required to obtain treaty benefits.

Sec. 2.47. Net Delta Exposure. Net delta exposure to an underlying security is the amount (measured in number of shares) by which (A) the aggregate number of shares in an underlying security that the QDD has exposure to as a result of positions in the underlying security (including as a result of owning the underlying security) with values that move in the same direction as the underlying security (the 'long positions') exceeds (B) the aggregate number of shares of in an underlying security that the QDD has exposure to as a result of positions in the underlying security with values that move in the opposite direction from the underlying security (the 'short positions'). The net delta exposure calculation only includes long positions and short positions that the QDD holds in its equity derivatives dealer business. Any long positions or short positions that are treated as effectively connected with the QDD's conduct of a trade or business in the United States for U.S. federal income tax purposes are excluded from the net delta exposure computation. The net delta exposure to an underlying security is determined at the end of the day on the date provided in §1.871-15(j)(2) for the applicable dividend. For purposes of this calculation, net delta must be determined in a commercially reasonable manner. If a QDD calculates net delta for non-tax business purposes, the net delta ordinary will be the delta used for this purpose, subject to the modifications required by this definition. Each QDD must determine its net delta exposure separately only taking into account transactions that exist and are attributable to that QDD for U.S. federal income tax purposes.

Sec. 2.48. Non-consenting U.S. Account. For purposes of a reporting Model 2 FFI, 'non-consenting U.S. account' has the meaning that such term has under an applicable Model 2 IGA.

Sec. 2.49. Non-exempt Recipient. A 'non-exempt recipient' means a person that is not an exempt recipient under the definition in section 2.26 of this Agreement.

Sec. 2.50. Non-financial Foreign Entity (NFFE). A 'non-financial foreign entity' or 'NFFE' means a foreign entity that is not a financial institution (including an entity that is incorporated or organized under the laws of any U.S. territory and that is not a financial institution). The term also means a foreign entity treated as an NFFE pursuant to a Model 1 or Model 2 IGA.

Sec. 2.51. Nonparticipating FFI. A 'nonparticipating FFI' means an FFI other than a participating FFI, a deemed-compliant FFI, or an exempt beneficial owner.

Sec. 2.52. Nonqualified Intermediary (NQI). A 'nonqualified intermediary' or 'NQI' is any intermediary that is not a qualified intermediary. An NQI includes any intermediary that is a foreign person unless such person enters an agreement to be a QI and acts in such capacity. An NQI also includes an intermediary that is a territory FI unless such institution agrees to be treated as a U.S. person.

Sec. 2.53. Non-U.S. Payor. A 'non-U.S. payor' means a payor other than a U.S. payor as defined in this section 2.81 of this Agreement.

Sec. 2.54. Non-withholding Foreign Partnership. A 'nonwithholding foreign partnership' means a foreign partnership other than a withholding foreign partnership as defined in §1.1441–5(c)(2)(i).

Sec. 2.55. Non-withholding Foreign Trust. A 'nonwithholding foreign trust' means a foreign trust (as defined in section 7701(a)(31)(B)) that is a foreign simple trust or a foreign grantor trust and that is not a withholding foreign trust.

Sec. 2.56. Overwithholding. The term 'overwithholding' means any amount actually withheld (determined before application of the adjustment procedures described in section 9 of this Agreement) from an item of income or other payment that is in excess of:

(A) The amount required to be withheld under chapter 4 with respect to such item of income or other payment, if applicable, and,

(B) In the case of an amount subject to chapter 3 withholding, the actual tax liability of the beneficial owner of the income or payment to which the withheld amount is attributable, regardless of whether such overwithholding was in error or appeared correct at the time it occurred.

For purposes of section 3406, the term 'overwithholding' means the excess of the amount actually withheld under section 3406 over the amount required to be withheld.

Sec. 2.57. Participating FFI. A 'participating FFI' means an FFI described in §1.1471-1(b)(91). The term participating FFI also includes a QI branch of a U.S. financial institution, unless such branch is a reporting Model 1 FFI.

Sec. 2.58. Payee. For chapter 4 purposes, a 'payee' means a person described in §1.1471-3(a). For purposes of chapter 61, a 'payee' means the person to whom a payment is made. For purposes of chapter 3, a 'payee' means a person described in §1.1441-1(c)(12).

Sec. 2.59. Payment. A 'payment' is considered made to a person if that person realizes income, whether or not such income results from an actual transfer of cash or other property. See §1.1441-2(e). For example, a payment includes crediting an amount to an account. For any payment of a dividend equivalent, a 'payment' has the meaning provided in §1.871-15(i).

Sec. 2.60. Payor. A 'payor' is defined in §31.3406(a)-2 and §1.6049-4(a)(2) and generally means any person required to make an information return under chapter 61. The term includes any person that makes a payment, directly or indirectly, to QI and to whom QI provides information, pursuant to this Agreement, so that such person can report a payment on Form 1099 and, if appropriate, backup withhold. See also sections 2.81 and 2.53 of this Agreement for the definition of U.S. payor and non-U.S. payor.

Sec. 2.61. Potential Section 871(m) Transaction. A 'potential section 871(m) transaction' is any securities lending or sale-repurchase transaction, notional principal contract (NPC), or equity linked instrument (ELI) that references one or more underlying securities. For purposes of this definition, securities lending or sale-repurchase transaction, NPC, ELI, reference, and underlying security have the meaning given to the terms in §§1.871-15(a)(13), (7), (4), (11), and (15), respectively.

Sec. 2.62. Private Arrangement Intermediary (PAI). A 'private arrangement intermediary' or 'PAI' is an intermediary described in section 4 of this Agreement.

Sec. 2.63. Qualified Derivatives Dealer (QDD). A 'qualified derivatives dealer' or 'QDD' is an eligible entity that agrees to meet the requirements of

§1.1441-1(e)(6)(i) and of this Agreement with respect to payments on potential section 871(m) transactions and underlying securities that it receives or makes as a principal. In order to act as a QDD, the home office or branch, as applicable, must qualify and be approved for QDD status and must represent itself as a QDD on its Form W-8IMY and separately identify the home office or branch as the recipient on a withholding statement (if necessary). Each home office or branch that obtains QDD status is treated as a separate QDD.

Sec. 2.64. QDD Tax Liability. A 'QDD tax liability' is the amount described in section 3.09 of this Agreement.

Sec. 2.65. Qualified Intermediary (QI). A 'qualified intermediary' or 'QI' is a person (or branch) described in §1.1441-1(e)(5)(ii) that has in effect an agreement with the IRS to be treated as a QI and acts as a QI.

Sec. 2.66. QI-EIN. A 'QI-EIN' means the employer identification number is assigned by the IRS to a QI. QI's QI-EIN is only to be used when QI is acting as a QI. For example, QI must give a withholding agent its EIN (other than its QI-EIN), if any, if it is receiving income as a beneficial owner (excluding when it receives income as a principal when acting as a QDD or as a QI assuming primary withholding responsibility for a substitute interest payment). QI must also use its non-QI EIN, if any, when acting as an NQI. Each signatory to this Agreement must have its own QI-EIN.

Sec. 2.67. Qualified Securities Lender (QSL). A 'qualified securities lender' or 'QSL' is a person described as a qualified securities lender in Notice 2010-46, 2010-24 I.R.B. 757. A QI that acts as a QSL with respect to a substitute dividend payment (as defined in §1.861-3(a)(6)) is required to act as a QSL for all U.S. source substitute dividends received by the QI when acting as an intermediary or dealer with respect to securities lending and similar transactions. A QI is only permitted to act as a QSL until December 31, 2017.

Sec. 2.68. Reportable Amount. A 'reportable amount' means U.S. source FDAP income that is an amount subject to chapter 3 withholding, U.S. source deposit interest, and U.S. source interest or original issue discount paid on the redemption of short-term obligations. The term does not include payments on deposits with banks and other financial institutions that remain on deposit for two weeks or less. It also does not include amounts of original issue discount arising from a sale and repurchase transaction completed within a period of two weeks or less, or amounts described in §1.6049-5(b)(7), (10), or (11) (relating to certain foreign targeted registered obligations and certain obligations issued in bearer form).

Sec. 2.69. Reportable Payment. For purposes of this Agreement, a 'reportable payment' means an amount described in section 2.69(A) of this

Agreement, in the case of a U.S. payor, and an amount described in section 2.69(B) of this Agreement, in the case of a non-U.S. payor.

(A) U.S. Payor. If QI is a U.S. payor, a 'reportable payment' means, unless an exception to reporting applies under chapter 61,—

(1) Any reportable amount;

(2) Any broker proceeds from a sale reportable under §1.6045-1(c); and

(3) Any foreign source interest, dividends, rents, royalties, or other fixed and determinable income.

(B) Non-U.S. Payor. If QI is a non-U.S. payor, a 'reportable payment' means, unless an exception to reporting applies under chapter 61,—

(1) Any reportable amount;

(2) Any broker proceeds from a sale effected at an office inside the United States, as

defined in §1.6045-1(g)(3)(iii); and

(3) Any foreign source interest, dividends, rents, royalties, or other fixed and determinable income if such income is not paid outside the United States as described under section 5.13(C)(1) of this Agreement.

Sec. 2.70. Reporting Model 1 FFI. A 'reporting Model 1 FFI' means an FFI with respect to which a foreign government or agency thereof agrees to obtain and exchange information pursuant to a Model 1 IGA, other than an FFI that is treated as a nonreporting Model 1 FFI (including a registered deemed-compliant Model 1 IGA FFI) or a nonparticipating FFI under an applicable Model 1 IGA.

Sec. 2.71. Reporting Pool. A 'reporting pool' is defined in section 8 of this Agreement.

Sec. 2.72. Responsible Officer. A 'responsible officer' of a QI means an officer of the QI with sufficient authority to fulfill the duties of a responsible officer as described in section 10 of this Agreement, including the requirements to periodically certify and to respond to requests by the IRS for additional information to review the QI's compliance.

Sec. 2.73. Section 871(m) Amount. For each dividend on each underlying security, the 'section 871(m) amount' is (A) the QDD's net delta exposure to the underlying security for the applicable dividend multiplied by (B) the applicable dividend amount per share.

Sec. 2.74. Section 871(m) Transaction. A 'section 871(m) transaction' is any securities lending or sale-repurchase transaction, specified NPC, or specified ELI described in §1.871-15(a)(13), (d), and (e), respectively.

Sec. 2.75. Short-Term Obligation. A 'short-term obligation' is any obligation described in section 871(g)(1)(B)(i).

Sec. 2.76. Substitute Interest. 'Substitute interest' means a substitute interest payment described in §1.861-2(a)(7).

Sec. 2.77. Underlying Security. For purposes of a QI acting as a QDD or any determination relating to section 871(m), 'underlying security' has the meaning provided in §1.871-15(a)(15).

Sec. 2.78. Underwithholding. 'Underwithholding' means the excess of the amount required to be withheld under chapter 3 or 4 or section 3406 over the amount actually withheld.

Sec. 2.79. Undocumented Account Holder. An 'undocumented account holder' is an account holder for whom QI does not hold valid documentation.

Sec. 2.80. U.S. Account. A 'U.S. account' is any financial account maintained by an FFI that is held by one or more specified U.S. persons or U.S.-owned foreign entities that such FFI reports or elects to report under the FFI Agreement or §1.1471-5(f), as applicable.

Sec. 2.81. U.S. Payor. The term 'U.S. payor' has the same meaning as in §1.6049-5(c)(5).

Sec. 2.82. U.S. Person. A 'U.S. person' (or 'United States person') is a person described in section 7701(a)(30), the U.S. government (including an agency or instrumentality thereof), a State of the United States (including an agency or instrumentality thereof), or the District of Columbia (including an agency or instrumentality thereof). An individual will not be treated as a U.S. person for purposes of this section for a taxable year or any portion of a taxable year that the individual is a dual resident taxpayer (within the meaning of §301.7701(b)-7(a)(1)) who is treated as a non-resident alien pursuant to §301.7701(b)-7 for purposes of computing his or her U.S. tax liability. The term 'U.S. person' or 'United States person' also means a foreign insurance company that has made an election under section 953(d), provided that either the foreign insurance company is not a specified insurance company (as described in §1.1471-5(e)(1)(iv)), or the foreign insurance company is a specified insurance company and is licensed to do business in any State of the United States.

Sec. 2.83. U.S. Reportable Account. A 'U.S. reportable account' means a financial account maintained by a reporting Model 1 FFI or registered deemed-compliant Model 1 IGA FFI that such FFI reports or elects to report under the applicable domestic law for compliance with and implementation of FATCA.

Sec. 2.84. U.S. Source FDAP. 'U.S. source FDAP' means amounts from sources within the United States that constitute fixed or determinable annual or periodical income, as defined in §1.1441-2(b)(1).

Sec. 2.85. U.S. TIN. A 'U.S. TIN' means a U.S. taxpayer identification number assigned under section 6109.

Sec. 2.86. Withholding Agent. A 'withholding agent' has the same meaning as set forth in §1.1441-7(a) for purposes of chapter 3 and as set forth in §1.1473-1(d) for purposes of chapter 4, and includes a payor (as defined in section 2.60 of this Agreement).

Sec. 2.87. Withholding Foreign Partnership (WP). A 'withholding foreign partnership' or 'WP' means a partnership, described in §1.1441-5(c)(2), that has entered into a withholding agreement with the IRS to be treated as a withholding foreign partnership.

Sec. 2.88. Withholding Foreign Trust (WT). A 'withholding foreign trust' or 'WT' means a trust, described in §1.1441-5(e)(5)(v), that has entered into a withholding agreement with the IRS to be treated as a withholding foreign trust.

Sec. 2.89. Withholdable Payment. A 'withholdable payment' means an amount described in §1.1473-1(a).

Sec. 2.90. Withholding Rate Pool. A 'withholding rate pool' is defined in section 6.03 of this Agreement and includes a chapter 3 withholding rate pool and a chapter 4 withholding rate pool.

Sec. 2.91. Other Terms. Any term not defined in this section has the same meaning that it has under the Code, including the income tax regulations under the Code, any applicable income tax treaty, or any applicable Model 1 or Model 2 IGA with respect to a QI's FATCA requirements as a participating FFI, registered deemed-compliant FFI, or registered deemed-compliant Model 1 IGA FFI. Except as expressly provided in this Agreement, any term relating to a QDD or section 871(m) has the same meaning given to the term in §1.871-15.

Section 3. Withholding Responsibility and QDD Tax Liability

Sec. 3.01. Chapters 3 and 4 Withholding Responsibilities.

(A) Chapter 4 Withholding. QI is a withholding agent for purposes of chapter 4 and subject to the withholding and reporting provisions applicable to withholding agents under sections 1471 and 1472 with respect to its accounts. QI is required to withhold 30% of any withholdable payment made after June 30, 2014, to an account holder that is an FFI unless either QI can reliably associate the payment (or portion of the payment) with documentation upon which it is permitted to rely to treat the payment as exempt from withholding under §1.1471-2(a)(4) or the payment is made under a grandfathered obligation described in §1.1471-2(b). See §1.1471-2(b)(2)(i)

(A)(2) for the definition of grandfathered obligation with respect to an obligation giving rise to a dividend equivalent. QI is also required to withhold 30% of any withholdable payment made after June 30, 2014, to an account holder that is an NFFE unless either QI can reliably associate the payment (or portion of the payment) with a certification described in §1.1472-1(b)(1)(ii) or an exception to withholding under §1.1472-1 otherwise applies.

If QI is a participating FFI or registered deemed-compliant FFI (other than a reporting Model 1 FFI), QI will satisfy its requirement to withhold under sections 1471(a) and 1472(a) with respect to direct account holders that are entities by withholding on withholdable payments made to nonparticipating FFIs and recalcitrant account holders to the extent required under its FATCA requirements as a participating FFI or registered deemed-compliant FFI. See the FFI Agreement, §1.1471-5(f)(1), or the applicable Model 2 IGA for the withholding requirements that apply to withholdable payments made to account holders of the FFI that are individuals treated as recalcitrant account holders or non-consenting U.S. accounts. If QI is a reporting Model 1 FFI or a registered deemed-compliant Model 1 IGA FFI, QI will satisfy its requirement to withhold under section 1471(a) with respect to direct account holders by withholding on withholdable payments made to nonparticipating FFIs to the extent required under its FATCA requirements as a registered deemed-compliant FFI or registered deemed-compliant Model 1 IGA FFI. QI must, however, withhold in the manner described in sections 3.02 and 3.03 of this Agreement for when QI assumes or does not assume primary withholding responsibility for purposes of chapters 3 and 4 regardless of its chapter 4 status.

(B) Chapter 3 Withholding. To the extent that QI makes a payment of an amount subject to chapter 3 withholding, QI is required to withhold 30% of the gross amount of any such payment made to an account holder that is (or is presumed) a foreign person unless QI can reliably associate the payment with documentation upon which it can rely to treat the payment as made to a payee that is a U.S. person or as made to a beneficial owner that is a foreign person entitled to a reduced rate of withholding. See section 5 of this Agreement regarding documentation requirements. With respect an amount subject to chapter 4 withholding that is also an amount subject to chapter 3 withholding, QI may credit any tax withheld under chapter 4 against its liability for any tax due under chapter 3 with respect to the payment so that no additional withholding is required on the payment for purposes of chapter 3. Nothing in chapter 4 or the regulations thereunder (including the FFI Agreement) or any applicable IGA relieves QI of its requirements to withhold under chapter 3 to the extent required in this Agreement.

Sec. 3.02. Primary Chapters 3 and 4 Withholding Responsibility Not Assumed.

Notwithstanding sections 1.01 and 3.01 of this Agreement, QI is not be required to withhold with respect to a payment of U.S. source FDAP income if it (a) does not assume primary withholding responsibility under section 3.03 of this Agreement by electing to be withheld upon under §1.1471-2(a)(2)(iii) for purposes of chapter 4, (b) provides the withholding agent from which QI receives the payment with a valid withholding certificate that indicates that QI does not assume primary withholding responsibility for chapters 3 and 4 purposes, and (c) provides correct withholding statements (including information regarding any account holders or interest holders of an intermediary or flow-through entity that holds an account with QI, other than a QI that assumes primary withholding responsibility, WP, or WT) as described in section 6.02 of this Agreement. Notwithstanding its election not to assume primary withholding responsibility under chapters 3 and 4, QI shall, however, withhold the difference between the amount of withholding required under chapter 3 or 4 and the amount actually withheld by another withholding agent if QI—

(A) Actually knows that the appropriate amount has not been withheld by another withholding agent; or

(B) Made an error which results in the withholding agent's failure to withhold the correct amount due (e.g., QI fails to provide an accurate withholding statement with respect to the payment, including a failure to provide information regarding any account holders or interest holders of an intermediary or flow-through entity that holds an account with QI to the extent required in section 6 of this Agreement), and QI has not corrected the underwithholding under section 9.05 of this Agreement.

Sec. 3.03. Primary Chapters 3 and 4 Withholding Responsibility Assumed.

(A) In General. QI may assume primary withholding responsibility for purposes of chapters 3 and 4 by providing a valid withholding certificate described in section 6 of this Agreement to a withholding agent that makes a payment of U.S. source FDAP income to QI and by designating on the withholding statement associated with such certificate the account(s) for which QI assumes primary withholding responsibility (if required). QI is not required to assume primary withholding responsibility for all accounts it holds with a withholding agent. If QI assumes primary withholding responsibility for any account, it must assume that responsibility under chapters 3 and 4 for all withholdable payments and amounts subject to chapter 3 withholding made by the withholding agent to that account.

If QI is acting as a QSL for a substitute dividend payment, QI must assume primary withholding responsibility for any such payment made to any account holder receiving a substitute dividend payment.

QI may assume primary withholding responsibility for U.S. source FDAP payments of substitute interest as described in §1.861-2(a)(7). If QI assumes primary withholding responsibility for payments of substitute interest (as described in this paragraph), it must assume primary withholding responsibility with respect to all such payments. QI assumes primary withholding responsibility for payments of substitute interest for purposes of this Agreement when it assumes such responsibility for payments of interest and substitute interest it receives in connection with a sale-repurchase or similar agreement, a securities lending transaction, or collateral that it holds in connection with its activities as a dealer in securities. As a result, QI may represent its status as a QI on the withholding certificate described in section 6.01 of this Agreement with respect to payments it receives of interest and substitute interest described in the preceding sentence regardless of whether it acts as an intermediary or as a principal with respect to these payments.

To the extent that QI assumes primary withholding responsibility, QI shall withhold as described in section 3.01 of this Agreement. QI is not required to withhold on amounts it pays to another QI that has assumed primary withholding responsibility with respect to the payment (including a QI acting as a QDD except for all payments with respect to underlying securities, other than dividend equivalents, paid to a QDD for which withholding is required) or to a WP or a WT.

(B) Assumption of Withholding Responsibility by a QDD. If QI is acting as a QDD, it must assume primary chapters 3 and 4 withholding responsibility for any dividend equivalent payment that it makes and must withhold with respect to a dividend equivalent payment on the dividend payment date for the applicable dividend (as determined in §1.1441-2(e)(4)). Notwithstanding the preceding sentence, a QDD remains liable for tax under section 881 and subject to withholding on all U.S. source FDAP payments with respect to underlying securities, other than dividend equivalents; however, with respect to dividends (including deemed dividends), a QDD will not be subject to withholding on those payments until January 1, 2018. A QDD must treat any dividend equivalent as a dividend from sources within the United States for purposes of section 881 and chapter 3 and chapter 4 consistent section 871(m) and the regulations thereunder. A QDD may reduce the rate of withholding under chapter 3 only based on a beneficial owner's claim of treaty-reduced withholding for portfolio dividends under the dividends article of an applicable income tax treaty. A QDD must also assume primary chapter 3 and chapter 4 withholding responsibility for payments made with respect to a potential section 871(m) transaction even if the payment is not a dividend equivalent if the amount paid is an amount subject to chapter 3 or 4 withholding. A QDD is not required to withhold under chapter 3 or 4 on amounts it pays to another QI that has assumed primary withholding responsibility with respect to the payment or to a WP or a WT. In addition, the QDD must notify each payee in writing that it will withhold on the dividend payment date before the time for determining the payee's first dividend equivalent payment (as determined under §1.871-15(j)(2)).

Sec. 3.04. Backup Withholding Under Section 3406 and Form 1099 Reporting Responsibility.

(A) Backup Withholding. QI is a payor under section 3406 with respect to reportable payments. Under section 3406, unless an exception to backup withholding applies, a payor is required to deduct and withhold 28% from a reportable payment to an account holder that is a U.S. non-exempt recipient if the U.S. non-exempt recipient has not provided its U.S. TIN in the manner required under that section; the IRS notifies the payor that the U.S. TIN furnished by the payee is incorrect; there has been a notified payee under-reporting described in section 3406(c); or there has been a payee certification failure described in section 3406(d).

(B) Coordination of Chapter 4 Withholding and Backup Withholding. With respect to a withholdable payment that is also a reportable payment subject to backup withholding under section 3406, QI is not required to withhold under section 3406 if QI withheld on such payment under chapter 4. See §31.3406(g)-1(e). Alternatively, if QI is a participating FFI or a registered deemed-compliant FFI (other than a reporting Model 1 FFI), it may elect to satisfy its obligation to withhold under chapter 4 (or the FFI Agreement) on a withholdable payment made to a recalcitrant account holder that is a U.S. non-exempt recipient by satisfying its backup withholding obligation under section 3406 provided that the payment is also a reportable payment. See section 4 of the FFI Agreement. Nothing in chapter 4 (including the FFI Agreement) or any applicable IGA relieves QI of its requirements to backup withhold under section 3406 to the extent required by this Agreement.

(C) Form 1099 Reporting. If QI applies backup withholding (as described in section 3.04(B) of this Agreement), it must report the amount subject to backup withholding on Form 1099 and not on Form 1042-S.

Sec. 3.05. Primary Form 1099 Reporting and Backup Withholding Responsibility for Reportable Payments Other Than Reportable Amounts. QI is responsible for Form 1099 reporting and backup withholding on reportable payments other than reportable amounts to the extent required under this section 3.05 and section 8.06 of this Agreement, whether or not QI assumes primary Form 1099 reporting and backup withholding responsibility with respect to reportable amounts under section 3.07 of this Agreement. Further, no provision of this Agreement which requires QI to provide another withholding agent with information regarding reportable amounts shall be construed as relieving QI of its Form 1099 reporting and backup withholding obligations with respect to reportable payments that are not reportable amounts. See, however, §31.3406(g)-1(e) providing that a payor (irrespective of whether the payor is a U.S. or non-U.S. payor) is not required to backup withhold under section 3406 on a reportable payment that is paid and received outside the United States with respect to an offshore obligation or on gross proceeds from a sale effected outside the United States, unless the payor has actual knowledge that the payee is a U.S. person.

(A) U.S. Payor. Except as provided in section 3.05(C) of this Agreement, if QI is a U.S. payor, QI has primary Form 1099 reporting and backup withholding responsibility for reportable payments other than reportable amounts. For example, if QI is a U.S. payor, it has primary Form 1099 reporting and backup withholding responsibility for payments of foreign source income as well as all broker proceeds paid to account holders that are, or are presumed to be, U.S. non-exempt recipients.

(B) Non-U.S. Payor. If QI is a non-U.S. payor, QI has primary Form 1099 reporting and backup withholding responsibility for broker proceeds described in section 2.69(B)(2) of this Agreement and foreign source fixed and determinable income other than income paid and received outside United States as described in section 2.69(B)(3) of this Agreement, if such payments are made (or presumed made) to U.S. non-exempt recipients.

(C) Special Procedure for Broker Proceeds. If QI is a U.S. payor, QI may request another payor that is either a U.S. financial institution or another QI to report on Form 1099 and, if required, backup withhold with respect to broker proceeds from a sale that is effected at an office outside the United States (as defined in §1.6045-1(g)(3)(iii)) that QI is otherwise required to report under section 3.05(A) and section 8.05 of this Agreement, provided the other payor actually receives the broker proceeds. In such a case, QI will not be responsible for primary Form 1099 reporting and backup withholding with respect to broker proceeds, provided that the other payor agrees to do the reporting and backup withholding and QI provides all of the information necessary for the other payor to properly report and backup withhold. QI, however, remains responsible for primary Form 1099 reporting and backup withholding if the other payor does not agree to report and backup withhold, or if QI knows that the other payor failed to do so. If, however, QI is a participating FFI or registered deemed-compliant FFI (other than a reporting Model 1 FFI) that reports an account on Form 1099 in order to satisfy its U.S. account reporting requirement under chapter 4, as described in section 8.04 of this Agreement, QI is responsible for reporting on Form 1099 with respect to reportable payments made to such U.S. account and must report in the manner described in the FFI Agreement.

Sec. 3.06. Primary Form 1099 Reporting and Backup Withholding Responsibility for Reportable Amounts Not Assumed. Notwithstanding sections 1.01 and 3.04 of this Agreement, QI shall not be required to report on Form 1099 and backup withhold with respect to a reportable amount if QI does not assume primary Form 1099 reporting and backup withholding responsibility and it provides a payor from which it receives a reportable amount the Forms W-9 of its U.S. non-exempt recipient account holders (or, if a U.S. non-exempt recipient fails to provide a Form W-9 or information regarding the account holder's name, address, and U.S. TIN, if a U.S. TIN is available) together with the withholding rate pools attributable to U.S. non-exempt recipient account holders so that such payor may report on Form 1099 and, if required, backup withhold. If QI elects to backup withhold on withholdable payments that are also reportable amounts made to recalcitrant account holders that are also U.S. non-exempt recipients, QI shall not be required to report on Form 1099 and backup withhold with respect to a reportable amount if it provides a payor from which it receives a reportable amount information regarding such recalcitrant account holders. See section 6.03 of this Agreement and section 4 of the FFI Agreement. If QI reports its U.S. accounts on Forms 1099 under its FATCA requirements as a participating FFI or registered deemed-compliant FFI, see section 8.04(A) of this Agreement providing that QI cannot delegate to a withholding agent its requirement to report its U.S. accounts. If QI elects not to assume primary Form 1099 reporting and backup withholding responsibility, QI must provide the withholding agent with such information regarding any account holders or interest holders of an intermediary or flow-through entity that holds an account with QI. Notwithstanding its election not to assume primary Form 1099 reporting and backup withholding responsibility, QI shall backup withhold and report a reportable amount to the extent required under sections 3.04 and 8.06 of this Agreement if—

(A) QI actually knows that a reportable amount is subject to backup withholding and that another payor failed to apply backup withholding, or

(B) Another payor has not applied backup withholding to a reportable amount because of an error made by QI (e.g., QI failed to provide the other payor with information regarding the name, address, U.S. TIN (if available), and withholding rate pool for a U.S. non-exempt recipient account holder subject to backup withholding, including a failure to provide information regarding any account holders or interest holders of an intermediary or flow-through entity that holds an account with QI to the extent required in section 6 of this Agreement).

Sec. 3.07. Primary Form 1099 Reporting and Backup Withholding Responsibility Assumed. QI may assume primary Form 1099 reporting backup withholding responsibility with respect to reportable amounts without obtaining approval from the IRS. QI that assumes such responsibility is subject to all of the obligations imposed by chapter 61 and section 3406, as modified by this Agreement, and QI shall be subject to any applicable penalties for failure to meet those obligations. QI shall inform a payor from which it receives a reportable amount that it has assumed primary Form 1099 reporting and backup withholding responsibility by providing the payor with a valid withholding certificate described in section 6 of this Agreement and by identifying on the withholding statement associated with such certificate the account(s) for which QI assumes primary Form 1099 reporting and backup withholding responsibility (if required).

QI is not required to assume primary Form 1099 reporting and backup withholding responsibility for all accounts it holds with a payor. However, if QI assumes primary Form 1099 reporting and backup withholding responsibility for any account, it must assume that responsibility for all reportable amounts made by a payor to that account.

If QI is acting as a QDD, it must assume primary Form 1099 reporting and backup withholding responsibility for any reportable payments that are made with respect to a potential section 871(m) transaction. Thus, for example, if QI acts as a QDD with respect to an NPC that is a potential section 871(m) transaction and makes a payment pursuant to the NPC to a U.S. person that is a U.S. non-exempt recipient, QI must backup withhold and report any amount paid to the U.S. person to the extent required under section 3406 and §1.6041-1(d)(5).

In addition, if QI is assuming primary withholding responsibility for payments of substitute interest (as described in section 3.03(A) of this Agreement), it must assume primary Form 1099 reporting and backup withholding responsibility with respect to all such payments.

QI is not required to backup withhold on a reportable amount it makes to a WP, WT, or another QI that has assumed primary Form 1099 reporting and backup withholding responsibility with respect to the reportable amount. QI is also not required to backup withhold on a reportable amount that QI makes to an intermediary or flow-through entity that is a participating FFI, registered deemed-compliant FFI, or another QI that does not assume primary Form 1099 reporting and backup withholding responsibility with respect to the payment provided that such intermediary or flow-through entity allocates the payment on its withholding statement to a chapter 4 withholding rate pool of U.S. payees and the withholding statement is associated with a valid Form W-8IMY that provides the applicable certification(s) for allocating the payment to this pool or allocates the payment on its withholding statement to a chapter 4 withholding rate pool of recalcitrant account holders.

Sec. 3.08. Deposit Requirements. If QI assumes primary withholding responsibility under chapters 3 and 4 or primary Form 1099 reporting and backup withholding responsibility, it must deposit amounts withheld under chapter 3 or 4 or section 3406 at the time and in the manner provided under section 6302 (see §1.6302-2) by electronic funds transfer as provided under §31.6302-1(h). If QI is a non-U.S. payor that does not assume primary withholding responsibility under chapters 3 and 4 or primary Form 1099 reporting and backup withholding responsibility, QI must deposit amounts withheld by the 15th day following the month in which the withholding occurred.

Sec. 3.09. QDD Tax Liability. In addition to satisfying its withholding tax liability as described in this Agreement and its section 881 tax on dividends received as a QDD, a QDD must satisfy its QDD tax liability. The QDD's QDD tax liability is the sum of:

(A) its tax liability under section 881 for its section 871(m) amount (as defined in section 2.73 of this Agreement) for each dividend on each underlying security reduced (but not below zero) by the amount of tax paid by the QDD under section 881(a)(1) on dividends received with respect to that underlying security on that same dividend in its capacity as an equity derivatives dealer;

(B) its tax liability under section 881 for dividend equivalent payments received as a QDD in its non-equity derivatives dealer capacity; and

(C) its tax liability under section 881 for any payments, such as dividends or interest, received as a QDD with respect to potential section 871(m) transactions or underlying securities that are not dividend equivalent payments, to the extent the full liability was not satisfied by withholding.

A QDD that is a foreign branch of a U.S. financial institution does not have a QDD tax liability. Instead, such a QDD must determine and report its tax liability in accordance with chapter 1 and the appropriate U.S. tax return for the U.S. corporation.

For calendar year 2017, the QDD will not be liable for tax under section 881(a)(1) on actual dividends on physical shares or deemed dividends or dividend equivalents that the QDD receives in its equity derivatives dealer capacity. The QDD is liable for tax on actual dividends on physical shares or deemed dividends or dividend equivalents received in its non-equity derivatives dealer capacity and on any other U.S. source FDAP payments received by the QDD.

(D) Timing for Determining QDD Tax Liability. A QDD must determine its QDD tax liability due under sections 3.09(A) and (B) on the date provided in §1.871-15(j)(2) for the applicable dividend. A QDD must determine its QDD tax liability due under section 3.09(C) at the time the payments are treated as received under the Code and the regulations promulgated thereunder.

See section 7.01(C) of this Agreement regarding a QI that is acting as a QDD's responsibility to report QDD tax liability on the appropriate U.S. tax return and to maintain a reconciliation schedule for its section 871(m) amount and other amounts related to its QDD tax liability.

Section 4. Private Arrangement Intermediaries and Certain Partnerships and Trusts

Sec. 4.01. Private Arrangement Intermediaries—In General. If QI is an FFI, QI may enter into a private arrangement with another intermediary under which the other intermediary agrees to perform all of the obligations of QI under this Agreement, except as modified in section 4.02 of this Agreement. QI, however, may not enter into a private arrangement under this section 4.01 with any account holder for which it acts as a QDD. The agreement between QI and the other intermediary shall be between QI and all the offices of the other intermediary located in a particular jurisdiction, which must be one for which the IRS has approved the know-your-customer rules. Such an intermediary is referred to in this Agreement as a private arrangement intermediary (PAI). By entering into a PAI agreement, QI is not assigning its liability for the performance of any of its obligations under this Agreement. Therefore, QI shall remain liable for any tax, penalties, interest, and any other sanctions that may result from the failure of the PAI to meet any of the obligations imposed by its agreement with QI. QI agrees not to assert any defenses against the IRS for the failures of the PAI or any defenses that the PAI may assert against QI. For purposes of this Agreement, the PAI's actual knowledge or reason to know of facts relevant to withholding or reporting shall be imputed to QI. QI's liability for the failures of the PAI shall apply even though the PAI is itself a withholding agent under chapters 3 and 4 and a payor under chapter 61 and section 3406 and is itself separately liable for its failure to meet its obligations under the Code. Notwithstanding the foregoing, QI shall not be liable for tax, interest, or penalties for failure to withhold and report under chapters 3, 4, and 61 and section 3406 unless the underwithholding or the failure to report amounts correctly on Forms 945, 1042, 1042-S, 1099, or 8966 is due to QI's or its PAI's failure to properly perform its obligations under this Agreement. The PAI is not required to enter into an agreement with the IRS but must respond (either directly or through QI) to IRS inquiries related to its compliance, as described in section 10.08 of this Agreement. The IRS may, however, in its sole discretion, refuse to permit an intermediary to operate as a PAI by providing notice to QI. QI may, however, appeal the IRS's determination by following the notice and cure provisions in section 11.06 of this Agreement. For purposes of this Agreement, an intermediary shall be considered a PAI only if the following conditions are met:

(A) The PAI is a certified deemed-compliant FFI (other than a registered deemed-compliant Model 1 IGA FFI) that acts as an intermediary with respect to reportable amounts and has provided QI with a certification that it has maintained such certified deemed-compliant FFI status during each certification period;

(B) The PAI does not act as an intermediary for a direct account holder that is a QI, WP, WT, participating FFI, registered deemed-compliant FFI, or a registered deemed-compliant Model 1 IGA FFI;

(C) The PAI is, pursuant to a written agreement between QI and the PAI (PAI agreement), subject to all the obligations of QI under this Agreement, except to the extent modified by sections 4.02 and 4.03 of this Agreement;

(D) For purposes of chapter 4, the PAI agrees to comply with the FATCA requirements applicable to its chapter 4 status as a certified deemed-compliant FFI, as modified by sections 4.02 and 4.03 of this Agreement, and is not required to fulfill QI's FATCA requirements as a participating FFI, registered deemed-compliant FFI, or registered deemed-compliant Model 1 IGA FFI;

(E) QI identifies the PAI on the QI/WP/WT Application and Accounts Management System before the first payment for which the PAI is operating under the PAI agreement;

(F) The PAI agrees, to the extent necessary for QI to satisfy its compliance obligations (i.e., if QI does not receive a waiver described in section 10.07 of this Agreement), either to provide its documentation and other information to QI for inclusion in QI's periodic review described in section 10.04 of this Agreement or to conduct an independent periodic review in accordance with the procedures described in section 10.05 of this Agreement and provide QI with the same certification as is required for QI's responsible officer under section 10.03 of this Agreement for each certification period in order to allow the responsible officer of QI to make a certification to the IRS regarding PAI's compliance. The PAI agrees to respond (either directly or through QI) to IRS inquiries regarding its periodic review and agrees to provide QI (and the IRS, upon request) with a periodic review report (as described in section 10.06 of this Agreement);

(G) The PAI furnishes QI with a Form W-8IMY and withholding statement described in section 6 of this Agreement as modified by this section 4.01(G). The PAI is required to provide QI with Forms W-9 (or, in absence of the form, the name, address, and U.S. TIN (if available)) of the PAI's U.S. non-exempt recipient account holders and the withholding rate pool information for those account holders as required by section 6.03(D) of this Agreement so that the QI (or the payor) may report on Form 1099 and, if required, backup withhold. In addition, the PAI is required to disclose to QI any account holder of PAI that is a passive NFFE with one or more substantial U.S. owners (or one or more controlling persons that is a specified U.S. person) as defined in §§1.1471-1(b)(74) and 1.1473-1(b), respectively (or in the applicable IGA), and the account holders or interest holders of any non-qualified intermediary or flow-through entity, respectively, which has an account with the PAI, and provide all of the documentation and other information relating to those account holders and interest holders that is required for the QI, or another withholding agent, to report the payments made to those account holders and interest holders to the extent required by sections 8.02(B) and 8.05 of this Agreement. Except to the extent the PAI provides its information to QI for purposes of performing the periodic review, the PAI is not required to disclose to QI, or another withholding agent, its direct account holders that are foreign persons other than a passive NFFE with one or more substantial U.S. owners (or one or more controlling persons that is a specified U.S. person); and

(H) The PAI agrees to notify QI if the PAI no longer meets the requirements for certified deemed-compliant status, and upon such notification, the agreement between the PAI and QI will terminate.

Sec. 4.02. Modification of Obligations for PAI Agreements.

(A) Payments Reportable Under Chapters 3 and 4. The agreement between QI and a PAI must provide that QI shall report all payments of amounts subject to chapter 3 or 4 withholding made by the PAI on QI's Forms 1042 and 1042-S as if QI had made the payments directly to the PAI's account holders. Therefore, QI shall report payments made to each of the following types of a PAI's account holders as follows:

(1) A direct account holder of the PAI that is a nonparticipating FFI, QI shall report an amount subject to chapter 4 withholding using the chapter 4

reporting pool described in section 8.03 of this Agreement with the PAI reported as the recipient with respect to the pool.

(2) A direct foreign account holder of the PAI for which no withholding is required under chapter 4 (other than an intermediary, custodian, nominee, agent, or flow-through entity described below), QI shall report an amount subject to chapter 3 withholding using the chapter 3 reporting pools as described in section 8.03 of this Agreement with the PAI reported as the recipient.

(3) A direct foreign account holder of the PAI that is a nonqualified intermediary or flow-through entity, QI shall report payments of amounts subject to chapter 4 withholding with respect to any indirect account holders of the PAI that the nonqualified intermediary or flow-through entity includes in a chapter 4 withholding rate pool of nonparticipating FFIs using the chapter 4 reporting pool for such account holders described in section 8.03 of this Agreement with the nonqualified intermediary or flow-through entity reported as the recipient and shall report payments of amounts subject to chapter 3 withholding made with respect to indirect foreign account holders of the PAI that are not subject to chapter 4 withholding by reporting the payments as made to specific recipients under the rules of section 8.02 of this Agreement.

(B) Form 1099 Reporting and Backup Withholding. The agreement between QI and a PAI must also provide that QI shall report all reportable payments made by the PAI on QI's Forms 945 and 1099 to the extent required under this section 4.02(B). QI shall file Forms 1099 and backup withhold, if required, on reportable payments made by QI (including by a PAI) to U.S. non-exempt recipients that are direct or indirect account holders of a PAI in accordance with the terms of this Agreement.

(C) Form 8966 Reporting. The agreement between QI and a PAI must also provide that QI shall report all withholdable payments made by the PAI on Form 8966 to the extent required under this section 4.02(C). QI shall file Forms 8966 to report withholdable payments made by QI (including by a PAI) to passive NFFEs with one or more substantial U.S. owners (or one or more controlling persons that is a specified U.S. person) that are direct or indirect account holders of a PAI in accordance with section 8.05 of this Agreement.

Sec. 4.03. Other Requirements of PAI Agreements. QI shall require a PAI to provide QI with all the information necessary for QI to meet its obligations under this Agreement. No provisions shall be contained in the agreement between QI and a PAI that preclude, and no provisions of this Agreement shall be construed to preclude, the PAI's joint and several liability for tax, penalties, and interest under chapters 3, 4, and 61 and section 3406 to the extent that underwithholding, penalties, and interest have not been collected from QI and the underwithholding or failure to report amounts correctly on Forms 945, 1042, 1042-S, 1099, or Form 8966 are due to a PAI's failure to properly perform its obligations under its agreement with QI. Nothing in the agreement between QI and a PAI shall be construed to limit the PAI's requirements under chapter 4 or an applicable IGA. Further, nothing in the agreement between QI and a PAI shall permit the PAI to assume primary chapters 3 and 4 withholding responsibility or assume primary Form 1099 reporting and backup withholding responsibility.

Sec. 4.04. Termination of Arrangement. Except as otherwise provided in section 4.01(H) of this Agreement, QI shall cease to treat an intermediary as a PAI within 90 days from the day QI knows that the PAI is in default of its agreement with QI unless the PAI has cured the event of default prior to the expiration of such 90-day period. QI must provide the IRS with notice of any PAI agreement that has been terminated within 30 days of the termination by removing the intermediary as a PAI on the QI/WP/WT Application and Accounts Management System.

Sec. 4.05. Joint Account Treatment for Certain Partnerships and Trusts.

(A) In General. If QI is an FFI, QI may enter an agreement with a non-withholding foreign partnership or non-withholding foreign trust that is either a simple or grantor trust described in this section 4.05(A) to apply the simplified joint account documentation, reporting, and withholding procedures provided in section 4.05(B) of this Agreement. QI and a partnership or trust that apply this section 4.05 to any calendar year must also apply these rules to the calendar year in its entirety. QI and the partnership or trust may not apply this section 4.05 to any calendar year in which the partnership or trust has failed to make available to QI or QI's reviewer the records described in this section 4.05(A) within 90 days after these records are requested, and the partnership or trust must waive any legal prohibitions against providing such records to QI. If the partnership or trust has failed to make these records available within the 90-day period, or if QI and the partnership or trust fail to comply with any other requirements of this section 4.05, QI must apply the provisions of §§1.1441-1(c) and 1.1441-5(e) to the partnership or trust as a non-withholding foreign partnership or non-withholding foreign trust, must correct its withholding for the period during which the failure occurred in accordance with section 9.05 of this Agreement, and cannot apply this section 4.05 to subsequent calendar years. QI and a partnership or trust that apply this section 4.05 to any calendar year are not required to apply this section 4.05 to subsequent calendar years. A partnership or trust is described in this section 4.05(A) of this Agreement if the following conditions are met:

(1) The partnership or trust has a chapter 4 status as a certified deemed-compliant FFI (other than a registered deemed-compliant Model 1 IGA FFI), an owner-documented FFI with respect to QI, an exempt beneficial owner, or an NFFE or is covered as an account that is excluded from the definition of financial account under Annex II of an applicable IGA or under §1.1471-5(a) and has provided QI with a certification that it has maintained such chapter 4 status at all times during each certification period;

(2) The partnership or trust is a direct account holder of QI;

(3) None of the partnership's or trust's partners, beneficiaries, or owners is a flow-through entity or is acting as intermediary for a payment made by QI to the partnership or trust;

(4) None of the partnership's or trust's partners, beneficiaries, or owners is a U.S. person and none of its foreign partners, beneficiaries, or owners is subject to withholding or reporting under chapter 4 (e.g., a nonparticipating FFI and certain passive NFFEs); and

(5) The partnership or trust agrees to make available upon request to QI or QI's reviewer for purposes of QI's periodic review under section 10 of this Agreement (including to respond to IRS inquiries regarding its compliance review) records that establish that the partnership or trust has provided QI with documentation for purposes of chapters 3 and 4 for all of its partners, beneficiaries, or owners.

(B) Modification of Obligations for QI.

(1) QI may rely on a valid Form W-8IMY provided by the partnership or trust and may rely on a withholding statement that meets the requirements of §1.1441-5(c)(3)(iv) or (e)(5)(iv), and §1.1471-3(c)(3)(iii)(B) (if the payment is a withholdable payment) and that provides information for all partners, beneficiaries, or owners together with valid Forms W-8 or, in the case of a partnership or trust that is a certified deemed-compliant FFI, documentary evidence permitted under the applicable know-your-customer rules from each partner, beneficiary, or owner, and, for a withholdable payment, documentation that meets the requirements of §1.1471-3(d) to establish the partner's, beneficiary's, or owner's chapter 4 status. The withholding statement need not provide any allocation information.

(2) QI must treat payments to the partnership or trust as allocated solely to a partner, beneficiary, or owner that is subject to the highest rate of withholding under chapter 3 and must withhold at that rate.

(3) QI may pool report amounts distributed to, or included in the distributive share of, the partnership's or trust's direct partners, beneficiaries, or owners in chapter 3 reporting pools on Form 1042-S as described in section 8.03(B) of this Agreement.

(4) After QI has withheld in accordance with section 4.05(B)(2) of this Agreement, it may file a separate Form 1042-S for any partner, beneficiary, or owner who requests that it do so. If QI issues a separate Form 1042-S for any partner, beneficiary, or owner, it cannot include such partner, beneficiary, or owner in its chapter 3 reporting pool. If QI has already filed a Form 1042-S and included the partner, beneficiary, or owner in a chapter 3 reporting pool, it must file an amended return to reduce the amount of the payment reported to reflect the amount allocated to the recipient on the recipient's specific Form 1042-S. QI may file a separate Form 1042-S for a partner, beneficiary, or owner only if the partnership or trust provides a withholding statement that includes allocation information for the requesting partner, beneficiary, or owner and only if the partnership or trust has agreed in writing to make available to QI or QI's reviewer the records that substantiate the allocation information included in its withholding statement.

(5) QI may not include any payments made to a partnership or trust to which QI is applying the rules of this section 4.05 in any collective refund claim made under section 9.04 of this Agreement.

Sec. 4.06. Agency Option for Certain Partnerships and Trusts.

(A) In General. QI may enter an agreement with a non-withholding foreign partnership or non-withholding foreign trust that is either a simple or grantor trust described in section 4.06(A) of this Agreement under which the partnership or trust agrees to act as an agent of QI with respect to its partners, beneficiaries, or owners, and, as QI's agent, to apply the provisions of the QI Agreement to the partners, beneficiaries, or owners. QI, however, may not enter an agreement under this section 4.06 with any account holder for which it acts as a QDD. By entering into an agreement with a partnership or trust as described in this section 4.06, QI is not assigning its liability for the performance of any of its obligations under this Agreement. QI and the partnership or trust to which QI applies the rules of this section 4.06 are jointly and severally liable for any tax, penalties, and interest that may result from the failure of the partnership or trust to meet any of the obligations imposed by its agreement with QI. QI and a partnership or trust that applies the agency option to any calendar year must apply these rules to the calendar year in its entirety. Generally, QI and a partnership or trust that applies the agency option to any calendar year are not required to apply the agency option to subsequent calendar years. If, however, QI withholds and reports any adjustments required by corrected information in a subsequent calendar year under section 4.06(B)(2) of this Agreement, QI must apply the agency option to that calendar year in its entirety. QI and a partnership or trust may not apply the agency option to any calendar year when the partnership or trust has failed to make available to QI or QI's reviewer the records described in section 4.06 of this Agreement within 90 days after these records are requested, and the partnership or trust must waive any legal prohibitions against providing such records to QI. If, for any calendar year, the partnership or trust has failed to make these records available within the 90-day period, or if QI and the partnership or trust fail to comply with any other requirement of this section 4.06, QI must apply §§1.1441-1(c) and 1.1441-5(e) to the partnership or trust as a non-withholding foreign partnership or non-withholding foreign trust, must correct its withholding for the period in which the failure occurred in accordance with section 9.05 of this Agreement, and cannot apply the agency option to subsequent calendar years.

A partnership or trust is described in this section 4.06(A) of this Agreement if the following conditions are met:

(1) The partnership or trust is either a direct account holder of QI or an indirect account holder of QI that is a direct partner, beneficiary, or owner of a partnership or trust to which QI also applies the agency option.

(2) The partnership or trust has a chapter 4 status as a certified deemed-compliant FFI (other than a registered deemed-compliant Model 1 IGA FFI), an owner-documented FFI, an NFFE, an exempt beneficial owner, or is covered as an account that is excluded from the definition of financial account under Annex II of an applicable IGA or under §1.1471-5(a) and has provided QI with a certification that it has maintained such chapter 4 status during each certification period;

(3) None of the partnership's or trust's partners, beneficiaries, or owners is a WP, WT, participating FFI, registered deemed-compliant FFI, registered deemed-compliant Model 1 IGA FFI, or another QI acting as an intermediary for a payment made by QI to the partnership or trust.

(4) The partnership or trust agrees to permit QI to treat its direct partners, beneficiaries, or owners as direct account holders of QI under this Agreement and to treat its indirect partners, beneficiaries, or owners as indirect account holders of QI under this Agreement.

(5) The partnership or trust agrees, to the extent necessary for QI to satisfy its compliance obligations (e.g., if the QI does not receive a waiver described in section 10.07 of this Agreement), either to provide its documentation and other information to QI for inclusion in QI's periodic review described in section 10.04 of this Agreement or to conduct an independent periodic review in accordance with the procedures described in section 10.05 of this Agreement, provide QI with the certification required under section 10.03 of this Agreement for each certification period in order to allow the responsible officer of QI to make a certification to the IRS regarding the partnership's or trust's compliance with this section 4.06, and respond (either directly or

through QI) to IRS inquiries regarding its compliance review, as described in section 10.08 of this Agreement, including providing the QI and the IRS with the results of the reviewer's testing of transactions and accounts described in section 10.06 of this Agreement.

(B) Modification of Obligations for QI.

(1) QI may rely on a valid Form W-8IMY provided by the partnership or trust, together with a withholding statement described in §1.1441-5(c)(3)(iv) or (e)(5)(iv) and §1.1471-3(c)(3)(iii)(B) (if the payment is a withholdable payment) that includes all information necessary for QI to fulfill its withholding, reporting, and filing obligations under this Agreement. The withholding statement may include chapter 3 withholding rate pools for partners, beneficiaries, or owners that are not intermediaries, flow-through entities (or persons holding interests in the partnership or trust through such entities), U.S. persons, or passive NFFEs with one or more substantial U.S. owners (or one or more controlling persons that is a specified U.S. person), and the partnership or trust need not provide to QI documentation for these partners, beneficiaries, or owners. The withholding statement may also include a chapter 4 withholding rate pool of nonparticipating FFIs described in section 6.03 of this Agreement for payments of amounts subject to chapter 4 withholding. Notwithstanding the preceding sentences of this section 4.06(B)(1), the partnership or trust is required to disclose to QI any interest holder that is a passive NFFE with substantial U.S. owners (or controlling persons that are specified U.S. persons) or that is a U.S. non-exempt recipient, as well as the account holders or interest holders of any nonqualified intermediary or flow-through entity, respectively, which has an interest in the partnership or trust, and to provide all of the documentation and other information relating to those account holders and interest holders that is required for the QI, or another withholding agent, to report the payments made to those account holders and interest holders to the extent required by sections 8.02(B) and 8.05 of this Agreement.

(2) **Timing of Withholding.** QI must withhold on the date it makes a payment to the partnership or trust based on a withholding statement provided by the partnership or trust on which QI is permitted to rely. The amount allocated to each partner, beneficiary, or owner in the withholding statement may be based on a reasonable estimate of the partner's, beneficiary's, or owner's distributive share of income subject to withholding for the year. The partnership or trust must correct the estimated allocations to reflect the partner's, beneficiary's, or owner's actual distributive share and must provide this corrected information to QI on the earlier of the date that the statement required under section 6031(b) (i.e., Schedule K-1) or the Beneficiary Statement or Owner

Statement is mailed or otherwise provided to the partner, beneficiary, or owner, or the due date for furnishing the statement (whether or not the partnership or trust is required to prepare and furnish the statement). If that date is after the due date (without regard to extensions) for QI's Forms 1042 and 1042-S for the calendar year, QI may withhold and report any adjustments required by the corrected information in the following calendar year.

(3) **Payments Reportable Under Chapters 3 and 4.** QI shall report on Form 1042-S all amounts subject to chapters 3 and 4 withholding distributed to, or included in the distributive share of, the partnership or trust as follows:

(a) For a direct partner, beneficiary, or owner of the partnership or trust that is a nonparticipating FFI, QI shall report an amount subject to withholding using the chapter 4 reporting pool described in section 8.03(A) of this Agreement with the partnership or trust reported as a recipient.

(b) For a direct partner, beneficiary, or owner of the partnership or trust that is a foreign person for which no withholding is required under chapter 4 (other than an intermediary, agent, or flow-through entity described below), QI shall report an amount subject to chapter 3 withholding using the chapter 3 reporting pools described in section 8.03(B) of this Agreement with the partnership or trust reported as a recipient.

(c) For a direct or indirect partner, beneficiary, or owner of the partnership or trust that is a nonqualified intermediary or foreign flow-through entity, QI shall report payments of amounts subject to chapter 4 withholding in a chapter 4 withholding rate pool of nonparticipating FFIs using the chapter 4 reporting pool for such partner, beneficiary, or owner with the nonqualified intermediary or foreign flow-through entity reported as the recipient, and QI shall report payments of amounts subject to chapter 3 withholding for which no chapter 4 withholding is required by reporting the payments as made to specific recipients as described in section 8.02 of this Agreement.

(4) **Form 1099 Reporting and Backup Withholding.** The agreement between QI and the partnership or trust must also provide that QI shall include all reportable payments made by the partnership or trust in QI's Forms 945 and 1099 to the extent required under this section 4.06(B)(4). QI shall file Forms 1099 and backup withhold, if required, on reportable payments made by QI to U.S. non-exempt recipient that are direct or indirect partners, beneficiaries, or owners of the partnership or trust in accordance with the terms of this Agreement.

(5) **Form 8966 Reporting Requirements.** The agreement between QI and the partnership or trust must also provide that QI shall report all withholdable payments made by the partnership or trust on Form 8966 to the extent required under this section 4.06(B)(5). If the partnership or trust is itself a

passive NFFE and if any of its partners, beneficiaries, or owners is a passive NFFE with one or more substantial U.S. owners (or one or more controlling persons that is a specified U.S. person), QI shall file Forms 8966 to report all withholdable payments made by QI to any such passive NFFE in accordance with sections 8.04 and 8.05 of this Agreement.

(C) **Other Requirements of Agency Agreement.** QI shall require the partnership or trust to provide QI with all the information necessary for QI to meet its obligations under this Agreement. No provisions shall be contained in the agreement between QI and the partnership or trust that preclude, and no provisions of this Agreement shall be construed to preclude, the partnership or trust's joint and several liability for tax, penalties, and interest under chapters 3, 4, and 61 and section 3406, to the extent that the underwithholding, penalties, and interest have not been collected from QI and the underwithholding or failure to report amounts correctly on Forms 945, 1042, 1042-S, 1099, or 8966 is due to the partnership's or trust's failure to properly perform its obligations under its agreement with QI. Nothing in the agreement between QI and the partnership or trust shall be construed to limit the partnership's or trust's requirements under chapter 4 as a certified deemed-compliant FFI, owner-documented FFI, NFFE, or exempt beneficial owner. Further, nothing in the agreement between QI and the partnership or trust shall permit the partnership or trust to assume primary chapters 3 and 4 withholding responsibility or primary Form 1099 reporting and backup withholding responsibility.

Section 5. Documentation Requirements

Sec. 5.01. Documentation Requirements.
(A) **General Documentation Requirements.** QI agrees to use its best efforts to obtain documentation from account holders that receive a reportable payment to determine whether withholding applies or whether a payment is reportable under this Agreement. Under section 11.06 of this Agreement, failure to obtain documentation from a significant number of direct account holders constitutes an event of default. If QI is an FFI obtaining documentary evidence, QI also agrees to adhere to the know-your-customer rules that apply to QI with respect to the account holder from whom the documentary evidence is obtained. If QI cannot reliably associate a reportable payment with valid documentation from the account holder, it must apply the applicable presumption rules to determine if withholding is required under chapter 3 or 4 or if backup withholding is required under section 3406. QI agrees to review

and maintain documentation in accordance with this section 5 and, in the case of documentary evidence obtained from direct account holders, in accordance with the applicable know- your-customer rules. QI also agrees, if the performance of an external review is requested by IRS (as described in section 10.08(D) of this Agreement), to make documentation (together with any associated withholding statements and other documents or information) available upon request for inspection by QI's external reviewer. QI represents that none of the laws to which it is subject prohibits disclosure of the identity of any account holder or account information to QI's reviewer.

If QI is acting as a QDD, QI is required to apply the rules of this section 5 to each account holder of an account for which it is acting as a QDD and to which it makes a reportable payment in accordance with the applicable requirements in section 5.01(A) and (B) of this Agreement.

(B) Coordination of Chapter 3 and Chapter 4 Documentation Requirements.

(1) QI That Is an FFI. If QI is an FFI, for each account holder for whom QI is acting under this Agreement, QI is required to perform the due diligence procedures under its FATCA requirements as a participating FFI, registered deemed-compliant FFI, or registered deemed-compliant Model 1 IGA FFI to determine if the account is a U.S. account (or U.S. reportable account) and to determine each account holder that is a nonparticipating FFI and, if applicable, recalcitrant account holder (or non-consenting U.S. account). If an account holder receiving the payment is not the payee, QI is also required to establish the chapter 4 status of the payee or payees to determine whether withholding applies under chapter 4. For purposes of this section 5, with respect to documenting an account holder for chapter 4 purposes, documentary evidence also includes any documentary evidence allowed under an applicable IGA.

To the extent an account holder receives a payment with respect to which QI has determined that withholding is not required under chapter 4, QI shall obtain, unless already collected, documentation that meets the requirements of this section 5 to determine whether the account holder is a foreign person for which QI is required to withhold under chapter 3 or a U.S. payee for which QI is required to backup withhold under section 3406 or report on Form 1099 under chapter 61. See, however, section 8.06 of this Agreement providing the circumstances in which reporting of U.S. accounts (or U.S. reportable accounts) under its FATCA requirements as a participating FFI, registered deemed-compliant FFI, or registered deemed-compliant Model 1 IGA FFI satisfies QI's Form 1099 reporting responsibilities. See Notice 2014-33, 2014-21 I.R.B. 1033, modifying the time in which QI is required to implement the applicable due diligence procedures under its FATCA requirements as a participating FFI, registered deemed-compliant FFI, or registered deemed-compliant Model 1 IGA FFI with respect to an obligation held by an entity that is opened, issued, or executed on or after July 1, 2014, and before January 1, 2015.

(2) QI That Is an NFFE. If QI is an NFFE, QI is required to document the chapter 4 status of each account holder for whom QI is acting to determine if withholding and reporting apply under section 1471 or 1472 on withholdable payments made to the account holder. QI is required to obtain, unless already collected, a valid Form W-8 or Form W-9 from each account holder to determine whether QI is required to withhold under chapter 3 or 4 or report on Form 1099 under chapter 61 and backup withhold under section 3406. The allowance in this section 5 for QI to obtain documentary evidence does not apply if QI is an NFFE. QI may, however, obtain appropriate documentary evidence as additional documentation to establish the foreign status of an account holder.

Sec. 5.02. Documentation for Foreign Account Holders. QI may treat an account holder as a foreign beneficial owner of an amount if the account holder provides a valid Form W-8 (other than Form W-8IMY unless provided by a QI that is acting as a QDD or assuming primary withholding responsibility for a substitute interest payment) or valid documentary evidence that supports the account holder's status as a foreign person. QI may not treat an account holder that provides documentation indicating that it is a bank, broker, intermediary, or agent (such as an attorney) as a beneficial owner unless QI receives a statement, in writing and signed by a person with authority to sign such a statement, stating that such account holder is the beneficial owner of the income. Further, QI may not reduce the rate of withholding with respect to an indirect account holder that is a foreign beneficial owner unless the certification provided by the direct account holder is a valid Form W-8IMY, and then only to the extent that QI can reliably associate the payment with valid documentation that establishes that withholding does not apply under chapter 4 in the case of a withholdable payment made to the account holder and establishes that the indirect account holder is entitled to a reduced rate of withholding under chapter 3.

Sec. 5.03. Beneficial Owner's Claim of Treaty Benefits. To the extent an account holder receives a payment that is not subject to withholding under chapter 4, QI may not reduce the rate of withholding under chapter 3 based on a beneficial owner's claim of treaty benefits unless QI obtains the documentation required by section 5.03(A) of this Agreement. In addition, QI agrees to establish procedures to inform account holders of the terms of limitation on benefits provisions of a treaty (whether or not those provisions are contained in a separate article entitled Limitation on Benefits) under which the account holder is claiming benefits. For accounts held by an entity opened or documented on or after January 1, 2017, QI is required to obtain a Form W-8BEN-E with the appropriate limitation on benefits certification or, if QI is allowed to and obtains documentary evidence, the written certification included in the treaty statement as described in section 5.03(B) of this Agreement. For accounts maintained by QI prior to January 1, 2017, that were documented with documentary evidence and for which treaty benefits are being claimed, QI is required to obtain the appropriate limitation on benefits statement prior to January 1, 2019.

(A) Treaty Documentation. The documentation required by this section 5.03(A) is as follows:

(1) The account holder has provided a properly completed Form W-8BEN or Form W-8BEN-E on which a claim of treaty benefits is made, including, for an entity, the appropriate limitation on benefits and section 894 certifications, as provided in §1.1441-6(b)(1). A U.S. TIN or foreign TIN shall not be required, however, if the beneficial owner is a direct account holder. An indirect account holder is required to have a either a U.S. TIN or foreign TIN to claim treaty benefits unless it is claiming treaty benefits on income from marketable securities;

(2) The account holder has provided documentary evidence that has been obtained pursuant to the know-your-customer rules that apply to the account holder, and the account holder, if it is an entity, has made the treaty statement (if applicable) required by section 5.03(B) of this Agreement; or

(3) The account holder provides the type of documentary evidence required under §1.1441-6 to establish entitlement to a reduced rate of withholding under a treaty, and the account holder, if it is an entity, has made the treaty statement (if applicable) required by section 5.03(B) of this Agreement.

(B) Treaty Statement. The treaty statement required by an entity account holder under this section 5.03(B) is as follows:

[Name of entity account holder] meets all provisions of the applicable treaty that are necessary to claim a reduced rate of withholding, including any limitation on benefits provisions, and derives the income within the meaning of section 894, and the regulations thereunder, as the beneficial owner.

QI is only required to obtain the treaty statement required by this section 5.03(B) from an account holder that is an entity. QI shall not be required to obtain a treaty statement required by this section 5.03(B) from an individual who is a resident of an applicable treaty country or from the government, or its political subdivisions, of a treaty country. QI is required to collect and report (as required on Form 1042-S) the specific category of limitation on benefits provision from all of its entity account holders, including a government (or its political subdivisions).

Sec. 5.04. Documentation for International Organizations. To the extent an account holder receives a payment that is not subject to withholding under chapter 4, QI may not treat the account holder as an international organization entitled to an exemption from withholding under section 892 unless the name provided on the documentation (including a Form W-8EXP) is the name of an entity designated as an international organization by executive order pursuant to 22 United States Code 288 through 288(f) and the documentation is valid under section 5.10 of this Agreement. If an international organization is not claiming benefits under section 892 but under another Code exception, the provisions of section 5.02 of this Agreement shall apply rather than the provisions of this section 5.04.

Sec. 5.05. Documentation for Foreign Governments and Foreign Central Banks of Issue.

(A) Documentation from a Foreign Government or Foreign Central Bank of Issue Claiming an Exemption from Withholding Under Section 892 or Section 895. To the extent an account holder receives a payment that is not subject to withholding under chapter 4, QI may not treat an account holder as a foreign government or foreign central bank of issue exempt from withholding under section 892 or 895 unless—

(1) QI receives from the account holder a Form W-8EXP or documentary evidence establishing that the account holder is a foreign government or foreign central bank of issue;

(2) The income paid to the account holder is the type of income that qualifies for an exemption from withholding under section 892 or 895; and

(3) QI does not know, or have reason to know, that the account holder is a controlled commercial entity as described in section 892, that the income owned by the foreign government or foreign central bank of issue is being received from a controlled commercial entity, or that the income is from the disposition of an interest in a controlled commercial entity.

(B) Treaty Exemption. To the extent an account holder receives a payment that is not subject to withholding under chapter 4, QI may treat an account holder as a foreign government or foreign central bank of issue entitled to a reduced rate of withholding under an income tax treaty for purposes of chapter 3 if it has valid documentation that is sufficient to obtain a reduced rate of withholding under a treaty as described in section 5.03 of this Agreement.

(C) Other Code Exception. If a foreign government or foreign central bank of issue is not claiming benefits under section 892 or under an income tax treaty but under another Code exception (e.g., the portfolio interest exception under section 871(h) or 881(c)), the provisions of section 5.02 of this Agreement apply rather than the provisions of this section 5.05.

Sec. 5.06. Documentation for Foreign Tax-Exempt Organizations. To the extent an account holder receives a payment that is not subject to withholding under chapter 4, QI may not treat an account holder as a foreign tax-exempt organization and reduce the rate of or exempt the account holder from withholding for purposes of chapter 3 unless it satisfies the requirements provided in section 5.06(A), (B), or (C) of this Agreement.

(A) Reduced Rate of Withholding Under Section 501. QI may not treat an account holder as a foreign organization described under section 501(c), and therefore exempt from withholding under chapter 3 (or, if the account holder is a foreign private foundation, subject to withholding at a 4% rate under section 1443(b)) unless QI obtains a valid Form W-8EXP on which Part IV of the form is completed.

(B) Reduced Rate of Withholding Under Treaty. QI may not treat an account holder as a foreign organization that is tax-exempt on an item of income pursuant to an income tax treaty unless QI obtains valid documentation as described under section 5.03 of this Agreement that is sufficient for obtaining a reduced rate of withholding under the treaty and the documentation establishes that the account holder is an organization exempt from tax under the treaty on that item of income.

(C) Other Exceptions. If a tax-exempt entity is not claiming a reduced rate of withholding because it is a foreign organization described under section 501(c) or under a treaty article that applies to exempt certain foreign organizations from tax, but is claiming a reduced rate of withholding under another Code or income tax treaty exception, the provisions of section 5.02 or 5.03 (as applicable) of this Agreement shall apply rather than the provisions of this section 5.06.

Sec. 5.07. Documentation from Intermediaries or Flow-Through Entities. QI must apply the presumption rules to a reportable payment made to a nonqualified intermediary or flow-through entity that is a direct account holder of QI to the extent QI fails to obtain the documentation set forth below. If QI receives documentation for the account holders or interest holders of an intermediary or flow-through entity, QI must apply the rules of this section 5 to determine the validity of such documentation.

(A) Withholdable Payments Made to Nonqualified Intermediaries and Flow-Through Entities. With respect to a withholdable payment made to a nonqualified intermediary or flow-through entity—

(1) QI receives a valid Form W-8IMY provided by the nonqualified intermediary or the flow-through entity receiving the payment that establishes the chapter 4 status of the intermediary or flow-through entity; and

(2) If the payment is not subject to withholding under chapter 4 based on such entity's chapter 4 status (or to the extent the payment is received on behalf of exempt beneficial owners), QI can reliably associate the payment with a withholding statement that meets the requirements of §1.1471-3(c)(iii)(B) that includes the account holders or interest holders of the intermediary or flow-through entity in chapter 4 withholding rate pools to the extent permitted or with valid documentation described in this section 5 provided by account holders or interest holders of the intermediary or flow-through entity that are not themselves nonqualified intermediaries or flow-through entities and that QI can treat as not subject to withholding under chapter 4.

(B) Reportable Payments Other Than Withholdable Payments Made to Nonqualified Intermediaries and Flow-Through Entities. With respect to a reportable payment that is not a withholdable payment made to a nonqualified intermediary or flow-through entity—

(1) QI receives a valid Form W-8IMY provided by the nonqualified intermediary or the flow-through entity regardless of whether the form includes a chapter 4 status of the nonqualified intermediary or flow-through entity unless such entity provides a withholding statement allocating a payment to a chapter 4 withholding rate pool of U.S. payees; and

(2) QI can reliably associate the payment with a chapter 4 withholding rate pool of U.S. payees or valid documentation described in this section 5 provided by account holders or interest holders of the nonqualified intermediary or flow-through entity that are not themselves nonqualified intermediaries or flow-through entities.

(C) Reportable Payments Made to QIs, WPs, and WTs. With respect to a reportable payment made to a QI, WP, or WT, QI receives a valid Form W-8IMY provided by the QI, WP, or WT that includes the entity's chapter 4 status for a payment that is a withholdable payment and, for those payments for which a QI has not assumed primary chapters 3 and 4 withholding responsibility or primary Form 1099 reporting and backup withholding responsibility, QI can reliably associate the payment with withholding rate pools, as described in section 6.03 of this Agreement.

(D) Payments Made to QIs Acting as QDDs. For payments with respect to potential section 871(m) transactions or underlying securities made to a QI acting as a QDD, if QI receives a valid Form W-8IMY provided by the QI acting as a QDD that includes the QI's chapter 4 status and the required certification that the QI is acting as a QDD and assumes primary withholding responsibility for payments it makes when the QI is acting as a QDD, then QI can reliably associate the payments as made to the QI acting as a QDD.

(E) Private Arrangement Intermediaries. If QI has an agreement with a PAI, QI obtains from the PAI a Form W-8IMY completed as if the PAI were a QI that is an FFI (with the exception that the PAI must not provide a QI-EIN on the Form W-8IMY) and QI can reliably associate the payment with a withholding statement, as described in section 4.01(G) of this Agreement and the information described in this section 5.07 for any account holders of the PAI that are intermediaries or flow-through entities and the documentation for any passive NFFE with one or more substantial U.S. owners (or one or more controlling persons that is a specified U.S. person if QI is a reporting Model 1 or reporting Model 2 FFI).

(F) Partnerships or Trusts to Which QI Applies the Agency Option. If QI has an agreement with a partnership or trust under which the partnership or trust agrees to act as an agent of QI, QI obtains from the partnership or trust a Form W-8IMY completed as if the partnership or trust were a QI (with the exception that the partnership or trust must not provide a QI-EIN on the Form W-8IMY) and QI can reliably associate the payment with a withholding statement, as described in section 4.06(B)(1) of this Agreement, and the information described in this section 5.07 for any account holders that are intermediaries or flow-through entities and the documentation for any passive NFFE with one or more substantial U.S. owners (or one or more controlling persons that is a specified U.S. person if QI is a reporting Model 1 or reporting Model 2 FFI).

Sec. 5.08. Documentation for U.S. Exempt Recipients. QI shall not treat an account holder as a U.S. exempt recipient unless QI obtains from the account holder—

(A) A valid Form W-9 on which the account holder includes an exempt payee code to certify that the account holder is a U.S. exempt recipient for purposes of chapter 4 reporting;

(B) Documentary evidence that is sufficient to establish that the account holder is a U.S. exempt recipient; or

(C) Documentary evidence that is sufficient to establish the account holder's status as a U.S. person and QI can treat the person as an exempt recipient under the rules of §§1.6045-2(b)(2)(i) or 1.6049-4(c)(1)(ii), as appropriate, without obtaining documentation.

Sec. 5.09. Documentation for U.S. Non-exempt Recipients. QI shall not treat an account holder as a U.S. non-exempt recipient unless QI obtains a valid Form W-9 or other similar agreed form under its FATCA requirements as a participating FFI, registered deemed-compliant FFI, or registered deemed-compliant Model 1 IGA FFI from the account holder, QI knows an account holder is a U.S. non-exempt recipient, or QI must presume a person is a U.S. non-exempt recipient to the extent required under section 5.13(C)(3) or (4) of this Agreement.

Sec. 5.10. Documentation Validity.

(A) In General. QI may not rely on documentation if QI has actual knowledge, or reason to know that the information or certifications contained in the documentation are unreliable or incorrect or that there is a change in circumstances with respect to the information or statements contained in the documentation or account information that affects the reliability of the account holder's claim. See §1.1441-1(e)(4)(ii)(D) for the definition of change in circumstances and a withholding agent's obligation with respect to a change in circumstances. See §31.3406(h)-3(e) for rules regarding when QI may rely on a Form W-9, §1.1441-7(b)(4) through (6) for rules regarding when QI may rely on a Form W-8, and §1.1441-7(b)(7) through (9) for rules regarding documentary evidence (including §1.1441-7(b)(8)(i) for rules regarding documentary evidence received prior to January 1, 2001). A change in circumstances affecting withholding information, including allocation information or withholding rate pools contained in a withholding statement, will also cause the documentation provided with respect to that information to no longer be reliable. Once QI knows, or has reason to know, that documentation provided by an account holder is unreliable or incorrect to establish foreign status or residency for purposes of claiming benefits under an applicable income tax treaty, it can no longer reliably associate a payment with valid documentation unless QI obtains the additional documentation described in §1.1441-7(b)(5), (b)(6), (b)(8), or (b)(9) (as applicable). With respect to a withholding agent's reason to know that a claim for treaty benefits is unreliable or incorrect based on the existence of a tax treaty, the rule in §1.1441-6(b)(1)(ii) will apply to pre-existing accounts for which QI held valid documentation upon a change in circumstances or, with respect to a pre-existing entity account, when it provides a written limitation on benefits statement (as described in section 5.03(B) of this Agreement). For all new accounts, this rule will apply on account opening. For purposes of this section 5.10(A), a 'pre-existing account' or 'pre-existing entity account' is an account documented by QI prior to January 1, 2017, for a QI with a QI Agreement in effect prior to that date. For a QI that did not have a QI Agreement in effect prior to January 1, 2017, a 'pre-existing account' or 'pre-existing entity account' means an account maintained (and for which QI has valid documentation) prior to the effective date of its QI Agreement.

In addition, if QI becomes aware of information resulting in the documentation no longer being reliable or correct and QI has not assumed primary withholding responsibility under chapters 3 and 4 or primary Form 1099 reporting and backup withholding responsibility, QI agrees that it will promptly provide a withholding agent with corrected information (e.g., corrected withholding rate pools, corrected Forms W-9, or corrected U.S. TINs) within 30 days after QI knows or has reason to know that the documentation upon which it has relied is unreliable or incorrect. If QI receives notification from the IRS that documentation provided by an account holder is unreliable or incorrect (e.g., that the U.S. TIN provided by an account holder is incorrect), QI shall follow the procedures set forth in §31.3406(d)-5. See also QI's FATCA requirements as a participating FFI, registered deemed-compliant FFI, or registered deemed-compliant Model 1 IGA FFI or an NFFE's requirements as a withholding agent under sections 1471 and 1472 following a change in circumstances.

(B) Reason to Know-Direct Account Holders. If QI is a financial institution as defined in §1.1471-5(e), an insurance company (without regard to whether such company is a specified insurance company), or a broker or dealer in securities, QI shall be considered to have reason to know that documentation provided by a direct account holder is unreliable or incorrect only as prescribed in §1.1441-7(b)(3). If QI is an NFFE (other than a NFFE described in the first sentence of this paragraph), see §1.1441-7(b)(2) for when QI shall be considered to have reason to know that a withholding certificate provided by a direct account holder is unreliable or incorrect.

(C) Reason to Know-Indirect Account Holders. QI shall be considered to have reason to know that relevant information or statements contained in documentation provided by an indirect account holder are unreliable or incorrect if a reasonably prudent person in the position of a QI would question the claims made. QI shall have reason to know that documentation provided by a nonqualified intermediary or a flow-through entity is unreliable or incorrect if the nonqualified intermediary or flow-through entity does not provide QI with, to the extent required, the names of the indirect account holders, their addresses, allocation information allocating payments to each indirect account holder, and sufficient information for QI to report payments on Forms 1042-S and 1099. In addition, QI shall have reason to know that an indirect account holder is not entitled to a reduced rate of withholding under an income tax treaty if the nonqualified intermediary or flow-through entity has not provided sufficient information so that QI can verify that the indirect account holder has provided a U.S. TIN or foreign TIN, if required, and made the necessary statements regarding limitations on benefits provisions and deriving the income under section 894 and the regulations thereunder. See §1.1441-7(b)(10) and section 5.03 of this Agreement.

Sec. 5.11. Documentation Validity Period.

(A) Documentation Other than Form W-9. QI may rely on valid documentary evidence obtained from account holders in accordance with applicable know-your-customer rules as long as the documentary evidence remains valid under those rules or until QI knows, or has reason to know, that the information contained in the documentary evidence is incorrect. However, QI may only rely on statements regarding entitlement to treaty benefits described in §1.1441-6(c)(5)(i) or the representations described in section 5.03 of this Agreement until the validity expires under §1.1441-1(e)(4)(ii)(A)(2). For establishing an account holder's chapter 3 status (as defined in §1.1441-1(c)(45)) or foreign status for chapter 61 purposes, QI may rely on a Form W-8 until its validity expires under §1.1441-1(e)(4)(ii) and may rely on documentary evidence (other than documentary evidence obtained pursuant to applicable know-your-customer rules) until its validity expires under §1.6049-5(c).

(B) Form W-9. QI may rely on a valid Form W-9 as long as it has not been informed by the IRS or another withholding agent that the form is unreliable or incorrect. If QI has primary Form 1099 reporting and backup withholding responsibility, it may rely on a Form W-9 unless one of the conditions of §31.3406(h)-3(e)(2)(i) through (v) applies.

Sec. 5.12. Maintenance and Retention of Documentation.

(A) Maintaining Documentation. QI shall maintain documentation by retaining the original documentation, a certified copy, a photocopy, a scanned copy, a microfiche, or other means that allow reproduction (provided that the QI has recorded receipt of the documentation and is able to produce a hard copy). For a direct account, if QI is not required to retain copies of documentary evidence under its know-your-customer rules, QI may instead retain a notation of the type of documentation reviewed, the date the documentation was reviewed, the document's identification number (if any, e.g., a passport number), and whether such documentation contained any U.S. indicia. For direct accounts opened prior to January 1, 2001, if QI was not required under its know-your-customer rules to maintain originals or copies of documentation, QI may rely on its account information if it has complied with all other aspects of its know-your-customer rules regarding establishment of an account holder's identity, it has a record that the documentation required under the know-your-customer rules was actually examined by an employee of QI in accordance with the know-your-customer rules, and it has no information in its possession that would require QI to treat the documentation as invalid.

(B) Retention Period. QI shall retain a record of the account holder's documentation obtained under this section 5 for as long as the documentation is relevant to the determination of QI's tax liability or reporting responsibilities under sections 871, 881, 1461, 1474(a), and 3406.

Sec. 5.13. Application of Presumption Rules.

(A) In General. QI shall apply the presumption rules of section 5.13(C) of this Agreement if QI cannot reliably associate a payment with valid documentation from an account holder. The presumption rules cannot be used to grant a reduced rate of withholding. For example, the portfolio interest exception of sections 871(h) and 881(c) shall not apply to a person that is presumed to be foreign. Further, QI must apply the presumption rules when required and may not rely on its actual knowledge regarding an account holder's chapter 4 status or status as a U.S. or foreign person to apply a reduced rate of withholding. Failure to follow the presumption rules may result in liability for under-withholding, penalties, and interest. Notwithstanding the preceding sentences, QI must rely on its actual knowledge regarding an account holder rather than what is presumed if, based on such knowledge, it should withhold an amount greater than the withholding rate under the presumption rules or it should report on Form 1042-S or Form 1099 an amount that would otherwise not be reported.

(B) Reliably Associating a Payment with Documentation. Generally, QI can reliably associate a payment with documentation if, for that payment, it holds valid documentation from the account holder; it can reliably determine how much of the payment relates to the valid documentation provided by such account holder; and it has no actual knowledge or reason to know that any of the information, certifications, or statements in or associated with the documentation are incorrect. See §1.1441-1(b)(2)(vii) or, for a withholdable payment, §1.1471-3(c) for rules regarding when a payment can be reliably associated with documentation. See also §1.1471-3(e)(4)(vi)(B) for when a QI that is an FFI may rely on documentation and information permitted in an applicable IGA to document an account holder's chapter 4 status. Sections 5.13(B)(1) through (5) of this Agreement describe when a payment is reliably associated with documentation if the payment is made to an account holder that is an intermediary or flow-through entity (other than a nonparticipating FFI that is not acting on behalf of exempt beneficial owners).

(1) Reliably Associating a Payment with Documentation Provided by a Nonqualified Intermediary or Flow-Through Entity. Generally, QI can reliably associate a payment with documentation provided by a nonqualified intermediary or flow-through entity if it can reliably associate the payment with a valid Form W-8IMY provided by the nonqualified intermediary or flow-through entity, and it can determine the portion of the payment that relates to valid documentation associated with the Form W-8IMY for an account holder or interest holder of the nonqualified intermediary or flow-through entity that is not itself a nonqualified intermediary or flow-through entity; and the nonqualified intermediary or flow-through entity provides sufficient information for QI to report the payments on Form 1042-S, Form 1099, or Form 8966 if reporting is required.

If the payment is a withholdable payment, the Form W-8IMY must provide the nonqualified intermediary's or flow-through entity's chapter 4 status to the extent required for chapter 4 purposes. In lieu of the nonqualified intermediary or flow-through entity providing documentation for an account holder that is subject to chapter 4 withholding, QI can reliably associate a withholdable payment with valid documentation associated with the Form W-8IMY from the nonqualified intermediary or flow-through entity if it can determine the portion of the payment allocable to a chapter 4 withholding rate pool (to the extent permissible under §1.1471-3(c)(3)(iii)(B)).

If the payment is a reportable amount, QI can reliably associate such payment with valid documentation provided by a nonqualified intermediary or a flow-through entity that is a participating FFI or registered deemed-compliant FFI if, in lieu of providing documentation for its account holders that are U.S. persons, such nonqualified intermediary or flow-through entity allocates the payment to a chapter 4 withholding rate pool of U.S. payees and also certifies on a valid Form W-8IMY that it meets the requirements of §1.6049-4(c)(4)(iii) with respect to any account holder of an account it maintains within the meaning of §1.1471-5(d)(5) (i.e., a direct account holder) that receives a payment included in this pool or allocates a payment that is a withholdable payment to a chapter 4 withholding rate pool of recalcitrant account holders. Notwithstanding the preceding sentences in this section 5.13(B)(1), to the extent a payment is not subject to reporting on Form 1042-S, Form 1099, or Form 8966, QI can reliably associate the payment with valid documentation if it can determine the portion of the payment that is allocable to a group of account holders for whom QI holds valid documentation (other than nonqualified intermediaries or flow-through entities) for whom withholding and reporting is not required. For example, QI can treat a payment of short-term OID allocable to a group of documented foreign account holders as reliably associated with valid documentation. Further, if the documentation attached to a nonqualified intermediary's or flow-through entity's Form W-8IMY is documentation from another nonqualified intermediary or flow-through entity, then QI must apply the rules of this paragraph to that other nonqualified intermediary or flow-through entity.

(2) Reliably Associating a Payment with a Withholding Certificate Provided by Another QI that Does Not Assume Primary Chapters 3 and 4 Withholding or Primary Form 1099 Reporting and Backup Withholding Responsibility. Generally, QI can reliably associate a payment with documentation provided by another QI that does not assume either primary chapters 3 and 4 withholding responsibility or primary Form 1099 reporting and backup withholding responsibility if it can reliably associate the payment with a valid Form W-8IMY and, if the form is associated with a withholdable payment, it includes the QI's chapter 4 status to the extent required for chapter 4 purposes. Additionally, the Form W-8IMY must be associated with a withholding statement that allocates the withholdable payment among the chapter 4 withholding rate pools (to the extent permissible under §1.1471-3(c)(3)(iii)(B)), and with respect to a payment of an amount subject to chapter 3 withholding that is either not a withholdable payment or a withholdable payment for which no chapter 4 withholding is required, that allocates such payment among chapter 3 withholding rate pools for foreign account holders as described in section 6.03(C) of this Agreement.

If the payment is a reportable amount, QI can reliably associate the payment with documentation provided by another QI if the withholding statement allocates the payment to withholding rate pools attributable to U.S. non-exempt recipients and the documentation includes a valid Form W-9 for each U.S. non-exempt recipient account holder for which the other QI is required to report on Form 1099 and, if required, backup withhold. QI can also reliably associate a reportable amount with valid documentation provided by another QI that is a participating FFI or registered deemed-compliant FFI if, in lieu of providing documentation for each U.S. non-exempt recipient account holder, the QI allocates the payment to a chapter 4 withholding rate pool of U.S. payees and provides the applicable certification(s) on a valid Form W-8IMY for allocating the payment to this pool or allocates a payment that is a withholdable payment to a chapter 4 withholding rate pool of recalcitrant account holders. Notwithstanding the preceding sentences in this section 5.13(B)(2), the presumption rules shall not apply if a payment cannot be allocated to each U.S. non-exempt recipient account holder or to a chapter 4 withholding rate pool of U.S. payees to the extent the alternative procedures of section 6.03(D) of this Agreement apply.

(3) Reliably Associating a Payment with Documentation Provided by a QI that Assumes Primary Chapters 3 and 4 Withholding Responsibility and Does Not Assume Primary Form 1099 Reporting and Backup Withholding Responsibility. Generally, QI can reliably associate a payment with valid documentation provided by another QI that assumes primary chapters 3 and 4 withholding responsibility, but not primary Form 1099 reporting and backup withholding responsibility, if it can associate the payment with a valid Form W-8IMY from the QI and, if the form is associated with a withholdable payment, it includes the QI's chapter 4 status to the extent required for chapter 4 purposes. Additionally, the Form W-8IMY must be associated with a withholding statement that allocates a payment that is a withholdable payment or an amount subject to chapter 3 withholding that is not a withholdable payment among a single withholding rate pool for all account holders with respect to which the QI assumes primary chapters 3 and 4 withholding responsibility.

If the payment is a reportable amount, QI can reliably associate the payment with documentation provided by another QI if the withholding statement allocates the payment to withholding rate pools attributable to each U.S. non-exempt recipient, as described in section 6.03(D), and the documentation includes a valid Form W-9 for each U.S. non-exempt recipient account holder for which the other QI is required to report on Form 1099 and, if required, backup withhold. QI can also reliably associate such payment with valid documentation provided by another QI that is a participating FFI or registered deemed-compliant FFI if, in lieu of providing documentation for each U.S. non-exempt recipient account holder, the QI allocates the payment made to the U.S. non-exempt recipient to a chapter 4 withholding rate pool of U.S. payees and provides the applicable certifications on a valid Form W-8IMY for allocating the payment to this pool or allocates a payment that is a withholdable payment to a chapter 4 withholding rate pool of recalcitrant account holders. Notwithstanding the preceding sentences in this section 5.13(B)(3), the presumption rules shall not apply if a payment cannot be allocated to each U.S. non-exempt recipient account holder or to a chapter 4 withholding rate pool of U.S. payees to the extent the alternative procedures of section 6.03(D) of this Agreement apply.

(4) Reliably Associating a Payment with Documentation Provided by a QI that Assumes Primary Form 1099 Reporting and Backup Withholding Responsibility. Generally, QI can reliably associate a payment with valid documentation provided by another QI that assumes primary Form 1099 reporting and backup withholding responsibility, but not primary chapters 3 and 4 withholding responsibility, to the extent it can associate the payment with a valid Form W-8IMY from the QI that, if the payment is a withholdable payment, includes the QI's chapter 4 status to the extent required for chapter 4 purposes. Additionally, the Form W-8IMY must be associated with a withholding statement that allocates a payment that is a withholdable payment among chapter 4 withholding rate pools (other than a pool of U.S.

payees and to the extent permissible under §1.1471-3(c)(3)(iii)(B) and, with respect to a payment that is an amount subject to chapter 3 withholding but is either not a withholdable payment or a withholdable payment for which no chapter 4 withholding is required, allocates the payment among chapter 3 withholding rate pools for foreign account holders as described in section 6.03(C) of this Agreement, and identifies the portion of the payment for which QI assumes primary Form 1099 reporting and backup withholding responsibility.

(5) Reliably Associating a Payment with Documentation Provided by a QI that Assumes Both Primary Chapters 3 and 4 Withholding Responsibility and Primary Form 1099 Reporting and Backup Withholding Responsibility. Generally, QI can reliably associate a payment with valid documentation provided by another QI that assumes both primary chapters 3 and 4 withholding responsibility and primary Form 1099 reporting and backup withholding responsibility if QI can associate the payment with a valid Form W-8IMY from the QI that, if the payment is a withholdable payment, includes the QI's chapter 4 status. Additionally, the Form W-8IMY must also designate the accounts for which the other QI is acting as a QI and is assuming primary chapters 3 and 4 withholding and primary Form 1099 reporting and backup withholding responsibility. If the other QI is acting as a QDD, the Form W-8IMY (or withholding statement) must also designate those accounts (1) for which the QDD is receiving payments with respect to potential section 871(m) transactions or underlying securities as a QDD, (2) for which the QDD is receiving payments with respect to potential section 871(m) transactions (and that are not also underlying securities) for which withholding is not required, and (3) for which the QDD is receiving payments with respect to underlying securities for which withholding is required. If the other QI is acting as a QDD, the Form W-8IMY (or withholding statement) must also identify the home office or branch acting as a QDD that is receiving the payment. If the QI receiving a payment assumes both primary chapters 3 and 4 withholding responsibility and primary Form 1099 reporting and backup withholding responsibility for substitute interest payments as described in section 3.03(A), the Form W-8IMY must indicate that the QI is assuming primary withholding responsibility for all such payments.

(C) Presumption Rules. With respect to a withholdable payment made to a foreign entity, if QI is an NFFE, it must follow the presumption rules of §1.1471-3(f) when it cannot reliably associate a withholdable payment with valid documentation.

With respect to a payment that is an amount subject to chapter 3 withholding that is either not a withholdable payment or a withholdable payment for which no chapter 4 withholding is required, the presumption rules are the rules under §1.1441-1(b)(3) that a withholding agent must follow to determine the status of a beneficial owner (i.e., as a U.S. person or foreign person and as an individual or entity (and the entity's classification)) when it cannot reliably associate a payment with valid documentation. With respect to a reportable payment (including a withholdable payment made to an entity) that is not an amount subject to chapter 3 withholding, the presumption rules are the rules of §1.6049-5(d) that a payor must follow to determine the status of a payee (e.g., as a non-exempt recipient) when it cannot reliably associate a payment with valid documentation. The presumption rules are as follows:

(1) Certain Withholdable Payments Made with Respect to an Offshore Obligation.

A withholdable payment paid outside of the United States as defined under §1.6049-5(e) with respect to an offshore obligation (as defined in §1.1471-1(b)(88)) that is made to an entity is presumed made to a nonparticipating FFI for purposes of chapter 4. A withholdable payment that is not an amount subject to chapter 3 withholding, that is paid outside the U.S. with respect to an offshore obligation, and that is treated as made to a payee that is an individual is presumed made to a U.S. person when the payee has any of the indicia of U.S. status that are described in §1.1441-7(b)(5). If QI is a participating FFI or registered deemed-compliant FFI (other than a reporting Model 1 FFI), see the rules under its FATCA requirements as a participating FFI or registered deemed-compliant FFI for classifying account holders as recalcitrant account holders. If QI is an FFI, see also section 8.06 of this Agreement for whether QI is required to report such payments on Form 1099.

(2) Amounts Subject to Withholding Under Chapter 3 that Are Paid with Respect to an Offshore Obligation. An amount that is subject to chapter 3 withholding that is not a withholdable payment is presumed made to an undocumented foreign account holder if the payment is made outside of the United States with respect to an offshore obligation. If QI is an NFFE or an FFI that is not required to withhold on recalcitrant account holders pursuant to the terms of an applicable Model 1 or Model 2 IGA, an amount subject to chapter 3 withholding that is a withholdable payment and that is treated as made to a payee that is an individual is also presumed made to an undocumented foreign account holder if the payment is made outside of the United States with respect to an offshore obligation. QI must treat an amount described in this section 5.13(C)(2) as subject to withholding under chapter 3 at a rate of

30% on the gross amount of the payment and must report the payment as made to an unknown recipient on Form 1042-S.

(3) Payments on Certain Short-Term Obligations and Bank Deposit Interest. An amount of U.S. source original issue discount on the redemption of a short-term obligation or U.S. source bank deposit interest not subject to chapter 4 withholding is presumed made to an undocumented U.S. non-exempt recipient account holder regardless of whether paid to an individual or entity. QI must report an amount described in this section 5.13(C)(3) on Form 1099. QI must backup withhold and report such amounts on Form 1099 unless it provides sufficient information to another payor from which it receives such amounts to backup withhold and report the payments and QI does not know that the other payor has failed to backup withhold or report.

(4) Foreign Source Income, Broker Proceeds, and Certain Other Amounts Made with Respect to an Offshore Obligation. A payment of an amount that is not a withholdable payment and is not an amount subject to chapter 3 withholding (other than payments of short-term OID and bank deposit interest described in section 5.13(C) of this Agreement) that is paid outside the United States with respect to an offshore obligation and that is made to a payee that is an individual is presumed made to a U.S. non-exempt recipient when the payee has any of the indicia of U.S. status that are described in section 5.10(B) of this Agreement. If the payment is made to a payee that is an entity, QI must apply the principles of §1.1441-1(b)(3)(ii), §1.1441-5(d)(2), or §1.1441-5(e)(6) (as applicable) without regard to §1.1441-1(b)(3)(ii)(D) for purposes of this paragraph 5.13(C)(4). For a payment of gross proceeds for which QI is a broker under §1.6045-1, similar rules apply to a payment made with respect to a sale that is effected at an office outside the United States under §1.6045-1(g)(1)(ii). QI must report an amount described in this section 5.13(C)(3) as paid to a presumed U.S. non-exempt recipient on Form 1099 to the extent required under section 8.06 of this Agreement. Backup withholding shall not be required, however, if the exception provided in §31.3406(g)-1(e) applies.

(5) Other Payments. For any payment not covered in sections 5.13(C)(1), (2), (3), or (4) of this Agreement, see the presumption rules provided in §1.1441-1(b)(3) or §1.6049-5(d)(2) (as applicable).

Section 6. Qualified Intermediary Withholding Certificate and Disclosure of Account Holders to Withholding Agent

Sec. 6.01. Qualified Intermediary Withholding Certificate. QI agrees to furnish a qualified intermediary withholding certificate to each withholding agent from which it receives a reportable amount as a QI. The qualified intermediary withholding certificate is a Form W-8IMY (or acceptable substitute form) that certifies that QI is acting as a QI, contains QI's QI-EIN, and provides all other information required by the form. If QI receives a withholdable payment, QI must certify to its chapter 4 status and provide its GIIN (if applicable). QI must also certify its chapter 4 status as a participating FFI or registered deemed-compliant FFI when QI provides a Form W-8IMY that certifies that it meets the requirements of §1.6049-4(c)(4)(iii) with respect to any account holder of an account it maintains that is included in a chapter 4 withholding rate pool of U.S. payees on QI's withholding statement.

If QI is acting as a QSL for a substitute dividend payment, QI must also certify that it is acting as a qualified securities lender and provide all other information required by Form W-8IMY.

If QI is acting as a QDD for payments with respect to potential section 871(m) transactions or underlying securities, it must certify that it is acting as a QDD for those payments and assumes primary chapters 3 and 4 withholding responsibility and primary Form 1099 reporting and backup withholding responsibility for any payments with respect to potential section 871(m) transactions that it makes as required by this Agreement, and it must provide all other information required by Form W-8IMY with respect to the certification.

If QI is acting with respect to payments of substitute interest as described in section 3.03(A) of this Agreement, it must certify that it is assuming primary chapters 3 and 4 withholding responsibility and primary Form 1099 reporting and backup withholding responsibility for all such payments, in addition to the other certifications it makes and information it provides as a QI as required by this Agreement.

Except as otherwise provided in section 6.02 of this Agreement, QI also agrees to furnish each withholding agent to whom it provides a Form W-8IMY with the withholding statement described in section 6.02 of this Agreement. QI is not required to disclose, as part of its Form W-8IMY or its withholding statement, any information regarding the identity of a direct or indirect account holder that is a foreign person or a U.S. exempt recipient or a holder of a U.S. account. To the extent QI does not assume primary Form 1099 reporting and backup withholding responsibility under section 3.04 of this Agreement or is not excepted from reporting under section 8.06 of this Agreement, for each U.S. non-exempt recipient account holder on whose behalf QI receives a reportable amount, QI must provide to a withholding agent the Form W-9, or if any such account holder has not provided a Form W-9, the name, address, and U.S. TIN (if available).

Sec. 6.02. Withholding Statement.

(A) In General. QI agrees to provide to each withholding agent from which QI receives reportable amounts as a QI a withholding statement described in this section 6.02 and §1.1441-1(e)(3)(iv). A withholding statement shall not be provided to a withholding agent if QI assumes both primary chapters 3 and 4 withholding responsibility and primary Form 1099 reporting and backup withholding responsibility for all of its accounts, unless QI is acting as a QDD. The withholding statement forms an integral part of the Form W-8IMY. The withholding statement shall be updated as often as necessary for the withholding agent to meet its reporting and withholding obligations under chapters 3, 4, and 61 and section 3406.

(B) Content of Withholding Statement. The withholding statement must contain sufficient information for a withholding agent to apply the correct rate of withholding on payments allocable to the accounts identified on the statement and to properly report such payments on Forms 1042-S and Forms 1099, as applicable. The withholding statement must—

(1) Designate those accounts for which QI acts as a QI;

(2) Designate those accounts for which QI assumes primary chapters 3 and 4 withholding responsibility or primary Form 1099 reporting and backup withholding responsibility (including accounts for which QI is acting with respect to payments of U.S. source substitute interest (as described in section 3.03(A) of this Agreement));

(3) If QI is acting as a QDD, designate the accounts (1) for which the QDD is receiving payments with respect to potential section 871(m) transactions or underlying securities as a QDD, (2) for which the QDD is receiving payments with respect to potential section 871(m) transactions (and that are not underlying securities) for which withholding is not required, and (3) for which QDD is receiving payments with respect to underlying securities for which withholding is required, and, if applicable, identifying the home office or branch that is treated as the owner for U.S. income tax purposes;

(4) If applicable, designate the accounts for which QI is acting as a QSL with respect to any U.S. source substitute dividend payments received from the withholding agent; and

(5) Provide information regarding withholding rate pools, as described in section 6.03 of this Agreement.

Sec. 6.03. Chapters 3 and 4 Withholding Rate Pools.

(A) In General. QI shall provide as part of its withholding statement withholding rate pool information in a manner sufficient for the withholding agent to meet its chapters 3 and 4 and backup withholding responsibilities and its Form 1042-S and Form 1099 reporting responsibilities.

(B) Chapter 4 Withholding Rate Pools. If QI receives a withholdable payment on behalf of its account holders, QI may allocate the payment to a chapter 4 withholding rate pool. A chapter 4 withholding rate pool is a payment of a single type of income (e.g., interest or dividends) that is allocated to payees that are nonparticipating FFIs. If QI is a participating FFI or registered deemed-compliant FFI (other than reporting Model 1 FFI), it may also allocate a withholdable payment to a chapter 4 withholding rate pool of recalcitrant account holders (if applicable). If QI is a participating FFI or registered deemed-compliant FFI receiving a reportable amount that is excepted from reporting under section 8.06(A) of this Agreement (excluding sections 8.06(A)(2) and (A)(3) of this Agreement when the payment is subject to chapter 4 withholding and section 8.06(A)(4) of this Agreement), QI may allocate the payment to a chapter 4 withholding rate pool of U.S. payees. See section 6.03(D) of this Agreement for the alternative procedures that may be used in this case. Except as otherwise provided in this section 6.03(B), if QI receives a withholdable payment, QI must provide the information required under §1.1471-3(c)(3)(iii)(B)(2).

Further, if QI elects under its FATCA requirements as a participating FFI or registered deemed-compliant FFI to backup withhold instead of withholding under chapter 4 with respect to certain recalcitrant account holders, QI's withholding statement must indicate the portion of such payment subject to backup withholding under section 3406 that is allocated to such account holders and must provide all other information relating to such account holders that is required under chapter 61 for the withholding agent to report with respect to the payment.

If QI has an account holder that is another intermediary (whether a QI, NQI, or PAI) or a flow-through entity, QI may combine the account holder information provided by the intermediary or flow-through entity with QI's direct account holder information to determine the amounts allocable to each of QI's chapter 4 withholding rate pools described in this section 6.03(B). If QI is an NFFE that has an account holder that is another intermediary or flow-through entity that is a participating FFI or registered deemed-compliant

FFI, QI may provide the account holder's chapter 4 withholding rate pools of recalcitrant account holders and U.S. payees to the extent applicable.

(C) Chapter 3 Withholding Rate Pools. With respect to any portion of the payment that is attributable to payees for which no chapter 4 withholding is required but is an amount subject to chapter 3 withholding, a chapter 3 withholding rate pool is a payment of a single type of income that is subject to a single rate of withholding (e.g., 0%, 10%, 15%, or 30%) and that is reported under a single chapter 4 exemption code on Form 1042-S. QI shall determine chapter 3 withholding rate pools based on valid documentation obtained under section 5 of this Agreement or, if a payment cannot be reliably associated with valid documentation, on the presumption rules of section 5.13(C) of this Agreement. If QI has an account holder that is another intermediary (whether a QI, NQI, or PAI) or a flow-through entity (other than a nonparticipating FFI that is not acting on behalf of any exempt beneficial owners), QI may combine the account holder information provided by the intermediary or flow-through entity with QI's direct account holder information to determine the amounts allocable to each of QI's chapter 3 withholding rate pools with respect to the portion of the payment allocable to an account holder to which chapter 4 withholding does not apply.

(D) U.S. Non-exempt Recipients Subject to Backup Withholding or Form 1099 Reporting and Alternative Procedures for Allocating Payments on Withholding Statements. To the extent QI does not assume primary Form 1099 reporting and backup withholding responsibility and is not excepted from reporting on Form 1099 under section 8.04 of this Agreement, QI's withholding statement must establish a separate withholding rate pool for each U.S. non-exempt recipient account holder that QI is required to report on Form 1099 and has disclosed to the withholding agent. QI may, by mutual agreement with the withholding agent, establish a single withholding rate pool (not subject to backup withholding) for all U.S. non-exempt recipient account holders for whom QI is required to report on Form 1099 and has provided Forms W-9 prior to the withholding agent paying any reportable amounts or, if applicable, designated broker proceeds to which backup withholding does not apply. QI must establish a separate withholding rate pool for all U.S. non-exempt recipient account holders subject to backup withholding prior to the withholding agent paying any reportable amounts or, if applicable, designated broker proceeds.

Alternatively, QI may include U.S. non-exempt recipients in a zero rate withholding pool that includes U.S. exempt recipients and foreign persons for which no withholding is required under chapters 3 and 4 and section 3406 and may include payments allocated to a chapter 4 withholding rate pool of

U.S. payees in this pool to the extent permitted to be provided by QI under section 6.03(B) of this Agreement. If QI chooses the alternative procedure of this paragraph, QI must provide sufficient information to the withholding agent no later than January 15 of the year following the year in which the reportable amounts and designated broker proceeds, if applicable, are paid in order to allocate to each U.S. non-exempt recipient account holder or to a chapter 4 withholding rate pool of U.S. payees (when applicable). Failure to provide such information will result in the application of penalties to QI under sections 6721 and 6722 and shall constitute an event of default under section 11.06 of this Agreement.

Section 7. Tax Return Obligations

Sec. 7.01. Form 1042 (or Other Tax Return) Filing Requirement.
   (A) In General. QI shall file a return on Form 1042, whether or not QI withheld any amounts under chapter 3 or 4, on or before March 15 of the year following any calendar year in which QI acts as a QI and makes a payment of an amount subject to chapter 3 or 4 withholding. A separate Form 1042 must be filed by each legal entity that is a QI covered by this Agreement. Form 1042 shall be filed at the address indicated on the form, at the address at which the IRS notifies QI to file the return, or in accordance with the instructions to file Form 1042 electronically. In addition to the information specifically requested on Form 1042 and the accompanying instructions, if QI made any overwithholding or underwithholding adjustments under §§1.1461-2 and 1.1474-2 and sections 9.02 and 9.05 of this Agreement, QI must attach a statement setting forth the amounts of any overwithholding or underwithholding adjustments and an explanation of the circumstances that resulted in the over- or underwithholding.
   (B) Extensions for Filing Returns. QI may request an extension of the time for filing Form 1042, or any of the information required to be attached to the form, by submitting Form 7004, *Application for Automatic Extension of Time to File Certain Business Income Tax, Information, and Other Returns*, on or before the due date of the return.
   (C) QDD Tax Liability Requirements for QDDs. In addition to its requirements under section 7.01(A) of this Agreement, a QI that is acting as a QDD (other than a foreign branch of a U.S. financial institution) also must report its QDD tax liability on the appropriate U.S. tax return (to be prescribed by the IRS), including separately identifying each part of the QDD tax liability described in section 3.09(A) through (C) of this Agreement separately

for the home office and each branch that is acting as a QDD (if applicable). A QDD must also report any other information required by the appropriate return with respect to its QDD tax liability (including any part thereof).

A QDD must also maintain, and make available to the IRS upon request, a reconciliation schedule that tracks across calendar years the section 871(m) amount for each dividend with respect to each underlying security referenced by a potential section 871(m) transaction separately for the home office and each branch that is a QDD (if applicable). The reconciliation schedule must separately state total amounts received as a QDD, as well as the dividends received in its equity derivatives dealer capacity and the section 881 tax paid on those amounts, the amount of dividends that were effectively connected with the conduct of a trade or business in the United States, the amount of stock owned in its equity derivatives dealer capacity that was not effectively connected with the conduct of a trade or business in the United States, the amount of dividend equivalent payments it received in its equity derivatives dealer capacity, its long positions, its short positions, its net delta for business purposes (if any), its adjustments to the net delta used for business purposes (if any, such as adjustments to exclude transactions that, for federal income tax purposes, are not treated as transactions of a QDD, do not exist, or that are effectively connected with the conduct of a trade or business in the United States), the dividend amount per share, its tax liability under section 881 for its section 871(m) amount, its net delta exposure, and the section 871(m) amount for each dividend with respect to each underlying security referenced by a potential section 871(m) transaction it received as a QDD, and any adjustments thereto, for transactions in its equity derivatives dealer capacity. The reconciliation schedule may be maintained in any manner or format that permits the IRS to reconcile the amount reported by the QDD for the calendar year.

Sec. 7.02. Form 945 Filing Requirement. QI shall file a return on Form 945 on or before January 31 following the calendar year in which QI backup withheld an amount under section 3406. Separate Forms 945 must be filed by each legal entity that is a QI covered by this Agreement. The form must be filed at the address specified in the instructions for Form 945, at the address at which the IRS notifies QI to file the return under the provisions of section 12.06 of this Agreement, or in accordance with the instructions to file Form 945 electronically.

Sec. 7.03. Retention of Returns. QI shall retain Forms 945 and 1042 (including, with respect to a QI acting as a QDD, its reconciliation schedule) for the applicable statute of limitations on assessment under section 6501.

Section 8. Information Reporting Obligations

Sec. 8.01. Form 1042-S Reporting. Except as otherwise provided in section 8.02 of this Agreement, QI is not required to file Forms 1042-S for amounts paid to each separate account holder for whom such reporting would otherwise be required. Instead, QI shall file a Form 1042-S reporting the pools of income (reporting pools) as determined in section 8.03 of this Agreement. QI must file its Forms 1042-S in the manner required by the regulations under chapters 3 and 4 (or in the case of a participating FFI, in the manner required under the FFI Agreement) and the instructions to the form, including any requirement to file the forms magnetically or electronically. Separate Forms 1042-S must be filed by each legal entity that is a QI covered by this Agreement. A QI acting as a QDD that also has QI activities must file separate Forms 1042-S in its QDD capacity and its QI capacity (i.e., other than when acting as a QDD). Each QI covered by this Agreement may also allow its individual branches not acting as QDDs to file Forms 1042-S provided that all Forms 1042-S contain the QI-EIN of the legal entity of which the branch forms a part and, to the extent required for chapter 4 purposes, the GIIN of the branch. If QI is acting as a QDD, the home office and each branch acting as a QDD must file separate Forms 1042-S for payments made as a QDD. Any Form 1042-S required by this section 8 shall be filed on or before March 15 following the calendar year in which the payment reported on the form was made. QI may request an extension of time to file Forms 1042-S by submitting Form 8809, *Application for Extension of Time to File Information Returns*, by the due date of Forms 1042-S in the manner required by (and to the extent permitted on) Form 8809.

Sec. 8.02. Recipient Specific Reporting. QI (whether or not it assumes primary chapters 3 and 4 withholding responsibility) is required to file separate Forms 1042-S for amounts paid to each separate account holder as described in this section 8.02. QI must file separate Forms 1042-S by income code, exemption code, recipient code, chapter 3 or 4 withholding rate pool, and withholding rate. In the case of a payment to a QDD, separate Forms 1042-S must be filed for each QDD, even if a single legal entity.

(A) QI must file a separate Form 1042-S for each account holder that is a QI (to the extent such payment is required to be reported under §1.1461-1) WP, WT, or QSL that receives from QI an amount subject to withholding under chapter 3 or 4 (or, in the case of a QSL, that receives a U.S. source substitute dividend payment), regardless of whether such account holder is a direct or indirect account holder of QI.

(B) QI must file a separate Form 1042-S for each account holder that is a nonqualified intermediary or flow-through entity that is a participating FFI, registered deemed-compliant FFI, or registered deemed-compliant Model 1 IGA FFI and that receives an amount subject to chapter 4 withholding from QI that is allocable to each of such FFI's chapter 4 withholding rate pools of recalcitrant account holders, nonparticipating FFIs, and pool of U.S. payees, if applicable, regardless of whether such FFI is a direct or indirect account holder of QI.

(C) QI must file a separate Form 1042-S for each account holder that is a nonqualified intermediary or flow-through entity that is not described in section 8.02(B) of this Agreement (other than a nonparticipating FFI) that receives from QI an amount subject to chapter 4 withholding allocable to such entity's chapter 4 withholding rate pool of payees that are nonparticipating FFIs, regardless of whether such intermediary or flow-through entity is a direct or indirect account holder of QI.

(D) QI must file a separate Form 1042-S for each account holder of QI that is a PAI or a partnership or trust to which QI applies the agency option that receives from QI an amount subject to chapter 4 withholding allocable to such entity's chapter 4 withholding rate pool of payees that are nonparticipating FFIs or an amount subject to chapter 3 withholding that is either not a withholdable payment or a withholdable payment for which no chapter 4 withholding is required and that is allocable to such entity's chapter 3 withholding rate pools.

(E) QI must file a separate Form 1042-S for each unknown recipient with respect to an account holder that is a nonqualified intermediary, flow-through entity, or QI that does not assume primary chapters 3 and 4 withholding responsibility and that receives an amount subject to chapter 4 withholding from QI that QI must presume is allocable to such entity's chapter 4 withholding rate pool of payees that are nonparticipating FFIs under the presumption rule of §1.1471-3(f)(5).

(F) QI must file a separate Form 1042-S for each foreign account holder (or interest holder) of a nonqualified intermediary or flow-through entity that is a nonparticipating FFI that is receiving a payment on behalf of an exempt beneficial owner (regardless of whether the nonqualified intermediary or flow-through entity is a direct or indirect account holder of QI) to the extent QI can reliably associate such amounts with valid documentation from such nonqualified intermediary or flow-through entity as to the payment allocable to one or more exempt beneficial owners. In addition, QI must file separate Forms 1042-S in the same manner for each foreign account holder (or interest holder) of a nonqualified intermediary or flow-through entity that is described in the preceding sentence and that is a direct or indirect account holder (or interest holder) of a PAI of QI or a partnership or trust to which QI applies the agency option.

(G) QI must file separate Forms 1042-S for each foreign account holder (or interest holder) of a nonqualified intermediary or flow-through entity that is receiving an amount subject to chapter 3 withholding that is either not a withholdable payment or a withholdable payment for which no chapter 4 withholding is required to the extent QI can reliably associate such amounts with valid documentation from an account holder that is not itself a nonqualified intermediary or flow-through entity. In addition, QI must file separate Forms 1042-S in the same manner for each foreign account holder (or interest holder) of a nonqualified intermediary or flow-through entity that is described in the preceding sentence and that is a direct or indirect account holder (or interest holder) of a PAI of QI or a partnership or trust to which QI applies the agency option.

(H) QI must file a separate Form 1042-S for each direct account holder that establishes its status as a passive NFFE but fails to provide the information regarding its owners as required under §1.1471-3(d)(12)(iii) unless such information was reported by the withholding agent.

(I) If QI is acting as a QDD, QI must file a separate Form 1042-S for any amount subject to chapter 3 withholding with respect to a potential section 871(m) transaction made to another QDD.

Sec. 8.03. Reporting Pools for Form 1042-S Reporting.

(A) Chapter 4 Reporting Pools. Except for amounts required to be reported under section 8.02 of this Agreement, if QI is an FFI, QI shall report all amounts subject to chapter 4 withholding by reporting pools on a Form 1042-S if those amounts are paid to direct account holders of QI. A separate Form 1042-S shall be filed for each type of reporting pool. A chapter 4 reporting pool is a payment of a single type of income, determined in accordance with the categories of income reported on Form 1042-S, that is allocable to a chapter 4 withholding rate pool consisting of either recalcitrant account holders or payees that are nonparticipating FFIs. QI must report recalcitrant account holders in pools based upon a recalcitrant account holder's particular status described in §1.1471-4(d)(6), with a separate Form 1042-S issued for each such pool. If QI is an FFI, it may report in a chapter 4 withholding rate pool of U.S. payees an account holder that is (or is presumed) a U.S. person and that QI reports as a U.S. account under its applicable FATCA requirements as a participating FFI or registered deemed-compliant FFI provided that QI is excepted from Form 1099 reporting with respect to the payment under section 8.06(A)(1) of this Agreement or section 8.06(A)(2) and (A)(3) of this Agreement if the payment is both excepted from Form 1099 reporting and not subject to withholding under chapter 4.

If QI is an NFFE, QI shall report all amounts subject to chapter 4 withholding by reporting pools on a Form 1042-S if those amounts are paid to direct account holders that are nonparticipating FFIs in a chapter 4 reporting pool of nonparticipating FFIs.

(B) Chapter 3 Reporting Pools. Except for amounts required to be reported under section 8.02 of this Agreement, QI shall report an amount subject to chapter 3 withholding that is either not a withholdable payment or a withholdable payment for which no chapter 4 withholding is required and that is paid to a foreign account holder by reporting pools on a Form 1042-S if those amounts are paid to direct account holders of QI or to direct account holders of a PAI of QI or a partnership or trust described in section 4 of this Agreement. A separate Form 1042-S shall be filed for each type of reporting pool. A chapter 3 reporting pool is a payment of a single type of income that falls within a particular withholding rate, chapter 3 exemption code, and, if the payment is a withholdable payment, chapter 4 exemption code as determined on Form 1042-S. QI may use a single chapter 3 pool reporting code (e.g., QI-withholding rate pool-general) for all reporting pools except for amounts paid to foreign tax-exempt recipients, for which a separate chapter 3 pool reporting code (e.g., QI-withholding rate pool-exempt organization) must be used. For this purpose, a foreign tax-exempt recipient includes any organization that is not subject to chapter 3 withholding and is not liable to tax in its jurisdiction of residence because it is a charitable organization, a pension fund, or a foreign government.

Sec. 8.04. FATCA U.S. Account Reporting.

(A) QI that Is an FFI. If QI is an FFI, QI is required to report each U.S. account (or, in the case of an FFI that is a reporting Model 1 FFI or a registered deemed-compliant Model 1 IGA FFI, each U.S. reportable account) that it maintains and for whom QI is acting consistent with its FATCA requirements as a participating FFI, registered deemed-compliant FFI, or registered deemed-compliant Model 1 IGA FFI. If QI is a participating FFI or registered deemed-compliant FFI (other than a reporting Model 1 FFI or registered deemed-compliant Model 1 IGA FFI), QI must report its U.S. accounts on Form 8966 in the time and manner required under its FATCA requirements as a participating FFI or registered deemed-compliant FFI except to the extent QI is reporting under §1.1471-4(d)(5) on Form 1099 with respect to its U.S. accounts. If QI is a reporting Model 1 FFI or registered deemed-compliant Model 1 IGA FFI, QI must report each U.S. reportable account on Form 8966 as required under the applicable Model 1 IGA. QI cannot delegate to its withholding agent its requirements to report U.S. accounts (or U.S. reportable accounts) regardless of whether QI does or does not assume primary Form 1099 reporting and backup withholding responsibility under section 3 of this Agreement. See section 8.06 of this Agreement for when the reporting described in this section 8.04 satisfies QI's Form 1099 reporting responsibilities with respect to reportable payments under chapter 61.

(B) QI that Is an NFFE. If QI is an NFFE acting as a QI on behalf of persons other than its shareholders, QI shall file Form 8966 to report withholdable payments made to an account holder that is an NFFE (other than an excepted NFFE) with one or more substantial U.S. owners if the NFFE is the beneficial owner of the withholdable payment received by QI. See §1.1471-1(b)(8) for the definition of beneficial owner. QI must report on Form 8966 in accordance with the form and its accompanying instructions. Such report must include the name of the NFFE that is owned by a substantial U.S. owner; the name, address, and U.S. TIN of each substantial U.S. owner; the total of all withholdable payments made to the NFFE during the calendar year; and any other information as required by the form and its accompanying instructions. If QI is acting as a sponsoring entity on behalf of an NFFE for chapter 4 purposes, QI is not required to report as described in this paragraph if QI reports the NFFE as part of QI's requirements as a sponsoring entity. See §1.1472-1(c)(5)(ii) for the reporting requirements of a sponsoring entity.

Sec. 8.05. Form 8966 Reporting for Payees that Are NFFEs. QI shall file Form 8966 to report withholdable payments made to an intermediary or flow-through entity that provides information regarding an account holder (or interest holder) that is an NFFE other than an excepted NFFE with one or more substantial U.S. owners (or one or more controlling persons that is a specified U.S. person under an applicable IGA). QI must report on Form 8966 in the time and manner provided in §1.1474-1(i)(2). Such report must include the name of the NFFE that is owned by a substantial U.S. owner (or controlling person); the name, address, and U.S. TIN of each substantial U.S. owner; the total of all withholdable payments made to the NFFE during the calendar year (or reportable period under the applicable IGA); and any other information as required by the form and its accompanying instructions. QI is not required to report, however, to the extent permitted under §1.1474-1(i)(2) on a payment made to a participating FFI or registered deemed-compliant FFI if such information is reported pursuant to section 8.04 of this Agreement or if the intermediary or flow-through entity certifies on its withholding statement that it is reporting the account holder (or interest holder) as a U.S.

account pursuant to its FATCA requirements as a participating FFI, registered deemed-compliant FFI, or registered deemed-compliant Model 1 IGA FFI.

Sec. 8.06. Form 1099 Reporting Responsibility. QI shall file Forms 1099 and, unless filing magnetically, Form 1096, *Annual Summary and Transmittal of U.S. Information Returns*, for reportable payments made to persons described in this section 8.06. Forms 1099 shall be filed on or before the date prescribed for the particular Form 1099 under chapter 61 and in the manner required by regulations under chapter 61 and the instructions to the forms (including the requirements for filing the forms magnetically or electronically). Extensions of the time to file Forms 1099 may be requested by submitting Form 8809 in the manner required by the form. If QI is required to file Forms 1099, it must file the appropriate form for the type of income paid (e.g., Form 1099-DIV for dividends, Form 1099-INT for interest, Form 1099-B for broker proceeds). QI must file Forms 1099 to report a reportable payment other than in the situations listed in sections 8.06(A) and (B) of this Agreement.

(A) Reportable Amount. QI must file a Form 1099 in accordance with the instructions to the form for the aggregate amount of a particular type of reportable amount paid to an account holder that is (or is presumed) a U.S. non-exempt recipient (whether a direct or indirect account holder). However, QI is not required to file a Form 1099 on a reportable amount if—

(1) QI is a non-U.S. payor reporting the account holder of a U.S. account under its FATCA requirements as a participating FFI or registered deemed-compliant FFI (including a reporting Model 1 FFI) and the other conditions of §1.6049-4(c)(4)(i) are satisfied;

(2) QI reports the account holder's account as held by a recalcitrant account holder or, in the case of a QI that is a reporting Model 2 FFI or nonreporting Model 2 FFI treated as registered deemed-compliant, as a non-consenting U.S. account under its FATCA requirements as a participating FFI or registered deemed-compliant FFI and the other conditions of §1.6049-4(c)(4)(ii) are satisfied;

(3) QI is a non-U.S. payor that is a reporting Model 1 FFI or registered deemed-compliant Model 1 IGA FFI and determines that the account has U.S. indicia for which appropriate documentation sufficient to treat the account as held by a specified U.S. person has not been provided and reports the account as a U.S. reportable account and the other conditions of §1.6049-4(c)(4)(ii) are satisfied;

(4) QI has not assumed primary Form 1099 reporting and backup withholding responsibility with respect to the account holder's account and has provided a Form W-9 to a withholding agent or has provided withholding rate pool information with respect to such account holder to a withholding agent to apply backup withholding and QI does not know that the withholding agent has failed to report or backup withhold as required;

(5) With respect to an account holder of an intermediary or flow-through entity (other than a QI) that is a direct or indirect account holder of QI, the intermediary or flow-through entity allocates the payment to a chapter 4 withholding rate pool of U.S. payees and provides a Form W-8IMY containing a certification that the entity meets the requirements of §1.6049-4(c)(4)(iii); or

(6) With respect to an account holder of another QI that is a direct or indirect account holder of QI, the QI allocates the payment to a chapter 4 withholding rate pool of U.S. payees and provides the applicable certification on a valid Form W-8IMY for allocating the payment to this pool.

(B) Reportable Payments Other than Reportable Amounts. QI must file a Form 1099 for a reportable payment (other than a reportable amount) paid to each U.S. non-exempt recipient (whether a direct or indirect account holder), or to any account holder that is presumed to be a U.S. non-exempt recipient under section 5.13(C) of this Agreement. Notwithstanding the previous sentence, QI is not required to file a Form 1099 for a reportable payment (other than a reportable amount) paid to a direct account holder that is (or is presumed) a U.S. non-exempt recipient if—

(1) QI is a non-U.S. payor reporting the account holder of a U.S. account under its FATCA requirements as a participating FFI or registered deemed-compliant FFI (including a reporting Model 1 FFI) and the other conditions of §1.6049-4(c)(4)(i) are satisfied;

(2) QI reports the account holder's account as held by a recalcitrant account holder or, in the case of a QI that is a reporting Model 2 FFI or nonreporting Model 2 FFI treated as registered deemed-compliant, as a non-consenting U.S. account under its FATCA requirements as a participating FFI or registered deemed-compliant FFI and the other conditions of §1.6049-4(c)(4)(ii) are satisfied;

(3) QI is a non-U.S. payor that is a reporting Model 1 FFI or registered deemed-compliant Model 1 IGA FFI and determines that the account has U.S. indicia for which appropriate documentation sufficient to treat the account as held by a specified U.S. person has not been provided and reports the account as a U.S. reportable account and the other conditions of §1.6049-4(c)(4)(ii) are satisfied; or

(4) With respect to a reportable payment that is broker proceeds paid to a U.S. non-exempt recipient, QI has applied the procedures of section 3.05(C) of this Agreement and QI does not know that the other payor has failed to report or backup withhold on the payment as required.

Section 9. Adjustments for Over- and Underwithholding; Refunds

Sec. 9.01. Adjustments for Overwithholding by Withholding Agent When QI Does Not Assume Primary Withholding Responsibility. QI may request that a withholding agent make an adjustment for amounts paid to QI when the withholding agent has overwithheld under chapter 3 or 4 by applying either the reimbursement procedure described in section 9.01(A) of this Agreement or the set-off procedure described in section 9.01(B) of this Agreement within the time period prescribed for those procedures. Nothing in this section shall be interpreted to require a withholding agent to apply the reimbursement or set-off procedures under sections 9.01(A) or (B) of this Agreement. See §1.1474-2(a)(2) for the definition of overwithholding that applies for purposes of this section 9 with respect to an amount withheld under chapter 4.

(A) Reimbursement Procedure. QI may request a withholding agent to repay QI for any amount overwithheld and for the withholding agent to reimburse itself under the reimbursement procedures described in §§1.1461-2(a)(2)(i) and 1.1474-2(a)(3) by making the request before the earlier of the due date (without regard to extensions) for the withholding agent to file Form 1042 and Form 1042-S for the calendar year of overwithholding or the date the Form 1042-S is actually filed with the IRS.

(B) Set-Off Procedure. QI may request a withholding agent to repay QI by applying the amount overwithheld against any amount which otherwise would be required to be withheld under chapter 3 or 4 from income paid by the withholding agent to QI under the set-off procedures of §§1.1461-2(a)(3) and 1.1474-2(a)(4). QI must make the request before the earlier of the due date (without regard to extensions) for the withholding agent to file Form 1042-S for the calendar year of overwithholding or the date that the Form 1042-S is actually filed with the IRS.

Sec. 9.02. Adjustments for Overwithholding by QI Assuming Primary Withholding Responsibility. QI may make an adjustment for amounts paid to its account holders when QI has overwithheld by applying either the reimbursement or set-off procedures described in this section 9.02 within the time period prescribed for those procedures.

(A) Reimbursement Procedure. QI may repay its account holders for an amount overwithheld under chapter 3 or 4 and reimburse itself by reducing, by the amount of tax actually repaid to the account holders, the amount of any subsequent deposit of tax required to be made by QI under section 3.08

of this Agreement. For purposes of this section 9.02(A), an amount that is overwithheld shall be applied in order of time (i.e., sequentially) to each of the QI's subsequent deposit periods in the same calendar year to the extent that the withholding taxes required to be deposited for a subsequent deposit period exceed the amount actually deposited. An amount overwithheld in a calendar year may be applied to deposit periods in the calendar year following the calendar year of overwithholding only if:

(1) The repayment occurs before the earlier of the due date (without regard to extensions) for filing Form 1042-S for the calendar year of overwithholding or the date that the Form 1042-S is actually filed by QI with the IRS;

(2) QI states on a Form 1042-S (issued, if applicable, to the account holder or otherwise to a chapter 3 or 4 reporting pool), filed by March 15 of the calendar year following the calendar year of overwithholding, the amount of tax withheld and the amount of any actual repayments; and

(3) QI states on a Form 1042, filed by March 15 of the calendar year following the calendar year of overwithholding, that the filing of the Form 1042 constitutes a claim for credit in accordance with §1.6414-1.

(B) Set-Off Procedure. QI may repay its account holders by applying the amount 107 Overwithheld against any amount which otherwise would be required under chapter 3 or 4 to be withheld from a payment made by QI to the account holders before the earlier of March 15 of the calendar year following the calendar year of overwithholding or the date that the Form 1042-S is actually filed with the IRS. For purposes of making a return on Form 1042 or 1042-S for the calendar year of overwithholding, and for purposes of making a deposit of the amount withheld, the reduced amount shall be considered the amount required to be withheld from such income under chapter 3 or 4.

Sec. 9.03. Repayment of Backup Withholding. If QI erroneously withholds, as defined under §31.6413(a)-3, an amount under section 3406 from an account holder, QI may refund the amount erroneously withheld as provided in §31.6413(a)-3.

Sec. 9.04. Collective Credit or Refund Procedures for Overwithholding. If there has been overwithholding on amounts subject to chapter 3 or 4 withholding paid to QI's account holders during a calendar year and the amount has not been recovered under the reimbursement or set-off procedures as described in section 9.01 or 9.02 of this Agreement, QI may request a credit or refund of the total amount overwithheld by following the procedures of this section 9.04. QI shall follow the procedures set forth under sections 6402 and 6414, and the regulations thereunder, to claim the credit or refund. No credit or refund will be allowed after the expiration of the statutory period of limitation for refunds under section 6511. If there has been an overwithholding and QI does not apply for a collective refund, it must provide a Form 1042-S for the payment that was subject to the overwithholding if requested by the account holder receiving the payment.

(A) **Payments for Which a Collective Refund Is Permitted.** Except as otherwise provided in this section 9.04, QI may use the collective refund procedures with respect to all amounts subject to chapters 3 and 4 withholding. With respect to amounts withheld under chapter 3 or 4, QI shall not include in its collective refund claim tax withheld on payments made to an indirect account holder or a direct account holder of QI that is a nonqualified intermediary or flow-through entity, and with respect to amounts withheld under chapter 4, if QI is a participating FFI or registered deemed-compliant FFI, QI shall not include in its collective refund claim tax withheld on payments made to any account holder described in the FFI agreement or in §1.1471-4(h)(2).

(B) **Requirements for Collective Refund.** QI may use the collective refund procedures under this section 9.04 only if the following conditions are met:

(1) QI must not have issued (and will not issue) Forms 1042-S to the account holders that received the payment that was subject to overwithholding;

(2) QI must submit together with its amended Form 1042 on which it provides a reconciliation of amounts withheld and claims a credit or refund, a copy of the Form 1042-S furnished to QI by its withholding agent reporting the taxes withheld to which the claim relates (if applicable) and a statement that includes the following information and representations—

(i) The reason(s) for the overwithholding;

(ii) QI deposited the tax for which a refund is being sought under section 6302 or received a Form 1042-S from its withholding agent showing the amount of tax withheld, and neither QI nor its withholding agent has applied the reimbursement or set-off procedure of §§1.1461-2 and 1.1474-2 to adjust the tax withheld to which the claim relates;

(iii) QI has repaid or will repay the amount for which refund is sought to the appropriate account holders;

(iv) QI retains a record showing the total amount of tax withheld, credits from other withholding agents, tax assumed by QI, adjustments for underwithholding, and reimbursements for overwithholding as its relates to each account holder and also showing the repayment (if applicable) to such account holders for the amount of tax for which a refund is being sought;

(v) QI retains valid documentation that meets the requirements of chapter 3 or 4 (as applicable) to substantiate the amount of overwithholding with respect to each account holder for which the refund is being sought; and

(vi) QI has not issued and will not issue a Form 1042-S (or such other form as the IRS may prescribe) to any account holder with respect to the payments for which the refund is being sought.

Sec. 9.05. Adjustments for Underwithholding. If QI knows that an amount should have been withheld under chapter 3 or 4 from a previous payment made to an account holder but was not withheld, QI may either withhold from future payments made pursuant to chapter 3 or chapter 4 to the same account holder or payee or satisfy the tax from property that it holds in custody for such person or property over which it has control. The additional withholding or satisfaction of the tax owed described in the previous sentence must be made before the due date (not including extensions) of the Form 1042 for the calendar year in which the underwithholding occurred. QI's responsibilities under this section 9.05 will be met if it informs a withholding agent from which it received the payment of the underwithholding and the withholding agent satisfies the underwithholding.

Sec. 9.06. Underwithholding After Form 1042 Filed. If, after a Form 1042 has been filed for a calendar year, QI, QI's reviewer, or the IRS determines that QI has underwithheld tax for such year, QI shall file an amended Form 1042 to report and pay the underwithheld tax. QI shall pay the underwithheld tax, the interest due on the underwithheld tax, and any applicable penalties at the time of filing the amended Form 1042. If QI fails to file an amended return, the IRS shall make such return under section 6020 and assess such tax under the procedures set forth in the Code.

Section 10. Compliance Procedures

Sec. 10.01. Compliance Program

(A) In General. QI is required to adopt a compliance program under the authority of a responsible officer or, if QI adopts a consolidated compliance program, under the authority of a responsible officer of a Compliance QI (as described in section 10.02(B) of this Agreement). QI's compliance program must include policies, procedures, and processes sufficient for QI to satisfy the documentation, reporting, and withholding requirements of this Agreement and sufficient for a responsible officer of QI (or a Compliance QI) to make the certifications required under section 10.03 of this Agreement. If QI is acting as a QDD, QI's compliance program must also include policies, procedures, and processes sufficient for it to satisfy and report its QDD tax liability and other reporting required as a condition of its status as a QDD. QI must also perform or arrange for the performance of a periodic review described in section 10.04 of this Agreement to the extent required by that section. As part of the responsible officer's certification, QI must provide to the IRS the factual information as required by and referenced in sections 10.04 and 10.05 and in Appendix 1 to this Agreement. QI must also satisfy the requirements of section 10.06 of this Agreement with respect to the report covering the periodic review and must comply with the IRS review described in section 10.08 of this Agreement. With respect to QI that, prior to January 1, 2017, was a limited FFI (as defined in §1.1471-1(b)(77)) or a limited branch (as defined in §1.1471-1(b)(76)), references in this section 10 (and in Appendix 1 to this Agreement) to QI's FATCA Requirements as a participating FFI, registered deemed-compliant FFI, or registered deemed-compliant Model 1 IGA FFI include its requirements under §1.1471-4(e)(4) for purposes of its initial certification period.

(B) Coordination with FATCA Requirements as a Participating FFI, Registered Deemed-Compliant FFI, or Registered Deemed-Compliant Model 1 IGA FFI and, for a Direct Reporting NFFE, the Requirements of §1.1472-1(c)(3). As a condition for maintaining QI status, QI must maintain its chapter 4 status with respect to each branch of QI operating under this Agreement. Therefore, QI must, as part of the compliance procedures described in this section 10 determines whether it is compliant with its FATCA requirements as a participating FFI, registered deemed-compliant FFI, or registered deemed-compliant Model 1 IGA FFI.

(C) Phase-In Year for QDD. For purposes of the IRS's enforcement and administration of the QDD rules in the section 871(m) regulations and the relevant provisions of this Agreement for calendar year 2017, the IRS will take into account the extent to which the QDD made a good faith effort to comply with sections 871 and 881, chapters 3 and 4 with respect to section 871(m) transactions, and the relevant provisions of this Agreement. For calendar year 2017, a QDD is not required to perform a periodic review with respect to its QDD activities (as otherwise required by section 10.04 of this Agreement) or provide the factual information specified in Appendix 1. In addition, the QDD is not required to make the certification of internal controls as applicable to its QDD activities for the certification period ending in calendar year 2017 but rather is required to certify for this period that it has made a good faith effort to comply with the relevant provisions of this Agreement in accordance with Notice 2016-76. A QDD is not required to file the certification described in the preceding sentence with the IRS; however, a QDD must retain a record of the certification (and information in support of the certification) until the end of the calendar year 2022. As a result, the certification of internal controls (and factual information and other certifications) applicable to a QI's QDD activities are not included in Appendix 1 and will be added to the QI agreement for purposes of certification periods ending after December 31, 2017. For 2017, a material failure relevant to a QDD has not occurred unless the QDD failed to make a good faith effort to comply with the section 871(m) regulations and the relevant provisions of the QI agreement.

The QDD will be considered to satisfy its obligations for purposes of section 10 that apply specifically to a QDD under this Agreement for calendar year 2017 provided that the QDD made a good faith effort to comply with the relevant terms of this Agreement. Any QDD that has not made a good faith effort to comply with its QDD obligations will not be given any relief from IRS administration or enforcement during calendar 2017, including penalties.

Sec. 10.02. Responsible Officer. QI must appoint an individual as a responsible officer as defined in section 2.72 of this Agreement. The responsible officer must be identified on the QI/WP/WT Application and Accounts Management System as QI's responsible party, and such person may, but is not required to, be the same responsible officer for purposes of compliance with QI's FATCA requirements as a participating FFI, registered deemed-compliant FFI, or registered deemed-compliant Model 1 IGA FFI. The responsible officer must establish a compliance program that meets the requirements of this section 10.02 and must make the periodic certifications to the IRS described in section 10.03 of this Agreement. The responsible officer of QI must be an officer of QI with sufficient authority to fulfill the duties of a responsible officer described in this section 10. The responsible officer (or a delegate appointed by the responsible officer) must also serve as the point of contact for the IRS for all issues related to this Agreement and for complying with IRS requests for information or additional review procedures under section 10.07 of this Agreement. References in this section 10.02 to the responsible officer include a responsible officer's designee, where appropriate.

(A) Compliance Program. The responsible officer must establish a program for QI to comply with the requirements of this Agreement that includes the following:

(1) Written Policies and Procedures. The responsible officer must ensure the drafting and updating, as necessary, of written policies and procedures sufficient for QI to satisfy the documentation, withholding, reporting, and other obligations of this Agreement, including, with respect to QI that is acting as a QDD, satisfying its QDD tax liability. Such written policies and procedures must include a process for employees of QI to raise issues to the responsible officer (or the responsible officer's designee) that concern QI's compliance with this Agreement.

(2) Training. The responsible officer must communicate such policies and procedures to any line of business of QI that is responsible for obtaining, reviewing, and retaining a record of documentation under the requirements of section 5 of this Agreement; making payments subject to withholding under section 3 of this Agreement; reporting payments and accounts as required under sections 7 and 8 of this Agreement; or entering into potential section 871(m) transactions, in the case of QI that is acting as a QDD.

(3) Systems. The responsible officer must ensure that systems and processes are in place that will allow QI to fulfill its obligations under this Agreement. For example, in order to fulfill QI's obligations to report on Forms 1042-S, 1099, and 8966 under section 8 of this Agreement, QI must establish systems for documenting account holders and for recording the information with respect to each such account that QI is required to report under that section.

(4) Monitoring of Business Changes. The responsible officer must monitor business practices and arrangements that affect QI's compliance with this Agreement, including, for example, QI's acquisition of lines of businesses or accounts that give rise to documentation, withholding, or reporting obligations under this Agreement.

(5) QDD Tax Liability Determinations. If QI is acting as a QDD, the responsible officer must ensure that the QDD has appropriate systems in place to make the necessary determinations and calculations to identify section 871(m) transactions, potential section 871(m) transactions, the amount of dividends received in its QDD equity derivatives dealer capacity and the section 881 taxes paid thereon, its net delta exposure, the dividend amount per share, the stock owned by the QDD included in its net delta exposure long position, its long position, its short position, its section 871(m) amount and the section 881 taxes paid thereon, its QDD tax liability amount, and the amount of dividend equivalent payments made by the QDD. In addition, the responsible officer must ensure that the QDD has appropriate systems in place to determine whether a transaction is as a principal or non-principal, whether a transaction is in an equity derivatives dealer or non-equity derivatives dealer capacity, whether the transaction exists for federal income tax purposes, whether transaction is owned by the QDD, and whether the transaction is effectively connected with the conduct of a trade or business in the United States. This includes appropriate systems to, where required, calculate the delta for a potential section 871(m) transaction, perform the substantial equivalence test described in §1.871-15(h), calculate the amount of a dividend equivalent, determine any QDD tax liability amount (and each part thereof) and its timing, and determine what payments are received or made with respect to potential section 871(m) transactions and underlying securities as a principal and whether in its equity derivatives dealer capacity or non-equity derivatives dealer capacity and by which home office or branch that is acting as a QDD. The systems must also take into account information received pursuant to §1.871-15(p).

(6) Periodic Review. Unless QI receives a waiver (the requirements of which are described in section 10.07(B) of this Agreement), the responsible officer must designate a reviewer that meets the qualifications described in section 10.04(A) of this Agreement to perform the periodic review as described in section 10.05 of this Agreement, to the extent required.

(7) Certification of Internal Controls. The responsible officer must make the periodic certification as described in section 10.03 of this Agreement, including ensuring that corrective actions are taken in response to any material failures (as defined in section 10.03(B) of this Agreement) of QI's compliance with this Agreement.

(B) Consolidated Compliance Program. The IRS, in its discretion, may permit a consolidated compliance program that includes two or more QIs that are members of a group of entities under common ownership when the QIs: (i) operate under a uniform compliance program for purposes of this Agreement; (ii) share practices, procedures, and systems subject to uniform monitoring and control; and (iii) are subject to a consolidated periodic review that includes a review of internal controls and testing of transactions relevant to this Agreement with respect to each QI in the consolidated compliance program. Each QI that is a member of a consolidated compliance program must designate a Compliance QI to act on its behalf, and the responsible officer of the Compliance QI must identify itself as such when making its periodic certification and must comply with the identification, certification of internal controls, and periodic review requirements for the QI consolidated compliance program as the IRS may prescribe. The Compliance QI must also agree to be jointly and severally liable for the obligations and liabilities of any QI in its consolidated compliance program relating to the QI's obligations under this Agreement. QIs that want to operate a consolidated compliance program must contact the IRS Foreign Intermediaries Program for approval.

Sec. 10.03. Certification of Internal Controls by Responsible Officer. A QI's responsible officer must make the certification described in either Part II.A (Certification of Effective Internal Controls) or Part II.B (Qualified Certification) of Appendix 1 to this Agreement and must disclose any material failures that occurred during the certification period or during any prior period if the material failure was not disclosed as part of a prior certification or written disclosure made by QI to the IRS. If the responsible officer has identified an event of default or a material failure that has not been corrected as of the date of the certification, the responsible officer cannot make the certification in Part II.A (Certification of Effective Internal Controls) and must make the certification in Part II.B (Qualified Certification).

For a QI that uses the third year of the certification period for its periodic review, the certification is due on or before December 31 of the year following the certification period. For a QI that uses the first or second year of the certification period for its periodic review or a QI that obtains a waiver of the periodic review requirement, the certification is due on or before July 1 of the year following the certification period. The initial certification period is the period ending on the third full calendar year that this Agreement is in effect (including renewals of this Agreement). Subsequent certification periods will be every three calendar years following the initial certification period (including renewals of this Agreement).

The certification of internal controls required by this section 10.03 applies only to the internal controls related to QI's compliance with this Agreement and its FATCA requirements as a participating FFI, registered deemed-compliant FFI, or registered deemed-compliant Model 1 IGA FFI and, in the case of a direct reporting NFFE, its requirements under §1.1472-1(c)(3), with respect to accounts for which it acts as a QI, and does not relate to any other obligations or requirements. The responsible officer may rely on any reasonable procedure, process, review, or certification that enables the responsible officer to make the certification described in this section 10.03. If the responsible officer relies on an internal or external review for this purpose (i.e., for purposes of determining whether QI has effective internal controls), the internal or external reviewer must be independent, as described in section 10.04 of this Agreement. The responsible officer must document the procedures, processes, reviews, or certifications relied upon in making the certification. QI's responsible officer (or the responsible officer of its Compliance QI) must make the certifications of compliance in such manner as the IRS may prescribe.

(A) PAIs and Partnership or Trust to Which QI Applies the Agency Option. Unless QI has received a waiver of the periodic review requirement, any PAI with which QI has an agreement and any partnership or trust to which QI applies the agency option must provide its documentation and other information to QI for inclusion in QI's periodic review or conduct an independent periodic review and provide a written certification to QI regarding its compliance with the requirements of the PAI or agency agreement. Such certification must be available to the IRS upon a request made as part of the review described in section 10.08 of this Agreement (with a certified translation into English if the certification is not in English).

(B) Material Failures.

(1) Material Failures Defined. A material failure is generally a failure of QI to fulfill the requirements of this Agreement or its FATCA requirements as a participating FFI, registered deemed-compliant FFI, or registered deemed-compliant Model 1 IGA FFI. For purposes of the certifications described in Parts II.A and B of Appendix 1 to this Agreement, a material failure is limited to the following:

(i) QI's establishing of, for financial statement purposes, a tax reserve or provision for a potential future tax liability related to QI's failure to comply with this Agreement, including its FATCA requirements as a participating FFI, registered deemed-compliant FFI, or registered deemed-compliant Model 1 IGA FFI, and with respect to QI that is acting as a QDD, failure to satisfy its QDD tax liability and its obligations pursuant to section 871(m) and the regulations under that section.

(ii) QI's failure to establish written policies, procedures, or systems sufficient for the relevant personnel of QI to take actions consistent with QI's obligations under this Agreement, or if QI is acting as a QDD, its obligations as a QDD under this Agreement or pursuant to section 871(m) and the regulations under that section.

(iii) A criminal or civil penalty or sanction imposed on QI (or any branch or office thereof) by a regulator or other governmental authority or agency with oversight over QI's compliance with AML/KYC procedures to which QI (or any branch or office thereof) is subject and that is imposed due to QI's failure to properly identify account holders under the requirements of those procedures.

(iv) A finding (including a finding noted in the periodic review report described in section 10.06 of this Agreement) for one or more years covered by this Agreement that QI failed to—

(a) Withhold an amount that QI was required to withhold under chapter 3 or 4 or under section 3406 as required under section 3 of this Agreement or, if QI is acting as a QDD, failing to timely pay its QDD tax liability;

(b) Provide information sufficient for another withholding agent to perform withholding and reporting to the extent required when QI does not assume primary chapters 3 and 4 withholding responsibility or primary Form 1099 reporting and backup withholding responsibility;

(c) Provide allocation information as described in section 6.03(D) of this Agreement (regarding U.S. non-exempt recipient account holders) by January 15 as required by that section when QI applies the alternative withholding rate pool procedures;

(d) Make deposits in the time and manner required by section 3.08 of this Agreement or make adequate deposits to satisfy its withholding obligations, or, if QI is acting as a QDD, timely satisfy its QDD tax liability, taking into account the procedures under section 9 of this Agreement;

(e) Report or report accurately on Forms 1099 as required under section 8.06 of this Agreement or provide information to the payor to the extent QI does not assume primary Form 1099 reporting and backup withholding responsibilities;

(f) Report or report accurately on Forms 1042 and 1042-S under sections 7 and 8 of this Agreement;

(g) Report or report accurately on Form 8966 under sections 8.04 and 8.05 of this Agreement; or

(h) Withhold an amount required to be withheld or report accurately with respect to U.S. source substitute dividend payments or make timely and adequate deposits of tax due with respect to such payments for which QI is a QSL and acts as a dealer or intermediary.

(2) Limitations on Material Failures. A failure described in section 10.03(B)(1)(iv) of this Agreement is a material failure only if the failure was the result of a deliberate action on the part of one or more employees of QI to avoid the requirements of this Agreement with respect to one or more account holders of QI, or was an error attributable to a failure of QI to establish or implement internal controls necessary for QI to meet the requirements of this Agreement. Regardless of these limitations for certification purposes, QI is required to correct a failure to withhold or deposit tax under section 3 of this Agreement, or to report under section 7 or 8 of this Agreement, or, for a QI that is acting as a QDD, to timely pay its QDD tax liability and timely file the appropriate return (or amended return).

Sec. 10.04. Periodic Review Absent Waiver. Unless the QI receives a waiver (the requirements of which are described in section 10.07(B) of this Agreement), at the time QI provides the certification described in section 10.03 of this Agreement, QI must also provide certain factual information regarding its accounts, withholdable payments, amounts subject to chapter 3 withholding, and, if QI is acting as a QDD, section 871(m) transactions, potential section 871(m) transactions, and its QDD tax liability based on the results of a periodic review. The factual information requested is included in Appendix 1 to this Agreement.

(A) Independent Reviewer. The periodic review may be performed by an internal reviewer (such as an internal auditor) that is an employee of QI or an employee of an affiliate of QI (including an employee of a Compliance QI in the case of a consolidated compliance program) ('internal reviewer'), or a certified public accountant, attorney, or third-party consultant ('external reviewer'), or any combination thereof.

(1) Internal Reviewer. QI may designate an internal reviewer to perform the periodic review (or a portion of the periodic review) only when the internal reviewer is competent with respect to the requirements of this Agreement. The internal reviewer must also be able to report findings that reflect the independent judgment of the reviewer. The internal reviewer must not be reviewing its own work, procedures, or results (e.g., the internal reviewer, in reviewing QI's documentation cannot be part of the team primarily responsible for collecting and validating documentation). The results of the periodic review and the internal reviewer's reporting of such results to the responsible officer cannot influence or affect the compensation, bonus, employment status, or employee review of the internal reviewer. The IRS has the right to request the performance of the periodic review by an alternative reviewer if the IRS, in its sole discretion, reasonably believes that the reviewer selected by QI was not independent, as described in this Agreement, or did not perform an effective periodic review under this Agreement. In the case of a consolidated compliance program, the Compliance QI may designate an internal reviewer to perform the consolidated periodic review (or a portion of the consolidated periodic review). See section 10.02(B) of this Agreement. The internal reviewer of the Compliance QI must meet the requirements of this section with respect to both the Compliance QI and each QI that is a member of the consolidated compliance program.

If QI designates an internal reviewer that is an employee of an affiliate of QI but is not part of a consolidated compliance program, QI must ensure that the internal reviewer has access to all necessary information in order to complete the review. In addition, QI must permit the IRS to communicate directly with such internal reviewer.

(2) External Reviewer. QI may engage an external reviewer that is a certified public accountant, attorney, or third-party consultant that is regularly engaged in the practice of performing reviews of clients' policies, procedures, and processes for complying with accounting, tax, or regulatory requirements (including assisting clients in determining such compliance). The external reviewer cannot be reviewing systems, policies, or procedures or the results thereof that it (or the firm with which it is affiliated) was involved in designing, implementing, or maintaining. The external reviewer must be in good standing with and comply with any applicable professional standards for maintaining its license as an accountant or attorney (or other third-party consultant that has similar professional standards or requirements). The external reviewer is not required to make an attestation or render an opinion regarding

QI's compliance with this Agreement or QI's compliance with its FATCA requirements as a participating FFI, registered deemed-compliant FFI, or registered deemed-compliant Model 1 IGA FFI, but the reviewer must be able to perform the periodic review as specified in section 10.05 of this Agreement. QI must permit the external reviewer to have access to all relevant records of QI for purposes of performing the review, including information regarding specific account holders. Additionally, the engagement between the external reviewer and QI must impose no restrictions on QI's ability to provide the results of the review to the IRS. However, the external reviewer is not required to divulge the identity of QI's account holders to the IRS, except as otherwise provided under QI's FATCA requirements as a participating FFI, registered deemed-compliant FFI, or registered deemed-compliant Model 1 IGA FFI. QI must permit the IRS to communicate directly with the external reviewer, and any legal prohibitions that prevent the IRS from communicating directly with the reviewer must be waived.

Sec. 10.05. Scope and Timing of Review. The responsible officer of QI (or of the Compliance QI) must require the reviewer to test accounts related to QI's documentation, withholding, reporting, and other obligations under this Agreement, including its QDD tax liability with respect to QI that is acting as a QDD, and its FATCA requirements as a participating FFI, registered deemed-compliant FFI, or registered deemed-compliant Model 1 IGA FFI for accounts for which it is acting as a QI, and to identify deficiencies in meeting these obligations. Any PAI with which QI has an agreement and any partnership or trust to which QI applies the agency option must provide the information necessary for QI to test accounts and transactions of such entity as part of QI's periodic review unless such entity conducts an its own periodic review and provides QI with the report documenting the results of such review as described in section 10.06 of this Agreement. Unless otherwise approved by the IRS, the review must include the steps described in section 10.05(A) of this Agreement.

QI is required to arrange for the performance of one review for the certification period to evaluate QI's documentation, withholding, and reporting practices. If QI is acting as a QDD, this should also include a review of its determination as to whether transactions are section 871(m) transactions, its computations and determinations of dividend equivalent amounts, dividends and taxes paid thereon, whether transactions are in its equity derivatives dealer capacity, net delta exposure, its section 871(m) amount, and its calculation of its QDD tax liability, as well as any other amounts required to be included on the reconciliation schedule. The review may be conducted for any calendar year covered by the certification period. However, all results of the review must relate to one calendar year. QI may conduct a review for a particular calendar year if, on the due date for reporting the factual information relating to the periodic review (provided in section 10.04 of this Agreement), there are 15 or more months available on the period for assessment under section 6501(a) of the calendar year for which the review is to be conducted or the QI's submits, upon request, a Form 872, *Consent to Extend the Time to Assess Tax*, that will satisfy the 15-month requirement. The Form 872 must be submitted to the IRS at the address provided in section 12.06 of this Agreement.

QI may use a sample to test accounts if there are more than 60 accounts to review. If QI has fewer than 60 accounts, it must review all accounts and cannot use a sample to test accounts. To the extent applicable, the reviewer must separately review its QI activities (when not acting in its QDD capacity) and QDD activities. The reviewer is required to record its sampling procedures and to maintain the ability to reconstruct the sample. Further, the review is not required to include statistical sampling procedures for testing transactions, but the reviewer must document its methodology for sampling determinations. A safe harbor methodology and additional information on the use of statistical sampling is provided in Appendix 2 to this Agreement.

If the reviewer determines that underwithholding has occurred, QI shall report and pay any amount due. QI must also notify the IRS Foreign Intermediaries Program at the address provided in section 12.06 of this Agreement of the underwithholding discovered as a result of the review. See Appendix 2 to this Agreement for information required to be provided when reporting underwithholding and information regarding any projection of underwithholding determined using a sampling method.

(A) Documentation. The reviewer must—

(1) Review QI's accounts, to ensure that QI obtained documentation that meets the requirements described in sections 5.01–5.09 of this Agreement;

(2) Review QI's accounts for which treaty benefits are claimed, to ensure that QI obtained the treaty statements and limitation on benefits information required by section 5.03(B) of this Agreement;

(3) Review information contained in account holder files to determine if the documentation validity standards of section 5.10 of this Agreement have been met. For example, the reviewer must verify that changes in account holder information (e.g., a change of address to a U.S. address or change of account holder status from foreign to U.S. or a change in chapter 4 status from participating FFI to nonparticipating FFI) are being conveyed to QI's withholding agents;

(4) Review the accounts for which QI is acting as a QI to ensure that QI is obtaining, reviewing, and maintaining documentation in accordance with its

FATCA requirements as a participating FFI, registered deemed-compliant FFI, or registered deemed-compliant Model 1 IGA FFI;

(5) Review accounts held by U.S. non-exempt recipient account holders, to determine if QI obtained Forms W-9, and, if QI does not assume primary Form 1099 reporting and backup withholding responsibility, that QI transmitted those forms to a withholding agent consistent with this Agreement;

(6) For a QI that is a QDD, review accounts for which QI is acting as a QDD and that received a reportable payment to determine whether QI has documented the status of account holders under the requirements described in sections 5.01 through 5.09 of this Agreement;

(7) For a QI that makes payments of U.S. source substitute interest and assumes primary chapters 3 and 4 withholding responsibility for such amounts, review accounts of persons to which QI pays U.S. source substitute interest to determine whether QI has documented the status of such persons under the requirements described in sections 5.01 through 5.09 of this Agreement; and

(8) For QI that is a QSL, review a sample of transactions for which QI acts as a QSL to determine whether QI has documented the status of persons to which QI pays U.S. source substitute dividends.

(B) **Withholding Rate Pools.** The reviewer must—

(1) Perform checks using account holders assigned to each withholding rate pool, and cross check that assignment against the documentation provided by, or the presumption rules applied to, the account holder, the type of income earned, and the withholding rate applied;

(2) Verify, if QI is using the procedure for U.S. non-exempt recipients described in 119

section 6.03(D) of this Agreement, that QI is providing sufficient and timely information to withholding agents that allocates reportable payments to U.S. non-exempt recipients; and

(3) With respect to a partnership or trust described in section 4.05 of this Agreement, if applicable, perform test checks, using account holder documentation for the selected partners, beneficiaries, or owners and records of each type of reportable amount paid by QI to the entity, to determine whether the highest rate of withholding applicable to each type of reportable amount was applied.

(C) **Withholding Responsibilities.** The reviewer must—

(1) To the extent QI has assumed primary chapters 3 and 4 withholding responsibilities, perform test checks, using recalcitrant account holders and nonparticipating FFIs, to verify that QI withheld the proper amounts under chapter 4;

(2) To the extent QI has assumed primary chapters 3 and 4 withholding responsibility, perform test checks, using foreign account holders for which no withholding is required under chapter 4 based on the payees chapter 4 status, to verify that QI withheld the proper amounts under chapter 3 and properly applied the exemptions from chapter 4 withholding;

(3) To the extent QI has not assumed primary chapters 3 and 4 withholding responsibility, verify that QI has fulfilled its responsibilities under section 3.02 of this Agreement (including withholding if QI failed to provide the required information to a withholding agent to withhold on payments);

(4) To the extent QI has assumed primary Form 1099 reporting and backup withholding responsibility, perform checks using U.S. non-exempt recipient account holders to verify that QI backup withheld when required;

(5) To the extent QI has not assumed primary Form 1099 reporting and backup withholding responsibility, perform test checks using U.S. non-exempt account holders to verify that QI fulfilled its backup withholding responsibilities under sections 3.04 through 3.06 of this Agreement;

(6) Verify that amounts withheld by QI were timely deposited in accordance with section 3.08 of this Agreement;

(7) To the extent that QI is acting as a QDD, determine that QI withheld when required on payments that it made with respect to potential section 871(m) transactions;

(8) To the extent that QI makes payments of U.S. source substitute interest and assumes chapter 3 and 4 withholding responsibility for such amounts, determine that QI withheld when required on such payments; and

(9) To the extent QI acts as a QSL, determine that QI withheld when required on U.S. source payments of substitute dividends.

(D) Return Filing and Information Reporting. The reviewer must—

(1) Obtain copies of original and amended Forms 1042 and 945, and any schedules, statements, or attachments required to be filed with those forms, verify that the forms have been filed, and determine whether the amounts of income, taxes, and other information reported on those forms are accurate by—

(i) Reviewing copies of Forms 1042-S that withholding agents have provided QI to determine whether QI properly reported the amount of taxes withheld by other withholding agents on Form 1042;

(ii) Reviewing account statements and correspondence from withholding agents;

(iii) Determining that adjustments to the amount of tax shown on Form 1042 (and any claim by QI for refund or credit) properly reflect the adjustments to withholding made by QI using the reimbursement or set-off procedures under section 9.02 of this Agreement and are supported by sufficient documentation;

(iv) Reconciling amounts shown on Forms 1042 with amounts shown on Form 1042-S (including the amount of taxes reported as withheld);

(v) If QI is acting as a QDD, reviewing the reconciliation schedule described in section 7.01(c) of this Agreement and any information used to prepare such schedule or compute its QDD tax liability, including information received pursuant to §1.871-15(p), reviewing the amounts required to determine its section 871(m) amounts and its QDD tax liability over the applicable period, and reviewing such information to determine whether the section 871(m) amounts and QDD tax liability have been properly calculated;

(vi) If QI is acting as a QDD, reviewing amounts shown on Forms 1042 (including the reconciliation schedule) and Forms 1042-S, as well as any information received pursuant to §1.871-15(p), to determine whether the QDD properly took the information into account (e.g., to calculate its QDD tax liability);

(vii) To the extent QI acts as a QSL, determine that QI properly reported the gross amount of the U.S. source payments of substitute dividends to which the recipient would have otherwise been entitled before consideration of any withholding tax obligations; the amount of tax withheld by the withholding agent; and the amount of tax withheld by other withholding agents in the series of securities lending or sale-repurchase transaction;

(viii) In the case of collective credits or refunds, reviewing the statements attached to amended Forms 1042 filed to claim a collective refund, determine whether those forms are accurate, and—

(a) Determine the causes of any overwithholding reported and ensure QI did not issue Forms 1042-S to persons whom it included as part of its collective credit or refund;

(b) Determine that QI repaid the appropriate account holders and that the amount of the claim is accurate and supported by adequate documentation; and

(c) Determine that QI did not include payments made to a partnership or trust described in section 4.05 of this Agreement.

(2) Obtain copies of original and corrected Forms 1042-S and Forms 1099 filed by QI together with the work papers used to prepare those forms, and determine whether the amounts reported on those forms are accurate by—

(i) Reconciling payments and tax reported on Forms 1042-S received from withholding agents with amounts (including characterization of income) and taxes reported by QI as withheld on Forms 1042-S and determining the reason(s) for any variance;

(ii) Reviewing the Forms W-8IMY, and the associated withholding statements, that QI has provided withholding agents;

(iii) Reviewing account statements issued by QI to account holders;

(iv) Determining, in the case in which QI utilized the reimbursement or set-off procedure, that QI satisfied the requirements of section 9.02 of this Agreement and that the adjusted amounts of tax withheld are properly reflected on Forms 1042-S.

(3) Obtain copies of original and amended Forms 8966 (or, for QI that is a reporting Model 1 FFI, any analogous forms used for reporting account information pursuant to the applicable Model 1 IGA) of accounts for which QI is acting as a QI, and determine whether the amounts of income and other information reported on Forms 8966 are accurate by—

(i) Reviewing U.S. accounts (or U.S. reportable accounts for which QI acts as a QI) to determine that such accounts were reported in accordance with QI's FATCA requirements as a participating FFI, registered deemed-compliant FFI, or registered deemed-compliant Model 1 IGA FFI;

(ii) If QI is an NFFE acting as a QI on behalf of persons other than its shareholders, confirming that if QI is acting on behalf of a passive NFFE with substantial U.S. owners, withholdable payments made to the passive NFFE and the information regarding its substantial U.S. owners were reported;

(iii) Confirming with respect to any nonqualified intermediary or flow-through entity that provides information regarding an account holder (or interest holder) that is an NFFE (other than an excepted NFFE) with one or more substantial U.S. owners that such substantial U.S. owners were reported to the extent required under section 8.04(B) of this Agreement;

(iv) Reviewing the documentation provided by a PAI or a partnership or trust to which QI applied the agency option to determine that QI reported on Form 8966 to the extent required under section 4 of this Agreement; and

(v) Reviewing work papers used to prepare these forms.

(4) If QI is acting as a QDD, the reviewer must also review accounts designated as accounts for which QI acted as a QDD to determine whether QI is acting as a QDD with respect to all potential section 871(m) transactions and underlying securities for which it is required to act as a QDD and not any other transactions and whether the section 871(m) amount includes the amounts in its equity derivatives dealer capacity and not amounts in its non-equity derivatives dealer capacity.

(E) Significant Change in Circumstances. The reviewer must verify that in the course of the review it has not discovered any significant change in circumstances, as described in section 11.04(A), (D), (E), or (J) of this Agreement.

Sec. 10.06. Periodic Review Report.

(A) In General. The results of the periodic review must be documented in a written report addressed to the responsible officer of QI and must be available to the IRS upon request (with a certified translation into English if the report is not in English). The report must describe the scope of the review and the actions performed to satisfy each requirement of section 10.05(A) through (E), including the methodology for sampling determinations. The report may include explanatory footnotes to clarify the results of the report. Recommendations may be included but are not required to be provided in the report. The periodic review report should form the basis for the factual information provided by QI that is set forth in Appendix 1.

In addition to the findings of section 10.05 of this Agreement, the periodic review report should also include details regarding the documentation and tax deposit and payment failures identified by the reviewer but then cured before the periodic review report is finalized. While the curing of inadequate documentation is permissible, the factual information reported (as set forth in Appendix 1) should report the results of the review as it was performed and should not reflect the results after curing. Any curing process should not delay certification of internal controls or factual information required in Appendix 1 to this Agreement. To the extent necessary, the periodic review report should include the dates on (or time period during) which curative documentation was received for accounts with respect to which the reviewer determined that underwithholding had occurred, the number of accounts for which curative documentation was obtained and a revised calculation of the underwithholding or additional backup withholding.

(B) Periodic Review Report for QDDs. If QI is acting as a QDD, the periodic review report should also include the number of accounts that were not correctly treated as (i) principal accounts (except accounts that are effectively connected with the conduct or a trade or business within the United States within the meaning of section 864), (ii) non-principal accounts, (iii) principal accounts that are effectively connected with the conduct or a trade or business within the United States within the meaning of section 864, (iv) equity derivatives dealer accounts, and (v) non-equity derivatives dealer accounts. The report should also include any other issues related to the QDD tax liability (e.g., incorrect determination of whether an account is a potential section 871(m) transaction or a section 871(m) transaction, the dividends received in the QDD's equity derivatives dealer capacity and the taxes paid on those dividends, the net delta exposure, the section 871(m) amount and the taxes on the section 871(m) amount, the amount of dividend equivalent payments made, or any other amounts subject to tax (or required to compute the tax liability) under section 871(a) and 881 (including the QDD tax liability)) for each QDD.

(C) PAI Certification and Partnership or Trust to Which QI Applies the Agency Option. Any PAI with which QI has an agreement and any partnership or trust to which QI applies the agency option that does not provide its documentation and other information to QI for inclusion in QI's periodic review described in section 10.04 of this Agreement, must conduct an independent periodic review in accordance with the compliance procedures described in section 10.05 of this Agreement. The performance results of the periodic review must be documented in a written report addressed to the responsible officer of QI and must be available to the IRS upon request (with a certified translation into English if the report is not in English).

(D) Retention of Report and Certifications. The report and certifications described in this section 10.06 must be retained by QI (or the Compliance QI) for as long as this Agreement is in effect.

Sec. 10.07. Waiver of Periodic Review Requirement.

(A) In General. A QI that is not acting as a QDD and that is an FFI that meets the requirements of section 10.07(B) may apply for a waiver of the periodic review requirement. QI must request a waiver of the periodic review requirement under this section 10.07 at the time the responsible officer makes the certification described in section 10.03 of this Agreement. QI's application for such a waiver must be approved by the IRS, and waiver applications are not approved automatically. QI must apply for a waiver for each certification period for which a waiver is requested. If QI's request for a waiver of the periodic review requirement is granted, such approval is only to waive QI's obligations under sections 10.04 and 10.05 of this Agreement, and QI is still required to make the certification described in section 10.03 of this Agreement. The waiver also does not preclude the IRS from requesting information or conducting a correspondence review as described in section 10.07 of this Agreement. QI must include the information of any PAI with which QI has an agreement and any partnership or trust to which QI applies the agency option in its waiver application which is set forth in Part III of Appendix 1 to this Agreement.

(B) Eligibility. QI is eligible to apply for a waiver of the periodic review requirement if it meets the following requirements—

(1) QI must be an FFI that is not also acting as a QDD;

(2) QI cannot be part of a consolidated compliance program;

(3) For each calendar year covered by the certification period, the reportable amounts received by QI cannot exceed $5 million;

(4) QI must have timely filed its Forms 1042, 1042-S, 945, 1099, and 8966, as applicable, for all calendar years covered by the certification period;

(5) QI must have made all periodic certifications and reviews required by sections 10.02 and 10.03 of this Agreement as well as all certifications required pursuant to QI's FATCA requirements as a participating FFI, registered deemed-compliant FFI, or registered deemed-compliant Model 1 IGA FFI; and

(6) QI must have made the certification of effective internal controls in section 10.02(A).

(C) Documentation Required with Waiver Application. When applying for a waiver under this section 10.07, QI must include the information described in Appendix 1 to this Agreement using the most recent calendar year covered by the certification period and reporting such results without any curing or remediation.

(D) Approval. If QI's request for a waiver of the periodic review requirement is approved, the IRS will notify QI. If QI requests a waiver but such request is not approved, QI will be granted a six month extension from the date of denial of the waiver to complete the periodic review. Such extension will not be granted if QI has made the request for waiver in bad faith.

Sec. 10.08. Periodic Review.

(A) In General. Based upon the certifications made by the responsible officer and the disclosure of material failures, the information reported on Forms 945, 1042, 1042-S, 1099, and 8966 filed with the IRS during the certification period, or otherwise at the IRS's discretion for compliance purposes, the IRS may initiate requests of QI under this section 10.08. The IRS may preemptively request remediation or the conduct of a limited periodic review earlier than the time period provided in this section 10 if, based on the information described above, the IRS identifies, in its discretion, a presence of factors indicating systemic or significant compliance failures by QI. The IRS may also request that QI designate a replacement responsible officer if QI's responsible officer has not complied with its responsibilities (including responding to requests by the IRS for additional information) or the IRS has information that indicates the responsible officer may not be relied upon to comply with its responsibilities.

(B) Periodic Review Report. The IRS may request, through written correspondence to the responsible officer of QI (or the Compliance QI), a copy of the results of QI's periodic review for any prior certification period or the periodic review report of any PAI or partnership or trust to which QI applied the agency option that QI has an agreement during the current certification period (with a certified translation into English if the report is not in English). QI is required to provide the results within 30 calendar days of such request.

(C) Correspondence Review. The IRS may, in its discretion, conduct additional fact finding through a correspondence review. In such a review, the IRS will contact the responsible officer of QI (or the Compliance QI) in writing and request information about QI's compliance with this Agreement or the compliance of a PAI or a partnership or trust to which QI applied the agency option, including, for example, information about documentation, withholding, or reporting processes, its periodic review, and information about any material failures that were disclosed to the IRS (including remediation plans). The IRS may request phone or video interviews with employees of QI (and the Compliance QI), a PAI, or a partnership or trust to which QI applied the agency option as part of the IRS's correspondence review. QI is required to respond in a reasonable time to any such requests.

(D) Additional Review Procedures. In limited circumstances, the IRS may direct QI (or the Compliance FFI) or any PAI or partnership or trust to which QI applies the agency option to perform additional, specified review procedures. The IRS reserves the right to require QI (or the Compliance QI) or a PAI, or a partnership or trust to which QI applied the agency option to engage an external reviewer to perform the additional review procedures regardless of whether such reviewer performed the periodic review. The IRS will provide the responsible officer of QI with a written plan describing the additional review procedures and will provide a due date of not more than 120 days for the QI to provide to the IRS a report covering the reviewer's findings.

Section 11. Expiration, Termination, Merger, and Default

Sec. 11.01. Term of Agreement. This Agreement begins on the effective date and expires at the end of the sixth full calendar year the Agreement is in effect, unless terminated under section 11.02 of this Agreement. This Agreement may be renewed as provided in section 11.08 of this Agreement.

Sec. 11.02. Termination of Agreement.

(A) In General. This Agreement may be terminated by either the IRS or QI prior to the end of its term by delivery of a notice, in accordance with section 12.06 of this Agreement, of termination to the other party. The IRS, however, shall not terminate this Agreement unless there has been a significant change in circumstances, as defined in section 11.04 of this Agreement, or an event of default has occurred, as defined in section 11.06 of this Agreement, and the IRS determines, in its sole discretion, that the significant change in circumstances or the event of default warrants termination of this Agreement. The IRS shall not terminate this Agreement if QI can establish to the satisfaction of the IRS that all events of default for which it has received notice have been cured within the time period agreed upon. The IRS shall notify QI that an event of default has occurred and that the IRS intends to terminate the Agreement unless QI cures the default or establishes that no event of default occurred. A notice of termination sent by either party shall take effect on the date specified in the notice, and QI is required to notify its withholding agent of the date that its status as a QI is terminated.

The termination of the Agreement shall not affect any of QI's reporting, tax filing, withholding, depositing, or payment responsibilities arising in the calendar years for which this Agreement was in effect and the portion of the calendar year in which termination is requested. The IRS shall revoke QI's QI-EIN within a reasonable time after the reporting, tax filing, and depositing requirements for such years are satisfied. The termination of this Agreement is not intended to affect any other federal income tax consequences.

(B) Final Certification After a Termination of the Agreement. Upon a termination of this Agreement, QI must provide to the IRS the certification described in section 10.03 of this Agreement covering the period from the end of the most recent certification period (or, if the first certification period has not ended, the effective date of this Agreement) to the date of termination within six months of the date of termination, regardless of whether a periodic review has been completed for such period.

Sec. 11.03. Loss of QDD Status. If QI is acting as a QDD and the home office or branch, as applicable, fails to qualify as an eligible entity during the term of this Agreement, the home office or branch shall lose its QDD status immediately upon the QDD failing to qualify as an eligible entity and as of that date can no longer act as a QDD. QI is required to notify its withholding agent of the date that the QDD failed to qualify as an eligible entity and no longer was permitted to act as a QDD. The QDD's loss of QDD status shall not affect any of QI's QDD reporting, tax filing, withholding, depositing, or payment responsibilities for the period QI was acting as a QDD as provided in this Agreement, including paying its QDD tax liability.

Sec. 11.04. Significant Change in Circumstances. For purposes of this Agreement, a significant change in circumstances includes, but is not limited to—

(A) An acquisition of all, or substantially all, of QI's assets in any transaction in which QI is not the surviving legal entity;

(B) A change in U.S. federal law, or applicable foreign law, that affects the validity of any provision of this Agreement, materially affects the procedures contained in this Agreement, or affects QI's ability to perform its obligations under this Agreement;

(C) A ruling of any court that affects the validity of any material provision of this Agreement;

(D) A material change in the applicable know-your-customer rules and procedures;

(E) A significant change in QI's business practices that affects QI's ability to meet its obligations under this Agreement;

(G) If QI is an FFI, QI's failure to maintain its status as a participating FFI, registered deemed-compliant FFI, or registered deemed-compliant Model 1 IGA FFI;

(H) If QI is acting as a sponsoring entity on behalf of a sponsored FFI or sponsored direct reporting NFFE, if it fails to comply with the due diligence, withholding, reporting, and compliance requirements of a sponsoring entity; or

(I) If QI is acting as a QDD, the home office or branch, as applicable, ceases to qualify as an eligible entity, including as a result of a change in its business or regulatory status (see section 11.03).

Sec. 11.05. Merger. If QI merges with or is acquired by another QI and the successor QI assumes all the rights, debts, and obligations of the predecessor QI as it relates to such QI's QI agreement, the predecessor or acquired QI must notify the IRS that it intends to terminate this Agreement prior to the end of its term by delivery of a notice of termination and merger, in accordance with section 12.06 of this Agreement. A notice of termination and merger shall take effect on the date specified in the notice, and QI is required to notify its withholding agent of the date that its status as a QI is terminated and designate the successor QI to receive payments in its capacity as a QI for any accounts previously covered by predecessor QI's QI Agreement.

The successor QI must ensure that all reporting and tax filing obligations are fulfilled and any withholding is deposited, in accordance with the procedures outlined in Rev. Proc. 99-50, 1999-2 C.B. 757, when applicable, that arose in the calendar years and portion of the calendar year in which termination is requested and for which this Agreement was in effect (including for Form 1042-S filed to report withholding under chapter 4). To the extent QI is acting as a QDD, it must use the standard procedure outlined in Rev. Proc. 99-50 and cannot use the alternative procedures. See QI's FATCA Requirements as a participating FFI, registered deemed-compliant FFI, or registered deemed-compliant Model 1 IGA FFI for the procedures, if any, for reporting on Form 8966 in the case of a merger or acquisition. In addition, the successor QI must provide the certification required by section 10.03 for the predecessor QI's compliance period prior to the merger (and must include the predecessor QI in its review following the merger).

The IRS shall revoke the predecessor QI's QI-EIN within a reasonable time after the reporting, tax filing, and depositing requirements for such years are satisfied. The termination of this Agreement is not intended to affect any other federal income tax consequences

Sec. 11.06. Event of Default. For purposes of this Agreement, an event of default occurs if QI fails to perform any material duty or obligation required under this Agreement and the responsible officer had actual knowledge or should have known of the facts relevant to the failure to perform any material duty. An event of default includes, but is not limited to, the occurrence of any of the following:

(A) QI fails to implement adequate procedures, accounting systems, and internal controls to ensure compliance with this Agreement;

(B) QI underwithholds a material amount of tax that QI is required to withhold under chapter 3 or 4 or backup withhold under section 3406 and fails to correct the underwithholding or to file an amended Form 1042 or 945 reporting, and paying, the appropriate tax;

(C) QI makes excessive refund claims;

(D) Documentation described in section 5 of this Agreement is lacking, incorrect, or unreliable for a significant number of direct account holders;

(E) QI files Forms 945, 1042, 1042-S, 1099, or 8966 that are materially incorrect or fraudulent;

(F) If QI is an FFI, QI fails to materially comply with its FATCA requirements as a participating FFI, registered deemed-compliant FFI, or registered deemed-compliant Model 1 IGA FFI;

(G) If QI is a sponsoring entity, QI fails to materially comply with the due diligence, withholding, reporting, and compliance requirements of a sponsoring entity;

(H) QI fails to materially comply with the requirements of a nonqualified intermediary under chapters 3 and 61, and section 3406 with respect to any account for which QI does not act as a QI.

(I) QI fails to perform a periodic review when required or document the findings of such review in a written report;

(J) QI fails to cooperate with the IRS on its compliance review described in section 10.08 of this Agreement;

(K) QI fails to inform the IRS of any change in the applicable know-your-customer rules within 90 days of the change becoming effective;

(L) QI fails to inform the IRS within 90 days of any significant change in its business practices to the extent that change affects QI's obligations under this Agreement;

(M) QI fails to inform the IRS of any PAI of QI, as described in section 4 of this Agreement;

(N) QI fails to cure a material failure identified in the qualified certification described in Part II.B of Appendix 1 to this Agreement or identified by the IRS;

(O) QI makes any fraudulent statement or a misrepresentation of material fact with regard to this Agreement to the IRS, a withholding agent, or QI's reviewer;

(P) The IRS determines that QI's reviewer is not sufficiently independent, as described in this Agreement, to adequately perform its review function, and QI fails to arrange for a periodic review conducted by a reviewer approved by the IRS;

(Q) An intermediary with which QI has a PAI agreement is in default with that agreement and QI fails to terminate that agreement within the time period specified in section 4.04 of this Agreement;

(R) A partnership or trust to which QI applies the agency option is in default with that agreement and QI fails to terminate that agreement within the time period specified in section 4.06 of this Agreement; and

(S) If QI is acting as a QDD, after calendar year 2017, QI fails to timely pay a material amount of its QDD tax liability and fails to correct the underpayment and pay the appropriate tax amount.

Sec. 11.07. Notice and Cure. Upon the occurrence of an event of default, the IRS will deliver to QI a notice of default specifying each event of default. QI must respond to the notice of default within 60 days (60-day response) from the date of the notice of default. The 60-day response shall contain an offer to cure the event of default and the time period in which to cure or shall state why QI believes that no event of default occurred. If QI does not provide a 60-day response, the IRS will deliver a notice of termination as provided in section 11.02 of this Agreement. If QI provides a 60-day response, the IRS shall either accept or reject QI's statement that no default has occurred or QI's proposal to cure the event of default. If the IRS rejects QI's contention that no default has occurred or rejects QI's proposal to cure the event of default, the IRS may offer a counter-proposal to cure the event of default with which QI will be required to comply within 30 days. If QI fails to provide a 30-day response, the IRS will send a notice of termination in accordance with section 11.02 of this Agreement to QI, which QI may appeal within 30 days of the date of the notice by sending a written appeal to the address specified in section 12.06 of this Agreement. If QI appeals the notice of termination, this Agreement shall not terminate until the appeal has been decided. If an event of default is discovered in the course of a review, the QI may cure the default, without following the procedures of this section 11.07, if the external reviewer's report describes the default and the actions that QI took to cure the default and the IRS determines that the cure procedures followed by QI were sufficient. If the IRS determines that QI's actions to cure the default were not sufficient, the IRS shall issue a notice of default and the procedures described in this section 11.07 shall be followed.

Sec. 11.08. Renewal. If QI intends to renew this Agreement, it must submit an application for renewal to the IRS on the QI/WP/WT Application and Accounts Management System. This Agreement will be renewed only upon the agreement of both QI and the IRS. A QI that seeks to renew its QI agreement and also seeks to become a QDD (that was not previously acting as a QDD) must supplement the renewal request by providing a statement containing all information required by Form 14345 relating to a QDD.

Section 12. Miscellaneous Provisions

Sec. 12.01. QI's application to become a QI, all Appendices to this Agreement, and, if QI is an FFI, its FATCA requirements as a participating FFI, registered deemed-compliant FFI, or registered deemed-compliant Model 1 IGA FFI, are hereby incorporated into and made an integral part of this Agreement. This Agreement, QI's application, and the Appendices to this Agreement constitute the complete agreement between the parties.

Sec. 12.02. This Agreement may be amended by the IRS if the IRS determines that such amendment is needed for the sound administration of the internal revenue laws or internal revenue regulations. This Agreement will only be modified through published guidance issued by the IRS and U.S. Treasury Department. Any such modification imposing additional requirements will in no event become effective until the later of 90 days after the IRS provides notice of such modification or the beginning of the next calendar year following the publication of such guidance.

Sec. 12.03. Any waiver of a provision of this Agreement is a waiver solely of that provision. The waiver does not obligate the IRS to waive other provisions of this Agreement or the same provision at a later date.

Sec. 12.04. This Agreement shall be governed by the laws of the United States. Any legal action brought under this Agreement shall be brought only in a U.S. court with jurisdiction to hear and resolve matters under the internal revenue laws of the United States. For this purpose, QI agrees to submit to the jurisdiction of such U.S. court.

Sec. 12.05. QI's rights and responsibilities under this Agreement cannot be assigned to another person.

Sec. 12.06. Except as otherwise provided in the QI/WP/WT Application and Accounts Management System, notices provided under this Agreement shall be mailed registered, first class airmail. All notices sent to the IRS must include the QI's name, QI-EIN, GIIN (if applicable), and the name of its responsible officer. Such notices shall be directed as follows:

To the IRS:

Internal Revenue Service Foreign Payments Practice Foreign Intermediaries Program 290 Broadway, 12th Floor NW New York, New York 10007-1867

To the QI:

The QI's responsible officer. Such notices shall be sent to the address indicated in the QI's registration or application (as may be amended).

Sec. 12.07. QI, acting in its capacity as a QI or in any other capacity, does not act as an agent of the IRS, nor does it have the authority to hold itself out as an agent of the IRS.

SECTION 7. EFFECTIVE DATE

The effective date of the QI agreement contained in section 6 of this revenue procedure (as modified and superseded by any future published guidance) is on or after January 1, 2017.

Appendix 4: IGA Model 1A

There are three Model IGAs—Models 1A, 1B and 2. These Models have evolved due to a variety of factors associated with discussions between the U.S. government and other governments. Below is the template for a Model 1A Reciprocal IGA where the jurisdiction has a pre-existing Double Tax Treaty (DTT) and/or Tax Information Exchange Agreement (TIEA).

Agreement Between the Government of the United States of America and the Government of [FATCA Partner] to Improve International Tax Compliance and to Implement FATCA

Whereas, the Government of the United States of America and the Government of [FATCA Partner] (each, a 'Party', and together, the 'Parties') desire to conclude an agreement to improve international tax compliance through mutual assistance in tax matters based on an effective infrastructure for the automatic exchange of information;

Whereas, [Article []] of the Income Tax Convention between the United States and [FATCA Partner]/[the Convention on Mutual Administrative Assistance in Tax Matters] (the 'Convention')]/[Article []] of the Tax Information Exchange Agreement between the United States and [FATCA Partner] (the 'TIEA')], done at [__] on [__] authorizes the exchange of information for tax purposes, including on an automatic basis;

Whereas, the United States of America enacted provisions commonly known as the Foreign Account Tax Compliance Act ('FATCA'), which introduce a reporting regime for financial institutions with respect to certain accounts;

Whereas, the Government of [FATCA Partner] is supportive of the underlying policy goal of FATCA to improve tax compliance;

Whereas, FATCA has raised a number of issues, including that [FATCA Partner] financial institutions may not be able to comply with certain aspects of FATCA due to domestic legal impediments;

Whereas, the Government of the United States of America collects information regarding certain accounts maintained by U.S. financial institutions held by residents of [FATCA Partner] and is committed to exchanging such information with the Government of [FATCA Partner] and pursuing equivalent levels of exchange, provided that the appropriate safeguards and infrastructure for an effective exchange relationship are in place;

Whereas, an intergovernmental approach to FATCA implementation would address legal impediments and reduce burdens for [FATCA Partner] financial institutions;

Whereas, the Parties desire to conclude an agreement to improve international tax compliance and provide for the implementation of FATCA based on domestic reporting and reciprocal automatic exchange pursuant to the [Convention/TIEA], and subject to the confidentiality and other protections provided for therein, including the provisions limiting the use of the information exchanged under the [Convention/TIEA];

Now, therefore, the Parties have agreed as follows:

Article 1: Definitions

1. For purposes of this agreement and any annexes thereto ('Agreement'), the following terms shall have the meanings set forth below:

    (a) The term **'United States'** means the United States of America, including the States thereof, but does not include the U.S. Territories. Any reference to a '**State**' of the United States includes the District of Columbia.

(b) The term **'U.S. Territory'** means American Samoa, the Commonwealth of the Northern Mariana Islands, Guam, the Commonwealth of Puerto Rico or the U.S. Virgin Islands.

(c) The term **'IRS'** means the U.S. Internal Revenue Service.

(d) The term **'[FATCA Partner]'** means [full name of FATCA Partner].[2]

(e) The term **'Partner Jurisdiction'** means a jurisdiction that has in effect an agreement with the United States to facilitate the implementation of FATCA. The IRS shall publish a list identifying all Partner Jurisdictions.

(f) The term **'Competent Authority'** means:

  (1) in the case of the United States, the Secretary of the Treasury or his delegate; and
  (2) in the case of [FATCA Partner], [].

(g) The term **'Financial Institution'** means a Custodial Institution, a Depository Institution, an Investment Entity or a Specified Insurance Company.

(h) The term **'Custodial Institution'** means any Entity that holds, as a substantial portion of its business, financial assets for the account of others. An entity holds financial assets for the account of others as a substantial portion of its business if the entity's gross income attributable to the holding of financial assets and related financial services equals or exceeds 20% of the entity's gross income during the shorter of: (i) the three-year period that ends on December 31 (or the final day of a non-calendar year accounting period) prior to the year in which the determination is being made; or (ii) the period during which the entity has been in existence.

(i) The term **'Depository Institution'** means any Entity that accepts deposits in the ordinary course of a banking or similar business.

(j) The term **'Investment Entity'** means any Entity that conducts as a business (or is managed by an entity that conducts as a business) one or more of the following activities or operations for or on behalf of a customer:

  (1) trading in money market instruments (cheques, bills, certificates of deposit, derivatives, etc.); foreign exchange; exchange, interest rate and index instruments; transferable securities; or commodity futures trading;
  (2) individual and collective portfolio management; or
  (3) otherwise investing, administering or managing funds or money on behalf of other persons.

This subparagraph 1(j) shall be interpreted in a manner consistent with similar language set forth in the definition of 'financial institution' in the Financial Action Task Force Recommendations.

(k) The term **'Specified Insurance Company'** means any Entity that is an insurance company (or the holding company of an insurance company) that issues, or is obligated to make payments with respect to, a Cash Value Insurance Contract or an Annuity Contract.

(l) The term **'[FATCA Partner] Financial Institution'** means (i) any Financial Institution [resident in]/[organized under the laws of] [FATCA Partner], but excluding any branch of such Financial Institution that is located outside [FATCA Partner], and (ii) any branch of a Financial Institution not [resident in]/[organized under the laws of] [FATCA Partner], if such branch is located in [FATCA Partner].

(m) The term **'Partner Jurisdiction Financial Institution'** means (i) any Financial Institution established in a Partner Jurisdiction, but excluding any branch of such Financial Institution that is located outside the Partner Jurisdiction, and (ii) any branch of a Financial Institution not established in the Partner Jurisdiction, if such branch is located in the Partner Jurisdiction.

(n) The term **'Reporting Financial Institution'** means a Reporting [FATCA Partner] Financial Institution or a Reporting U.S. Financial Institution, as the context requires.

(o) The term **'Reporting [FATCA Partner] Financial Institution'** means any [FATCA Partner] Financial Institution that is not a Non-Reporting [FATCA Partner] Financial Institution.

(p) The term **'Reporting U.S. Financial Institution'** means (i) any Financial Institution that is resident in the United States, but excluding any branch of such Financial Institution that is located outside the United States, and (ii) any branch of a Financial Institution not resident in the United States, if such branch is located in the United States, provided that the Financial Institution or branch has control, receipt or custody of income with respect to which information is required to be exchanged under subparagraph (2)(b) of Article 2 of this Agreement.

(q) The term **'Non-Reporting [FATCA Partner] Financial Institution'** means any [FATCA Partner] Financial Institution, or other Entity resident in [FATCA Partner], that is described in Annex II as a Non-Reporting [FATCA Partner] Financial Institution or that otherwise qualifies as a deemed-compliant FFI or an exempt beneficial owner under relevant U.S. Treasury Regulations [in effect on the date of signature of this Agreement].

(r) The term **'Nonparticipating Financial Institution'** means a nonparticipating FFI, as that term is defined in relevant U.S. Treasury Regulations, but does not include a [FATCA Partner] Financial Institution or other Partner Jurisdiction Financial Institution other than a Financial Institution treated as a Nonparticipating Financial Institution pursuant to subparagraph 2(b) of Article 5 of this Agreement or the corresponding provision in an agreement between the United States and a Partner Jurisdiction.

(s) The term **'Financial Account'** means an account maintained by a Financial Institution, and includes:

(1) in the case of an Entity that is a Financial Institution solely because it is an Investment Entity, any equity or debt interest (other than interests that are regularly traded on an established securities market) in the Financial Institution;

(2) in the case of a Financial Institution not described in subparagraph 1(s)(1) of this Article, any equity or debt interest in the Financial Institution (other than interests that are regularly traded on an established securities market), if (i) the value of the debt or equity interest is determined, directly or indirectly, primarily by reference to assets that give rise to U.S. Source Withholdable Payments, and (ii) the class of interests was established with a purpose of avoiding reporting in accordance with this Agreement; and

(3) any Cash Value Insurance Contract and any Annuity Contract issued or maintained by a Financial Institution, other than a non-investment-linked, non-transferable immediate life annuity that is issued to an individual and monetizes a pension or disability benefit provided under an account that is excluded from the definition of Financial Account in Annex II.

Notwithstanding the foregoing, the term 'Financial Account' does not include any account that is excluded from the definition of Financial Account in Annex II. For purposes of this Agreement, interests are 'regularly traded' if there is a meaningful volume of trading with respect to the interests on an ongoing basis, and an 'established securities market' means an exchange that is officially recognized and supervised by a governmental authority in which the market is located and that has a meaningful annual value of shares traded on the exchange. For purposes of this subparagraph

1(s), an interest in a Financial Institution is not 'regularly traded' and shall be treated as a Financial Account if the holder of the interest (other than a Financial Institution acting as an intermediary) is registered on the books of such Financial Institution. The preceding sentence will not apply to interests first registered on the books of such Financial Institution prior to July 1, 2014, and with respect to interests first registered on the books of such Financial Institution on or after July 1, 2014, a Financial Institution is not required to apply the preceding sentence prior to January 1, 2016.

(t) The term **'Depository Account'** includes any commercial, checking, savings, time, or thrift account, or an account that is evidenced by a certificate of deposit, thrift certificate, investment certificate, certificate of indebtedness or other similar instrument maintained by a Financial Institution in the ordinary course of a banking or similar business. A Depository Account also includes an amount held by an insurance company pursuant to a guaranteed investment contract or similar agreement to pay or credit interest thereon.

(u) The term **'Custodial Account'** means an account (other than an Insurance Contract or Annuity Contract) for the benefit of another person that holds any financial instrument or contract held for investment (including, but not limited to, a share or stock in a corporation, a note, bond, debenture or other evidence of indebtedness, a currency or commodity transaction, a credit default swap, a swap based upon a non-financial index, a notional principal contract, an Insurance Contract or Annuity Contract, and any option or other derivative instrument).

(v) The term **'Equity Interest'** means, in the case of a partnership that is a Financial Institution, either a capital or profits interest in the partnership. In the case of a trust that is a Financial Institution, an Equity Interest is considered to be held by any person treated as a settlor or beneficiary of all or a portion of the trust, or any other natural person exercising ultimate effective control over the trust. A Specified U.S. person shall be treated as being a beneficiary of a foreign trust if such Specified U.S. person has the right to receive directly or indirectly (e.g., through a nominee) a mandatory distribution or may receive, directly or indirectly, a discretionary distribution from the trust.

(w) The term **'Insurance Contract'** means a contract (other than an Annuity Contract) under which the issuer agrees to pay an amount upon the occurrence of a specified contingency involving mortality, morbidity, accident, liability or property risk.

(x) The term **'Annuity Contract'** means a contract under which the issuer agrees to make payments for a period of time determined in whole or in part by reference to the life expectancy of one or more individuals. The term also includes a contract that is considered to be an Annuity Contract in accordance with the law, regulation or practice of the jurisdiction in which the contract was issued, and under which the issuer agrees to make payments for a term of years.

(y) The term **'Cash Value Insurance Contract'** means an Insurance Contract (other than an indemnity reinsurance contract between two insurance companies) that has a Cash Value greater than $50,000.

(z) The term **'Cash Value'** means the greater of (i) the amount that the policyholder is entitled to receive upon surrender or termination of the contract (determined without reduction for any surrender charge or policy loan), and (ii) the amount the policyholder can borrow under or with regard to the contract. Notwithstanding the foregoing, the term 'Cash Value' does not include an amount payable under an Insurance Contract as:

(1) a personal injury or sickness benefit or other benefit providing indemnification of an economic loss incurred upon the occurrence of the event insured against;

(2) a refund to the policyholder of a previously paid premium under an Insurance Contract (other than under a life insurance contract) due to policy cancellation or termination, decrease in risk exposure during the effective period of the Insurance Contract or arising from a redetermination of the premium due to correction of posting or other similar error; or

(3) a policyholder dividend based upon the underwriting experience of the contract or group involved.

(aa) The term **'Reportable Account'** means a U.S. Reportable Account or a [FATCA Partner] Reportable Account, as the context requires.

(bb) The term **'[FATCA Partner] Reportable Account'** means a Financial Account maintained by a Reporting U.S. Financial Institution if: (i) in the case of a Depository Account, the account is held by an individual resident in [FATCA Partner] and more than $10 of interest is paid to such account in any given calendar year; or (ii) in the case of a Financial Account other than a Depository Account, the Account Holder is a resident of [FATCA Partner], including an Entity that certifies that it is resident in [FATCA Partner] for tax purposes, with respect to which U.S. source income that is subject to reporting under chapter 3 of subtitle A or chapter 61 of subtitle F of the U.S. Internal Revenue Code is paid or credited.

(cc) The term **'U.S. Reportable Account'** means a Financial Account maintained by a Reporting [FATCA Partner] Financial Institution and held by one or more Specified U.S. persons or by a Non-U.S. Entity with one or more Controlling Persons that is a Specified U.S. person. Notwithstanding the foregoing, an account shall not be treated as a U.S. Reportable Account if such account is not identified as a U.S. Reportable Account after application of the due diligence procedures in Annex I.

(dd) The term **'Account Holder'** means the person listed or identified as the holder of a Financial Account by the Financial Institution that maintains the account. A person, other than a Financial Institution, holding a Financial Account for the benefit or account of another person as agent, custodian, nominee, signatory, investment advisor or intermediary is not treated as holding the account for purposes of this Agreement, and such other person is treated as holding the account. For purposes of the immediately preceding sentence, the term 'Financial Institution' does not include a Financial Institution organized or incorporated in a U.S. Territory. In the case of a Cash Value Insurance Contract or an Annuity Contract, the Account Holder is any person entitled to access the Cash Value or change the beneficiary of the contract. If no person can access the Cash Value or change the beneficiary, the Account Holder is any person named as the owner in the contract and any person with a vested entitlement to payment under the terms of the contract. Upon the maturity of a Cash Value Insurance Contract or an Annuity Contract, each person entitled to receive a payment under the contract is treated as an Account Holder.

(ee) The term **'U.S. Person'** means a U.S. citizen or resident individual, a partnership or corporation organized in the United States or under the laws of the United States or any State thereof, a trust if (i) a court within the United States would have authority under applicable law to render orders or judgments concerning substantially all issues regarding administration of the trust, and (ii) one or more U.S. persons have the authority to control all substantial decisions of the trust, or an estate of a decedent that is a citizen or resident of the United States. This subparagraph 1(ee) shall be interpreted in accordance with the U.S. Internal Revenue Code.

(ff) The term **'Specified U.S. Person'** means a U.S. person, other than: (i) a corporation the stock of which is regularly traded on one or more established securities markets; (ii) any corporation that is a member of the same expanded affiliated group, as defined in section 1471(e)(2) of the U.S. Internal Revenue Code, as a corporation described in clause (i); (iii) the United States or any wholly owned agency or instrumentality thereof; (iv) any State of the United States, any U.S. Territory, any political subdivision of any of the foregoing or any wholly owned agency or instrumentality of any one or more of the foregoing; (v) any organization exempt from taxation under section 501(a) of the U.S. Internal Revenue Code or an individual retirement plan as defined in section 7701(a)(37) of the U.S. Internal Revenue Code; (vi) any bank as defined in section 581 of the U.S. Internal Revenue Code; (vii) any real estate investment trust as defined in section 856 of the U.S. Internal Revenue Code; (viii) any regulated investment company as defined in section 851 of the U.S. Internal Revenue Code or any entity registered with the U.S. Securities and Exchange Commission under the Investment Company Act of 1940 (15 U.S.C. 80a-64); (ix) any common trust fund as defined in section 584(a) of the U.S. Internal Revenue Code; (x) any trust that is exempt from tax under section 664(c) of the U.S. Internal Revenue Code or that is described in section 4947(a)(1) of the U.S. Internal Revenue Code; (xi) a dealer in securities, commodities or derivative financial instruments (including notional principal contracts, futures, forwards and options) that is registered as such under the laws of the United States or any State; (xii) a broker as defined in section 6045(c) of the U.S. Internal Revenue Code; or (xiii) any tax-exempt trust under a plan that is described in section 403(b) or section 457(g) of the U.S. Internal Revenue Code.

(gg) The term **'Entity'** means a legal person or a legal arrangement such as a trust.

(hh) The term **'Non-U.S. Entity'** means an Entity that is not a U.S. person.

(ii) The term **'U.S. Source Withholdable Payment'** means any payment of interest (including any original issue discount), dividends, rents, salaries, wages, premiums, annuities, compensations, remunerations, emoluments, and other fixed or determinable annual or periodical gains, profits, and income, if such payment is from sources within the United States. Notwithstanding the foregoing, a U.S. Source Withholdable Payment does not include any payment that is not treated as a withholdable payment in relevant U.S. Treasury Regulations.

(jj) An Entity is a '**Related Entity**' of another Entity if either Entity controls the other Entity, or the two Entities are under common control. For this purpose control includes direct or indirect ownership of more than 50% of the vote or value in an Entity. Notwithstanding the foregoing, [FATCA Partner] may treat an Entity as not a Related Entity of another Entity if the two Entities are not members of the same expanded affiliated group as defined in section 1471(e)(2) of the U.S. Internal Revenue Code.

(kk) The term '**U.S. TIN**' means a U.S. federal taxpayer identifying number.

(ll) The term '**[FATCA Partner] TIN**' means a [FATCA Partner] taxpayer identifying number.

(mm) The term '**Controlling Persons**' means the natural persons who exercise control over an Entity. In the case of a trust, such term means the settlor, the trustees, the protector (if any), the beneficiaries or class of beneficiaries and any other natural person exercising ultimate effective control over the trust, and in the case of a legal arrangement other than a trust, such term means persons in equivalent or similar positions. The term 'Controlling Persons' shall be interpreted in a manner consistent with the Financial Action Task Force Recommendations.

2. Any term not otherwise defined in this Agreement shall, unless the context otherwise requires or the Competent Authorities agree to a common meaning (as permitted by domestic law), have the meaning that it has at that time under the law of the Party applying this Agreement, any meaning under the applicable tax laws of that Party prevailing over a meaning given to the term under other laws of that Party.

Article 2: Obligations to Obtain and Exchange Information with Respect to Reportable Accounts

1. Subject to the provisions of Article 3 of this Agreement, each Party shall obtain the information specified in paragraph 2 of this Article with respect to all Reportable Accounts and shall annually exchange this information with the other Party on an automatic basis pursuant to the provisions of Article [] of the [Convention/TIEA].

2. The information to be obtained and exchanged is:

(a) In the case of [FATCA Partner] with respect to each U.S. Reportable Account of each Reporting [FATCA Partner] Financial Institution:

(1) the name, address and U.S. TIN of each Specified U.S. person that is an Account Holder of such account and, in the case of a Non-U.S. Entity that, after application of the due diligence procedures set forth in Annex I, is identified as having one or more Controlling Persons that is a Specified U.S. person, the name, address and U.S. TIN (if any) of such entity and each such Specified U.S. person;

(2) the account number (or functional equivalent in the absence of an account number);

(3) the name and identifying number of the Reporting [FATCA Partner] Financial Institution;

(4) the account balance or value (including, in the case of a Cash Value Insurance Contract or Annuity Contract, the Cash Value or surrender value) as of the end of the relevant calendar year or other appropriate reporting period or, if the account was closed during such year, immediately before closure;

(5) in the case of any Custodial Account:

   (A) the total gross amount of interest, the total gross amount of dividends and the total gross amount of other income generated with respect to the assets held in the account, in each case paid or credited to the account (or with respect to the account) during the calendar year or other appropriate reporting period; and

   (B) the total gross proceeds from the sale or redemption of property paid or credited to the account during the calendar year or other appropriate reporting period with respect to which the Reporting [FATCA Partner] Financial Institution acted as a custodian, broker, nominee or otherwise as an agent for the Account Holder;

(6) in the case of any Depository Account, the total gross amount of interest paid or credited to the account during the calendar year or other appropriate reporting period; and

(7) in the case of any account not described in subparagraph 2(a)(5) or 2(a)(6) of this Article, the total gross amount paid or credited to the Account Holder with respect to the account during the calendar year or other appropriate reporting period with respect to which the Reporting [FATCA Partner] Financial Institution is the obligor or debtor, including the aggregate amount of any redemption payments made to the Account Holder during the calendar year or other appropriate reporting period.

(b) In the case of the United States, with respect to each [FATCA Partner] Reportable Account of each Reporting U.S. Financial Institution:

(1) the name, address and [FATCA Partner] TIN of any person that is a resident of [FATCA Partner] and is an Account Holder of the account;
(2) the account number (or the functional equivalent in the absence of an account number);
(3) the name and identifying number of the Reporting U.S. Financial Institution;
(4) the gross amount of interest paid on a Depository Account;
(5) the gross amount of U.S. source dividends paid or credited to the account; and
(6) the gross amount of other U.S. source income paid or credited to the account, to the extent subject to reporting under chapter 3 of subtitle A or chapter 61 of subtitle F of the U.S. Internal Revenue Code.

Article 3: Time and Manner of Exchange of Information

1. For purposes of the exchange obligation in Article 2 of this Agreement, the amount and characterization of payments made with respect to a U.S. Reportable Account may be determined in accordance with the principles of the tax laws of [FATCA Partner], and the amount and characterization of payments made with respect to a [FATCA Partner] Reportable Account may be determined in accordance with principles of U.S. federal income tax law.
2. For purposes of the exchange obligation in Article 2 of this Agreement, the information exchanged shall identify the currency in which each relevant amount is denominated.
3. With respect to paragraph 2 of Article 2 of this Agreement, information is to be obtained and exchanged with respect to 2014 and all subsequent years, except that:

    (a) In the case of [FATCA Partner]:

    (1) the information to be obtained and exchanged with respect to 2014 is only the information described in subparagraphs 2(a)(1) through 2(a)(4) of Article 2 of this Agreement;
    (2) the information to be obtained and exchanged with respect to 2015 is the information described in subparagraphs 2(a)(1) through 2(a)(7) of Article 2 of this Agreement, except for gross proceeds described in subparagraph 2(a)(5)(B) of Article 2 of this Agreement; and

(3) the information to be obtained and exchanged with respect to 2016 and subsequent years is the information described in sub-paragraphs 2(a)(1) through 2(a)(7) of Article 2 of this Agreement.

(b) In the case of the United States, the information to be obtained and exchanged with respect to 2014 and subsequent years is all of the information identified in subparagraph 2(b) of Article 2 of this Agreement.

4. Notwithstanding paragraph 3 of this Article, with respect to each Reportable Account that is maintained by a Reporting Financial Institution as of the Determination Date, and subject to paragraph 4 of Article 6 of this Agreement, the Parties are not required to obtain and include in the exchanged information the [FATCA Partner] TIN or the U.S. TIN, as applicable, of any relevant person if such taxpayer identifying number is not in the records of the Reporting Financial Institution. In such a case, the Parties shall obtain and include in the exchanged information the date of birth of the relevant person, if the Reporting Financial Institution has such date of birth in its records.
5. Subject to paragraphs 3 and 4 of this Article, the information described in Article 2 of this Agreement shall be exchanged within nine months after the end of the calendar year to which the information relates.
6. The Competent Authorities of [FATCA Partner] and the United States shall enter into an agreement or arrangement under the mutual agreement procedure provided for in Article [] of the [Convention/TIEA], which shall:

(a) establish the procedures for the automatic exchange obligations described in Article 2 of this Agreement;
(b) prescribe rules and procedures as may be necessary to implement Article 5 of this Agreement; and
(c) establish as necessary procedures for the exchange of the information reported under subparagraph 1(b) of Article 4 of this Agreement.

7. All information exchanged shall be subject to the confidentiality and other protections provided for in the [Convention/TIEA], including the provisions limiting the use of the information exchanged.
8. Following entry into force of this Agreement, each Competent Authority shall provide written notification to the other Competent Authority when it is satisfied that the jurisdiction of the other Competent Authority has in place (i) appropriate safeguards to ensure that the information received pursuant to this Agreement shall remain confidential and be used solely for tax purposes, and (ii) the infrastructure for an effective exchange rela-

tionship (including established processes for ensuring timely, accurate and confidential information exchanges, effective and reliable communications, and demonstrated capabilities to promptly resolve questions and concerns about exchanges or requests for exchanges and to administer the provisions of Article 5 of this Agreement). The Competent Authorities shall endeavor in good faith to meet, prior to September 2015, to establish that each jurisdiction has such safeguards and infrastructure in place.

9. The obligations of the Parties to obtain and exchange information under Article 2 of this Agreement shall take effect on the date of the later of the written notifications described in paragraph 8 of this Article. Notwithstanding the foregoing, if the [FATCA Partner] Competent Authority is satisfied that the United States has the safeguards and infrastructure described in paragraph 8 of this Article in place, but additional time is necessary for the U.S. Competent Authority to establish that [FATCA Partner] has such safeguards and infrastructure in place, the obligation of [FATCA Partner] to obtain and exchange information under Article 2 of this Agreement shall take effect on the date of the written notification provided by the [FATCA Partner] Competent Authority to the U.S. Competent Authority pursuant to paragraph 8 of this Article.

10. This Agreement shall terminate on September 30, 2015, if Article 2 of this Agreement is not in effect for either Party pursuant to paragraph 9 of this Article by that date.

Article 4: Application of FATCA to [FATCA Partner] Financial Institutions

1. **Treatment of Reporting [FATCA Partner] Financial Institutions.** Each Reporting [FATCA Partner] Financial Institution shall be treated as complying with, and not subject to withholding under, section 1471 of the U.S. Internal Revenue Code if [FATCA Partner] complies with its obligations under Articles 2 and 3 of this Agreement with respect to such Reporting [FATCA Partner] Financial Institution, and the Reporting [FATCA Partner] Financial Institution:

    (a) identifies U.S. Reportable Accounts and reports annually to the [FATCA Partner] Competent Authority the information required to be reported in subparagraph 2(a) of Article 2 of this Agreement in the time and manner described in Article 3 of this Agreement;

    (b) for each of 2015 and 2016, reports annually to the [FATCA Partner] Competent Authority the name of each Nonparticipating Financial

Institution to which it has made payments and the aggregate amount of such payments;
(c) complies with the applicable registration requirements on the IRS FATCA registration website;
(d) to the extent that a Reporting [FATCA Partner] Financial Institution is (i) acting as a qualified intermediary (for purposes of section 1441 of the U.S. Internal Revenue Code) that has elected to assume primary withholding responsibility under chapter 3 of subtitle A of the U.S. Internal Revenue Code, (ii) a foreign partnership that has elected to act as a withholding foreign partnership (for purposes of both sections 1441 and 1471 of the U.S. Internal Revenue Code), or (iii) a foreign trust that has elected to act as a withholding foreign trust (for purposes of both sections 1441 and 1471 of the U.S. Internal Revenue Code), withholds 30% of any U.S. Source Withholdable Payment to any Nonparticipating Financial Institution; and
(e) in the case of a Reporting [FATCA Partner] Financial Institution that is not described in subparagraph 1(d) of this Article and that makes a payment of, or acts as an intermediary with respect to, a U.S. Source Withholdable Payment to any Nonparticipating Financial Institution, the Reporting [FATCA Partner] Financial Institution provides to any immediate payor of such U.S. Source Withholdable Payment the information required for withholding and reporting to occur with respect to such payment.

Notwithstanding the foregoing, a Reporting [FATCA Partner] Financial Institution with respect to which the conditions of this paragraph 1 are not satisfied shall not be subject to withholding under section 1471 of the U.S. Internal Revenue Code unless such Reporting [FATCA Partner] Financial Institution is treated by the IRS as a Nonparticipating Financial Institution pursuant to subparagraph 2(b) of Article 5 of this Agreement.

2. **Suspension of Rules Relating to Recalcitrant Accounts.** The United States shall not require a Reporting [FATCA Partner] Financial Institution to withhold tax under section 1471 or 1472 of the U.S. Internal Revenue Code with respect to an account held by a recalcitrant account holder (as defined in section 1471(d)(6) of the U.S. Internal Revenue Code), or to close such account, if the U.S. Competent Authority receives the information set forth in subparagraph 2(a) of Article 2 of this Agreement, subject to the provisions of Article 3 of this Agreement, with respect to such account.

3. **Specific Treatment of [FATCA Partner] Retirement Plans.** The United States shall treat as deemed-compliant FFIs or exempt beneficial owners, as appropriate, for purposes of sections 1471 and 1472 of the U.S. Internal

Revenue Code, [FATCA Partner] retirement plans described in Annex II. For this purpose, a [FATCA Partner] retirement plan includes an Entity established or located in, and regulated by, [FATCA Partner], or a predetermined contractual or legal arrangement, operated to provide pension or retirement benefits or earn income for providing such benefits under the laws of [FATCA Partner] and regulated with respect to contributions, distributions, reporting, sponsorship and taxation.

4. **Identification and Treatment of Other Deemed-Compliant FFIs and Exempt Beneficial Owners.** The United States shall treat each Non-Reporting [FATCA Partner] Financial Institution as a deemed-compliant FFI or as an exempt beneficial owner, as appropriate, for purposes of section 1471 of the U.S. Internal Revenue Code.

5. **Special Rules Regarding Related Entities and Branches That Are Nonparticipating Financial Institutions.** If a [FATCA Partner] Financial Institution, that otherwise meets the requirements described in paragraph 1 of this Article or is described in paragraph 3 or 4 of this Article, has a Related Entity or branch that operates in a jurisdiction that prevents such Related Entity or branch from fulfilling the requirements of a participating FFI or deemed-compliant FFI for purposes of section 1471 of the U.S. Internal Revenue Code or has a Related Entity or branch that is treated as a Nonparticipating Financial Institution solely due to the expiration of the transitional rule for limited FFIs and limited branches under relevant U.S. Treasury Regulations, such [FATCA Partner] Financial Institution shall continue to be in compliance with the terms of this Agreement and shall continue to be treated as a deemed-compliant FFI or exempt beneficial owner, as appropriate, for purposes of section 1471 of the U.S. Internal Revenue Code, provided that:

   (a) the [FATCA Partner] Financial Institution treats each such Related Entity or branch as a separate Nonparticipating Financial Institution for purposes of all the reporting and withholding requirements of this Agreement and each such Related Entity or branch identifies itself to withholding agents as a Nonparticipating Financial Institution;

   (b) each such Related Entity or branch identifies its U.S. accounts and reports the information with respect to those accounts as required under section 1471 of the U.S. Internal Revenue Code to the extent permitted under the relevant laws pertaining to the Related Entity or branch; and

   (c) such Related Entity or branch does not specifically solicit U.S. accounts held by persons that are not resident in the jurisdiction where such Related Entity or branch is located or accounts held by Nonparticipating Financial Institutions that are not established in the jurisdiction where

such Related Entity or branch is located, and such Related Entity or branch is not used by the [FATCA Partner] Financial Institution or any other Related Entity to circumvent the obligations under this Agreement or under section 1471 of the U.S. Internal Revenue Code, as appropriate.

6. **Coordination of Timing.** Notwithstanding paragraphs 3 and 5 of Article 3 of this Agreement:

   (a) [FATCA Partner] shall not be obligated to obtain and exchange information with respect to a calendar year that is prior to the calendar year with respect to which similar information is required to be reported to the IRS by participating FFIs pursuant to relevant U.S. Treasury Regulations;
   (b) [FATCA Partner] shall not be obligated to begin exchanging information prior to the date by which participating FFIs are required to report similar information to the IRS under relevant U.S. Treasury Regulations;
   (c) the United States shall not be obligated to obtain and exchange information with respect to a calendar year that is prior to the first calendar year with respect to which [FATCA Partner] is required to obtain and exchange information; and
   (d) the United States shall not be obligated to begin exchanging information prior to the date by which [FATCA Partner] is required to begin exchanging information.

7. **Coordination of Definitions with U.S. Treasury Regulations.** Notwithstanding Article 1 of this Agreement and the definitions provided in the Annexes to this Agreement, in implementing this Agreement, [FATCA Partner] may use, and may permit [FATCA Partner] Financial Institutions to use, a definition in relevant U.S. Treasury Regulations in lieu of a corresponding definition in this Agreement, provided that such application would not frustrate the purposes of this Agreement.

Article 5: Collaboration on Compliance and Enforcement

1. **Minor and Administrative Errors.** A Competent Authority shall notify the Competent Authority of the other Party when the first-mentioned Competent Authority has reason to believe that administrative errors or other minor errors may have led to incorrect or incomplete information

reporting or resulted in other infringements of this Agreement. The Competent Authority of such other Party shall apply its domestic law (including applicable penalties) to obtain corrected and/or complete information or to resolve other infringements of this Agreement.

2. **Significant Non-compliance.**

    (c) A Competent Authority shall notify the Competent Authority of the other Party when the first-mentioned Competent Authority has determined that there is significant non-compliance with the obligations under this Agreement with respect to a Reporting Financial Institution in the other jurisdiction. The Competent Authority of such other Party shall apply its domestic law (including applicable penalties) to address the significant non-compliance described in the notice.

    (d) If, in the case of a Reporting [FATCA Partner] Financial Institution, such enforcement actions do not resolve the non-compliance within a period of 18 months after notification of significant non-compliance is first provided, the United States shall treat the Reporting [FATCA Partner] Financial Institution as a Nonparticipating Financial Institution pursuant to this subparagraph 2(b).

3. **Reliance on Third-Party Service Providers.** Each Party may allow Reporting Financial Institutions to use third-party service providers to fulfill the obligations imposed on such Reporting Financial Institutions by a Party, as contemplated in this Agreement, but these obligations shall remain the responsibility of the Reporting Financial Institutions.

4. **Prevention of Avoidance.** The Parties shall implement as necessary requirements to prevent Financial Institutions from adopting practices intended to circumvent the reporting required under this Agreement.

Article 6: Mutual Commitment to Continue to Enhance the Effectiveness of Information Exchange and Transparency

1. **Reciprocity.** The Government of the United States acknowledges the need to achieve equivalent levels of reciprocal automatic information exchange with [FATCA Partner]. The Government of the United States is committed to further improve transparency and enhance the exchange relationship with [FATCA Partner] by pursuing the adoption of regulations and

advocating and supporting relevant legislation to achieve such equivalent levels of reciprocal automatic information exchange.
2. **Treatment of Passthru Payments and Gross Proceeds.** The Parties are committed to work together, along with Partner Jurisdictions, to develop a practical and effective alternative approach to achieve the policy objectives of foreign passthru payment and gross proceeds withholding that minimizes burden.
3. **Documentation of Accounts Maintained as of the Determination Date.** With respect to Reportable Accounts maintained by a Reporting Financial Institution as of the Determination Date:

   (a) The United States commits to establish, by January 1, 2017, for reporting with respect to 2017 and subsequent years, rules requiring Reporting U.S. Financial Institutions to obtain and report the [FATCA Partner] TIN of each Account Holder of a [FATCA Partner] Reportable Account as required pursuant to subparagraph 2(b)(1) of Article 2 of this Agreement; and

   (b) [FATCA Partner] commits to establish, by January 1, 2017, for reporting with respect to 2017 and subsequent years, rules requiring Reporting [FATCA Partner] Financial Institutions to obtain the U.S. TIN of each Specified U.S. Person as required pursuant to subparagraph 2(a)(1) of Article 2 of this Agreement.

Article 7: Consistency in the Application of FATCA to Partner Jurisdictions

1. [FATCA Partner] shall be granted the benefit of any more favorable terms under Article 4 or Annex I of this Agreement relating to the application of FATCA to [FATCA Partner] Financial Institutions afforded to another Partner Jurisdiction under a signed bilateral agreement pursuant to which the other Partner Jurisdiction commits to undertake the same obligations as [FATCA Partner] described in Articles 2 and 3 of this Agreement, and subject to the same terms and conditions as described therein and in Articles 5 through 9 of this Agreement.
2. The United States shall notify [FATCA Partner] of any such more favorable terms, and such more favorable terms shall apply automatically under this Agreement as if such terms were specified in this Agreement and effective as of the date of signing of the agreement incorporating the more favorable terms, unless [FATCA Partner] declines in writing the application thereof.

Article 8: Consultations and Amendments

1. In case any difficulties in the implementation of this Agreement arise, either Party may request consultations to develop appropriate measures to ensure the fulfillment of this Agreement.
2. This Agreement may be amended by written mutual agreement of the Parties. Unless otherwise agreed upon, such an amendment shall enter into force through the same procedures as set forth in paragraph 1 of Article 10 of this Agreement.

Article 9: Annexes

The Annexes form an integral part of this Agreement.

Article 10: Term of Agreement

1. This Agreement shall enter into force on the date of [FATCA Partner]'s written notification to the United States that [FATCA Partner] has completed its necessary internal procedures for entry into force of this Agreement.
2. Either Party may terminate this Agreement by giving notice of termination in writing to the other Party. Such termination shall become effective on the first day of the month following the expiration of a period of 12 months after the date of the notice of termination.
3. The Parties shall, prior to December 31, 2016, consult in good faith to amend this Agreement as necessary to reflect progress on the commitments set forth in Article 6 of this Agreement.

In witness whereof, the undersigned, being duly authorized thereto by their respective Governments, have signed this Agreement.
Done at [_____], in duplicate, this [__] day of [_____], 20[__].
FOR THE GOVERNMENT OF
THE UNITED STATES OF AMERICA:
FOR THE GOVERNMENT OF [FATCA PARTNER]:

Appendix 5: Template AI Agreement (TRACE IP)

AGREEMENT AUTHORISING FINANCIAL INTERMEDIARY TO ACT AS AN AUTHORISED INTERMEDIARY WITH RESPECT TO INCOME ARISING IN [COUNTRY]

WHEREAS, [Financial Intermediary] (the——Applicant) has submitted an application to become an Authorised Intermediary with respect to certain types of income arising in [Country] (the——Source Country);

WHEREAS, the Applicant and the Affiliates of the Applicant designated in Appendix A to this Agreement that are signatories to this Agreement (individually and collectively referred to as——the AI), and [the competent authority of the Source Country] (the——Competent Authority) desire to enter into an agreement (this——Agreement) to establish the AI's rights and obligations regarding documentation, information reporting and compliance with respect to certain types of income arising in the Source Country;

WHEREAS, the AI and the Competent Authority (the——Parties) have accepted the procedures designated in Appendix B to this Agreement (the—— Procedures), as such Procedures may be modified by this Agreement;

NOW, THEREFORE, in consideration of the following terms, representations and conditions, the Parties agree as follows:

1. The AI agrees to undertake the responsibilities and assume the liabilities of an Authorised Intermediary as set out in the Procedures, as they may be modified by this Agreement, and the Competent Authority agrees to allow the AI to act as an Authorised Intermediary in accordance with, and subject to, those Procedures.
2. The Parties agree that the definition of Covered Payment set forth in the Procedures shall be modified to include the following types of income: [ ];
    and to exclude:
    [ ].
3. The Parties agree that the definition of Reportable Payment set forth in the Procedures shall be modified to include the following types of income: [ ]; and to exclude: [ ].
4. The Parties agree that the term——Eligible Countries‖ shall mean: [list of countries and jurisdictions identified by the Source Country, taking into account factors including whether the Source Country has with that country or jurisdiction an effective exchange of information relationship, whether that country or jurisdiction has in effect adequate

Know-Your-Customer Rules and whether the country or jurisdiction is a member of a multilateral organisation or community or grouping of countries that adopt common standards and approaches to issues of tax compliance, including mutual assistance (such as the Member States of the European Union or Organisation for Economic Co-Operation and Development)];

5. [The Parties agree that the AI will/will not undertake [primary] withholding responsibilities unless specified otherwise in Appendix A. [In undertaking such [primary] withholding responsibilities, the AI agrees to comply with the additional procedures set out in Appendix C to this Agreement.]]

6. For purposes of providing Tax Rate Information to a Payor in accordance with Paragraph IV.A of the Procedures, the rate of withholding that will apply to:

   (a) a Covered Payment in respect of a resident of the Source Country with respect to which the AI has received a valid Investor Self-Declaration, either directly from the AI's own Direct Account Holder that is an Investor, or indirectly through a Contractual Intermediary, is/are [the applicable rate(s) provided in the Source Country's domestic law at the time this Agreement is entered into for the relevant category or categories of residents of the Source Country with respect to each relevant income type], as such rate may be modified by [reference to relevant provision(s) of domestic law];

   (b) a Covered Payment in respect of a resident of the Source Country with respect to which the AI has not received a valid Investor Self-Declaration either directly from the AI's own Direct Account Holder that is an Investor, or indirectly through a Contractual Intermediary is/are [the back-up rate(s) provided in the Source Country's domestic law at the time this Agreement is entered into for the relevant category or categories of residents of the Source Country with respect to each relevant income type, if applicable], as such rate may be modified by [reference to relevant provision(s) of domestic law];

   (c) a Covered Payment in respect of a non-resident of the Source Country with respect to which the AI has received a valid Investor Self-Declaration, either directly from the AI's own Direct Account Holder that is an Investor, or indirectly through a Contractual Intermediary, is/are the [lower of the] applicable rate(s) provided in the relevant tax treaty with respect to income of that type, but excluding lower rates applicable to companies receiving dividends from companies in which they own a specified percentage of the capital or voting rights (or some combination thereof)[, or in [cross-reference to relevant provisions of domestic law providing a reduction or an exemption from withholding tax]];

(d) [a Covered Payment with respect to which the AI has assumed [primary] withholding responsibilities [or with respect to which the AI has received a valid Intermediary Declaration from a Withholding agent] is zero;]

(e) a Covered Payment with respect to which the AI has received from an Authorised Intermediary a valid Intermediary Declaration and Tax Rate Information is/are the rates specified in that Tax Rate Information; and

(f) all other Covered Payments, is/are [standard rate(s) for the relevant income types provided under Source Country law at the time this Agreement is entered into for undocumented investors], as such rate(s) may be modified by [reference to relevant provision(s) of domestic law].

7. The Parties agree that the period for retention of Tax Rate Information for purposes of Paragraph IV.C of the Procedures shall be [description of applicable document retention period in the Source Country, including starting date] and for retention of documentation for purposes of Paragraph V.E of the Procedures shall be [description of applicable document retention period in the Source Country, including starting date].

8. The Parties agree that claims made under paragraph VI.A.3 of the Procedures will be processed only if they are filed by [description of applicable statute of limitations in the Source Country, including starting date].

9. The Parties agree that the applicable period for purposes of Paragraph II.B (regarding claims against the AI for under-withholding) shall be [description of applicable statute of limitations in the Source Country for an assessment by the Competent Authority with respect to under-withholding on an Investor, including starting date].

10. The Parties agree that, unless changed in accordance with Paragraph VIII.B.6 of the Procedures, the Independent Reviewer shall be: [ ] If different from the above, the Independent Reviewer of each Affiliate is set out in Appendix A.

11. Notices shall be directed as follows:

To the Competent Authority:

Contact:

_____

Address:

_____

City: _____ Province, State or Locality:

_____ Country: _____

Postal Code: _____

Telephone: _____ Fax: _____

e-mail: _____

To the AI:

Contact:

_____

Address:

_____

City: _____

Province, State or Locality: _____

Country: _____

Postal Code: _____

Telephone: _____ Fax: _____

e-mail: _____

To the Independent Reviewer: Contact:

_____

Address:

_____

_____

IMPLEMENTATION PACKAGE

City: _____ Province, State or Locality:

_____

Country: _____ Postal Code:

_____

Telephone: _____ Fax: _____ e-mail:

_____

If different from the above, the address of the Affiliates' Independent Reviewers is set out in Appendix A.

12. The Agreement shall be governed by the laws of the Source Country. Any legal action brought under this Agreement shall be brought only in [appropriate court of the Source Country]. For this purpose, the AI agrees to submit to the jurisdiction of such court.
13. This Agreement shall enter into effect on [ ] and shall remain in effect indefinitely unless terminated by either Party in accordance with Section IX of the Procedures.
14. The AI's application to become an Authorised Intermediary and all the Appendices to this Agreement and Annexes to the Procedures are hereby incorporated into and made an integral part of this Agreement, which shall constitute the entire agreement between the Parties.
15. Terms used in this Agreement shall have the meaning given to them in the Procedures, except as explicitly modified by this Agreement.

16. The Applicant's Authorised Intermediary Identification Number shall be [ ] and those of its Affiliates designated in Appendix A to this Agreement shall be as set out therein.
17. The AI hereby give permission to the Competent Authority to disclose its status as an Authorised Intermediary or to make such information publicly available and, if the Competent Authority designates the Applicant or any Affiliate designated in Appendix A as an Excluded Intermediary, to disclose such Excluded Intermediary's status as such to any person or to make such information publicly available.

THIS AGREEMENT is made in duplicate by and between the Applicant, any Affiliates of the Applicant designated in Appendix A to this Agreement and the Competent Authority by:

On behalf of the Competent Authority:

_____

Signature Date

_____ Name of Signatory in block capitals or
type _____ Title of Signatory

On behalf of the Applicant:

_____

IMPLEMENTATION PACKAGE

AGREEMENT AUTHORISING FINANCIAL INTERMEDIARY TO ACT AS AN AUTHORISING INTERMEDIARY WITH RESPECT TO INCOME ARISING IN [COUNTRY]

_____

IMPLEMENTATION PACKAGE

_____

Signature Date

_____ Name of Signatory in block
capitals or type _____ Title of Signatory

[Additional signature blocks, if necessary, for affiliates]

_____

APPENDIX A: AFFILIATES OF THE APPLICANT AUTHORISED TO ACT AS AUTHORISED INTERMEDIARIES

The following Affiliates of the Applicant are authorised to act as Authorised Intermediaries with respect to Covered Payments arising in the Source Country, and their AIINs are as indicated:

Name of Affiliate Address of Affiliate AIIN of Affiliate [[Primary]
Withholding Responsibility: Yes/No] Independent Reviewer (if different from
Applicant's Independent Reviewer) Address of Independent Reviewer

[to be repeated for each Affiliate]

Index

A

Account designation, 25, 44–45
Actual knowledge, 6, 13, 29, 43, 56, 59, 62, 196–197, 306, 310, 328, 331, 375
Anti-Money Laundering (AML), xxvi, 5, 6, 11, 13, 40, 43, 58, 62, 112, 166, 173, 178, 181, 183, 184, 187, 191, 240, 360
Authorised intermediary, 238–245, 247, 252, 256, 398–403
Automatic exchange of information (AEoI), xxv, xxx, 182, 184, 239, 245, 267, 271, 272, 378

B

Benchmarking, 149
Beneficial owner, xxiv, xxv, xxix, xxx, 3–8, 12–14, 17, 26, 28, 31, 36, 42, 44, 45, 47, 48, 50, 51, 55, 60, 66, 70, 73, 75, 77, 85–89, 91, 92, 123, 125, 131, 132, 134–138, 143, 144, 192–194, 210, 218, 238, 239, 246, 248–253, 256, 270, 289–291, 293, 296–298, 302, 304, 315, 317, 320, 322–324, 326, 331, 336, 341, 345, 348, 381–382, 392, 393

C

Certification, 6, 18, 24, 26, 27, 29, 32, 41–43, 48, 87, 101, 105, 106, 109–117, 169, 173, 175, 185, 196, 200–202, 211, 214, 302, 305, 309, 311, 312, 315, 317, 322, 323, 326, 328, 331, 333, 334, 338, 350, 354–356, 358–361, 363, 369–371, 373, 374, 376
Collective investment vehicles (CIVs), xxix, 171, 190, 194–195, 201, 237, 241, 242
Common Reporting Standard (CRS), xxv, xxx, 50, 182, 184, 187, 193, 225–227, 229, 267, 271
Compliance program, 354–356, 358, 361, 362, 370
Country attachments, 42

D

Data privacy, 178, 207, 214, 249
Deposits, 6, 10, 14, 19, 28, 34, 63, 66, 71–74, 112, 120, 122, 129, 133, 285, 298, 309, 337, 351, 352, 361, 369, 380, 383
Documentary evidence, 5, 6, 13, 27, 30, 39, 40, 42, 45, 291, 292, 315, 320–324, 327, 328, 330
Documentation, xxiv, xxv, xxx, 5, 6, 12–13, 16, 25–27, 29, 30, 33, 34, 36, 39–63, 68, 69, 73, 76, 79–81, 85, 90–92, 99, 105, 107, 110–112, 116, 131–133, 135, 137–138, 142, 179, 181, 183, 191, 195–197, 202, 206, 208, 218, 219, 228, 247, 249–253, 266, 270, 271, 285, 287, 291, 292, 295, 300–302, 311, 312, 314, 315, 317, 318, 320–337, 341, 345, 346, 349, 350, 353, 354, 356, 357, 359, 362–365, 367–369, 371, 372, 375, 396, 398, 400
Double tax treaty (DTT), 3, 4, 55, 160, 161, 170, 172, 378

E

871(m), xxiv, 80, 145–154, 226, 228, 287, 289, 292, 297–301, 304, 305, 308–310, 326, 335, 338, 339, 343, 346, 355–357, 360, 361, 363, 366–369
Electronic Federal Tax Payment System (EFTPS), 66, 71, 72, 74, 81, 133
Electronic signature, 39, 48, 49, 185
Employer Identification Number (EIN), 16, 17, 87, 88, 99, 123, 142, 298
Enforcement, 4, 6, 7, 16, 18–19, 158, 355, 356, 394–395
Entitlement, 3–5, 9, 106, 130, 131, 238, 249, 250, 252, 253, 291, 323, 330, 385
Equity linked instrument (ELI), 14, 146, 148, 149, 152, 297, 299
eW-8, 49
Expanded affiliate group (EAG), 37, 174, 193, 205, 211, 212, 216, 218, 267
Extended mark-up language (xml), 162, 178, 223, 225, 228, 251, 256
Extension, 29, 74, 82–84, 90, 106, 117, 120, 142, 188, 193, 226, 266, 319, 342, 344, 349, 351, 352, 354, 371

F

Factual information, 110–111, 117, 355, 361, 364, 369
FFI Agreement, xxvi, 102, 117, 161, 172, 173, 177, 188, 207, 214, 217, 285, 286, 293, 300, 302, 305, 307, 344, 353
Filing Information Returns Electronically (FIRE), 15, 92, 96, 270
Fixed, Determinable, Annual or Periodic (FDAP), xxii–xxv, xxviii, 7, 9, 10, 21, 23, 25–28, 44, 45, 55, 61, 62, 64, 65, 80, 86–88, 90, 91, 102, 103, 105, 106, 120, 122, 138, 144, 163, 165, 172, 173, 175, 176, 181, 187, 200, 201, 215, 218–220, 259, 266, 290, 298, 300, 303, 304, 310
Flow-through, xxii, 8, 30, 65, 104, 106, 289, 293, 294, 303, 307–309, 313, 315, 318, 319, 325–327, 329, 331, 332, 340, 341, 345, 346, 348, 350, 353, 368

Index

G
Gross proceeds, 7, 177, 220, 224, 228, 290, 306, 337, 388, 389, 396

H
High value accounts, 227
HIRE Act, xxix, 55, 157, 159–161, 165, 166
Home rule, 11

K
Know-your-customer (KYC), xxvi, 5, 6, 11–13, 16, 18, 23, 24, 27, 29, 33, 36, 40–44, 46, 47, 57, 58, 62, 68, 90, 112, 113, 127, 129, 166, 173, 178, 181, 183, 184, 187, 191, 240, 249, 250, 260, 288, 291, 295, 310, 315, 320, 323, 330, 360, 374, 399

L
Late-filing penalties, 84, 93, 120–122
Limitation of benefits (LOB), 46
Low-value accounts, 201, 206–207, 211, 212

M
Memorandum of Understanding (MoU), 39, 49, 62, 185, 240, 269

N
Non-duplicative taxation, xxiii, 218, 221
Non-withholding QI (NWQI), 10, 13, 25, 28, 36, 45, 67–73, 76, 77, 89, 93, 95, 104, 120, 123, 267

Notional principal contract (NPC), 14, 147–149, 152, 293, 297, 299, 308, 383, 386

O
Obama, Barrack, xxv, 11, 128
Organisation for Economic Co-operation and Development (OECD), xxv, xxx, 79, 225, 229, 233, 234, 237–247, 252, 254, 255, 257, 271, 399
Oversight, xxv, 4, 6, 14, 16, 18, 24, 31, 36, 61, 79, 101–117, 119, 190, 250, 251, 360

P
Partnerships, xxii, 10, 26, 30, 65, 106, 113, 131, 293, 296, 301, 310–320, 327, 345–347, 359, 363, 365, 367, 368, 370–372, 376, 383, 385, 392
Penalties, viii, xxvi, xxx, 4–6, 12, 18–21, 24, 28, 30, 48, 50, 72, 73, 80, 81, 83, 84, 86, 87, 93, 99, 102, 105, 119–125, 129, 133–136, 142, 144, 158, 163, 165, 173, 175–177, 179, 185, 188, 202, 215, 218–222, 225, 226, 228, 243, 251, 260, 266, 271, 308, 310, 311, 313, 314, 316, 320, 331, 342, 354, 356, 360, 395
Periodic review (PR), 6, 18–20, 24, 26, 32, 35, 41, 61, 62, 79, 101, 110, 111, 113–117, 182, 311, 312, 315, 317, 354, 355, 358–364, 369–373, 375, 376
Presumption rules, 6, 13, 26, 29, 51, 59, 62, 70, 176, 186, 188, 203, 320, 325, 331–337, 341, 345, 365

Private arrangement intermediary (PAI), 10, 29, 37, 113, 114, 297, 310–320, 327, 340, 341, 345–347, 359, 363, 368, 370–372, 376

Proprietary accounts, 8, 89

Q

QI Agreement, xxiii, xxv, xxvi, xxviii, 5, 6, 9, 18, 19, 21, 23–37, 42, 45, 46, 57, 59, 61, 75, 77, 101–103, 105, 107, 109–112, 114–117, 119, 123, 127, 129, 134, 145, 146, 151, 153, 172, 179, 272, 285–378

Qualified derivatives dealer (QDD), 13, 14, 25–28, 30, 37, 45, 110, 113, 117, 145–154, 226, 267, 285, 287–290, 292, 295–310, 316, 321, 322, 326, 335, 338, 339, 342–344, 346, 354–358, 360, 361, 363–370, 373, 374, 376, 377

Qualified intermediary EIN (QIEIN), 16, 27, 36, 87, 110, 373

Qualified investment vehicle (QIV), 208, 210, 213

Qualified Securities Lender (QSL), 13, 14, 27, 28, 30, 37, 153, 287, 289, 295, 298, 304, 338, 339, 344, 361, 365–367

Quick refund, 4, 5, 250, 256

R

Rate pool accounts, 8–9, 13, 36, 68–71, 76, 89, 104, 109, 131, 136, 138, 203, 215, 267

Reason to know, 6, 29, 43, 56, 59, 62, 184, 186, 194, 196–197, 204, 310, 324, 328–331

Recalcitrance, 217, 218

Recalcitrant, xxvi, 59, 80, 87, 102, 165, 173, 175, 176, 178–181, 203, 204, 215, 217, 219–222, 266, 302, 305, 307, 309, 321, 332–334, 336, 340, 341, 345, 346, 349, 350, 365, 392

Reciprocity, 169, 178–180, 395

Relief at source, 3–23, 26, 79, 131–133, 137, 138, 240–242, 244, 245, 249, 250, 252, 253, 256

Responsible officer (RO), 6, 18, 31, 61, 79, 101–103, 117, 191, 215, 251, 260, 299, 311, 312, 317, 354–359, 362, 363, 369–372, 375, 378

S

Safe harbour, 27, 107

Sampling, 27, 105, 107, 364, 369

Securities lending, 13, 14, 145–147, 150, 152, 287, 297–299, 304, 367

Segregated accounts, 8, 9, 88, 89, 130, 134, 138

Self-certification, 5, 12, 16, 40–44, 51, 52, 185, 186, 190, 191, 199, 200, 202, 247, 249

Self-declaration, 50, 239, 242

Social Security Numbering Agency (SSNA), 17, 60

Social security number (SSN), 17, 58–60, 70, 104, 168, 200

SS-4, 36

Standard refund, 4, 5, 75, 76

Substantial ownership, 178, 196, 201, 202

Substitute dividends, 14, 146, 287, 289, 295, 298, 304, 338, 339, 361, 365–367

Substitute W-8, 47–48

T

Tax Barriers Business Advisory Group (T-BAG), 234, 246–248, 250, 252–254

Tax evasion, xxv, xxx, 11, 40, 55, 57, 59, 117, 128, 144, 159, 162, 166–168, 170, 173, 174, 185, 192–195, 200, 201, 207, 212, 213, 219, 234, 260, 268, 271

Tax Identification Number (TIN), 17, 60, 70, 104, 177, 223, 239, 250, 251, 294, 295, 301, 305, 307, 312, 323, 329, 339, 348, 387–390, 396

Tax liability, 26, 28, 58, 67, 72, 93, 112, 113, 151, 152, 154, 201, 219, 285, 288, 297, 298, 300–310, 331, 342, 354, 356–358, 360, 361, 363, 367, 369, 370, 373, 376

Tax Relief and Compliance Enhancement Implementation Protocol (TRACE IP), xxx, 233, 235–246, 255, 256, 271, 398–403

1042, 15, 26, 29, 33, 72, 74, 80, 82–93, 105, 106, 112, 117, 123, 134, 142, 152, 173, 181, 215, 221, 222, 226, 266, 288, 294, 311, 312, 314, 319, 320, 342–343, 351–354, 361, 366, 367, 371, 375

1042-S, 15, 26, 29, 30, 33, 74, 75, 80, 82–95, 97–99, 105, 112, 117, 120–123, 125, 134–136, 142–144, 173, 181, 215, 221, 222, 226, 260, 266, 270, 294, 305, 311, 312, 314–316, 319, 320, 324, 329, 331, 332, 337, 339–341, 344–347, 351–354, 357, 361, 366–368, 371, 374, 375

1099, xxiv, 15, 28, 33, 52, 59, 60, 85, 94, 96, 104, 112, 117, 121, 151, 181, 287, 290, 293–295, 297, 305–309, 311–314, 319–322, 326, 329–342, 346–350, 357, 360, 361, 365–367, 371, 375

Training, xxviii, 31, 33, 35, 56, 101, 105, 110, 111, 116, 184, 194, 272, 357

Transmitter control code (TCC), 17, 142

Treasury, 6, 9, 10, 13, 14, 19, 26, 66, 71, 72, 79–81, 120, 122, 129, 133, 152, 195, 219, 377, 380

Treaty, xxii, xxiii, 3–5, 11, 12, 29, 31, 40, 46, 55, 64, 76, 88, 91, 95, 131, 136, 138, 144, 170, 187, 237–239, 241, 243, 250, 251, 256, 291, 294, 295, 301, 304, 322–325, 328–330, 364, 399

Trusts, xxii, 12, 24, 26, 30, 51, 65, 82, 106, 113, 131, 201, 202, 293, 296, 301, 310–320, 327, 345–347, 359, 363, 365, 367, 368, 370–372, 376, 383, 385–387, 392

U

US indicia, 49, 50, 57, 167, 168, 173, 185, 188, 200, 203–205, 218, 330, 336, 337, 349, 350

US withholding agent (USWA), xxix, 6–10, 14, 16, 18, 19, 21, 25, 29, 36, 40, 63, 64, 66–72, 74, 75, 81, 83, 85, 87–91, 94, 95, 104, 122–124, 128, 130–134, 136–138, 142–144, 173, 191, 215, 218, 267

V

Validation on the face, 43, 53–55

W

W-8BEN, 42, 47, 51, 52, 55, 59, 73, 134, 138, 187, 323
W-8BEN-E, 8, 42, 59, 195, 201, 294, 323
W-8ECI, 42, 65, 294
W-8EXP, 42, 65, 294, 324, 325
W-8IMY, xxiii, 8, 16, 29, 42, 45, 51–54, 59, 66, 85, 90–92, 123, 124, 132–138, 142, 144, 176, 188, 190, 191, 201, 218, 294, 298, 309, 312, 315, 318, 322, 326, 327, 331–335, 338, 339, 350, 368
W-9, 6, 12, 13, 27, 29, 39, 40, 44, 46, 47, 59, 60, 62, 65, 70, 90, 104, 181, 183, 266, 270, 291, 292, 294, 307, 312, 322, 327–330, 333, 334, 339, 341, 349, 365
Waiver, 6, 101, 116–117, 311, 317, 358, 359, 361, 370–371, 377
Withholding agent, 10, 11, 16, 25, 27, 31, 61, 64, 65, 68, 70, 71, 75, 76, 79, 86, 87, 94–96, 99, 113, 123, 142, 185, 211, 214, 243–245, 249, 285, 286, 289, 294, 295, 298, 301, 303, 306, 307, 310, 312, 318, 328–330, 336, 338–342, 346, 348–351, 353, 354, 360, 364–368, 373, 374, 376, 393, 400
Withholding certificate, 40, 52, 99, 303, 304, 308, 329, 333, 338–342
Withholding foreign partnership (WFP), 24, 117, 131, 293, 296, 301, 392
Withholding foreign trust (WFT), 24, 131, 293, 296, 301, 392
Withholding QI (WQI), 6, 10, 13, 14, 25, 28, 45, 52, 64, 66–67, 71, 73–75, 89, 93, 122, 131, 132, 267, 301, 302, 305, 318, 332
Withholding Rate Pool Statement (WRPS), 36, 68–71, 76, 132
Withholding statement, 33, 40, 66, 91, 92, 104, 112, 131, 132, 136, 142–144, 176, 218, 266, 270, 298, 303, 308, 309, 312, 315, 316, 318, 321, 326–328, 333–335, 338–342, 348, 368

The manufacturer's authorised representative in the EU is Springer Nature Customer Service Centre GmbH, Europaplatz 3, 69115 Heidelberg, Germany. If you have any concerns regarding our products, please contact ProductSafety@springernature.com

Printed and bound by CPI Group (UK) Ltd, Croydon, CR0 4YY

23/03/2026

02076745-0006